INDIA: NATION ON THE MOVE

An Overview of India's People, Culture,
History, Economy, IT Industry, & More

Manish Telikicherla Chary

iUniverse, Inc.
New York   Bloomington

India: Nation on the Move
An Overview of India's People, Culture,
History, Economy, IT Industry, & More

iUniverse books may be ordered through booksellers or by contacting:

iUniverse
1663 Liberty Drive
Bloomington, IN 47403
www.iuniverse.com
1-800-Authors (1-800-288-4677)

Because of the dynamic nature of the Internet, any Web addresses or
links contained in this book may have changed since publication and
may no longer be valid. The views expressed in this work are solely those
of the author and do not necessarily reflect the views of the publisher,
and the publisher hereby disclaims any responsibility for them.

ISBN: 978-1-4401-1635-3 (sc)
ISBN: 978-1-4401-1636-0 (ebk)

Printed in the United States of America

iUniverse rev. date: 01/27/2009

In Memory of My Mother, Indira

In Memory of My Mother, Indira

Contents

List of Tables

Preface

India has long been known for its rich and diverse culture, venerable history, spirituality, and unwavering commitment to democracy. American author Mark Twain[1] called India "cradle of the human race, the birthplace of human speech, the mother of history, the grandmother of legend, and the great-grandmother of tradition." Albert Einstein[2] said: "we owe a lot to the Indians, who taught us how to count, without which no worthwhile scientific discovery could have been made."

India's greatness was never in doubt. The West has admired India since time immemorial. However, slow economic growth and acute poverty remained a sore point for nearly half a century after India became independent from British colonial rule. All that changed in 1991, when this nation of over a billion people unleashed groundbreaking economic reforms that transformed it, along with China, into one of the fastest growing economies of the world.

The apparent rise of India, like the rise of China, has stimulated great interest among economists, business leaders, policymakers, and journalists. Many books have been written about India. Some focus exclusively on Indian history, which is always a fascinating topic, while others focus on Indian culture; recent books focus on India's growth story. Only few books have comprehensively covered all aspects of India. This book aims to fill that gap. *India: Nation on the Move* aims to provide entertaining and illuminating insights into India's people, culture, history, economy, and outsourcing industry, as well as myriad other topics. It covers anything that a person would want to know about India.

The early 1990s were arguably the most tumultuous years for India since the years after gaining independence. The nation was in the throes of caste and religious conflict, and on the brink of economic meltdown. The first Gulf War and the implosion of the Soviet Union, which had been the main source of India's aid and trade, made matters even worse. Frustrated by the lack of job opportunities in India and influenced by the Hollywood depiction of the American lifestyle, I decided to embark on my journey to the United States to pursue an advanced degree. I must confess that I came under the influence of the 1987 hit comedy *Secret of my Success*, in which Michael J. Fox, who plays the role of Brantley Foster, leaves his hometown in Kansas City to try to make it big in New York City. I wanted to emulate Fox and was eager to leave my own Kansas City in India. I was not alone in taking this journey. Over the years, thousands of doctors, engineers, students, and professionals have left India for the United States in search of greener pastures. For them, India represented the "land of wasted opportunities" whereas the United States represented the "the land of unlimited opportunities."

My first attempt at securing a student visa ended in dismal failure, for reasons beyond my control and comprehension. On that fateful day, I stood in line outside the U.S. consulate in Bombay (now Mumbai) for nearly nine hours, only to be told that my visa was rejected for unspecified reasons. It took the U.S. immigration official just over eighty seconds to shatter my American dream. Although crestfallen, I decided to take my failure in stride and reapply at a later date. My perseverance paid off, and I managed to get the coveted student visa in my second attempt. I wasted no time and secured a bank loan for 100,000 rupees (roughly $4,700) to cover the tuition fee and living expenses for one semester. In order to secure the loan, my mother had to mortgage our ancestral home that she inherited from her father.

In June 1991, P. V. Narasimha Rao took over as the new prime minister of India. In his first speech as India's new leader, Rao announced that the nation was facing its worst economic situation in decades and vowed to take tough measures to restore the health of the economy. I didn't realize at the time that I would soon be at the receiving end of the government's new policies. Within a week of Rao's speech, the rupee had depreciated by almost 20 percent vis-à-vis the U.S. dollar, thus effectively shaving off $1,000 from the money I was going to carry to the United States (my loan of 100,000 rupees yielded only $3,700, instead of $4,700). Fortunately, my family once again came to my rescue and made up for the shortfall. I was finally airborne, en route to the United States, in August 1991.

Since my arrival, I have watched with keen interest as India embarked on its new journey as a market economy. I was quite thrilled by the fact that the economic reforms program launched by the government in 1991 has started paying huge dividends, and there has been a marked improvement in living standards. What had been a casual interest in rediscovering my homeland has become a full-blown obsession for me in the past few years. I have spent countless hours researching and learning new things about India. Eventually, I decided to organize my thoughts into to book for the benefit of others. My initial goal was to write about India's growth story. But I quickly realized that to put the growth story into the right context, I would have to explain history, culture, politics, and other related topics. Having spent my entire childhood and part of my adulthood in pre-reform India, I believe I am uniquely qualified to tell India's story.

Why call India the "nation on the move"? I will provide some random facts and let you be the judge. India is the second-fastest-growing major economy in the world. Four Indians are among the ten richest in the world. The world's biggest steel company is owned by an Indian. Two women of Indian origin made it to space. Indian Americans account for one in twenty doctors practicing medicine in the United States. Indian American children have won six National Spelling Bee titles in the past ten years. India sends more students to the United States than any other country in the world. India has recently launched an unmanned spacecraft to orbit the moon. A person of Indian origin heads the world's largest bank. A person of Indian origin is currently the governor of Louisiana. India finally managed to win its first Olympic individual gold medal. The list goes on and on.

Without a question, the economic reforms of 1991 have changed the face of the nation. The India of 2008 bears little resemblance to the India of 1991, especially in its urban areas. India is currently the most exciting place in the world. It's changing by the day, by the hour, and by the second. Hardly a day passes without a news report highlighting an achievement by India or Indians.

Why should you learn more about India? I'll answer that question with another: Can you afford *not* to? Today, pundit after pundit is predicting that the nation of over a billion people will become the third-largest economy in the world, behind China and the United States. According to a study by Goldman Sachs[3], the Indian economy will grow at the rate of 5 percent or more until 2050, assuming that the nation continues its pro-growth policies. By developing a deep understanding of India, we can take advantage of the unprecedented opportunities this nation provides.

This book consists of nine chapters and a brief epilogue. Chapter 1, the introductory chapter, sets the stage for this book. It briefly contrasts the pre-reform and post-reform India and highlights the achievements of economic reforms of 1991. Then it tackles questions such as these: How does India stack up against China? Is India an emerging world power? What does the rise of India and China mean to the world? The chapter briefly summarizes the challenges that India faces as it attempts to shake off its third-world image.

Chapter 2, "Land & People," covers topics including India's unique caste system, religions, languages, food habits, cultures and traditions, festivals, marriage system, architecture, literature, and sports. Did you know that India is perhaps the only nation on the planet where you can unapologetically be a vegetarian? The last section is devoted entirely to Bollywood, the world's largest film industry in terms of number of movies produced per year. The primary aim of this chapter is to provide a broad and sophisticated understanding of India, a country understood by many only in terms of stereotypes: snake charmers, spiritual leaders, and poverty.

Chapter 3 sweeps through nearly five thousand years of Indian history, from the Indus Valley Civilization to present-day India. My goal was to give equal emphasis to all periods, both ancient and modern. Chapter 4 briefly touches on India's polity and answers the question of why India is the world's largest democracy. Did you know that India has 671 million registered voters, more than any other nation in the world? Chapter 5 provides a comprehensive discussion about India's economy and its transition from a government-controlled economy to a market-oriented economy. This chapter also presents a deep exploration into India's burgeoning automobile, airline, and mobile phone industries. Consider this: India currently has a vehicle ownership rate of 8 per thousand. That number is expected to reach 140 per thousand by 2030. For a nation of more than a billion people, India's domestic airlines carry merely sixty million passengers per year. That number is expected to reach two hundred million by 2020, mainly driven by urban, middle-class consumers. India's mobile phone industry is growing by leaps and bounds, adding six million new subscribers each month.

Chapter 6 focuses on India's outsourcing industry, which has been in the forefront of India's rapidly growing economy. It is one of the few areas where India's domination is complete. Consider this: India's software export revenues have increased from a paltry $100 million in 1992 to $40 billion in 2008. Topics covered in this chapter include a brief history of India's information technology industry, the factors behind India's emergence as an information technology superpower, and the changing landscape of the outsourcing industry. A special section is devoted to India's Big 3 information technology powerhouses: TCS, Infosys, and Wipro.

Chapter 7 deals with India's foreign relations. The greater part of this chapter is devoted to India's relations with the United States, China, Russia, and Pakistan. Rather than merely stating the current state of affairs, it takes a historical perspective. Since people of Indian origin have become a force to be reckoned with in the United States in recent times, I have devoted an entire chapter to them. Consider this: the median household income for Indians in the United States was $78,315 in 2006, the highest of any ethnic group.

The last chapter is a reality check. It explains why it will take many more decades for India to break out of the third-world mold. I have identified ten serious challenges that India currently faces, including poverty, population explosion, pollution, HIV/AIDS, and crumbling infrastructure. Lastly, I have attempted to fill the appendix with a number of interesting and insightful topics, including the chronology of India, India's twelve proudest moments, and fifty prominent Indians of the present time.

What is unique about this book? I would say simplicity. I was guided by the philosophy that a book should never become a burden on the reader. Therefore, I tried to keep the content engaging, entertaining, and highly informative by summarizing key points after every major section and using tables to convey key messages. My goal was to provide content about India that is much more nuanced than a typical news story. This is a thoroughly researched book, with lots of facts and figures. I have three hundred endnotes and forty tables to prove it. Although India is my birthplace and therefore holds a special place in my heart, I have tried hard to present a dispassionate and nonpartisan view of the country, such as in the section that takes an honest look at the Indian marriage system, including the evil practice of dowry.

Overall, it has been an exciting and exasperating experience to write on a difficult topic such as India. The main challenge was keeping pace with the developments of a nation that is growing so fast. Just when I thought I had finished the manuscript, word came that an Indian national won the Booker Prize, India successfully launched its first unmanned spacecraft to orbit the moon, and President Bush signed an India-specific nuclear deal into law, ending India's nuclear isolation once and for all. I had to grudgingly make changes to my manuscript to account for the new information. The other challenge was how to condense five thousand years of history into little more than twenty thousand words without compromising its accuracy and integrity.

It is my hope that this book will serve as a solid primer for anyone interested in knowing about India, its fascinating past, and its exciting future.

I could not have written this book without the help, support, patience, understanding, and encouragement of my wife, Madhavi. Special thanks are reserved for my daughter Nidhi who pushed Daddy hard to complete the manuscript. My kids, Nidhi and Ved, provided me with the necessary motivation to complete the manuscript. I also want to thank my father T. K. Nammalvar, sister Mythili, and brother Giriraj for their encouragement throughout my life. I have no doubt in my mind that my mother, Indira, is watching me and blessing me every day from heaven.

I want to express my sincere gratitude to my trusted friend Srinivas Chalasani for his guidance and advice since my college days. The entire team at iUniverse has been terrific. I especially want to thank George Nedeff and Samantha Hale for their help and consultation.

Manish Chary

Chapter 1: Introduction

India, a multi-ethnic, multi-religious, multi-linguistic, pluralistic, free-market democracy of over one billion people, has come a long way since it jettisoned its quasi-socialistic economic policies in 1991. The metaphor "sleeping elephant," which was once used to describe India, has become a thing of the past. It was coined at a time when India's GDP was averaging 2–4 percent over much of the period since India gained its independence. Today, India is growing at 8–10 percent annually, making it the world's fastest-growing free-market democracy. A new metaphor may well be "elephant on the move" or, even better, "elephant on steroids." Japan saw explosive growth in the 1950s and 1960s, South Korea excelled in the 1970s, and China is having its best years since the early 1980s. Many Indians feel that it is their turn now.

It was a dramatic turnaround for a nation that until sixteen years ago was not known for its economy or trade but known instead for snake charmers, gurus, the Taj Mahal, and perhaps Gandhi. For its first forty-five years of existence as an independent country, India's potential was largely unknown to the outside world. Its biggest achievement was surviving as a functioning democracy without any military coups. While other countries traded goods with the West, India was spreading the virtues of universal nuclear disarmament, nonalignment, spirituality, yoga, and meditation. No American president, with the exceptions of Dwight Eisenhower, Richard Nixon, and Jimmy Carter, considered India important enough to make a visit let alone make a serious attempt to engage it in business.

Truth be told, until a decade and a half ago, India had little or nothing to offer to the West. India's economic policies after independence were marked by suspicion toward capitalism and foreign trade. Indian leaders, influenced by socialist ideas, opted for a centrally planned, mixed economy in which both the public and private sector coexisted. Industrial policy emphasized import substitution, a protectionist strategy that emphasizes the growth of domestic industries by discouraging imports using tariff and nontariff measures. Although the government protected domestic companies from foreign competition, it put several burdensome controls on them, which constrained their growth and profitability. The private industry had to go through a cumbersome government licensing process for investing in new ventures and expanding existing capacity. India's quasi-socialistic economic policies led to rapid industrialization, but they also caused considerable economic stagnation. The Indian economy grew at an anemic rate of 3.5 percent between 1950 and 1980, giving rise to the famous expression of "Hindu growth rate."[4]

While democratic India continued to cling to its socialist economic policies, communist China was taking pragmatic steps to lift its people out of acute poverty. Led by the visionary leader Deng Xiaoping, China embarked on an ambitious economic reform program in 1978, transforming itself from a planned economy to a market-oriented economy. The results were nothing but dramatic. Between 1979 and 2004, China experienced an annual GDP growth rate of 9.6 percent.[5]

Ironically, India refused to learn from the success of its neighbor. Instead, it took a number of retrograde steps. In 1977, India virtually declared war on the few multinationals who dared to operate on its soil. Both Coke and IBM were banished from the country after they refused to dilute their equity in their Indian operations to 40 percent.[6]

Even worse, Coke was asked to reveal its secret formula. Coke chose to leave. (It should be noted that both IBM and Coke re-entered India with a bang after India liberalized its economy in 1991. Today, Coke commands a large share of India's soft-drink market.)

Starting in the late 1970s, successive governments sought to reduce state control of the economy. However, progress toward that goal was slow. In the 1980s, India increasingly relied on external borrowings to finance its development plans. Piecemeal reforms and government spending helped boost the average GDP growth rate to 5.6 percent.[7]

India celebrated its forty years of independence in 1987, but at forty, India was still an impoverished nation. The nation of 850 million people remained locked in enormous poverty, illiteracy, overpopulation, unemployment, economic inequality, strangling bureaucratic controls, and corruption at all levels. Although India built great institutions of higher learning, such as IITs and IIMs, and produced the best and brightest graduates, it did not provide enough job opportunities for them, resulting in "brain drain." While China hogged the limelight as the "factory of the West," India made news for wrong reasons: natural calamities, religious and social tensions, industrial accidents, assassination of political leaders, and violent separatist movements. Indians did not have much to cheer about other than India's upset victory in the 1983 Cricket World Cup, the movie *Gandhi* sweeping the 1982 Oscars, and an Indian man making it to space aboard the Soviet Soyuz T-11, courtesy of the Soviet Union. India was not on anybody's radar screen. The Reagan administration, guided by cold-war-era politics, largely ignored India and, even worse, preferred Pakistan's military generals to India's democratic leaders. Despite all these problems, India remained steadfast in its commitment to democracy, individual liberties, and religious freedom and therefore earned the badge as "the most admired" third-world country. But the situation on the ground was worsening and required decisive leadership to turn things around. India's economic woes were self-inflicted wounds. Somebody had to stop the bleeding. Who would do it?

Economic Reforms of 1991

By all accounts, the year 1991 will go down as the most significant year for India since independence. The day was June 21, 1991. On this day, P. V. Narasimha Rao was sworn in as India's new prime minister, just a week short of his seventieth birthday. A month earlier, Rao was busy packing for retirement, when word came that his party leader had been assassinated while campaigning for the general election. Riding on the sympathy wave, Rajiv's Congress Party won the election and Rao, a Congress Party loyalist who had earlier held important positions as foreign and home minister, was chosen by the party elders to lead the party and the government.

At first, Rao, a slight, enigmatic, southern Indian Brahmin widower with eight children, was viewed as a caretaker prime minister while the Congress Party searched for a more decisive leader. Rao, known more for his extraordinary linguistic skills (he spoke anywhere between six and seventeen languages, including French, Spanish, and German) than political skills, had no real political base and was already known to be in frail health. On the eve of his election to the highest office in the land, the *New York Times* described him as a curious choice to lead a nation of 850 million that was suffering from poverty, illiteracy, and increasing violence.[8]

At the time Rao took office, India was facing its worst economic situation in decades in the form of high internal public debt, high inflation, dwindling foreign exchange reserves, plunging credit rating, and GDP growth of less than 1 percent. Decades of financial mismanagement had begun to take their toll. The foreign currency reserves fell to $1.2 billion in January 1991, and by June the reserves could cover only two weeks of imports. In an indication of how low India's credibility had sunk, the government had to airlift forty-seven tons of gold to London and pledge it as collateral to secure emergency loans and ride out the financial crisis.[9]

With loans came obligations to both the World Bank and International Monetary Fund to undertake fundamental restructuring of the economy. Unlike his predecessors, Rao agreed to undertake reform. One of Rao's first acts was the appointment Dr. Manmohan Singh, an Oxford-educated economist, as his new finance minister (equivalent to the U.S. treasury secretary). Together, Rao and Singh ushered in groundbreaking economic reforms, which brought India out of the economic mess and put on a path of growth. Singh devalued the rupee, removed restrictions on foreign trade and investment, slashed import tariffs, eliminated subsidies, abolished industrial licensing, and freed the economy from controls.

The government took two years to get over the immediate macroeconomic crisis. The era of stifling controls (also known as "License Raj") became a thing of the past, and India was finally open for business. Competition brought new players into the market. Waiting lists for most products and services virtually disappeared overnight, prices came down, quality went up, and service improved. The reform process helped jump-start the economy, resulting in higher growth rates, lower inflation, and significant increases in foreign direct and portfolio investments. In January 2007, India finally clawed back from "non-investment grade" to "investment grade" in Standard & Poor's long-term sovereign credit rating.[10]

The success of Rao's economic reforms is still evident today. The GDP has grown at over 8 percent annually and is set to continue at the same pace. Growth rates of 9–10 percent are within reach. India's foreign exchange reserves increased from around $1 billion in 1991 to nearly $300 billion in 2008.[11]

Foreign direct investment has risen to $5–$6 billion a year as compared to $100 million in 1991. The information technology sector is going gangbusters, and the manufacturing sector has become a key engine of the economy. The number of wealthy people is growing, and a substantial middle class with 300 million people (the size of the entire U.S. population) has emerged. Four Indians (Lakshmi Mittal, Mukesh Ambani, Anil Ambani, and K. P. Singh) with a combined net worth of $160 billion are among the ten richest in the world, according to the 2008 *Forbes* list of the world's billionaires. Businesses in metropolitan cities are booming, hotels are fully booked, stock markets are at record levels, airports are clogged, and flights are oversold.

In a sign of the middle class's rising purchasing power, 6 to 8 million new cell phone users are added each month, taking the mobile telephone subscription base to 233 million, behind China and United States. Domestic passenger car sales have jumped from 707,000 in 2002 to 1.5 million in 2007. Many foreign automakers have entered the Indian market by way of joint ventures, collaborations, or wholly owned subsidiaries. Even the luxury automaker BMW is building its first assembly plant in India to produce 3 Series and 5 Series vehicles. The number of airline passengers jumped from eight million in 1996 to sixty million in 2005. The number of carriers operating in India has grown from two state-owned airlines in 1991 to over a dozen airlines today. The booming aviation sector has made India one of the most attractive markets for the aircraft industry. Hundreds of new aircrafts are being ordered each year. Due to high growth rates, poverty levels have fallen by nearly a third in both rural and urban areas. Consumers have benefited from improved quality, lower prices, better customer service, and a wider selection of products and services. While Mahatma Gandhi brought political independence for India, Rao brought economic freedom. Every newly rich Indian owes a debt of gratitude to Rao.

With the economy booming, Indian companies are flexing their financial muscle on the global scene. The past few years have seen a number of high-profile acquisitions involving Indians and Indian companies. Tata Steel acquired Anglo-Dutch steelmaker Corus for $8 billion; Hindalco acquired Novelis for $6 billion; Mittal Steel, owned by Indian businessman Lakshmi Mittal, acquired European steel giant Arcelor for $33 billion; and Tata Motors acquired luxury auto brands Jaguar and Land Rover from Ford Motor Company for $2.3 billion. Tata Motors has recently unveiled the world's cheapest car, costing as little as $2,500, a move intended to lure millions of two-wheeler owners to the automobile segment. The Tata group was recently selected by *Business Week* as the sixth most innovative company in the world behind Apple, Google, Toyota, GE, and Microsoft.

The period following reforms also led to the birth of India's envied information technology (IT) outsourcing industry. In the past decade and half, India has established itself as the top outsourcing destination in the world, and it will be years before India's number-one status will be seriously contested. India's comparative advantage in IT is the availability of a huge pool of highly skilled, English-speaking workers at low cost. Indian IT workers have become so indispensable to Microsoft that Bill Gates himself routinely visits Capitol Hill to urge Congress to increase or eliminate quotas on the temporary H-1B visas. Software and outsourcing industries have created hundreds of thousands of high-paying jobs and billions in export revenues. India's IT exports are expected to reach $80 billion by 2010. The industry makes up nearly 5 percent of GDP and employs two million people. Like China in the manufacturing sector, India has attained critical mass in the IT sector and therefore has become indispensable.

Indians Shining at Home and Abroad

Indians are shining both at home and abroad. The Indian American community, which crossed the two-million mark in 2005, has emerged as one of the most successful immigrant groups in America. High levels of education and command of the English language have enabled them to secure high-paying jobs in fields including medicine, science, technology, and software engineering. The median household income for Asian Indians in United States in 2006 was $78,315, the highest for any ethnic group. According to a *San Jose Mercury News* report, Indian Americans own the most valuable real estate in Santa Clara County, home of Silicon Valley. Indian Americans with origins in the western Indian state of Gujarat virtually rule the hotel industry in the United States, with ownership of 43 percent of the forty-seven thousand motels and hotels across the country.

There are around forty thousand Indian American physicians in America, accounting for one in twenty doctors practicing medicine in the United States. They make up the largest non-Caucasian segment of the American medical community. Two women of Indian origin (Kalpana Chawla and Sunita Williams) made it to space. Astronaut Sunita Williams even set a record for the most time spent in space by a woman. Indian American children have dominated the Scripps National Spelling Bee Championship by winning six titles in the past ten years. India also has the unique distinction of sending the highest number of students to the United States to pursue advanced degrees in engineering, computer science, and business. There are currently more than eighty thousand Indian students enrolled in various universities across United States. Indians virtually rule the H-1B nonimmigrant visas awarded to temporary workers. About 36 percent of recipients of these visas are Indians.

It may be hard to find an Indian in the roster of the NBA, which had eighty-three international players from thirty-seven countries outside the United States. But it is becoming increasingly easy to find Indians in the boardrooms of Fortune 500 companies. From Indra Nooyi (chairman and CEO of PepsiCo) to Vikram Pandit (CEO of Citigroup) and from Raj Gupta (chairman and CEO of Rohm & Haas) to Rajat Gupta (former managing director of McKinsey & Company), Indians are making their presence felt in corporate America. India also has international business leaders in Lakshmi Mittal (president and CEO of the world's largest steelmaker, ArcelorMittal) and Arun Sarin (former CEO of the world's leading mobile telecom company). With a net worth of $45 billion, Mittal ranks fourth among the ten richest people in the world behind Warren Buffet, Carlos Slim Helú, and Bill Gates.

People of Indian origin are also shining as venture capitalists, entrepreneurs, and professors at prestigious universities. Pramod Haque (managing partner of Northwest Venture Partners) and Vinod Khosla (partner of Kleiner Perkins Caufield & Byers) earned the top two spots in the 2004 Forbes Midas List of the world's top venture capitalists. Amar Bose (founder of a company that makes the world-famous Bose speakers) and Sabeer Bhatia (cofounder of the pioneering webmail service Hotmail) are notable entrepreneurs of Indian origin. Professor

C. K. Prahlad, the India-born management guru and distinguished professor at the University of Michigan Ross School of Business, was voted in 2007 as the world's most influential management thinker ahead of Bill Gates, Alan Greenspan, Michael Porter, and Tom Peters by Suntop Media. Indian minds are behind the immensely popular Scrabulous game (an Internet version of the board game Scrabble), which attracted half a million daily users on Facebook, a leading social networking site.

Indians and Indian Americans have also made it big in media, film, and politics. Dr. Sanjay Gupta (CNN's chief medical correspondent) and Fareed Zakaria (an ABC political analyst and editor of *Newsweek International*) are perhaps the most prominent Indian faces on American television. India-born M. Night Shyamalan, who created the blockbuster movie *The Sixth Sense*, has earned a reputation as Hollywood's "modern-day Hitchcock." Bollywood movie director Shekhar Kapur gained international prominence as the director of Academy Award-winning movies *Elizabeth* (1998) and its sequel. Aishwarya Rai, an Indian model, beauty pageant queen, and Bollywood movie star, is widely regarded as one of the most beautiful women in the world.

No person of Indian origin has ever occupied a cabinet-level position in the U.S. government. The only person who came close was Karan Bhatia, who served in the Bush Administration as deputy U.S. trade representative. In October 2007, Indian American Republican Congressman Bobby Jindal made history by winning the Louisiana gubernatorial race. He is also the youngest current governor in the United States, the first nonwhite governor of the state since reconstruction in 1870, and the first Indian American head of an American state.

India Versus China

How does India stack up against China? China and India account for 2.4 billion people, or 36 percent of the world's population. With economic growth rates of 8–10 percent annually, both countries are poised to become major economic powerhouses within a decade. China's GDP topped $3 trillion, whereas India's crossed $1 trillion

(China ranks fourth and India ranks twelfth in the world). Both nations have radically different political systems. India is the world's largest democracy, while China is still under tight communist party control. China began its economic transformation in the early 1980s, a decade earlier than India initiated its first-generation reforms. It grew at 8–9 percent between 1981 and 1991. In contrast, India grew at 5–6 percent during that period. China's growth is mainly driven by manufacturing, whereas India's growth is driven by knowledge-based industries.

China's economic boom is mainly due to the government, which carefully nurtures and directs economic activity within the country. In contrast, India owes its economic success to the private entrepreneurs who emerged with little or no government assistance. Communist China embraces foreign direct investment (FDI), whereas democratic India remains cautious and still maintains some restrictions on FDI. China routinely receives $50–$60 billion in FDI annually, more than any other country in the world. India receives a tenth of what China receives in FDI. China beats India on the hard infrastructure such as roads, power, airports, and ports. On the soft infrastructure, such as availability of highly skilled workers and well-established financial and legal systems, India beats China. Education continues to be an Achilles' heel for India, which has a literacy rate of only 65 percent as compared to 91 percent of China. Both nations face serious problems that can impede growth. India faces infrastructure-related issues: lack of power, roads, and water. China has massive bad bank loans that will come to haunt it in the future. Also, China is facing a demographic squeeze due to its one-child policy.

India's Advantages

India has several advantages. It has well-established democratic institutions, which have survived the test of time. It is one of the few countries in South Asia where democracy has taken root and is thriving. India has never had a military coup in its sixty years of existence as an independent country. Elections are held at regular intervals. Political parties respect election results, and there is always an orderly transfer of power. India has an independent judiciary and fiercely independent media. India adopted universal suffrage at the time of independence. It is also one of the freest societies in the world, on par with the United States and United Kingdom.

India is a melting pot of various cultures and religious traditions. There is complete religious and political freedom. Although 80 percent of the people belong to the Hindu religion, India is also home to a large number of people of Islamic faith. In fact, India has the second-largest Muslim population in the world, second only to Indonesia. It is truly an inclusive democracy. India's secular constitution mandates a separation between religion and politics. Indian politicians take great pride in promoting minorities, women, and people from lower castes into the highest positions in the government. Predominantly Hindu India is now led by a Sikh prime minister and an Italian-born Catholic woman who is the president of the powerful ruling Congress Party. India in the past had three Muslim presidents and a female prime minister. In 2007, India elected its first female president (a largely ceremonial post). The architect of India's missile program, A. P. J. Abdul Kalam, is a Muslim.

After a period of political uncertainty, India successfully underwent a transformation from single-party rule to multi-party rule. The current government consists of a coalition of seventeen disparate parties with varying ideologies; therefore, the decision-making process is slow and tedious and involves building consensus. India is by no means perfect. Caste discrimination still exists despite the implementation of the world's largest affirmative-action program. Communal riots happen from time to time. India has its own share of corrupt politicians. But all issues tend to get resolved within the established democratic parameters.

The justice system is slow, but it works. There is no summary execution of people. Since independence, India has been witnessing a tremendous power shift from upper-caste to lower-caste people. Over the past five years, India's domestic situation has shown considerable improvement. Separatist violence in Punjab and Assam is a thing of the past. Kashmir has become relatively peaceful as a result of peace talks with Pakistan. India is arguably witnessing its most peaceful time in decades. But terrorism still poses a threat, as is evident from recent terrorist attacks in Hyderabad, Bangalore, and Ahmedabad.

Foreign Policy Successes

On the foreign policy front, India has had remarkable successes over the past decade. India was able to forge a close relationship with the United States without antagonizing its cold-war-era ally, Russia. Similarly, it was able to establish full diplomatic relations with Israel without upsetting the Palestinians. Today, Israel has emerged as one of the biggest suppliers of military hardware to India. Relations with China and Pakistan are also largely normalized. With trade dominating its foreign policy, India is making new friends in Brazil, Mexico, South Africa, and Saudi Arabia. India's Look East policy, which was launched in the early 1990s, is already paying rich dividends for the country. India is set to become a "full-dialogue partner" of ASEAN.

Although India continues to maintain a close relationship with Russia, a lot has changed since the cold-war era when Russia enjoyed a near monopoly as the central arms supplier to India. Now Russia is facing stiff competition from the United States, France, and other countries, which are eager to tap into India's lucrative arms market. The Indo-China relationship has come a long way since the border war of 1962. India and China, the world's fastest-growing economies and the world's two most populous nations, are making a conscious effort to improve their trade relationship, putting contentious issues on the back burner. In a sign of changing times, a direct air link has been operating between the nations since 2002. Bilateral trade quadrupled from $5 billion in 2002 to $20 billion in 2006. Although India still hosts the Dalai Lama and his 150,000 followers, much to the chagrin of the Chinese government, it consistently promotes the Chinese line that Tibet is an integral part of China to keep Beijing happy.

Relations between archrivals India and Pakistan, who were involved in three major wars and numerous other conflicts in their six decades of existence as independent countries, are on the upswing. Pakistan has been a thorn in India's side for many years. Not powerful enough to defeat India in an all-out war but emboldened by military support from China and North Korea in the form of missile and nuclear technologies and the Reagan administration's arms largesse, Pakistan launched and sustained a low-intensity but deadly terrorist campaign against India for nearly two decades to dislodge it from the disputed Kashmir region. Fortunately for India, Pakistan's "bleed India" campaign ran out of steam after the 9/11 attacks against the United States. Pakistan is increasingly unable or unwilling to openly support the jihadi groups operating on Indian-controlled Kashmir. With India catching world attention and admiration as the next China, Pakistan has little choice but to build good relations with India, lest it face marginalization in this increasingly globalized world.

The India-Pakistan peace process, which was initiated in 2004, is going well, with both sides pledging that the process is irreversible. For the first time in the history of the Kashmir dispute, both sides are discussing various "options" to solve the dispute. In 2005, India and Pakistan launched a landmark bus service linking the towns of Srinagar (Indian Kashmir) and Muzaffarabad (Pakistan Kashmir), thus reuniting families who were divided after bus service was halted in 1947. In 1998, following the tit-for-tat nuclear tests by India and Pakistan, the Doomsday Clock was advanced by five minutes to 11:51 p.m., with midnight representing a worldwide nuclear holocaust. It is too soon to tell if the new bonhomie between the nations warrants a turning back of the Doomsday Clock.[12]

The Indo-U.S. relationship is on the upswing, and there is even talk of forging a strategic partnership. The end of cold-war hostilities and the opening of the Indian economy to foreign trade have created unprecedented opportunities for cooperation at government and business levels. There is a general consensus that the bilateral relationship is in its best shape in decades. The United States is drawn to India due to its economic and military potential. Only India has the depth and size to act as a counterweight to the rising power of China. Ironically, the United States started talking to India only after the 1998 nuclear tests, which confirmed India as a major power in the world, a power that could not be ignored for too long.

Bilateral trade between the countries tripled since 2000 to reach $41 billion in 2007. India's sizable population and its burgeoning middle class make it a potentially lucrative market for American goods and services. India's expected overhaul of its largely dilapidated and underdeveloped infrastructure provides unique opportunity for those companies in infrastructure-related industries. So far India has not disappointed. Air India ordered sixty-eight Boeing planes worth a staggering $11.6 billion. It is not only the largest single purchase in Air India's history, but the single-largest order in Boeing's history as well. Although bilateral trade between India and the United States is growing at a rapid pace, the countries have taken the opposite position in the World Trade Organization's multilateral Doha trade negotiations. The talks reached an impasse over the reluctance of rich nations to cut farm subsidies and the refusal of developing countries to reduce import duties and open markets for goods.

The defense ties between India and the United States, which were nonexistent before the 1990s, have also begun to blossom. In 2007, the Indian Navy conducted one of its largest military exercises with the United States in the Bay of Bengal, along with Japan, Australia, and Singapore.[13] American defense companies are in stiff competition with Russian and European rivals for a lucrative $10 billion fighter jet contract. India recently decided to buy six C-130J military transport planes from Lockheed for about $1 billion. It is also set to sign a $2.2 billion deal to purchase Boeing long-range maritime reconnaissance aircraft.

The Bush administration deserves a lot of credit for pushing Indo-U.S. ties to a new level. In March 2006, President Bush signed a historic but controversial nuclear deal with India under which energy-hungry India would get access to U.S. civil nuclear technology and fuel, even though it has not signed the Non-Proliferation Treaty

(NPT). In return, India pledged to open its civilian nuclear facilities to international inspection.

Everyone from Australia to Germany, Mexico to Japan is courting India. Politicians around the world are leading business delegations to try to drum up more trade. India has global ambitions and is increasingly flexing its muscles on the international diplomatic front. India's goal of attaining a permanent seat in the U.N. Security Council remains elusive, although many countries have enthusiastically supported India's bid. Ironically, it is India's new friend Washington who is opposing such a move. When Secretary-General Kofi Annan retired in 2007, India tried to get its candidate Shashi Tharoor elected. Once again, Washington thwarted India's moves and instead supported Ban Ki-moon's candidacy. India did score a small diplomatic victory when its candidate Kamlesh Sharma was elected as the secretary-general of the Commonwealth.

Is India an Emerging World Power?

Is India an emerging superpower? Perhaps. For starters, India is a regional power, nuclear power, space power, military power, and, now, an economic power. It has all the ingredients necessary to be a major power in the twenty-first century. While India is forging ahead, many of the current world powers are losing their prominence or declining in stature. The United States is neck-deep in its war on terrorism. It can't hope to lower its guard any time soon, and military and homeland security expenses will continue to drain its resources. Russia, a former superpower, is now facing a critical decline in its relatively small population base of 140 million. Russia also has not made up its mind whether to go for a full-fledged democracy or stay with its own version of a quasi-dictatorship-style democracy.

A dwindling birthrate is expected to reduce the Japanese population to one hundred million by 2050.[14] Japan already has the highest number of elderly people and the lowest number of young as a percentage of its population. The imbalance is threatening Japan's future economic growth. Western European countries have neither the depth nor the scale to compete with either China or India. The entire population of Europe (seven hundred million) is less than that of India or China. Moreover, nothing exciting is going on in Europe. Their growth rates have either stabilized or stagnated for years. Only China will continue to outpace India, both economically and militarily. But, going forward, China will have its own issues. It will sooner or later face the issue of how to provide political freedom without losing grip on its authoritarian regime. In contrast, India has been a vibrant democracy for the past sixty years and therefore has a stronger foundation on which to build.

What Does India's Rise Mean to the World?

What does the rise of India and China mean to the world? The simple answer is that the world will have to make room for them, not out of magnanimity but out of necessity. When the United Nations is expanded, India will likely land a permanent seat on the Security Council. India's nuclear status has now been formally acknowledged by the international community. Sooner or later, India and China will become part of the G-8 (it will then be called the G-10) group of the world's leading industrialized nations.

China is already a major power, and India is poised to bolster its geopolitical clout in the next few decades. As China and India continue to grow at a breakneck speed, the world will see its natural resources deplete at a faster rate. The International Energy Agency predicts that China and India together may increase their oil consumption to 23.1 million barrels in 2030, up from 9.3 million a day in 2005. Global commodity prices, from oil to base metals, are already going up. Developed countries like the United States are bracing for more job losses, as blue-collar jobs move to China, white-collar jobs move to India, and multinational companies rush to Asia to take advantage of the growth opportunities. It will be tough to reverse this trend in the near future. Just as America got used to low-priced Chinese goods, American big businesses are getting used to cheap Indian labor for their back-office work. American politicians have more or less resigned themselves to the fact that the exodus of white-collar jobs to low-cost destinations can't be reversed. As a result, there is much talk about creating green-collar jobs involving products and services that are environmentally friendly.

Challenges Remain

For all its economic successes of the past decade, India will continue to be a developing nation for the foreseeable future. The overall growth numbers are no doubt impressive, but the devil is in the details. India's boom is very narrowly based and is mainly concentrated in urban areas and some key states. India's much-vaunted IT sector, which employs just over two million people and accounts for 5 percent of the GDP, is largely irrelevant to the people who live in rural areas and derive their income from agriculture. The people in rural areas are yet to see improvement in their lives as they grapple with issues such as poverty, illiteracy, unemployment, corruption, and lack of basic amenities such as healthcare, clean drinking water, sanitation, and electricity.

Poverty is among the biggest challenges that India faces today. If John Edwards, a former U.S. presidential candidate, were Indian rather than American, he would have talked about at least six "Indias," including acutely poor, poor, lower-middle class, upper-middle class, rich, and super-rich. India has the world's largest number of poor people living in a single country. About one-third of population (370 million people) lives below the internationally accepted poverty line of $1 a day, compared to 85 million in China. Nearly 80 percent earn a daily wage of $2 or less a day. Compare this to the U.S. minimum wage, which is set to reach $7.25 per hour in 2009.

At the other end of the spectrum, India has fifty-three billionaires with a total wealth of $335 billion between them, according to the 2008 *Forbes* list of billionaires. India accounts for 5 percent of the world's billionaires. The problem with India is not a lack of money but the concentration of money in the hands of a small percentage of people at the top. The gulf between rich and poor has become more pronounced than ever in the past decade or so since the launch of the reforms. The market reform movement, without a doubt, has created many new millionaires; but at the same time, the country has witnessed suicides by thousands of debt-ridden farmers. Also, there is a huge gap between states.

While investor-friendly states like Karnataka, Andhra Pradesh, Tamil Nadu, and Maharashtra are forging ahead, states like Bihar, Orissa, and Jharkhand are trailing behind, due to various reasons. The situation is especially grim in Bihar, which is home to ninety million Indians (roughly the size of Germany), where 43 percent of the people are below the poverty line. In the lawless Bihar state, kidnapping for ransom is still the easiest way of making money. Closely tied to poverty is India's overflowing population. Even with a modest growth rate of 1.6 percent, India adds about eighteen million people a year (the combined population of Norway, Sweden, and Finland) to its tally, putting enormous strain on already scarce resources.

India produces more engineers and college graduates than any other country in the world. Yet sixty years after independence, one out of three Indians cannot read or write. There is also a huge disparity between male and female literacy rates. India sends its own satellites to space, maintains one of the world's largest armies, and has well-developed nuclear and missile programs. Yet an overwhelming number of its citizens do not have access to proper healthcare, sanitation, or drinking water. More women die during childbirth in India than anywhere else in the world. India has more malnourished children than any other country in the world. Less than a third of India's homes have a toilet. Mumbai City, widely known as the financial and glamour capital of India, is home to Asia's largest slum, Dharavi, where one million people live in appalling conditions.

Pollution is also a fact of life in Indian cities. A recent study concluded that 70 percent of the eighteen million inhabitants of Kolkota (formerly Calcutta) suffer from respiratory disorders caused by air pollution. An estimated 2.5 million Indians are infected with the HIV/AIDS virus, putting India in the third spot behind South Africa and Nigeria in the list of nations most badly affected by the epidemic. Bill Clinton called India the epicenter of the global HIV/AIDS epidemic.[15]

To be fair to the Indian government, India has made giant strides since independence. All social indicators have shown improvement. Life expectancy has nearly doubled, and the infant mortality rate has been halved. According to India's Planning Commission, the percentage of people living in acute poverty has dropped considerably, from 36 percent in 1994 to 22 percent in 2005. India's per capita income in nominal terms has surged from $460 (2001) to $950 (2007).

India's infrastructure is largely dilapidated and remains underdeveloped. The country doesn't have enough electricity to meet its demand, roads are crumbling, ports and airports are clogged, and water shortages are common. Power outages are common in India, despite the fact that an average Indian consumes one-fifteenth as much energy per year as a typical American. In response to the growing power crisis, the Indian government has set an ambitious goal to provide power for all by 2012. Only time will tell whether this is an empty slogan or a genuine commitment. According to a report released by KPMG[16], the energy sector needs investments to the tune of $120–$150 billion to keep pace with the current demand. Former U.S. ambassador to India David Mulford listed energy, infrastructure, and agriculture as India's three main challenges.[17]

India, land of Mahatma Gandhi, ranks among the most corrupt nations in the world. A study by Transparency International found that more than half of those surveyed had firsthand experience in paying bribes and using influence to get a job done in a government office. Furthermore, the rich, powerful, and connected operate virtually above the laws. They are rarely prosecuted; and even if they are prosecuted, they rarely serve out their terms. The likes of Andrew Fastow (former Enron CFO) and Dennis Kozlowski (former Tyco CEO) would never be prosecuted in India.

Perhaps one of the biggest challenges India faces pertains to global warming and greenhouse gas emissions. Recent studies have shown that India and China will be the world's greatest emitters of greenhouse gases by 2050 due to their increasing reliance on fossil fuels to meet their growing energy needs. With half of India's population lacking regular, uninterrupted access to electricity, environmental issues are taking a backseat to developmental issues. Interestingly, as developing nations, India and China are not required to make any cuts in carbon emissions under the Kyoto Protocol. However, both countries are coming under increasing international pressure to implement a mandatory limit on harmful emissions. Jacques Chirac argued that India needs nuclear power to prevent the country from becoming "an enormously polluting chimney"[18] for greenhouse gases. India continues to argue that its per-capita greenhouse emissions are very small compared to the gas-guzzling United States. But the reality is that in aggregate terms, it figures among the top emitters of carbon dioxide. A recent U.N. report[19] warned that India is likely to be one of the first major countries to be the most severely affected by climate change and could face severe water shortages, widespread drought, and famine.

Chapter 2: Land & People

India is the seventh-largest country in the world by land area and covers about 1.3 million square miles. Only Russia, Canada, China, the United States, Brazil, and Australia have more land than India. India is about one-third the size of the United States. Located in South Asia, India is the largest of the countries in the Indian subcontinent, encompassing India, Pakistan, Bangladesh, Nepal, Bhutan, Maldives, and Sri Lanka. The country measures 1,997 miles from north to south and 1,860 miles from east to west. India also has a coastline of about 4,349 miles.[20]

India's neighbors include China, Nepal, and Bhutan on the northeast, Pakistan on the northwest, and Myanmar on the east. India's eastern and northeastern states surround Bangladesh. Just south of peninsular India is Sri Lanka. The word "peninsula" is used to describe a piece of land surrounded by water on three sides. India is surrounded by water on three sides: the Bay of Bengal in the east, the Arabian Sea in the west, and the Indian Ocean in the south. The Indian Ocean is the third-largest ocean in the world after the Pacific and Atlantic Oceans.

The Himalayas form a natural barrier between India and China. They form the highest mountain range in the world, extending 1,500 miles over northern India. The tallest mountain in India, Kanchenjunga, stands at 28,169 feet (8,586 meters) high on the border of India and Nepal in the Himalayas. It is also world's third-highest peak and stands 866 feet below the world's highest peak, Mount Everest.[21]

The Himalayas, Northern Plains, and Deccan or Southern Plateau are the three main land regions of India. The Northern Plains lie between the Himalayas and southern peninsula. The plains include the valleys carved by the Brahmaputra, Indus, and Ganges rivers and their branches. The Thar Desert (also called the Great Indian Desert) lies in the western part of the Northern Plains. It covers much of the state of Rajasthan and parts of Gujarat.

The Deccan Plateau forms most of the southern peninsula. It is separated from the Northern Plains by a mass of mountain and hill ranges. Rugged mountain ranges called the Eastern Ghats and Western Ghats form the eastern and western boundaries of Deccan Plateau. Nilgiri Hills form the southernmost point of the plateau, where the Eastern and Western Ghats meet. The soil in the Northern Plains and Deccan Plateau is fertile and is used as farmland. Parts of the Eastern and Western Ghats are heavily forested and are home to wildlife.

India also controls the Andaman and Nicobar Islands in the Bay of Bengal and Lakshadweep and Minicoy Islands in the Arabian Sea. The Andaman and Nicobar Islands were among the areas that bore the brunt of the 2004 tsunamis triggered by an undersea earthquake whose epicenter was off the west coast of Sumatra, Indonesia.

India has many large rivers. These are classified into two major types: Himalayan and Deccan. The Himalayan rivers are snow- and rain-fed and flow throughout the year. The Ganges is the most famous river in India. It originates in the Himalayas and flows into the Bay of Bengal. The Deccan rivers are generally rain-fed; they are nonperennial and fluctuate greatly in volume. Major Deccan rivers include Krishna, Godavari, and Cauvery.

Climate

India has three main seasons: summer, monsoon season, and winter. Each of these seasons lasts about four months. The Himalayan states of Kashmir, Himachal Pradesh, and Sikkim also experience autumn and spring.

The summer season usually lasts from March to June. Summer months are very hot in most parts of India. The heat can be severe, and the temperature routinely hovers around 90–110°F. April and May are the hottest months. The only exception is the Himalayan states and other hilly areas, where the climate is pleasant during summer. Most of the hill resorts in Himachal Pradesh, Kashmir, and Nilgiri hills are very popular destinations for summer holiday travel.

The rainy season lasts from June to September. By the first week of July, the entire country experiences rain. During the rainy season, seasonal winds called "monsoons" blow across the Indian Ocean and bring heavy downpours. Monsoon rains are vital to agricultural production and, therefore, the overall health of India's economy.

The winter season lasts from October to February. Winters are much more severe in northern India than southern India. However, temperatures in northern India rarely fall below freezing. India, with the exception of areas in the foothills of the Himalayas, doesn't receive any snow during the winter.

Ancestry

People of India belong to a number of ethnic groups. Most people belong to either the Indo-Aryan or the Dravidian group. The Aryans live in north and central India, and the Dravidians live in southern India. The Dravidians are believed to be descendents of some of the earlier inhabitants of India. The Indo-Aryans, who trace their ancestry to central Asian people called Aryans, started arriving in India around 1500 BC. The Aryan invasion led to the movement of the Dravidians toward southern India. India is also home to a number of tribal or native groups. The physical appearances of the people vary with the regions.

Population

India has the second-largest population in the world; 16 percent of the world's population lives in India. Only China has a larger population. These are the only counties in the billion-dollar population club. Chindia (a new term being used for India and China together) is now home to 36 percent of humanity.

India's population growth (1.6 percent) is much higher than that of China (0.6 percent) or the United States (0.9 percent).[22] Each year, twenty-six million new babies are added to the population, the largest number of babies born in a single country. China's adoption of the one-child policy helped it to reduce its population growth. There are no such restrictions in democratic India. As per the U.N. estimates, India is set to eclipse China as the most populous country in the world by 2050. In 1950, India's population was only 371 million.[23] This number was closely tied to the life expectancy at that time, which was only thirty-two. Since that time, advances in medicine and increased food production have pushed life expectancy to about sixty-four years and helped increase the population.

Social Structure

The social structure of India is based on the caste system. The Hindu caste system of India dates back to the time of Indo-Aryans. Castes are essentially social groups. A person is born into a caste, and this caste determines his or her social status and influences what occupation he or she might hold. Hindu society is traditionally divided into four major castes: the Brahmins, the Kshtriyas, the Vaishyas, and the Shudras. There are many sub-casts within each of these castes.

The Brahmins are priests and scholars and for centuries occupied a preeminent position in the caste system. Even today, almost all the priests in Hindu temples are Brahmins. The Kshtriyas are rulers or warriors; the Vaishyas are merchants; and the Shudras are laborers, servants, or artisans. A large group of people belong to no particular caste. They are the so-called *untouchables*, who were subjected to terrible discrimination for centuries. Mahatma Gandhi was greatly moved by the plight of the untouchables and made their emancipation one of the cornerstones of his freedom movement.

Since independence, India has made tremendous progress toward uplifting its disadvantaged population. Caste-based discrimination was outlawed, and the Indian constitution guarantees equal rights to all citizens. The government has also set aside a significant percentage of government jobs, legislative seats, and seats in educational institutions to the disadvantaged groups of people. Today, caste barriers are coming down like never before, especially in the cities. Caste-based discrimination is on the wane, but caste continues to play a major role in every sphere of life. For example, marriage decisions are almost always made on the basis of caste. Intercaste marriages in India are as rare as interracial marriages in United States. Political leaders are also elected on the basis of caste.

Languages

The Indian constitution recognizes twenty-two languages (Hindi, English, and twenty others).[24] These are spoken in over 1,600 dialects. Hindi is India's most popular language, spoken by about 40 percent of the population: a whopping four hundred million people. The states in India are divided on linguistic lines. Some states even get their names from the language spoken. Tamil Nadu state gets its name from the language Tamil. Gujarat state gets its name from the language Gujarati.

Hindi, which is derived from an ancient Indian language called Sanskrit, is mainly spoken in the so-called Hindi-belt states, situated in northern and central India. Penetration of Hindi is very low in southern states. Four regional languages, Telugu, Tamil, Kannada, and Malayalam, are spoken in the southern states of Andhra Pradesh, Tamil Nadu, Karnataka, and Kerala, respectively. These belong to the

Dravidian family of languages. Urdu is the state language of Jammu and Kashmir. It is also the language used by the majority of Muslims in India, as well as the people of neighboring Pakistan.

English, which was brought into India by the British, still maintains an associate status in India. Federal government uses both Hindi and English for communication purposes. English also serves as a common language for interstate communication involving non-Hindi-speaking states. About a third of India's population, about three hundred million people, have the ability to read, write, and carry on a simple conversation in English. English is also widely used in courts, universities, the press, and businesses. Indian parents often take pride in sending their children to English-language schools; they strongly believe that a child's future success is closely tied to his or her mastery of English. The availability of millions of English-speaking workers at low cost is the main reason why India has become the hottest destination for outsourcing of IT jobs from the United States.

Religions

India is a secular state and therefore has no official religion. India's constitution doesn't give any preferential treatment to any particular religion, and people of various faiths are allowed to practice their religion freely. The main religions in India are Hinduism, Islam, Christianity, Sikhism, Buddhism, and Jainism. India is the birthplace of two of the greatest religions of the world, Hinduism and Buddhism. The religious breakup of India's population is as follows: Hindus, 80.5 percent; Muslims, 13.4 percent; Christians, 2.3 percent; Sikhs, 1.9 percent; Buddhists, 0.8 percent; and Jains, 0.4 percent.[25]

Hinduism

Hinduism dominates India's religious landscape. Practiced by eight hundred million people, about 80 percent of India's population, Hinduism is one of the oldest religions in the world, with roots dating back thousands of years. A unique aspect of this religion is that it has no founder or fixed set of beliefs. Hindus pray to hundreds of gods and goddesses, which they believe are the different manifestations of one supreme god. Three gods, Vishnu (the protector), Shiva (the destroyer), and Brahma (the creator) are the most prominent.

Hindus believe in the concept of divine incarnation, called *avatar*. It is essentially Lord Vishnu, or god, appearing in human form to protect the world from evil. Lord Ram, hero of the Hindu epic *Ramayana*, is considered the seventh avatar. Lord Krishna, whose spiritual discourses are contained Hinduism's holy book *Bhagavad Gita*, is considered to be the eighth avatar. Gautama Buddha, founder of Buddhism, is considered to be the ninth avatar. In all there are ten avatars of Lord Vishnu: Matsya (the fish), Kurma (the tortoise), Varaha (the boar), Narasimha (the half-man/half-lion), Vamana (the dwarf), Parashurama (the man with the axe), Rama (hero of the epic *Ramayana*), Krishna (hero of epic *Mahabharata*), Buddha (founder of Buddhism), and Kalki (eternity). The Kalki avatar is expected to appear at the end of Kali Yuga, the time period in which we currently exist.

Hindus also believe in reincarnation. Each time a person dies, he or she is reborn. That means that only the body dies, while the soul of the person is reborn in a new body. The cycle of birth and death may continue for thousands of years, until one attains *moksha* (liberation) from this cycle. In order to attain moksha, a person has to lead a good life. Hinduism doesn't have one single sacred book, but rather has several, including the *Vedas, Puranas, Bhagavad Gita, Ramayana*, and *Mahabharata*. The *Vedas*, religious scriptures dating back to 1500 BC, form the basis for Hinduism and the caste system.

Key Things to Know About Hinduism:

- The Hindu religion is generally regarded as the world's oldest organized religion. It is considered more a way of life than a religion. It doesn't have an identifiable founder or a fixed set of beliefs.

- Hinduism is a set of codes of conduct written in ancient texts known as the *Vedas*. The *Bhagavad Gita* is considered the holiest of the holy books.
- Hindus pray to many gods and goddesses. They believe that these gods are different manifestations of one supreme god. Hindus worship idols. The Hindu religion respects other religions and does not seek any converts.
- The cow is sacred in Hinduism, and the slaughtering of cows is outlawed in many Indian states. Hindus don't eat beef.
- It is estimated that over sixty million Hindus live outside India. More than a million Hindus live in the United States.

Islam

Islam is the second most popular religion of India. India has the second-largest population of Muslims in the world, after Indonesia. Hindu India has more Muslims than the neighboring Muslim state of Pakistan. Islam arrived in India around AD 700[26] and flourished thereafter. Indian Muslims are the descendents of either the Muslim clans that invaded India or the Hindus who converted to Islam.

Christianity

India is home to twenty-five million Christians, more than the combined population of Norway, Sweden, and Belgium. Christianity was first introduced to India with the arrival of Saint Thomas the Apostle in the southern Indian state of Kerala in AD 52, when southern India had maritime trade with the West. In 1498, Portuguese explorer Vasco da Gama arrived in Calicut, India, becoming the first person to find a sea route from Europe to India. The discovery of a sea route not only gave boost to the spice trade but also encouraged Roman Catholic missionaries to travel to India to spread their faith. The Portuguese conquest of the western coastal region of Goa in 1510 led to the gradual introduction of the Christian faith there, under the auspices of Saint Francis Xavier. Under British rule, the Church of England was introduced in India, and numerous churches came into existence in major cities.

Like other religions of India, Christians differ in ethnicity, language, social customs, and forms of worship. They are mainly concentrated in the southern states of Kerala, Tamil Nadu, and Goa. Of the total Christian population, Kerala state accounts for a quarter of the population, or six million people. Indian Christians are widely credited with playing a positive role in the areas of education, social work, and nursing. Since the 1990s, Christian missionaries operating in India have come under increased criticism and scrutiny for their role in converting people of Hindu faith into Christianity. Pope John Paul II, on his second visit to India in 1999 amid rising tensions between the Hindus and Christians, defended the conversions on the grounds that religious freedom constitutes the very heart of human rights, and people have a right to change their religion if their conscience so demands.[27]

Sikhism

Sikhism, founded by Guru Nanak in the sixteenth century, is widely practiced in the north Indian state of Punjab. Sikhs believe in one god, follow ten gurus, do not believe in the caste system, and uphold the right to bear arms to defend their faith. Sikhs worship in places called *Gurudwaras*, which contain the religion's sacred book called *Guru Granth Sahib*. Facing persecution from Muslim rulers of India, the tenth and final Guru Gobind Singh founded the *Khalsa* (community) of Sikhs who took vows of loyalty and were ready to use weapons to defend themselves and their people. Sikhs pride themselves on their bravery, and many of them serve in the Indian army. They wear turbans, and all men use the same last name Singh. Five K's are mandatory for all Sikh men: *kesh* (leave hair or beard untrimmed), *kangha* (always carry a comb), *kirpan* (carry a sword to be ready for battle), *kachcha* (wear underwear), and *kada* (wear an iron bangle).[28]

In the 1980s, some Sikh groups were involved in a violent separatist movement in Punjab state to gain independence from India. This movement turned violent and culminated in the assassination of India's prime minister Indira Gandhi by her Sikh security staff. In the aftermath of Indira Gandhi's death, riots broke out in Delhi, which resulted in thousands of deaths. After a decade of bloodshed and thousands of innocent lives lost, peace finally returned to Punjab state in the early 1990s.

Buddhism

Buddhism was founded in India by Siddhartha Gautama (563–483 BC)[29] and became popular in ancient India. Gautama was an Indian prince who renounced his royal life to search for an end to human suffering, including sickness, old age, and death. He became enlightened after meditating for six years under a banyan tree. He was given the title of Buddha (the enlightened one) by his followers. Like Hindus, Buddhists believe that life is a cycle of births, deaths, and rebirths. The goal of a person is to be released from the seemingly endless cycle of birth-death-rebirth by living a life of detachment. Buddha introduced four noble truths, or four facts of life,[30] which form the foundation of Buddhism:

- Life is suffering (*dukkha*). All human beings are subject to suffering and pain.
- The root cause of suffering is attachment.
- Suffering does have an end. That means there is a way to end the suffering.
- The fourth noble truth explains the eight-fold path that leads to an end of suffering.

The eight-fold path that leads to detachment and which, in turn, ends human suffering can be broken down into eight parts: right understanding, right intention, right speech, right action, right livelihood, right effort, right-mindedness, and right concentration.

Key Things to Know About Buddhism:

- Buddhism was founded 2,500 years ago by an Indian Hindu prince named Siddhartha Gautama, who renounced everything (his royal life, his wife and son) to understand the meaning of life and find an answer to human suffering.
- Buddha introduced the concept of four noble truths, which acknowledge that life is full of suffering and provide a path to end suffering. Buddha preached an eight-fold path that leads to detachment and an end of suffering.
- Emperor Ashoka, who ruled India in the third century BC, is widely credited with spreading Buddha's teachings around the world.
- Buddhism later spread to China and other countries of Southeast Asia but declined in India.
- There are four pilgrimage sites for Buddhism: Lumbini (birthplace of Buddha), Bodh Gaya (site where Buddha attained enlightenment), Sarnath (site of Buddha's first discourse), and Kushinagar (site where Buddha passed away or attained *nirvana*). Lumbini is in Nepal, and the other three places are in India.

Jainism

Jainism was founded in India by a reformer named Mahavira (599 BC–527 BC).[31] It currently has about four million followers, mostly confined to northern and western India. Jainism preaches the doctrine of *ahimsa*, which includes nonviolence and respect for all life.

Zoroastrianism

India has the largest population of Zoroastrians in the world. Usually called the *Parsis* in India, the Zoroastrians fled Persia (present-day Iran) over one thousand years ago when it was being converted to Islam. The Parsis excel in industry and commerce and contribute richly to the intellectual and artistic life of the nation. Prominent people among the Indian Parsi community include the head of India's illustrious industrial group Ratan Tata, the well-known conductor Zubin Mehta, and the lead singer Freddie Mercury of the rock band Queen.

Clothing/Dress

India's traditional clothing styles are unique and varied when compared to the West. Cultural, regional, and religious differences account for these variations. Clothing comes in different colors, textures, and designs.

The majority of Indian women wear traditional Indian clothing. There are basically two types of traditional garments for women: the *saree* and the *salwar-kameez*. The saree is one of the garments most commonly worn by Indian women, especially married and elderly women. The origin of the saree dates back to the Indus Valley Civilization. It is essentially a rectangular, unstitched cloth, five to six yards long, that is draped around the body with the loose end flung over the shoulder. It is worn with a blouse. There are many varieties of sarees manufactured in different types of cloth, including silk, cotton, polyester, and synthetic. They can be handwoven or woven on mechanical looms. *Salwar-kameez* or *churidar* is the other type of garment that is gaining popularity with younger Indian women. Originating in the northern state of Punjab, it is a combination of *salwar* (loose trousers) and a *kameez* (long shirt). A piece of cloth called a *dupatta*, worn over the shoulders, completes this outfit. A variation of salwar involves tightly fitting trousers called *churidar*, which are wide at the top and narrow at the ankle.

Indian women complement their traditional clothing with several types of ornamentation, including *bindi, mehendi, mangalsutra*, toe rings, nose rings, earrings, bangles, and other jewelry. A *bindi* is an essential part of a Hindu woman's makeup. It is derived from the Sanskrit word *bindu* (a drop) and consists of a red dot made with vermilion powder that is worn by women on their forehead, between their eyebrows. A bindi is considered a highly auspicious mark in the Hindu religion and has been part of India's culture and heritage for thousands of years. *Mehendi* is the traditional art of decorating palms and feet with a paste made from finely ground leaves from a henna plant. The green leaves from the plant give the skin a red color. A *mangal-sutra* (auspicious thread) is a sacred necklace with a pendant worn strictly by married Hindu women as a symbol of their marriage. Toe rings are traditional Indian jewelry, worn by married Hindu women to adorn their feet. They are generally circular bands made of silver and worn in pairs on the second toe of both feet. Nose pins or nose rings are quite popular in Indian culture.

Indian women's love affair with gold is widely acknowledged throughout the world. Gold is worn on a daily basis, although heavy jewelry is generally reserved for special occasions such as festivals and religious ceremonies. India, the world's largest importer of gold, routinely imports eight hundred to nine hundred tons of gold, three-quarters of which is used by India's thriving jewelry industry.[32]

Table 1:
Top Five Gold-Importing Nations by Value (2005) $ Billions

India	10.9
U.S.A.	4.4
Turkey	3.9
Italy	3.5
Canada	2.3

Source: International Trade Center

Men are less traditional when it comes to clothing. Men in southern India wear a garment called a *dhoti*, which is a rectangular cloth wrapped between the legs to form a type of loose trousers. Men in northern India wear loose trousers called *pajama*. Both of these garments are worn with a short shirt or a long, loose shirt known as a *kurta*. On special occasions, such as a marriage, men in northern India wear *sherwani* (a long coatlike garment), fastened in the front with buttons. Men belonging to the Sikh community wear turbans. Western-style clothing is becoming increasingly popular for urban men and women. The majority of men have adopted trousers and shirts in both formal and informal settings. Jeans are quite common among the younger generations.

Food Habits

India is truly a diverse country, and its varied nature can be observed in culture, religion, racial makeup, language, geography, and climate. As a result, Indian cuisine is also diverse, and food preferences and traditions vary from region to region and from culture to culture. It is entirely possible that dishes from one part of the country may be completely unknown to other parts of the country. Due to India's large vegetarian population, Indians over the years have perfected the art of vegetarian cooking like no other country in the world. Unlike in the West, where vegetarian dishes are often equated with salads and raw vegetables, India offers vegetarian dishes that are rich in taste, color, flavor, and calories.

A typical Indian meal consists of rice or wheat bread served with fried vegetables or meat, lentil soup, and plain yogurt. Generally, people of northern India eat wheat bread, whereas people of southern India prefer rice. The preference is mainly dictated by both age-old traditions and availability of the commodities. Since rice crops require more water and sunshine than wheat crops, they are mainly produced in southern and eastern parts of the country. Similarly, wheat is mainly produced in the northern states of Punjab, Haryana, and Uttar Pradesh, where the rainfall is generally less. Indian homemade wheat breads, also known as *chapathis*, are thin, round, flat breads with the look and feel of Mexican flour tortillas. In southern India, rice is consumed in different forms: steamed; made into crispy, paper-thin crepes known as *dosas*; or streamed rice cakes called *idlies*.

Indian dishes are generally cooked in vegetable oil or *ghee* (clarified butter). Indian cuisine also uses large varieties of pulses such as peas, beans, and lentils. They are used in whole, split, or powdered form. For many vegetarian Indians, pulses are an excellent low-fat, low-cost source of necessary dietary proteins. Fresh fruits like bananas, mangoes, and guavas or desserts round out the meal.

One thing that is common to all types of Indian foods, both vegetarian and meat-based, is the extensive uses of spices. If you walk into a traditional Indian home or restaurant during mealtime, you are guaranteed to experience the aroma of distinct spices. India's love affair with spices is thousands of years old. Spices have both aromatic and medicinal value and are generally considered good for the body, mind, and soul. Indian spices are generally used in ground form, since they release more fragrance when grounded. *Masala* refers to a mixture of spices in ground form. The spices used in preparing masala include black pepper, turmeric, cumin, mustard, fenugreek, cloves, and cardamom. Indians typically top off their spicy dishes with cilantro leaves to bring additional flavor.

India is home to the famous *tandoori* chicken and basmati rice. Originating in the northern Indian state of Punjab, tandoori chicken is made by roasting marinated chicken in a unique, smoky clay oven called a *tandoor*. The chicken is marinated in yogurt, lemon juice, and unique spices. The tandoori chicken is served with either *tandoori naan* (special bread made in a tandoori oven) or basmati rice. *Basmati* rice is long-grained, aromatic rice grown in the foothills of the Himalayas in northern India and parts of Pakistan. *Bas* in the Hindi language means "aroma" or "smell" and *Mati* means "full of"; the combined word *basmati* means "full of aroma." Basmati rice is more expensive than regular rice and is mainly consumed on special occasions.

Tea (*chai*) is the most popular beverage in northern India, whereas coffee is popular in southern India. Both tea and coffee are consumed in hot form with milk and a generous amount of sugar. Indian tea or chai is a hot, spiced, milk beverage, very different to the iced tea available in the United States. Various spices, including cardamom, cinnamon, cloves, and pepper, are used in chai. Chai is becoming increasingly popular in the United States, with chai lattes emerging as an alternative to coffee-based beverages offered in coffeehouses like Starbucks. A chai latte (*latte* in Italian means "milk") is a spiced tea mixed with milk steamed from an espresso machine.

Religion and caste play a huge part in the food habits of Indians. In general, Hindu Brahmins and Jains are strictly vegetarian, excluding all forms of meat, fish, and even eggs from their diet. It is generally believed that about 20 percent of the Indian population is strictly vegetarian.[33]

That still adds up to two hundred million vegetarians in the nation, making India the largest vegetarian country in the world. Even those who eat meat do so sparingly. The reason may be economic or cultural. Meats like chicken and lamb can be very expensive for an average Indian and therefore are eaten only on special occasions such as festivals and family get-togethers. In India, most meat-eaters are perfectly happy eating a complete vegetarian meal. Hindus do not eat meat, as they consider the cow to be holy. Muslims do not eat pork because they consider it unclean. When the fast-food giant McDonald's entered the Indian market, it had no choice but to dump its flagship hamburgers in favor of chicken and vegetarian fast-food offerings.

Table 2: McDonald's Menu in India

Vegetarian Offerings	Non-Vegetarian Offerings
McVeggie™	Chicken Maharaja Mac™
McAloo Tikki™	McChicken™
Paneer Salsa Wrap	Filet-O-Fish™
Crispy Chinese	Chicken Mexican Wrap
Veg McCurry Pan™	Chicken McGrill™
Pizza McPuff™	Chicken McCurry Pan™

Source: McDonald's India Web Site

India is also known for its simple cooking methods and dining traditions. Cooking is generally done on a two-burner gas stove connected to an external cooking gas (LPG) metal cylinder. A traditional Indian eats his or her meal sitting cross-legged on the kitchen floor or on low wooden stools. Indians generally eat with the fingers of their right hand, without using their palm. It is considered offensive to eat food with the left hand. Spoons and forks are seldom used, so washing hands before and after meals is fairly common in India.

Until recently, most Indians cooked everything from scratch with fresh ingredients. Cooking is considered an art perfected by the women in the family, and recipes are passed from generation to generation. Also, Indians traditionally prefer eating at home to eating out. But there are growing signs that modern India is going through a culinary revolution decades after India decided to open its doors to foreign trade and investment. India's burgeoning middle-class families, with high disposable incomes, are increasingly showing preference to eating out, which is contributing to a boom in restaurant business in cities and towns. Global fast-food chains like McDonald's and Pizza Hut have opened up outlets in all the major cities across India.

Key Things to Know About Indian Cuisine:

- Indian cuisine is very diverse, and food habits and preference vary by region, culture, and religion. It is known for its extensive use of spices. The term *masala* refers to a blend of spices in ground form.
- *Curry* is the term popularized by the British to refer to any sauced Indian vegetable and meat dish with lots of spices.
- India is home to the famous *tandoori* chicken and aromatic *basmati* rice. Tandoori chicken is marinated chicken roasted in a unique, smoky clay oven.
- Contrary to popular belief, only 20 percent of Indians, or two hundred million people, are strictly vegetarian. That still makes India the largest vegetarian country in the world.
- There is no beef-farming in India. Hindus don't eat beef because they consider the cow to be holy.

Cultures and Traditions [34]

India, site of one of the oldest civilizations in the world, is a melting pot of diverse races, religions, languages, and cultures. The rich diversity of India is the result of an assimilation of unique cultures brought by foreign invaders into native Indian culture. India's diverse cultures gave rise to many customs and traditions, which vary considerably from region to region. Yet many customs and traditions transcend race, caste, religious, linguistic, or regional boundaries and bind all Indians.

Key Traditions:

- Lighting of a lamp: In almost every Indian household, a traditional oil lamp is lit daily before the altar of the Lord. Light symbolizes knowledge in Hindu custom, and darkness, ignorance.
- *Namaste,* Indian salutation: *Namaste* is the most widely used salutation for greeting people, welcoming somebody, or even bidding farewell. In this salutation, both palms are placed together and raised below the face and the word *namaste* is uttered. The word *namaste* ("I bow to you" in Sanskrit) has the spiritual significance of reducing one's ego in the presence of another.
- Respect for parents, elders and guests: From early childhood, Indian children are taught to show the utmost respect for their parents and elders. It is customary for Indians to touch the feet of their parents and elders to seek their blessings. Indian hospitality is legendary and is guided by a Sanskrit saying, *Athithi Devo Bhava*, which means that a guest is truly your god and therefore should be treated like one. Indians rarely let their guests leave their homes unfed or hungry.
- Respect for cows: Cows are considered sacred by India's majority Hindu community. Therefore, slaughtering of cows is outlawed in many Indian states. In Hindu mythology, cows are associated with Lord Krishna, the reincarnation of Vishnu, who is believed to have appeared as a cowherd and protector of cattle.
- Cremation upon death: In the Hindu tradition, a person is cremated rather than buried after death. However, cremation is forbidden in Islam, and Indian Muslims bury their dead. Cremation is the practice of disposing of a corpse by burning.

- Beliefs and superstitions: For many Indians, daily life is governed by many beliefs and superstitions, which can take many forms and shapes. Indians have a lot of faith in astrology (the belief that distant cosmic objects like stars and planets influence human lives). Even routine activities, such as leaving on a journey or depositing money in a bank, are undertaken at auspicious times as per the Hindu calendar. Indians also believe in palmistry, or hand-reading.

Yoga

India is the birthplace of yoga, an exercise system that consists of a series of postures, breathing techniques, and meditation. Many sacred Hindu texts such as *Vedas*, *Upanishads*, and *Bhagavad Gita* discuss various aspects of yoga. The yoga as we know it today is based on the *Yoga Sutras*, believed to be written by Sage Patanjali in the second century BC.

Yoga is not just a workout; it can be a whole way of life. The word *yoga* comes from Sanskrit (the language of ancient India) and means "union." The goal is to create union between body, mind, and spirit, thus achieving a state of enlightenment. This is done through exercise, breathing, and meditation. In yoga terminology, *asana* means "posture" or "pose" and *pranayama* is the science of proper breathing. Pranayama goes hand in hand with the asana or pose. Popular asanas or postures include *padma-asana* (lotus posture), *matsya-asana* (fish posture), *dhanura-asana* (the bow pose), *sirsha-asana* (headstand posture), and *shava-asana* (corpse posture). A balanced diet complements yoga practice.

Although yoga has been around for thousands of years, only in the past two decades has it become popular in the West. Today, millions of people around the world are adding yoga to their exercise routine to reduce stress and improve their health and well-being. A Harris poll commissioned by *Yoga Journal* estimated that 7.5 percent of U.S. adults (some 16.5 million people) practiced yoga in 2003.[35]

The health and fitness benefits of yoga are now being confirmed by scientific research. A study by the American Council on Exercise

(ACE) concluded that yoga improves strength and endurance as well as balance and flexibility.[36]

Ayurveda

Ayurveda is an ancient system of medicine that originated in India more than five thousand years ago. The word *ayurveda* comes from Sanskrit and means "the science of life." Ayurveda is a form of holistic medicine that views the body and the mind as a whole. The goal is to integrate body, mind, and spirit because physical health can't be achieved without emotional or mental health.

According to Ayurveda, the five elements of nature (space, air, fire, water, and earth) combine in the body as three *doshas* (components) known as *vatta* (air and space), *pitta* (fire and water), and *kapha* (earth and water). Illness results if imbalance occurs in any of the three components. Restoring the balance of these components is required for optimal health. The Ayurvedic system of medicine combines yoga, meditation, herbs, and dietary advice to restore the balance and bring about healing. In India, there are many undergraduate and graduate colleges for Ayurveda, where training can involve up to five years of study. India is home to almost four hundred thousand Ayurvedic doctors and fifteen thousand medical facilities dedicated to this form of medicine.[37]

In North America, Ayurveda is considered a form of alternative medicine, and its popularity is growing. Many spas and salons offer Ayurvedic treatments for relaxation and healing.

Indian Holidays/Festivals

Indians celebrate many festivals, perhaps more than any country in the world. There are three "secular" national holidays that are celebrated throughout the country: Republic Day (January 26), Independence Day (August 15), and Mahatma Gandhi's birthday (October 2). In the spirit of India's religious pluralism, a number of religious festivals of all the major religions (Hinduism, Islam, Christianity, Sikhism, Jainism, and Buddhism) are celebrated each year. These festivals are celebrated according to the lunar calendar and therefore do not occur on the same date each year.

Table 3: Major Indian Festivals (Based on 2008 Calendar)

January 13, 14	Makara Sankranti/Pongal
February 11	Vasant Panchami
March 6	Mahashivratri
March 22	Holi
April 6	Gudi Padwa/Ugadi
April 14	Baisakhi/Ram Navami
April 18	Mahavir Jayanti
May 20	Buddha Purnima
July 18	Guru Purnima
August 6	Nag Panchami
August 16	Raksha Bandhan
August 24	Sri Krishna Janmashtami
September 3	Ganesh Chaturthi
September 12	Onam
September 29	Navratri Begins
October 9	Dussehra
October 18	Karwa Chawth
October 28	Diwali
November 13	Guru Nanak Jayanti

The Hindu calendar forms the basis for Hindu festivals. It follows a lunar year, which consists of twelve lunar months. Each month has a unique name and is associated with a sign of the *rashi* (zodiac). The lunar months are: *Chaitra, Vaisakha, Jyaistha, Asadha, Shravana, Bhadra, Asvina, Kartika, Agrahayana, Pausa, Magha,* and *Phalguna*. Each month is divided into two *pakshas* (fortnights). There are fifteen days in each *paksha*, called *tithis*. Each *tithi* (day) has a unique name. The use of the Hindu calendar is largely limited to setting up the dates for the festivals each year. Indians still follow the Gregorian or Christian calendar for day-to-day activities.

The Hindu calendar is filled with festivals. Some of the festivals, such as *Diwali*, *Dussehra*, and *Holi*, are celebrated throughout the country. *Diwali* or *Deepawali* (row of lamps) is arguably the biggest and most well-known Hindu festival around the world. It commemorates the return of Lord Ram to his kingdom in Ayodhya after spending fourteen years in exile. The festival generally lasts for five days, with the third day celebrated on a grand scale. On the third day, rows of lamps (generally clay oil lamps) are lit around homes and rooftops. Fireworks light up the night sky.

Key Things to Know About Indian Festivals:

- India celebrates more festivals than any other country in the world. The Hindu lunar calendar forms the basis for Hindu festivals.
- *Diwali* or *Deepawali* (row of lamps) is arguably the biggest festival celebrated by Hindus around the world. It commemorates the return of the Hindu god Lord Ram to Ayodhya after spending fourteen years in exile.
- *Ganesha* (elephant-headed god) is arguably one of the most worshipped Hindu gods. Hindus deeply believe in his powers as remover of obstacles and therefore worship him before undertaking a journey or any important task.
- Not all festivals are celebrated in every part of India. For example, the *Onam* festival is celebrated only in the southern state of Kerala.
- The *Kumbh Mela* (*Kumbh* means "pitcher" and *Mela* means "fair"), which is held once every three years at one of four designated locations, attracts millions of people and is considered the largest religious gathering in the world.

Indian Marriages

Arranged or traditional (or family-assisted) marriages have been part and parcel of Indian culture for thousands of years. Unlike the courtship or love-marriage system practiced in Western cultures, in which people choose their own partners, the arranged-marriage system relies on the matchmaking skills of parents, relatives, and close friends. India's arranged-marriage system has been a topic of great interest in the West for centuries. Most people in West deride the system as backward due to its perceived lack of choice, freedom, and individuality.

The arranged-marriage system came into existence at a time when child marriages were common in India. In those days, parents married off their children at an early age, even before puberty. Since the child was too young to give consent to the marriage, the parents would give consent on his or her behalf. The main purpose of securing marriage at a young age was to prevent the child from marrying outside his or her caste, religion, and social status. The system is essentially a by-product of India's rigid caste system. Child marriages are now banned in India, and a boy must be twenty-one and a girl eighteen before they can marry. As per Indian laws, once a person attains the legal marriage age, he or she is free to choose his or her marriage partner. However, a majority of Indians continue to prefer the arranged-marriage route to find their spouses.

Here is how the system works. Parents and family members take the initiative and search for the prospective bride or groom through personal contacts, advertisements in the newspapers, or Internet marriage portals. If there is an apparent match, a contact is established between the parents of the boy and girl to gather more details and fix a date for a face-to-face meeting. The boy and the girl see and talk to each other for the first time in the presence of both families. After the face-to-face meeting, if the boy and girl like each other and give their consent to the marriage, an engagement ceremony is typically held at a later date. If they do not feel they are a good fit, the search will continue until a suitable bride or groom is found. At some point during the process, the horoscopes of the boy and girl are compared to gauge compatibility. This age-old custom is still followed in India. At the time of a child's birth, a horoscope is created (with a chart representing the positions of the sun, moon, and planets) at the precise time of birth. For many Hindu Indian families, even the most educated, it is important that the horoscopes of the prospective bride and groom be compatible; otherwise, the marriage is a nonstarter. The date and time of the wedding is fixed as per the astrological chart of both the bride and the groom.

A typical Hindu marriage consists of several religious ceremonies performed over two to three days. The main ceremony typically lasts for five to six hours. At the end of the ceremony, the groom ties a *mangalsutra* (sacred thread) around the neck of the bride to symbolize their union. Legally, the marriage is now final and binding. The majority of Indian marriages are not registered because the government recognizes the legality of religious marriages. Recently, however, India's Supreme Court ruled that all marriages, regardless of their religion, be registered with state authorities. The goal is to prevent underage marriages and polygamy.

What is the success rate of arranged marriages? Pretty good, it seems, if one goes by the low divorce rates in India, which are among the lowest in the world. Does this mean that all married couples are happy in India? Certainly not. So what accounts for its success? Men in India are generally breadwinners, and women take the role of full-time homemakers. Due to a lack of educational and job opportunities, Indian women find it financially difficult to survive on their own outside of marriage. Also, the social stigma of divorce makes it difficult for a woman to walk away from an abusive or incompatible relationship. It is very hard for a divorced woman to get remarried in India. But arranged marriages offer some protections to women. For example, it is equally difficult for a man to walk away from a relationship, due to a fear of what society and elders may think. the fear of society and elders. All these factors contribute to lower divorce rates in India. In summary, Indian society generally discourages divorces except as a last resort.

The main drawback of the arranged-marriage system is that the marriage happens without the boy or girl knowing each other well. This may lead to incompatibility and unhappiness down the road as the couples uncover the finer details of their partner's behaviors and attitudes. Also, social evils such as the age-old dowry system continue to flourish in some parts of India under the guise of the arranged-marriage system.

Anatomy of India's Dowry System

A *dowry* is an illegal payment either in cash or in kind made by a bride's parents to a groom's parents at the time of their wedding. In many Indian households, a marriage is a nonstarter without this payment, even if the boy and girl like each other and want to get married. Paying and accepting a dowry has been illegal in India for more than four decades, but the law is routinely ignored even by the educated and wealthy.

What is considered a reasonable dowry payment? It depends on several factors. Doctors, engineers, computer professionals, and Indian men working abroad command huge dowries in the marriage market due to their high future earnings potential. The payments can add up to hundreds of thousands of dollars, and they are often adjusted to inflation rates and rupee/dollar exchange rates. Needless to say, the dowry system has become such an enormous financial burden that many women try to avoid having daughters. The accepted notion in India is that a daughter is a financial burden, while a son is a cash cow. In India, female fetuses are routinely aborted after a prenatal sex determination. Some women often end up aborting fetus after fetus until they have a baby boy. This perilous trend led to a steep drop in the female population, which stood at just 933 women for every 1,000 men in India. In 1996, the government finally acted by banning sex determination tests. But like the antidowry legislation, legislation against sex determination is largely ignored by the Indian population.

The dowry system often leads to violence against newly married women in India. Government statistics show that over seven thousand women died in 2001 in mysterious circumstances, presumably killed by their in-laws and husbands over inadequate dowry payments. This type of crime is often called "bride-burning" in India. After the death of their wives, the men can remarry and can get another dowry. Although the number of deaths is small compared to the size of India's population, the fact that such practices are still occurring in the twenty-first century brings shame to the society. Many other brides in India live under constant harassment over the dowry. Recently, many women have been striking back at this evil practice. In 2003, Nisha Sharma, a young college graduate, caused quite a stir and gained international prominence when she had her would-be husband and in-laws arrested for demanding $25,000 more than the agreed-upon dowry on the day of wedding. But the dowries are not going away any time soon. They are deeply ingrained in Indian culture, and the laws of the land are treated with contempt.

Indian Marriages: New Trends

Although the basic concept of arranged marriage continues to be popular in India, there are definite signs that it is undergoing significant changes, particularly with the advent of the Internet and the noticeable increase in girls' education levels. Arranged marriages are giving way to "assisted marriages," in which parents still do the basic groundwork, such as screening the candidates based on caste, religion, and social status, but the children have ultimate veto power over who they would like to marry. Many young people, especially those in urban areas who tend to come under Western influence, are increasingly adopting an ambivalent approach toward arranged marriages. With the proliferation of matrimonial portals on the Internet, many boys and girls are looking for matches themselves. The estimated market for online matchmaking is estimated at $250–$300 million.[38] It is expected to go up sharply with the rapid increase in computer penetration in India and favorable youth demographics, with 60 percent of Indians or six hundred million people below the age of thirty. Dating is still taboo in India, and live-in relationships are very rare.

It is also widely acknowledged that divorce rates are steadily climbing in India, especially among the affluent middle classes. Women are becoming more educated and hold high-paying jobs and are therefore less dependent economically on their husbands. Also, the social stigma associated with divorce is receding, and remarriages are becoming more common. The concept of marriage is also undergoing a paradigm shift among young people. More emphasis is placed on the quality of the marriage than the longevity of the marriage.

Key Things to Know About the Indian Marriage System:

- The institution of marriage is considered very sacred in Indian culture. Arranged marriages have been an integral part of Indian culture for thousands of years.
- In addition to looking for a person belonging to same caste, religion, and social status, Indians generally want to marry somebody from the same community who can speak the same language, shares the same culture, and shares similar traditions.
- A typical Indian wedding ceremony lasts for days and showcases India's rich culture and tradition. Generally, all the wedding costs are borne by the parents of the bride.
- Although banned under Indian law, the dowry system continues to flourish under the arranged-marriage system. The parents of the bride are often required to make huge cash payments to the groom's family at the time of the wedding.
- Love marriages or courtship marriages do happen in India, but these are not the norm. Dating is still taboo in India, although it is becoming increasingly popular in urban areas.

Architecture

Indian architecture can be classified into four types or styles: Buddhist, Hindu, Muslim, and Colonial. Buddhist architecture is the oldest and dates back to the fourth century BC. Hindu architecture started to develop in the sixth century AD. Muslim invaders brought Islamic architecture to India after AD 1000. Colonial architecture came into existence during the British rule of India. India is now home to a number of UNESCO World Heritage Sites.[39]

Vaastu Shastra (dwelling treatise) is the ancient Indian science of architecture. The principles of Vaastu date back thousands of years, and the Vedas dealt with the subject extensively. Even today, Indians depend on this system for building homes, businesses, and temples. The Vaastu system relies on balancing the manmade environment with nature. For instance, the system stipulates that the main entrance of a home should always face east. Indians deeply believe that for the family's peace and happiness, one should abide by the principles of Vaastu. The system is very similar to the Chinese system of *feng shui*, which attaches importance to gadgets such as fish tanks and mirrors to achieve harmony with one's environment.

Buddhist Architecture

Buddhist architecture flourished during the reign of Mauryan Emperor Ashoka (270–232 BC), who conquered a great portion of India during the third century. Under Ashoka, Buddhism emerged as the dominant religion, overshadowing Hinduism. Ashoka's period marked the introduction of stone architecture in India. Two examples of Buddhist architecture are the cave temples of Ajanta and the monuments of Sanchi. Kushan King Kanishka, who ascended the throne in AD 120, embraced Buddhism and played a key role in spreading Buddhist architecture in his empire, which included Bactria (Afghanistan), Punjab, and Sind. Kushan rulers constructed two Buddha statues at Bamiyan between the second and fifth century AD. In 2001, the Taliban regime of Afghanistan caused an international outrage by destroying the two priceless Buddha statues at Bamiyan, as they viewed them as contrary to Islam.[40]

With Buddhism disappearing from India by thirteenth century AD, Buddhist architecture suffered a decline due to a lack of patronage from the ruling classes.

Hindu Architecture

Hindu architecture began to flourish in the sixth century AD with the growth of Hindu dynasties in both the north and the south. Initially, Hindu architecture drew heavily from the Buddhist styles; later, however, it became very ornate, with intricate carvings and sculptures. The rock-cut temples of the Elephanta caves, the Kailasa Temple of Ellora, the temple complex in Khajuraho, and the Sun temple at Konark are some of the examples of Hindu architecture that flourished between the sixth and eleventh centuries.

Hindu architecture began to decline in the north following Muslim invasions starting AD 1000. However, it continued to flourish in the south with the patronage of powerful Hindu rulers. All major rulers, including Pallavas (AD 600–900), Cholas (AD 900–1250), Hoysala (AD 1100–1350), and Vijayanagara (AD 1350–1565), brought their own distinct style to Hindu architecture. These rulers constructed thousands of temples across Tamil Nadu state, making it "the land of temples."

Pallavas are considered pioneers of southern Indian or Dravidian architecture, and they started the trend of building stone temples. The rock-cut temples of Mahabalipuram and the Kailasanatha temple at Kanchipuram are the finest examples of Pallava architecture. Kanchipuram (known as the land of one thousand temples) was the capital city of Pallava rulers and is filled with temples dating from the eight to seventeenth century AD. The Meenakshi temple in the ancient southern Indian city of Madurai is nearly two thousand years old and offers a marvelous example of Dravidian architecture.[41] Madurai was the capital city of the Pandyan rulers, who ruled parts of southern India until the twelfth century. The temple was almost completely destroyed by Muslim invaders in 1310 but was brought back to glory by Hindu Nayak rulers in AD 1560. The ancient temple draws thousands of pilgrims every day.

All Dravidian temples have at least three distinct features that differentiate them from other temple types. *Vimana* is the pyramidal tower over the shrine. *Gopura* is the gateway tower of the temple, ten or twelve stories in height. *Prakara* is the outer wall that envelops the main shrine and smaller shrines of the temple.

Rajasthani Architecture

The western Indian state of Rajasthan is known for its splendid forts and palaces. The warrior Hindu-Rajput community, which exerted influence over Rajasthan since AD 700, is mainly credited for the architectural developments there. Since many Rajput rulers served as vassals of the powerful Delhi-based Mughal rulers, they were able to protect their palaces and forts from the destructive attacks of the Mughal army. Therefore, many of the structures remain intact even today.

All major cities—Jaipur, Chittorgarh, Bikaner, Udaipur, Jodhpur, and Jaisalmer—have world-famous forts and palaces built by various rulers and architects. Built between the eighth and fifteenth century AD, many of the palaces have since been converted into luxury palace hotels. For instance, Udaipur (also known as the "city of lakes") is home to the world-famous Lake Palace Hotel, which was originally built in 1743 as a royal summer palace. It attained international recognition as the setting for the James Bond movie *Octopussy*, which was released in 1983.

Muslim Architecture

Indian architecture took on a new shape with the arrival of Islamic rule at the end of the twelfth century AD. During the early period of Islamic rule, Persian style was directly imported into India. But during the period of Mughal rule, starting the sixteenth century, an amalgamation of Islamic and Indian styles led to the creation of native Indo-Islamic architecture. The Mughal rulers constructed numerous mosques, mausoleums, palaces, forts, and other buildings. Although Mughal architecture can be found in many places in northern India, the principle sites are in Delhi, Agra, and Lahore.

Delhi is home to world-famous monuments such as the Qutb-Minar, Humayun Tomb, Red Fort, and Jama Masjid. Agra is known for its universally admired masterpiece, the Taj Mahal (Crown Palace), considered the jewel of Indo-Islamic architecture. In July 2007, the Taj Mahal was chosen as one of the "Seven New Wonders of the World" by a nonprofit foundation headed by Swiss adventurer Bernard Weber.[42] The selection was based on over one hundred million votes cast via the Internet and text massages.

Table 4: Seven Wonders of the World: Original Versus New

Original	New
The Great Pyramid	The Great Wall of China
The Hanging Gardens of Babylon	Petra, Jordan
The Temple of Zeus	The Christ Redeemer Statue, Brazil
The Colossus of Rhodes	Machu Picchu, Peru
The Lighthouse of Alexandria	The Pyramid at Chichen Itza, Mexico
The Temple of Artemis	The Roman Coliseum, Italy
The Mausoleum of Halicarnassus	The Taj Mahal, India

Source: www.new7wonders.com

Key Things to Know About the Taj Mahal:

- The Taj Mahal is a white marble mausoleum built in memory of Mumtaz Mahal, the wife of the fifth Mughal Emperor, Shah Jahan.
- The mausoleum houses the grave of Queen Mumtaz Mahal (who died in AD 1631). The grave of Shah Jahan (who died AD 1666) was added later.

- The Taj Mahal is an example of Mughal architecture, which combines elements of Persian, Indian, and Islamic architectural styles. It took nearly twenty-two years (AD 1631–53) and twenty thousand workers to build this monument, known as the "symbol of eternal love."
- The Taj Mahal is located along the banks of the Yamuna River in Agra city, two hundred kilometers south of Delhi. The tomb rises about 187 feet (higher than a modern twenty-storey building) from a platform of around 313 square feet.
- The Indian government imposed restrictions on industrial activity and motor vehicles near the Taj Mahal amid growing concerns that the air pollution around the monument is giving a yellow tinge to the white marble structure.[43]

Colonial Architecture

After Mughal architecture, major Indian cities saw the advent of Indo-European architecture. The Portuguese, who brought the Roman Catholic Church to India in the sixteenth century, built many churches and monasteries in Goa and Cochin. The British brought the Church of England to India and built cathedrals and churches in various places. They also built massive civic buildings and monuments, such as Rashtrapati Bhavan and India Gate in Delhi, Victoria Terminus and Gateway of India in Bombay (now Mumbai), and Victoria Memorial in Calcutta (now Kolkota).

Indian Literature

The *Vedas* (*Veda* means "knowledge") are the earliest examples of Indian literature. They are Hindu religious scriptures composed between 2000–1000 BC in *Vedic*, or old Sanskrit. The Vedas consists of four texts: the *Rig Veda*, the *Yajur Veda*, the *Sama Veda*, and the *Atharva Veda*. They are essentially hymns and chants about Vedic gods, the universe, rituals, and various aspects of life. After Vedas, *Brahmanas* and *Upanishads* came into existence between the eighth and fifth century BC. Brahmanas provide detailed information about rituals, whereas Upanishads are commentaries and explanations of Vedas. The emergence of Buddhism and Jainism in the sixth century BC gave rise to literature in several dialects of Sanskrit known as *Prakrit* ("natural" language). *Pali* is the most prominent Prakrit language. It was used for many Buddhist literary works, including the ancient *Jataka* tales, encompassing 547 stories of former incarnations or births of Buddha. It is believed that Jataka tales were composed around 300 BC.

The great Hindu epics, *Ramayana* and *Mahabharata*, were composed in Sanskrit between 300 BC and AD 400. The period between 400 BC and AD 600 is also referred to as the epic period. Hindus ascribe the authorship of *Ramayana* to Valmiki and *Mahabharata* to Ved Vyas. These epics evolved through several centuries before being put into writing. The *Ramayana* centers on the story of the Hindu god Lord Ram, who kills the demon king Ravana and rescues his abducted wife Sita with the help of the monkey god Hanuman. The *Mahabharata* recounts the heroic struggle of five brothers (Pandavas) against their evil paternal cousins (Kauravas). The Pandavas represent *dharma* (good) and the Kauravas *adharma* (evil). In the decisive battle of Kurukshetra, fought over eighteen days, Pandavas defeat Kauravas with the help of Lord Krishna and win control of the kingdom of Hastinapura.

The Hindu religious text *Bhagavad Gita* (Song of God), which is part of *Mahabharata*, was composed between the third and fourth century AD. It is arguably the most sacred and popular religious text in Hinduism. Like the *Ramayana* and *Mahabharata*, it was also composed in Sanskrit. The *Bhagavad Gita* is a divine discourse spoken by Lord Krishna in the form of a long dialogue between him and Arjuna, in the middle of the battlefield of Kurukshetra.

Table 5: Indian Literature (Pre-Bhakti Era)

Type	Period	Significance
Vedas	2000–1000 BC	Original scripture of the Hindu religion
Brahmanas	800–500 BC	Details about the rituals of Vedas
Upanishads	800–500 BC	Commentaries and explanations of Vedas
Jataka Tales	300 BC	Collection of Buddhist tales
Ramayana	300 BC–AD 400	The great Hindu epic; story of Lord Ram
Mahabharata	300 BC–AD 400	The great Hindu epic; story of a great war
Bhagavad Gita	AD 200–300	Holy book; contains the essence of Hinduism
Arthashastra	322–185 BC	Chanakya's treatise on politics and economics
Shakuntala	AD 300–400	Kalidasa's poetic drama
Kamasutra	AD 300–500	Vatsyayana's manual of love
Puranas	AD 500	Short, simple stories about Hindu gods
Panchatantra	300 BC–AD 500	Collection of children's stories

Source: Various

The *Arthashastra* by Chanakya Kautilya came into existence during the Mauryan rule (322–185 BC). Chanakya was believed to be the Brahmin prime minister in the court of India's first emperor, Chandra Gupta Maurya. *Arthashastra* is a treatise on politics and economics.

The Gupta period (AD 320–550) is considered the golden age of classical Sanskrit literature. The famous poet and playwright Kalidasa, whose works include *Raghuvamsha* (Dynasty of Raghu),

Kumarasambhava (Birth of Kumar Kartikeya), *Meghaduta* (Cloud Messenger), and *Shakuntala* (Story of Shakuntala), is generally associated with the reign of Chandra Gupta II. Kalidasa is often referred to as the Shakespeare of India. Other works of the Gupta period include the *Kamasutra* by Vatsyayana, which is a comprehensive text covering the entire spectrum of lovemaking.

A class of Sanskrit literary texts called the *Puranas* attained their final form around AD 500. Puranas are tales of ancient times. They are short, simple stories intended to convey the essence of the Vedas to common people.

The *Panchatantra* (Five Strategies) was written in classical Sanskrit between 300 BC and AD 500. It is a collection of popular children's stories featuring animal characters; much like Aesop's fables, they teach moral values.

From about AD 500 to 1600, a social and religious movement called the *bhakti* (personal devotion to god) movement swept across India.[44] It originated in southern India with the Nayanmars (devotees of Siva) and Alvars (devotees of Vishnu). They introduced the concept of *bhakti* as a means of attaining *moksha* (liberation from rebirth). This concept resonated well with the masses because it provided a good alternative to the Vedic and epic-era Hinduism, which had become too ritualistic and was dogged by the caste system. The bhakti movement had a profound influence on the development of regional languages, since the reformers preached in local languages. As a result, there was a remarkable growth of literature in all Indian languages.

Table 6: The Bhati Movement: Reformers/Poets/Saints

Poet/ Reformer	Language	Period (AD)	Significance
Nayanmars	Tamil	7th–12th century	Devotees of Lord Siva
Alvars	Tamil	7th–12th century	Devotees of Lord Vishnu
Ramanuja	Sanskrit	1017–1137	Proponent of Vaishnavism
Namdev	Marathi	1270–1350	Devotee of Lord Vithoba
Ramanand	Hindi	1400–70	Disciple of Ramanuja
Kabir	Hindi	1440–1518	Composer of popular poems in Hindi
Surdas	Hindi	15th century	Prominent poet, saint, and singer
Tulsi Das	Hindi	1532–1623	Author of the Hindi version of Ramayana
Tukaram	Marathi	1598–1647	Composer of popular devotional songs
Mira Bai	Rajasthani	1498–1547	Composer of popular devotional songs
Chaitanya	Bengali	1485–1533	Devotee of Lord Krishna

Source: Various

Indian literature came under the influence of Islam starting in the twelfth century. The Muslim rulers of India, including the powerful Mughal rulers (1526–1707), patronized the Persian language and made it the language of their administration. As a result, some of the Indian languages came under the influence of the Persian language. A new language called Urdu, a mixture of Hindi and Persian, emerged.

Hindi and Urdu are almost identical, except that Hindi is written in *Devanagari* script and draws heavily from Sanskrit, whereas Urdu is written in Persian script and contains large number of Persian and Arabic words.

Islamic rulers also brought to northern India a new form of poetry called the *Ghazal* (which means "converse with beloved" in Arabic). This is a form of poetry that was originally written in Persian but was later adapted into Urdu. It consists of five to fifteen couplets (two-line poems) called *Sher*. The Ghazals were made famous by Mirza Ghalib (1797–1869), a famous Indian poet of Turkish ancestry. He is considered to be the most popular and influential poet of the Urdu language.

By the early 1800s, the British had gained control of much of the Indian subcontinent. At the behest of Lord Macaulay, English education was formally introduced in India in 1835.

English education enabled Indian youth to explore Western ideas and literary works. The creation of printing presses around the country led to a rapid growth of newspapers and publications in both English and vernacular languages.

The later period of nineteenth century witnessed an intellectual awakening of Bengali Indians in and around Calcutta, a city founded by the British that later became the imperial capital of British Raj. This phenomenon, known as the Bengal Renaissance, produced an array of writers, painters, scholars, thinkers, and socioreligious reformers. The Bengali writers took the lead in blending Western ideas into Indian literature, thus laying the foundation for the era of modern Indian literature. Prominent among them were Bankim Chandra Chatterjee (1838–94), considered the father of the Bengali literary renaissance; and the literary genius Rabindranath Tagore (1861–1941), the first Indian and first non-European to receive the coveted Nobel Prize for literature in 1913 for his collection of poems called *Gitanjali* (Song Offerings).

Indian literature has come of age in the twentieth century. Prominent writers, including Premchand (Hindi), Amrita Pritam

(Punjabi), Subramanya Bharati (Tamil), Kaifi Azami (Urdu), Shiv Shankar Pillai (Malayalam), and Gurajada Appa Rao (Telugu), all contributed to the development of modern literature in their respective languages. Munshi Premchand (1880–1936) is one of the greatest literary figures of modern Hindi literature. His numerous works are credited with bringing realism into Hindu literature, which until then was dominated by religious works and fantasy. Amrita Pritam (1919–2005) is considered the doyenne of Punjabi literature. Her novel *Pinjar* (The Skeleton) was made into a feature film a few years ago.

Many Indians writing in English have attained international acclaim for their innovative and creative writing. The trio of Mulk Raj Anand, Raja Rao, and R. K. Narayan are regarded as the founding fathers of the Indian English novel and brought a distinct Indian flavor to English literature. Mulk Raj Anand's pioneering English novel *Untouchable* (1935) brought him international recognition. Raja Rao's debut novel *Kanthapura* (1938) deals with India's independence movement. R. K. Narayan's simple yet elegant style of writing, laced with gentle humor, has won him accolades throughout India. Most of his works are set in a fictional southern Indian town called Malgudi and depict the lives of common individuals.

The 1980s and 1990s brought a new crop of Indian writers who left an indelible mark on the international literary scene. Prominent among them are Salman Rushdie, Anita Desai, Vikram Seth, Arundhati Roy, Jhumpa Lahiri, Kiran Desai, Shashi Tharoor, and Aravind Adiga. The list is literally growing by the day.

Table 7: Indian Authors in English

Author	Select Works	International Honors
Rabindranath Tagore	*Gitanjali*	Nobel Prize in Literature 1913
Salman Rushdie	*Midnight's Children*	Booker Prize 1981
Anita Desai	*Fasting, Feasting*	Booker Prize 1999 Finalist
Arundhati Roy	*The God of Small Things*	Booker Prize 1997
Jhumpa Lahiri	*Interpreter of Maladies*	Pulitzer Prize 2000
V. S. Naipaul	*The Mystic Masseur*	Nobel Prize in Literature 2001
Kiran Desai	*The Inheritance of Loss*	Booker Prize 2006
Aravind Adiga	*The White Tiger*	Booker Prize 2008

Source: Compiled from Media Reports

Indian Music

India has two unique classical music styles, *Hindustani* and *Carnatic*, which are performed either as vocal or as instrumental. Hindustani music, which is popular in northern India, is influenced by Persian and Arabic music, brought to India by the invading Muslim rulers of the twelfth century. Carnatic, or southern, classical music, however, was not influenced by outsiders and evolved mainly from Hindu traditions dating back thousands of years. *Ragas* (set compositions of five to seven notes) form the foundation of both Hindustani and Carnatic music styles. Each raga has a special meaning and may be associated with a particular mood, emotion, season, or time of day. India has a unique set of musical instruments. The traditional Indian string instruments consist of the *sitar, sarod,* and *veena,* whereas the percussion instruments consist of the *tabla* and *mrigangam*. The violin, originally a Western instrument, made its entry into Carnatic music in the eighteenth century and has since become a vital part of southern Indian music.

Perhaps the most popular form of Indian music is film music, or music generated for motion pictures. Song and dance sequences are a cornerstone of almost all Indian movies. India's most celebrated female playback singer is Lata Mangeshkar, who was featured in the Guinness Book of World Records from 1974 to 1991 for having made the most recordings in the world.[45]

Indian Dance

India has a rich tradition of classical dance. There are six prominent types of classical dances: *Bharatanatyam, Kathak, Kathakali, Kuchipudi, Odissi,* and *Manipuri*. Each of these classical dance styles can be traced to a particular region of the country, and none can claim to have nationwide appeal. Some of the classical dances draw upon Hindu epics and deities. Bharatanatyam is one of the oldest and most widely known classical dances of India. Although it originated from the southern state of Tamil Nadu, is has gained recognition throughout India. It is performed by both men and women. Kathak is the major classical dance form of northern India. The word *Kathak* means "to tell a story." It is derived from the dance dramas of ancient India and is performed by both men and women. Kathakali is a popular dance from Kerala state. The word *Kathakali* translates to "story-play." It is known for its colorful costumes and unique makeup and is traditionally performed by men only. Kuchipudi dance gets its name from a village in the southern state of Andhra Pradesh. It is known for its graceful movements and is generally performed by a solo female dancer. Odissi and Manipuri dances belong to Orissa and Manipuri states, respectively, and are performed by both men and women.

Indian Movies

The Indian film industry is the largest in the world, with over one thousand films released annually. Indian movies are made in fifteen different languages, but only Hindi-language movies have national appeal; these take the lion's share of box-office revenues. The Hindi-language industry based in Mumbai (formerly Bombay) is widely known as "Bollywood," a term coined by the Indian media by blending Bombay and Hollywood, the hub of American cinema. The word "Bollywood" was added to the *Oxford English Dictionary* in 2003 and *Merriam-Webster's Collegiate Dictionary* in 2007.[46]

Since Indian states are divided along linguistic lines, each state produces films in its own language for its own audiences. The majority of regional movies are made in the southern Indian languages Telugu, Tamil, Malayalam, and Kannada. Each of these regions has adopted a nickname for its film industry. For instance, the Telugu movie industry, based in Andhra Pradesh state, is known as "Tollywood," and the Tamil film industry, based in Tamil Nadu, is known as "Kollywood." Even India's neighbor Pakistan chose "Lollywood" to describe its film industry, which is originated in the city of Lahore. In 2003, India produced 877 movies, in languages including Hindi (222), Telugu (155), and Tamil (151).[47]

So, what makes Indian cinema unique? Here are few important characteristics:

- Indian cinema remains the most popular medium of entertainment for the country of one billion people. Around fifteen to twenty million people go to see a movie every day.
- A typical Indian movie contains a little bit of everything: tragedy, comedy, drama, action, romance, fights, and musical numbers. That's why the majority of Indian movies are known as *masala* movies (*masala* is a term in Indian cuisine used to describe a hodge-podge of ingredients mixed together).
- Indian movies tend to be long. Many movies are three-hour extravaganzas and have intermissions. Indian audiences expect to get full value for their money.

- All movies feature elaborate song-and-dance sequences and flashy costumes. Actors and actresses lip-synch to songs previously recorded by professional playback singers.
- Strict government censorship rules do not allow nudity or French kissing in Indian cinema. But modest kisses do appear in some movies.

Table 8: Indian Feature Films by Language (2003)

Language	City/Region	Movies Released
Hindi	Mumbai	222
Telugu	Hyderabad	155
Tamil	Chennai	151
Kannada	Bangalore	109
Malayalam	Kerala State	64
Bengali	Kolkota	49
Marathi	Mumbai	25
Other Languages	Rest of India	102
Total Indian Movies Released (2003)		877
Hollywood Movies Released (2005)		563

Source: Central Board of Film Certification, India

A Brief History of Bollywood

India's first full-length silent movie, *Raja Harishchandra*, was produced by Dhundiraj Govind Phalke in 1913. The movie was a resounding success and heralded the birth of the Mumbai-based Indian film industry. The first "talkie" movie (a movie with sound) made its appearance with the release of Ardeshir Irani's *Alam Ara* in 1931. Later on, talkie movies in regional languages appeared in Telugu, Tamil, and Bengali.

The Mumbai movie industry got a big boost with the establishment of a production company, Bombay Talkies Limited, by Himanshu Rai and Devika Rani in 1934. A stream of movies began to emerge from the Bombay Talkies, starting with a murder mystery, *Jawani Ki Hawa*, in 1935. The pre-independent movie era also saw the arrival of actor-singer K. L. Saigal (1904–47), who acted in several hit movies such as *Devdas*, *Bhakta Surdas*, and *Tansen*. His untimely death in 1947, at the age of forty-three, brought an end to a glorious film career.

The 1940s also saw the arrival of three immensely popular actors: Dilip Kumar, Raj Kapoor, and Dev Anand. Dilip Kumar made his debut as the hero of the Bombay Talkies production *Jwar Bhatta* in 1944. He shot to fame in 1947 with his highly successful movie *Jugnu*, opposite singer-actress Noor Jehan. Dilip Kumar is considered a living legend of Indian cinema, and he is arguably the most imitated actor in Bollywood.

Legendary director-actor Raj Kapoor (1924–88), who began his career as an assistant on the sets of Dilip Kumar's first movie, *Jwar Bhatta*, got his first major break as the hero in Kidar Sharma's *Neel Kamal* (1947), opposite the actress Madhubala. Mehboob Khan's *Andaz* (1949) established Raj Kumar as a major actor in Indian cinema. *Andaz* also featured Dilip Kumar, the only time the two legends acted together in a film. Not content with being an actor, Raj Kapoor, at the age of twenty-four, set up his own studio and launched his first movie, *Aag*, in 1948. In 1949, Raj Kapoor produced the hit movie *Barsaat*, which featured him in the lead role, opposite Nargis. His next venture, *Awara* (1951), was a huge hit in India and also became a cult favorite in China and Russia.

Dev Anand, regarded as one of the most handsome actors of Bollywood, began his acting career in 1946 but tasted his first success in the Bombay Talkies production *Ziddi* in 1948, opposite Kamini Kaushal. Like Raj Kapoor, Dev Anand also turned into a movie producer with the establishment of his own movie production company, Navketan Films. His first film under the Navketan banner was *Afsar* (1950), starring Dev and the singer-actress Suraiya; it was directed by his older brother Chetan Anand. The following year saw the release of Navketan's second movie, *Baazi*, which catapulted Dev Anand to stardom. After that, there was no looking back for Dev Anand, who went on to act in more than one hundred motion pictures in a career spanning five decades. The movie *Baazi* also marked the debut of Guru Dutt (1925–64) as film director. He later started his own production company and produced and acted in many classic movies such as *Pyaasa, CID, Kaagaz Ke Phool, Sahib Biwi Aur Ghulam*, and *Chaudhvin Ka Chand*. His movie *Pyaasa* (1957) was rated as one of the best one hundred movies of all time by *Time Magazine* in 2005. Dutt's brilliant career came to an end with his apparent suicide in 1964, at the age of thirty-nine.

The leading actresses of Bollywood's golden era include Nargis, Madhubala, Meena Kumari, Vyjayantimala, and Wahida Rahman. Nargis had lead roles in many popular movies, such as *Barsaat* (1949), *Andaz* (1949), *Awaara* (1951), *Shree 420* (1955), *Chori Chori* (1956), and *Mother India* (1957). In most of her films, she acted opposite actor Raj Kapoor. Madhubala was, without a doubt, the most beautiful Hindi actress of all time. She is often compared to Marilyn Monroe and occupies a similar position in Bollywood. Meena Kumari, who earned the title "tragedy queen" of Indian cinema, delivered memorable performances in several movies, including *Baiju Bawra, Parineeta, Sahib Biwi Aur Ghulam*, and *Pakeezah*.

The 1940s and 1950s also saw the emergence of playback singing in Indian cinema. A playback singer is an off-camera voice that performs a song to which the actors and actress mime in the movie. The male playback singers that dominated Indian cinema include Mohammad Rafi, Mukesh, and Kishore Kumar. On the female side, singers Noor Jahan, Suraiyya, Lata Mangeshkar, her sister Asha Bhosle, and Geeta Dutt dominated the field.

The 1950s also saw the evolution of art cinema in India, pioneered by ace Bengali director Satyajit Ray (1921–92). Ray's classic Bengali movie *Pather Panchali*, which features life in rural Bengal in the 1920s, won the Best Human Document Award at the 1956 Cannes Film

Festival. He was also honored with an Oscar for Lifetime Achievement in films in 1992. The following year, in 1957, Mehboob Khan's *Mother India*, starring Nargis, Raj Kumar, Sunil Dutt, and Rajendra Kumar, became the first Indian movie to be nominated for an Academy Award in the Best Foreign Language Film category.

While the 1960s continued the dominance of the famous trio of Dilip Kumar, Raj Kapoor, and Dev Anand, a new crop of actors and actresses had begun to emerge. Notable among them were actors Rajendra Kumar, Shammi Kapoor, Raj Kumar, and Sunil Dutt. Rajendra Kumar, who played a memorable role in Mehboob Khan's Oscar-nominated *Mother India* (1957), emerged as the most successful romantic actor of Bollywood between 1959 and 1966. Virtually every film in which he acted turned out to be a silver jubilee hit, and soon he earned the nickname "Jubilee Kumar." Shammi Kapoor, the younger brother of legendary actor-director Raj Kapoor, finally came out of his brother's shadow in the early 1960s and emerged as a major actor in his own right, capitalizing on his unique antics and dancing style.

Toward the end of the 1960s, a new phenomenon in the form of actor Rajesh Khanna was sweeping the nation. After a string of unsuccessful movies, starting with Chetan Anand's *Aakhri Khat* (1966), Rajesh Khanna achieved overnight stardom with Shakti Samanta's *Aradhana* in 1969. The movie also catapulted Kishore Kumar into the position as the top male playback singer of Bollywood, displacing legendary singer Mohammad Rafi. For the next five years, Rajesh Khanna delivered hit after hit, acting opposite all the leading ladies of the time, including Hema Malini, Mumtaz, Sharmila Tagore, Tanuja, Mala Sinha, and Nanda.

But the Rajesh Khanna phenomenon did not last beyond the mid-1970s. As his films began to fail at the box office, Bollywood was looking for the next big star to emerge. The release of Prakash Mehra's *Zanjeer* in 1973 changed all that. The movie not only jumpstarted the fledgling movie career of Amitabh Bachchan but also changed the look and feel of Indian movies by introducing a new kind of action hero known as the "angry young man." Prior to the release of *Zanjeer*, Amitabh had acted in over a dozen movies, but none were very successful. After *Zanjeer*, there was no looking back for Amitabh, who delivered a string of hits for the next decade, including *Deewar, Sholay, Muqaddar Ka Sikander, Don, Laawaris,* and *Shakti.* Amitabh's immense popularity with the Indian masses became evident when he was gravely injured during the filming of *Coolie* in 1982. While he battled for his life with a ruptured intestine in Mumbai's Breach Candy Hospital, the entire nation went through a period of grief and prayers. The 1970s saw a rapid transformation in Bollywood movie plots, away from romance and family drama and toward violence and revenge.

By the mid-1980s, popular stars like Amitabh Bachchan were clearly past their prime. The advent of national television and the proliferation of pirated videocassettes and tapes deeply hurt the motion-picture industry. The playback singing for the movies, which forms the basis of elaborate song-and-dance numbers, suffered a body blow with the death of legendary singers Mukesh, Mohammad Rafi, and Kishore Kumar, all within a decade. Hurt by mediocre plots and lack of quality music, the movie industry grossed only $650 million in 1987, a 20 percent drop from 1982 levels. Remarkably, the movie industry still produced 964 movies in 1987, but only a third of them made money. By the end of the 1980s, Bollywood had reached its lowest point in history.

In the face of challenges faced in the 1980s, Bollywood had begun the task of reinventing itself. The success of movies like *Qayamat Se Qayamat Tak* (1988) and *Maine Pyar Kiya* (1989) shifted the momentum away from violent and vulgar themes to family-oriented movies and love stories. India's youth began to rally around a new generation of young stars such as Aamir Khan, Salman Khan, and Shah Rukh Khan. Indian directors began to make movies focusing on realistic, contemporary themes such as religious tensions, terrorism in Kashmir, and family stories and themes that catered to nonresident Indians (NRI). With this new approach, Bollywood tried to create a niche for itself in the era of satellite and cable television.

Among the prominent directors that emerged in the 1990s are Mani Ratnam, Aditya Chopra, Karan Johar, Sanjay Leela Bhansali, and Ashutosh Gowariker. Both Sanjay Leela Bhansali and Ashutosh Gowariker created a niche for themselves in the increasingly crowded field of talented Bollywood directors. Bhansali's hit movies include *Hum Dil De Chuke Sanam, Devdas,* and *Black.* The movie *Devdas* (2002), considered one of the most ambitious and successful films in Bollywood history, became the first Bollywood movie to receive special screening at the Cannes Film Festival. Ashutosh Gowariker directed the movie *Lagaan* (2001), which received the nomination for an Academy Award in the Best Foreign Language Film category.

Among the leading actors to emerge in the 1990s are Shahrukh Khan and Aamir Khan. Shahrukh Khan, also known as King Khan, is the most successful actor of present times. At age forty-two, he had already acted in more than fifty movies, delivering an astounding number of hits. He became the third Bollywood star, after Amitabh Bachchan and Aishwarya Rai, to have his wax statue unveiled at Madame Tussauds in London. Like Shahrukh Khan, Aamir Khan is also a very successful Bollywood actor; his hits include *Lagaan* (2001) and *Rang De Basanti* (2006).

The women actresses who were largely sidelined in the violent movie era of the 1980s also made a huge comeback in the 1990s, with actresses including Madhuri Dixit, Aishwarya Rai, Rani Mukherjee, Kajol, and Manisha Koirala taking significant roles. The year 1994 turned out to be a watershed year for Indian women, when Sushmita Sen and Aishwarya Rai won the coveted Miss Universe and Miss World titles, respectively. India's winning streak continued when Diana Hayden won the Miss World title in 1997, and Yukta Mookhey repeated the feat in 1999. In the new millennium, India bagged two more titles, with Lara Dutta winning the Miss Universe title and Priyanka Chopra the Miss World title. Many of the beauty queens sought careers in movies, setting new standards for beauty in Bollywood. Of all the beauty queens that entered Indian movies, Aishwarya Rai had the most success.

Table 9: Indian Female Beauty Pageant Winners

1994	Sushmita Sen	Miss Universe
1994	Aishwarya Rai	Miss World
1997	Diana Hayden	Miss World
1999	Yukta Mookhey	Miss World
2000	Lara Dutta	Miss Universe
2000	Priyanka Chopra	Miss World

Source: Compiled from Media Reports

The 1990s also saw movie directors of Indian origin shining at the international level. Notable among them are Shekhar Kapur, Mira Nair, Gurinder Chadha, and Deepa Mehta.

Shekhar Kapur, who started his career producing movies in Bollywood, directed the Academy Award-winning film *Elizabeth* (1998) and its 2007 sequel, *Elizabeth: The Golden Age*. Mira Nair, who shot to fame in 1988 with her Academy Award-nominated movie *Salaam Bombay*, established herself as a successful director with popular movies like *Mississippi Masala* (1991) starring Denzel Washington, *The Perez Family* (1995) starring Marisa Tomei, *Monsoon Wedding* (2001), and, more recently, *The Namesake* (2007). Gurinder Chadha, a British director of Indian descent, became an international sensation with her highly successful comedy movie *Bend It Like Beckham* (2002). The movie went on to become the first film by a nonwhite Briton to reach the number-one spot at the British box office. Likewise, Indian Canadian filmmaker Deepa Mehta's critically acclaimed movie *Water* (2005) was nominated for an Academy Award for Best Foreign Language Film in 2006.

Bollywood: New Trends

India's film industry is quietly emerging as a major player at the international level. The nation currently spends around $2 billion on movie tickets each year,[48] and most analysts predict that number to double by 2010. So what is driving this boom? It is not a single factor but rather a confluence of factors that is fueling the explosive growth in Indian cinema. The movie industry is clearly benefiting from the booming Indian economy, which is growing at 8–9 percent, causing disposable income and leisure-related spending to go up. The demographic profile also favors the industry. Nearly two-thirds of the population is under the age of thirty-five, and forty million people are joining the ranks of the middle-class every year.

Trend 1: Movie Financing Undergoes Changes; Corporatization is the New Mantra

Funding for the Indian movie industry used to come from an unorganized sector and a few big studios. Banks were not allowed to lend money to the industry. This opened the door for illegitimate funding for movie production, including money from the Mumbai mafia and black money from tax evaders.

The government finally acted by according industry status to Bollywood in 2001. Now banks are allowed to lend money to the movie industry. Funds from legitimate sources helped professionalize the industry. Corporatization is the new order in Bollywood. Gone are the days when the film industry was dominated by a few film dynasties. UTV Communications, Adlabs Films, Yash Raj Films, Eros, Venus Entertainment, and Studio 18 are some of the big names in the newly corporatized world of Bollywood. They brought professionalism to movie production and helped improve both the quality and the variety of movies produced in India.

Trend 2: Growing Overseas Markets

Bollywood movies are popular not only in India but also among South Asian communities around the world. The overseas markets are becoming increasingly lucrative for Indian producers, accounting for 20 percent of box-office revenues. The latest Bollywood hit movie *Jodhaa Akbar* was released in twenty-five countries on 1,500 screens, underscoring Bollywood's increasing reliance on overseas box offices.

The movie buffs among the twenty-million-strong nonresident Indians (NRIs), with a combined wealth of $300 billion, are credited with revitalizing the Indian movie industry after a slump in the 1980s. Many new releases are tailor-made to their tastes.

There are plenty of movie theaters across the United States that feature Indian movies on evenings and weekends. They are heavily concentrated in wealthy South Asian communities in Illinois, New York, New Jersey, Michigan, and Texas. Many companies have sprung up to tap the lucrative market of distributing Bollywood movies internationally. For instance, Eros International distributes Bollywood movies in markets such as the United States, United Kingdom, Canada, Africa, United Arab Emirates, and Australia.

Trend 3: Increase in Number of Movies Shot Overseas[49]

Indian filmmakers are increasingly filming in Switzerland, Australia, New Zealand, the United Kingdom, and elsewhere. Almost every producer wants to shoot important song sequences and romantic scenes in lush, foreign locales. The Swiss Alps area is a popular film location for Bollywood directors. Many Western countries are rolling out the red carpet for Bollywood filmmakers, hoping to increase tourism. The locations tend to become tourist attractions for Indian travelers. For instance, after Switzerland was featured in a number of movies, the number of Indian tourists traveling to that country increased to seventy-five thousand annually.[50]

Table 10: Select Bollywood Movies Shot in Foreign Locations

Movie	Country
Dilwale Dulhaniya Le Jayenge	Switzerland, United Kingdom
Don	Malaysia
Fanaa	Poland
Gangster	South Korea
Kabhi Alvida Naa Kehna	United States (New York)

Kabhi Khushi Kabhi Gam	United Kingdom
Kaho Na Pyar Hai	New Zealand
Koi…Mil Gaya	Thailand
Krrish	Singapore
Salaam Namaste	Australia

Source: Compiled from Media Reports

Trend 4: Hollywood Goes Bollywood

India's emergence as the new global power player in movies is beginning to attract the attention of major Hollywood studios. With the expected doubling of the Indian movie industry from $2 billion in 2006 to $4.4 billion in 2011, many Hollywood studios want to have their piece of the pie. The reasons are simple. Hollywood's market inside the United States is facing near-saturation. Also, the proliferation of videogames, the Internet, and video-on-demand is hurting their revenue streams. India's five hundred million people under the age of twenty ensures that the market inside India will grow exponentially in the coming years. Here are some examples of growing Hollywood/Bollywood partnership:

- Walt Disney is partnering with India's Yash Raj Films to make animated movies for the Indian market. Their first film, *Roadside Romeo*, is currently in production.
- Sony Pictures Entertainment became the first Hollywood studio to produce a Hindi-language film. The movie *Saawariya* was based on Feodor Dostoevsky's short story "White Nights." Sony plans to create six more pictures in the coming years.
- News Corp and Disney bought stakes in India's UTV Motion Pictures, a production company set up by Ronnie Screwvala. UTV is partnering with Sony Pictures and Fox Searchlight on movies starring Chris Rock and Will Smith.

Trend 4: Multiplex Boom Sweeping India

India's multiplex (multiscreen cinema hall) revolution is only a decade old. Yet it has forever changed the movie-watching experience for millions of people in this movie-crazy nation. Multiplexes offer better comfort and ambience, state-of-the-art audio and projection technology, and, above all, a wide choice of films under one roof. Today, dozens of multiplexes have mushroomed in cities and towns across the country. Major players that are dominating the multiplex business include PVR, Adlabs, Fun Cinemas, and Inox Leisure. Among the key drivers contributing to the growth of multiplexes in India are higher disposable incomes brought about by the booming Indian economy; tax-exempt status accorded to multiplex owners; and the explosive growth of malls all over the country.

Trend 5: Bollywood Profile Is Increasing Worldwide

Bollywood is making a concerted effort to promote Indian cinema globally. In 2000, Bollywood created the International Indian Film Academy (IIFA), mirroring Hollywood's Academy of Motion Pictures. Each year, IIFA conducts an annual awards ceremony, the Bollywood equivalent of the Oscars, at a different location outside India. An estimated thirty thousand overseas visitors poured into Yorkshire for the 2007 IIFA festival held. The event, which was telecast globally, attracted five hundred million viewers in 110 countries. Besides the IIFA festival, the Cannes Film Festival and the Toronto International Film Festival (TIFF) are increasingly attracting a large gathering of Bollywood celebrities.

Sports in India

Indian youth play a variety of sports, including cricket, field hockey, tennis, chess, badminton, and soccer, but sports have never been India's forte. Sports like archery, chess, and wrestling are believed to have originated in India. Both field hockey and cricket were brought to the Indian subcontinent by the British. Field hockey is officially the national sport, but cricket is the de facto national sport due to its immense popularity. India won an impressive eight Olympic gold medals in field hockey, including six consecutive gold medals from 1928 to 1956. But Indian field hockey has witnessed a gradual decline and hasn't made it to an Olympic semifinal since 1980. Indian hockey plunged to a new low when it failed to qualify for the 2008 Beijing Summer Olympics after being trounced by Great Britain in the qualifier. India's track record in cricket is mixed.

The popularity of cricket surged after India pulled off a major upset by defeating the defending champions, the West Indies, to claim its first and only World Cup Cricket title in 1983. Since 1983, India managed two semifinals and one runner-up finish in the World Cup championships. In 2007, India won the inaugural Twenty20 Cricket World Cup, defeating its archrival Pakistan.

India also has several indigenous sports like *kabaddi* and *kho-kho* (a type of a tag game), for which teams compete at the national level. The kabaddi game was added for the first time to the Asian games held in Beijing in 1990. Some sports even have a regional flavor. For example, snake-boat races are popular in the state of Kerala during the Onam festival. Soccer is the most popular sport in West Bengal, Kerala, and Goa states, even when India is ranked 148 out of the 202 countries in the FIFA ranking list. Kolkota (formerly Calcutta) is the soccer capital of India and has a rich tradition of the sport.

India is home to several athletes of international repute. Prominent among them are Vishwanathan Anand (world's top chess player), Sachin Tendulkar (biggest cricket icon), Leander Paes and Mahesh Bhupathi (the world's most prominent doubles tennis players), and Sania Mirza (top-ranked women's tennis player in Asia).

With the opening up of India's economy since 1991, the sports landscape has undergone a gradual change. Major Indian companies are realizing the potential of sponsoring or owning sports teams. For instance, Satyam, a leading IT company, has recently signed up as a FIFA World Cup sponsor. India, backed by its booming economy, is also attracting the attention of Formula One organizers. Vijay Mallya, a prominent Indian businessman and an enthusiastic Formula One fan, brought the sport to India by purchasing a 50 percent stake in the Spyker team, which was subsequently renamed the Force India Formula One team. India is also slated to host its first-ever Formula Grand Prix in 2010. India launched its first cricket franchise, the Indian Premier League (IPL), which raked in an estimated $725 million from winning bids for eight teams representing eight major cities, while ten-year TV rights for the games were sold for over a billion dollars.[51]

Table 11: Select Indian Sports Personalities of Present Times

Name	Sport	Achievement(s)
Pankaj Advani	Snooker	World champion amateur player
Vishwanathan Anand	Chess	Number one player in the world
Abhinav Bindra	Shooting	First Indian to win an individual Olympic gold
Mahesh Bhupathi	Tennis	Winner of ten Grand Slam doubles titles
Mahendra Dhoni	Cricket	One-day captain; got highest bid in player auction
Narain Karthikeyan	Racing	India's first Formula One racer
Anil Kumble	Cricket	India's leading wicket taker
Sania Mirza	Tennis	Asia's number-one women's player
Leander Paes	Tennis	Winner of ten Grand Slam tennis titles
R. S. Rathore	Shooting	Winner of India's first individual Olympic silver
Jeev Milkha Singh	Golf	Highest-ranked Indian golfer in the world
Sachin Tendulkar	Cricket	India's top batsman and world record holder

Source: Various

Despite the recent infusion of corporate money, sports, with the exception of cricket, continue to languish in India. Except for sporadic achievements, India's progress in the sports arena since independence has been dismal during the last sixty-plus years. India's Olympic performance can be summed up in one sentence. "Indian Olympic medalist" is an oxymoron. That changed slightly in 2008 in Beijing, when India won an unprecedented three individual medals, including the first Olympic gold by shooter Abhinav Bindra. Still, the world's second most populous nation behind China managed to win only eighteen medals in the past 108 years. Of those eighteen medals, eleven came from field hockey and only seven came from individual events. India's performance in Asian games is equally dismal, but in Commonwealth games it fares slightly better.

In contrast, China has emerged as a leading sports nation over the past few decades. At the 2008 Summer Olympics in Beijing, China won a total of one hundred medals, including fifty-one gold medals. China is now a formidable force in track and field, gymnastics, swimming, and several other individual events. Even tiny nations like Slovenia (population 2 million) and Estonia (population 1.7 million) did considerably better than India in the 2004 Olympics.

Why doesn't India do well in sports? A recent government report has identified several problems, including a lack of sports culture in the country; nonintegration of sports with formal education; inadequacy of sporting infrastructure; and a lack of an effective system for talent identification. First and foremost is that the nation clearly lacks a sports culture. Sports have never been a priority in India. Indian youth would rather spend their free time watching a Bollywood movie than involving themselves in sports. Indian parents and teachers seldom push their children toward sports; rather, they view sports as a distraction from academics. Unlike in the United States, where college sports are followed with great fervor and prominent universities have stadiums that seat tens of thousands of spectators, India lacks a credible sports culture or infrastructure at the college or university level. It is very difficult to make a decent living in India if you are an athlete, unless you are an outstanding cricketer; cricket is the only sport that gets money, publicity, and public support. Other sports are generally relegated to the background. Some Indian athletes excel at the international level, but this is due only to their hard work and not to any support from the government or sports organizations.

India may be an IT superpower and may be on the cusp of becoming a major economic power. But as far as sports are concerned, the nation is unable to shed its third-world image. But things are bound to change for Indian sports. The economic reforms of the 1990s brought access to money. Going forward, India has some advantages. India is a young nation. Nearly 40 percent of the population (or four hundred million people) falls within the age group of fifteen to thirty-five, the age group that is most active in sports. If India can harness the youth power and develop a sports culture the way China has, it can make some headway in the international sports arena in the near future.

Furthermore, there must be a concerted effort at the national level to end the medal draught at the Olympics. India is hosting the Commonwealth Games in 2010 (the first major sporting event being hosted in the country since the 1982 Asian Games) with the hope that the multidiscipline event will serve as a catalyst for India's change from a one-sport country.

Table 12: India's Olympic Performance Summary

Event	Athlete	City	Year	Result
Field Hockey	Team event	Various	1928–56	Six golds
Field Hockey	Team event	Rome	1960	Silver
Field Hockey	Team event	Tokyo	1964	Gold
Field Hockey	Team event	Mexico City	1968	Bronze
Field Hockey	Team event	Munich	1972	Bronze
Field Hockey	Team event	Moscow	1980	Gold
Wrestling	K. Jadhav	Helsinki	1952	Bronze
Men's 400 m	Milkha Singh	Rome	1960	Fourth place
Women's 400 m	P. T. Usha	Los Angeles	1984	Fourth place
Tennis	L. Paes	Atlanta	1996	Bronze
Weightlifting	K.Malleshwari	Sydney	2000	Bronze
Shooting	R. Rathore	Athens	2004	Silver
10-Meter Air Rifle	A. Bindra	Beijing	2008	Gold
Boxing	V. Kumar	Beijing	2008	Bronze

Wrestling	S. Kumar	Beijing	2008	Bronze
Total Medals (1928–2008):	18			

Source: Various

Cricket: India's Obsession

America has many spectator sports: baseball, American football, basketball, ice hockey, and NASCAR. India has only one spectator sport: cricket. The sport is like a religion in India. It is not only successful in terms of the number of fans but also in commercial terms. Cricketers, like Bollywood stars, are given godlike status in India. Both cricketers and film stars endorse a large variety of products in India, including clothes, phones, soft drinks, and automobiles. Indians are very passionate about cricket, and losses in cricket tournaments are not received well by the nation. For instance, after India's surprise defeat by minnows Bangladesh in the 2007 World Cup tournament, the nation witnessed several incidents of player effigies being burned in the streets and vandalism of players' homes.

Cricket is a bat-and-ball sport played by two teams of eleven players each. A cricket match is played on an oval-shaped grass field, in the center of which is a twenty-two-yard flat strip called the cricket pitch. A wicket is placed at each of the pitch. The team that bats first tries to score as many runs as possible and bowl out the opposition for lesser runs. Similarly, the team that bowls first tries to bowl out the batting side and then outscore them. The team that scores more runs than the other is deemed the winner.

There are three forms of cricket: test cricket, one-day international, and Twenty20 cricket. Test cricket is the classic form, as well as the longest; it is played over a five-day period. Only full members of the International Cricket Council (ICC), cricket's world governing body, are allowed to compete in the test form. Currently, only ten nations—Australia, England, South Africa, West Indies, New Zealand, India, Pakistan, Sri Lanka, Zimbabwe, and Bangladesh—are full members.

The West Indies team consists of players from a number of Caribbean nations.

One-day international (ODI) cricket, the shorter form of the game, came into existence in the mid-1970s in response to demands for a shorter form of cricket. The game is played over fifty-overs per side, in sharp contrast to the customary five-day test match, and is short enough to conclude in less than eight hours in a single day. It almost always provides a result, as opposed to a test match, which may end up in a draw. ODI became immensely popular with cricket fans and created a vast television audience across the globe.

In recent years, another popular format of the game known as Twenty20 (T20) cricket has emerged under which the playing time is further compressed to about three hours, bringing the game closer to the time span of popular sports like soccer, basketball, or a five-set tennis match. The T20 format, which is the latest craze among cricket fans, has the potential to increase the popularity of the game beyond Commonwealth nations.

Over the years, India has produced some of the best batsmen and spin bowlers of all time. Sunil Gavaskar, Kapil Dev, Sachin Tendulkar, and Anil Kumble top the list of prominent cricketers from India. Widely acknowledged as one of the greatest opening batsman of all time, Gavaskar set several records during his career, including the world record for most runs and most centuries scored in test cricket. Kapil Dev, the greatest pace bowler India has ever produced, is also one of the best all-around cricketers of all time. He was named by Wisden as the Indian Cricketer of the Century for leading India to its first World Cup title in 1983. He also held the world record for most wickets in test cricket from 1994 to 1999.

Sachin Tendulkar (nicknamed "the master blaster") is widely regarded as one of the greatest batsman in the history of cricket. He holds several batting world records, including most runs and most centuries in test cricket and ODI combined. Tendulkar's demigod status in the cricket-crazy nation has yielded many product endorsement deals, including luxury cars, credit cards, shoes, and soft drinks.

A recent development in the cricketing world is the launch of the multimillion-dollar Indian Premier League (IPL), India's new domestic cricket league; it is similar to the National Basketball League (NBA) or National Football League (NFL) in the United States. The league follows a franchise model wherein private entities (corporations or individuals) own and run the teams. Currently, the league features eight franchises representing eight major Indian cities: Mumbai, Delhi, Kolkata, Bangalore, Jaipur, Chennai, Chandigarh, and Hyderabad. All the matches are played under lights, with play starting at 5 p.m. to attract prime-time television audiences. The inaugural tournament was played in April 2008 over forty-four days in a twenty-overs-a-side (T20 format). The franchises for the teams, auctioned off by India's cricket board in January 2008, fetched a whopping $700 million, with Mukesh Ambani of Reliance Industries snapping up the Mumbai team for $111 million.

Key Things to Know About Cricket:

- Cricket is a bat-and-ball game (similar to baseball) mainly played among ten Commonwealth nations (former British colonies).
- There are three forms of cricket: test cricket, one-day international, and Twenty20 cricket. A test cricket match, which is played over a five-day period between two nations, is the classic form.
- A rapidly compressed form of cricket known as Twenty20 (T20) cricket, in which the playing time is reduced to a little over three hours, is the latest craze among cricket fans.
- Cricket is followed with passion in India, Pakistan, and Sri Lanka. The popularity of cricket soared and the fan base expanded after India's success in the 1983 World Cup and the creation of a national television audience in the early 1980s.
- Cricket is India's de facto national sport, although field hockey is India's official national sport.

Tennis

Tennis is played by only a tiny fraction of India's population. However, some Indian tennis players, such as Ramanathan Krishnan, Vijay Amritraj, Ramesh Krishnan, Leander Paes, and Mahesh Bhupathi, have made a mark in the international tennis arena. Ramanathan Krishnan is a legendary tennis player who made two Wimbledon semifinal appearances in 1960 and 1961. During his career, he attained number-three seeding worldwide, a feat yet to be matched or bettered by any Indian player to date.

While the 1960s belonged to Ramanathan Krishnan, the 1970s saw the emergence of Vijay Amritraj as a major tennis phenomenon. Amritraj competed in seventeen consecutive Wimbledon tournaments, making it to quarterfinals in 1973 and 1981. He was also a quarterfinalist in the 1973 and 1974 U.S. Open tournaments. He rendered yeoman services to the nation by captaining the Indian Davis Cup team for much of the late 1970s and 1980s, helping India reach the finals in 1974 and 1987. Unfortunately for Amritraj, India refused to play the other finalist, South Africa, in the Davis Cup final in 1974 in protest against its apartheid policies, thus handing it a victory.

The 1980s saw the entry of tennis legend Ramanathan Krishnan's son Ramesh Krishnan into the tennis arena. He made history by winning both Junior Wimbledon as well as the Junior French title in 1979. Krishnan also made it to the quarters at Wimbledon in 1986 and the U.S. Open twice, in 1981 and 1987.

Since the early 1990s, Indian men's tennis has been dominated by Leander Paes and Mahesh Bhupathi. In 1990, Paes became the third Indian after Ramanathan and Ramesh Krishnan to win the Wimbledon Junior Championship. Since then, he has become the face of Indian tennis at the Davis Cup and various other international tournaments. Paes won a bronze medal at the 1996 Atlanta Olympics, becoming the first Indian in more than four decades to win an individual Olympic medal. In the late1990s, Paes teamed up with compatriot Mahesh Bhupathi at various doubles events, and together they became one of the most successful men's doubles pairings in the world. The Indian dynamic duo of Paes and Bhupathi, dubbed the "Indian Express," had a golden season in 1999; they became the first doubles pair in the world to reach the finals of all four Grand Slam doubles finals, winning at Roland Garros and Wimbledon. Both Paes and Bhupathi have also won several mixed-doubles championships. Bhupathi's mixed-doubles partners include the likes of Mary Pierce and Martina Hingis, whereas Paes teamed up with legendary women's tennis player Martina Navratilova and helped her win her record-equaling twentieth title at Wimbledon.

Indian women's tennis got a fillip with the arrival of teenage tennis sensation Sania Mirza, who turned professional in 2003. A rising star in the women's tennis circuit, Sania became the first and only Indian woman to reach the fourth round of a Grand Slam tournament at the 2005 U.S. Open. She is now the highest-ranked female tennis player ever from India.

Table 13: Indians at Grand Slam Tennis Singles Events

Player	Year(s)	Event	Result
Ramanathan Krishnan	1960 and 1961	Wimbledon	Semifinalist
Vijay Amritraj	1973 and 1981	Wimbledon	Quarterfinalist
Vijay Amritraj	1973 and 1974	U.S. Open	Quarterfinalist
Ramesh Krishnan	1986	Wimbledon	Quarterfinalist
Ramesh Krishnan	1981 and 1987	U.S. Open	Quarterfinalist

Source: Various

Field Hockey

Field hockey, popular around the world, is the national sport of India. Hockey has several prestigious tournaments, including the Summer

Olympics, the Hockey World Cup held every four years, and the Champions Trophy held annually.

Table 14: Field Hockey Olympic Performance

Nation	Gold	Silver	Bronze	Total	Remarks
India	8	1	2	11	Last won gold in 1980
Australia	4	3	4	11	2004 gold medalist
Netherlands	3	4	6	13	1996, 2000 gold medalist
Pakistan	3	3	2	8	Last won gold in 1984
Great Britain	3	2	5	10	Last won gold in 1988
Germany	1	3	2	6	Won 2008 gold

Source: Wikipedia

The period between 1928 and 1956, during which India won six consecutive gold medals at the Olympics, is considered the golden era for Indian hockey. India's winning streak of thirty consecutive games at the Olympics came to an end in 1960, when it lost to archrival Pakistan in the 1960 Rome Olympics finals. India reclaimed its gold medal from Pakistan in 1964 Tokyo Olympics, but in the next two successive Olympics it managed to get only bronze, marking the beginning of the end of India's supremacy in world hockey. Although India won its first-ever Hockey World Cup title in 1975, the following year it missed out on a hockey medal for the first time in forty-eight years at the 1976 Montreal Olympics.

One of the main contributing factors for India's dismal performance was the introduction of artificial turf, which favored power and speed over deft stick work and artistic ability, strong suits for India. Since artificial turf is expensive to build, players in developing nations like India and Pakistan have had very little access or exposure to the new surface, which puts them at a disadvantage to European or Australian players. In fact, the first artificial surface came to India six years after it was introduced. The switch to synthetic surfaces essentially ended Indian and Pakistani domination of the sport. India did win a gold medal in the 1980 Moscow Olympics, but the victory was largely facilitated by the absence of some heavyweight nations due to the American-led boycott of the games to protest the Soviet invasion of Afghanistan in the previous year.

In the past three decades, Western European teams, along with Australia, have become the powerhouses in the sport. In 2008, Indian hockey reached a new low when the national team failed to qualify for the Beijing Olympics after losing to Great Britain in the final of the Olympics qualifier.

Barring the Olympics, India's record in other international hockey tournaments has been less than stellar. For instance, India has won only one Hockey World Cup, while Pakistan has won an impressive four tournaments.

Chess

The game of chess is believed to have originated in northern India around AD 450, when it was known as *chaturanga*. It metamorphosed into its present form in the fifteenth century. Russia and Eastern European countries largely dominated the game in the twentieth century, except for a brief period of 1972 to 1975 when the American player Bobby Fischer held the world title. India's foray into the big league of chess started with the arrival of Vishwanathan Anand in the late 1980s. He became India's first grand master at the age of eighteen. The grand master title is the highest title a chess player can achieve. Once achieved, the title is held for life.

In 1995, Anand rose to international fame when he played and lost the PCA Championship title match against the defending champion, Garry Kasparov. The game was played on the 106th floor of the World Trade Center in New York City. After several near-misses, Anand became first Indian to win the 2000 FIDE World Chess Championship title, ending many years of Russian domination. But at that time, the title was split and disputed due to the existence of a rival chess federation, whose winner, Kramnik, was seen by many as the legitimate world champion. Anand eventually lost the federation title in 2001.

In 2007, seven years after he won his first world title, Anand became the undisputed world chess champion after winning the unified World Chess Championship tournament held in Mexico City. He is scheduled to defend the title against Kramnik in a match in 2008.

Anand's achievements have triggered huge public interest in the game in India, as reflected in the growing number of grand masters coming from India. Although India has only 17 grand masters (a far cry from Russia's 147 grand masters), the nation's position in chess appears bright in the near future, with many players making their presence known in international events. For instance, Humpy Konery, a chess grand master from India, is currently the number-two-ranking women's chess player in the world.[52]

Table 15: World's Top Five Men's Chess Players

Rank	Name	Country	Rating
1	Viswanathan Anand	India	2803
2	Vladimir Kramnik	Russia	2788
3	Alexander Morozevich	Russia	2774
4	Veselin Topalov	Bulgaria	2767
5	Magnus Carlsen	Norway	2765

Source: FIDE Web Site (July 2008)

Billiards, Snooker, and Badminton

India has produced only a few world champions in any sport, but the games of billiards and snooker have seen an unusually high number of Indian world champions. Unfortunately, the game neither receives government patronage nor generates public interest in India. Some of the prominent players from the past to the present include Wilson Jones, Michael Ferreira, Geet Sethi, and Pankaj Advani. Geet Sethi had a stellar career, winning a combined six titles in world amateur and professional championships. He is rated as one of the best billiards players the game has ever produced.

In badminton, Prakash Padukone of India won the prestigious All England Open Badminton Championship in 1980, a feat repeated by Pullela Gopichand in 2001.

Chapter 3: History

India is one of the oldest countries in the world, with roots reaching back to prehistoric times (the period in human history before the invention of writing). The discovery of stone tools points to human activity on the Indian subcontinent during the Stone Age.[53] It should be noted that India didn't become a single entity until its independence in 1947; rather, it consisted of a number of feuding kingdoms. The disunity among local rulers attracted invasions from various parts of Asia and Europe. The attackers included Persians, Greeks, Turks, Afghans, and, finally, the British. Present-day India was carved out of greater India, which consisted of the territories of India, Pakistan, and Bangladesh.

Indus Valley Civilization

The Indus Valley Civilization, which is named after the Indus River, is considered the first real landmark in the history of India. This civilization existed in the Indus River valley in present-day Pakistan. It is one of the world's oldest civilizations, existing at the same time as the ancient civilizations of Egypt and Sumer, although it far outlasted them. The existence of the Indus Valley Civilization was not known until 1856, when ruins were discovered accidentally by two British engineers who were building a rail track in the area. Their discovery prompted historians to rewrite the early history of India preceding the Aryan invasion.

Archeological evidence points to the existence of a highly urbanized society based on two ancient cities, Mahenjo-Daro and Harappa. Both cities were marvels of town planning, with well-planned streets, brick houses, and elaborate drainage systems. The economy was based on agriculture and commerce. The Indus script consisted of about four hundred characters, encompassing symbols and pictures. Artifacts discovered from this period include pottery, sculptures, and seals. The wide use of bronze tools suggests that this civilization belonged to the Bronze Age.

The Indus Valley Civilization ceased to exist by 1500 BC. Although details of the origin, rise, and decline of this civilization still remain a mystery, it is commonly believed that their decline coincided with the invasion of Aryans from central Asia. Another possible reason for its decline could be the flooding of its towns, caused by environmental changes.

Aryan Invasion

Aryans were the first people to invade India, around 1500 BC. Aryans were nomadic tribes who had originally lived in central Asia. They entered through the Khyber Pass and settled in the same area inhabited by people belonging to the Indus Valley. The Aryans brought with them new set of religious beliefs and traditions. For example, the Aryans regarded nature as their god and worshipped the five objects of nature: sun, moon, earth, fire, and water.

Aryans relied on religious texts known as Vedas, which consisted of hymns, poems, and prayers to Aryan gods. The earliest text in this series, the *Rig Veda*, is considered the oldest religious text in the world. Two other texts, the *Upanishads* and *Brahmanas*, were added to the Aryan literature in 1000 BC. The great epic poems *Ramayana* and *Mahabharata* came into existence around 400 BC. Together with Vedas, these epics form the basis for the Hindu religion as we know it today. Both Vedas and the epics were passed from generation to generation by word of mouth, using a language called Sanskrit, which gradually evolved into a written language. Most of the present-day Indian languages trace their origins to Sanskrit.

Aryans led their lives very differently from their predecessors. The urban sophistication of people from the Indus Valley was missing in the Aryans. They did not construct large cities or temples. They were war-mongering and considered themselves chosen people. In fact, the word *Arya* translates to "noble" or "chosen one." Ayrans believed that people are not created equal, and they divided their society into four different classes, with each class assigned a specific role based on its capabilities. Priests or Brahmins occupied the most exalted position in the caste tree, due to their knowledge of Vedas and sacred rites. The next level was the warrior class, followed by traders and artisans. The bottom class consisted of people called *shudras*, who were forced to take up menial jobs. This classification became a blueprint for the Hindu caste system, which still exists today. Other distinctive traits of the Ayrans include a great love of music, technical skill in the art of metal-working, and an affinity for gold ornaments.

By the end of the *Rig Veda* period, the Aryans, after having consolidated their position in the Indus Valley, had begun moving deeper into the heart of India, pushing the indigenous Dravidian inhabitants further south into the Indian peninsula. This brought some fundamental changes to the Indian ethnic mix. People of Dravidian ethnicity live almost entirely in peninsular India, even today. The old Vedic gods, consisting of deities associated with nature, were gradually replaced by the new gods of Hinduism: Brahma, Vishnu, and Shiva.

Emergence of Buddhism, Alexander Invasion, Mauryan Empire

The sixth century saw the birth of two new religions in India: Buddhism and Jainism. These religions came into existence in response to the discontent with various aspects of Hinduism based on the Vedas, which emphasized sacrificial rituals and castes. Both Buddhism and Jainism opposed violence and the caste system and preached tolerance and self-discipline. Siddhartha Gautama (563–483 BC) propounded Buddhism while Vardhaman Mahavira (599–527 BC) founded Jainism. While the geographic reach of Jainism was limited to western India, Buddhism gained popularity in India and other Asian countries.

By 500 BC, the tribal states of the Vedic period had been replaced by sixteen territorial states stretching from modern-day Afghanistan to Bangladesh. The most powerful of these were Magadha, Kosala, Kuru, and Gandhara. They lacked unity and fought among themselves. Eventually, Magadha emerged victorious and became a powerful kingdom in northern India. During that time, Persians conquered the Indus Valley. They were in turn conquered by the Greeks, led by Alexander the Great, who had set out in 327 BC to invade India after conquering Egypt, Persia, and Syria.

He inflicted crushing defeat on Indian king Porus and then set out to conquer kingdoms eastward, including the Magadha kingdom. Alexander's plans did not materialize due to troop discontent, and he was forced to turn back without completing his conquests. When Alexander died in 323 BC, his Indian empire disintegrated, giving rise to Indo-Greek kingdoms throughout northwestern India, led by his erstwhile generals.

Alexander's exit and death created instability in northwestern India. In 321 BC, shortly after Alexander's invasion, Chandragupta Maurya overthrew the unpopular Nanda King of Magadha to establish India's first large kingdom, which included the entire Indian subcontinent except for some areas in the south. He was helped by his brilliant Brahmin advisor and prime minister, Chanakya, who authored India's classic text, *Arthashastra*, which deals with subjects such as politics and government. Chandragupta's dynasty ruled India over the next two hundred years. No Indian dynasty before them had enjoyed so much power.

Chandragupta was succeeded by his son Bindusara (298–272 BC), who further extended the Mauryan empire. Bindusara was succeeded by his son Ashoka, who ruled the Indian subcontinent unchallenged for the next thirty-seven years. Ashoka is considered one of the greatest Indian rulers of all time. He conquered almost all of the Indian subcontinent, from Afghanistan in the west to present-day Bangladesh in the east, from the foothills of the Himalayas in the north to Mysore in the south. Only the Dravidian kingdoms of the south, led by Cholas and Pandyas, managed to remain independent. When Ashoka invaded the eastern region of Orissa, the battle turned gruesome, and much blood was shed. Although he won the battle, Ashoka was so disturbed by the bloodshed that he converted to Buddhism. Under Ashoka, Buddhism attained the status of the state religion of India, although other religions were also respected. He made a concerted effort to spread Buddhism throughout the region by sending emissaries to neighboring countries to spread the message and giving orders to inscribe Buddhist messages on rocks and pillars. Some of these have survived for over two thousand years. One such pillar, at Sarnath, was adopted as a national emblem of India after independence.[54] Ashoka's *dharma charka* also became part of India's national flag.

Post-Ashoka India

After Ashoka's death in 232 BC, his empire began to unravel and was repeatedly attacked by invaders from central Asia, leaving India weak and helpless for the next four hundred years. The Maurya dynasty ceased to exist by 185 BC. The foreign invaders competed for the territories of northern India, whereas the regional kings gained control of the south. Prominent among them were Satavahanas in south-central India and Cholas, and Pandyas in the far south.

The invaders of the post-Ashoka period include Greeks from Bactria and Shakas from central Asia. A nomadic tribe called the Kushans defeated the Shakas and established the Kushan kingdom. Unlike Mauryans, Kushans did not control the entire subcontinent but had to be content with controlling only parts. Kanishka was the most prominent ruler of the Kushans. Like Ashoka, Kanishka also converted to Buddhism. The Gandharan art, combination of Greek and Indian styles, came into existence during Kushan rule. The Kushan kingdom disintegrated by the third century.

The Gupta Empire

After four hundred years of uncertainty following the disintegration of the Maurya dynasty, India was once again united by a powerful Hindu dynasty called the Guptas. The Guptas brought an end to the invasions from the west and established a strong kingdom in essentially the same territory as the once-powerful Mauryas, with their capital at Patna. Peace and prosperity finally returned to India. The Guptas' rule, spanning two centuries, is considered to be the golden age of Indian history.

Hinduism, which was marginalized during Mauryan rule, once again gained prominence. The Hindu epics *Ramayana* and *Mahabharata* appeared in writing and spread throughout the region. Hindu temples were built throughout the country, and fine temple architecture and sculptures emerged. Sacred Hindu texts called Puranas came into existence during the Gupta period. Puranas contain tales of Hindu gods and are relevant even today.

The period of Gupta rule is also considered the classical age of Indian culture, as Guptas were great patrons of arts, literature, and science. The Buddhist paintings and sculptures in the Ajanta caves were created during this time.[55] Kalidasa, India's most famous Sanskrit playwright, is believed to have served in the court of Chandragupta Maurya II. Kalidasa's famous works include a play called *Shakuntala*, which was later translated into English and German in the eighteenth century. Kalidasa is known as the Shakespeare of India.

Under Gupta rule, India also excelled in mathematics and science. The decimal system of numbers and the concept of zero were invented. Aryabhatta (AD 476–550), a renowned mathematician and astronomer, lived during this era. To commemorate Aryabhatta's work in astronomy, India named its first satellite Aryabhatta.

The decline of the Gupta dynasty started around AD 455 due to a series of invasions by nomadic tribes called the Huns, who came from central Asia. Gupta ruler Skanda Gupta initially resisted the Huns' attacks, but they became increasingly ferocious, and he ultimately could not stop them. Although the Huns did not establish a lasting foothold in the Guptas' empire, they had sufficiently weakened it. The complete collapse of the Gupta dynasty came about in AD 550, and the empire became fragmented into smaller kingdoms ruled by Hindu kings.

The Harsha Vardhana Era

After the collapse of Gupta rule, uncertainty and chaos prevailed in India, as the Hindu kings engaged in warfare to gain control of larger territories. This ended when Harsha Vardhana assumed the throne and united the northern territories into a single empire. His rule was also marked by peace and prosperity. Although a devotee of Lord Shiva, Harsha Vardhana embraced the principles of Buddhism. He banned the slaughter of animals and the consumption of their meat. Harsha Vardhana died without an heir in AD 647, plunging India once again into anarchy and confusion.

Muslim Invasions

Post-Harsha Vardhana India consisted of number of Hindu dynasties in northern India. These dynasties lacked unity and fought among themselves. This same period saw the emergence of tribal groups in northwest India called Rajputs (son of kings). Rajputs saw themselves as descendants of the warrior caste of ancient India and began to play a prominent role in the history of northern and western India. The period of Indian history from Harsha Vardhana's death to Muslim invasions is also referred to as the Rajput period.

The first major Muslim invasions started with the Mahmud of Ghazni, who plundered India for its riches. He attacked India seventeen times between 1001 and 1027, destroyed many temples, and ransacked cities. His attacks brought an end to the Hindu Shahiyas dynasty in 1018. He captured and looted Mathura and Kanuj (1018), Bundelkhand (1021–22), and Somnath (1025–26). Ghazni died in

1030, but India's woes did not end there. The next series of attacks on India came from Muhammad Ghori in the late twelfth century; his army consisted of Turks, Afghans, Persians, and Arabs. He defeated Prithviraj Chauhan, the Tomar ruler of Delhi. He then returned to Afghanistan triumphant and left his territory in the control of his deputy and former slave, Qutbuddin Aibak. This heralded the creation of the Slave dynasty, with Delhi as the capital city.

The Delhi Sultanate

For the next three hundred years, the Muslim rulers of Delhi controlled northern India's destiny. Five Muslim dynasties ruled from Delhi, from the assumption of power by Qutbuddin Aibak to its conquest by Moghuls. The Khalji, Tughlaq, Sayyid, and Lodhi dynasties followed Qutbuddin Aibak's Slave dynasty.[56]

Known as the Sultanate of Delhi, it was during this period that the Islamic concepts of society and governance were imposed on northern India's largely Hindu population. India witnessed large-scale conversions to Islam during this period.

The Sultanate of Delhi faced several rebellions during its rule. Ala-ud-din Bahman Shah seceded from the Delhi Sultanate and founded the Bahmani dynasty in western Deccan, with his capital at Daulatabad. The Mongol conqueror, Timur the Great, invaded India in 1398 and plundered Delhi mercilessly, severely weakening the Delhi Sultanate's rule. Several independent kingdoms were established in Gujarat, Rajasthan, and other places. The last ruler of the Delhi Sultanate was Ibrahim Lodhi, who ruled for a short period between 1517 and 1526.

While northern India fell into the hands of Muslims, southern India set its own course. A powerful Hindu kingdom known as the Vijayanagar kingdom was founded in 1336 by Harihara, with Hampi as its capital. Under Krishna Deva Raya, Vijayanagara Empire gained control over almost all of southern India and successfully neutralized the Bahmani rulers of Deccan.

This period also saw the birth of two religious reformers: Kabir and Guru Nanak. Kabir (1440–1518) sought to promote Hindu-Muslim amity by using principles from both religions. Guru Nanak (1469–1539) founded the Sikh religion, which currently has twenty million followers in India. One other notable event of this period was the arrival of European traders to India. A Portuguese sailor called Vasco da Gama sailed into the harbor of Calicut on the Malabar coast in 1498, seeking spice and pepper trade. His visit marked the beginning of a European presence in India.

The Mughal Rule

The Mughal dynasty was founded by central Asian warlord Babur in 1526. Babur, a descendent of Genghis Khan and Timur, had earlier become the ruler of the central Asian kingdom of Fergana, a region of modern Uzbekistan, in 1494. Babar's army defeated the combined forces of the Ibrahim Lodi (ruler of Delhi) and Raja Vikramaditya (ruler of Gwalior) to establish the Mughal Empire in India.

Babur ruled only for five years and was succeeded by his son Humayun, who managed to reclaim in 1555 the throne that he had lost to his Afghan rival, Sher Shah. Humayun's death in 1556 propelled his thirteen-year-old son, Akbar, to the Mughal throne. Akbar, who ruled for nearly fifty years, is considered the greatest of the Mughal rulers and one of the best rulers in Indian history.

Akbar expanded his kingdom, which included two-thirds of the subcontinent, including Afghanistan. He initially set out to conquer the Rajput territories and later conquered Gujarat (1572), Bengal (1576), Kashmir (1586), Sind (1591), and Kandahar (1595). He turned his attention to Deccan and captured some parts of Ahmednagar. Akbar was the most tolerant ruler of all Mughals. Although he was a Muslim, he won over the Hindus by naming them to a number of important administrative positions. He even married a Hindu princess, Jodha Bai, of the Rajput clan. He tried unsuccessfully to create a new faith called Din Illahi (divine faith) in an attempt to blend Islam with other religions. Akbar was succeeded by his son Jahangir in 1605. He maintained the territorial gains made by his father and also continued the tradition of showing tolerance to other religions. Mughal arts, culture, and painting flourished during his rule. Jahangir married thirty-three-year-old Mihr un Nisa and renamed her Nur Jahan (light of the world).

Jahangir died in 1627 and was succeeded by his son Shah Jahan, who captured the throne even though he was third in line for succession. Like his father, Shah Jahan inherited a vast Indian empire with centralized control. Shah Jahan wasted no time and mounted a campaign to expand his territories in the south. Mughal architecture reached its peak during his reign.

The biggest contribution of Shah Jahan to world architecture is the Taj Mahal in Agra, which is regarded as one of the wonders of the world. Shan Jahan built the Taj Mahal, a mausoleum, as homage to his departed wife Mumtaz Mahal, who died during childbirth at the age of thirty-nine. The work on the Taj Mahal, which began in 1632, finally ended twenty years later in 1653. Shah Jahan was also responsible for building the famous Red Fort and Jama Masjid in Delhi.

The next Mughal ruler was Aurangzeb (1658–1707), who ascended to the throne at the age of forty by killing his elder brothers and imprisoning his father, Shah Jahan. Aurangzeb is considered the most intolerant of all Mughal rulers.

A strict follower of Islam, he banned un-Islamic acts such as gambling and consumption of alcohol. He also dismissed court dancers, musicians, and artists. He banned Hindus from celebrating their festivals. He ordered the destruction of Hindu schools and temples to prevent the spread of Hinduism. Many Hindus bowed to Islam to avoid the special tax imposed on them. He was equally harsh on followers of the Sikh religion. He ordered the execution of the ninth Sikh Guru in 1675 to prevent Muslims from embracing Sikhism. Under the leadership of Guru Gobind Singh, Sikhs later withdrew to the Himalayan foothills in Punjab and took up arms to challenge the Mughals.

A devout Sunni, Aurangzeb vowed to destroy the Shia ruling dynasties of Golkonda and Bijapur. After protracted battles, he ended the Adil Shahi dynasty of Bijapur in 1686 and Qutb Shahi dynasty of

Golkonda in 1687. However, Aurangzeb faced serious challenges from the Marathas of Maharastra, who became a major force in India between 1640 and 1680. Shivaji founded the Maratha kingdom by annexing a portion of the Bijapur Sultanate in 1674. Known for his heroism and guerilla warfare, Shivaji led a rebellion against the Mughal rule, thus becoming the symbol of Hindu resistance to oppressive Muslim rule. In a daring act, he killed a Muslim general called Afzal Khan with steel claws attached to his hands. He was captured and taken to Agra, but he escaped. Shivaji is considered a hero in Maharashtra state. Shivaji died in 1680 and was succeeded by his son Shambhaji, who was captured and executed by Aurangzeb's army in 1689.

Although Aurangzeb was largely successful on the battlefield, his oppressive governance, based on Muslim exclusivity, created a number of enemies throughout the country. After Aurangzeb's death in 1707, the Mughal empire was severely weakened, and the previously oppressed groups such as Rajputs, Sikhs, and Marathas regrouped and challenged the rulers who followed him.

Decline of Mughal Rule

Aurangzeb's death brought an end to any further expansion of Mughal rule. Nine Mughal emperors ruled after Aurangzeb, but none were effective. The last effective emperor was Bhadur Shah I, who succeeded Aurangzeb and ruled for only five years. After his death, the Mughal power declined steadily.

The decline in centralized Mughal authority led to the creation of independent kingdoms throughout India. Hyderabad, Bengal, and Oudh became independent states. At that time, Hyderabad was a district in the vast Mughal empire. Nizam-ul-Mulk, who had previously been the chief minister in the Mughal empire, rebelled against the Mughal rulers and formed an independent state of Hyderabad in 1725. Another Mughal noble established an independent Bengal state, creating a new regime and new capital.

The tottering Mughal empire, famous for its riches, attracted invaders from outside the boundaries. Nadir Shah of Persia attacked and plundered Delhi in 1739. He returned to Persia with gold and jewels, including the famed Kohinoor diamond and the Peacock throne of Shah Jahan. Delhi was again attacked in 1756 by Ahmad Shah of Afghanistan. The early eighteenth century also saw the resurgence of Maratha warriors. Taking advantage of the weakness of the Mughal regime, the Marathas, led by Peshwas, began taking over the territories previously held by Mughals. By 1750, the Marathas had expanded their influence beyond central India, deep into the north. However, Marathan dominance of India did not last long. Facing attacks from Ahmad Shah of Afghanistan, Mughals turned to their old enemy for help. The Marathas took on the Afghans in what is known as the third battle of Panipat in 1761. They were soundly defeated in this battle and lost control of northern territories. However, they held on to their territories in central India.

The late eighteenth century witnessed the revival of the Sikhs. The Sikhs, who faced persecution under the Mughal rule of Aurangzeb, consolidated their position. Taking advantage of the confusion and anarchy following the collapse of Mughal rule, they established a powerful Sikh kingdom comprising Punjab, Kashmir, and Afghanistan.

Rise of British Power

The arrival of Portuguese sailor Vasco da Gama in the southern port city of Calicut in 1498 heralded the beginning of a European presence in India. The main motivation of the Europeans was to engage Indians in spice trade; the value of spice as the preserver of food was an established fact by then. Unlike Muslims, who attacked India from the northwest frontier using land routes, the Europeans had to be content with using sea routes to access southern India. Sea routes also made sense because of the naval superiority of the Europeans.

Although the Portuguese were the first to arrive, their presence was limited to a few seaports in southern India. In 1503, the Portuguese built a fort in Cochin; in 1510, they captured Goa from the Bijapur Sultanate. Soon the Dutch, French, and British followed in the footsteps of the Portuguese and began arriving in the seaports of southern India.

In 1600, the British government authorized the creation of a company called the East India Company for the purpose of trading with India. The East India Company established its initial operations in Surat in 1612 and took control of Bombay in 1668. In 1674, the French established a trading settlement in Pondicherry, eighty-five miles south of Madras. The British faced off with Mughal ruler Aurangzeb in 1690 in what is now known as the first Anglo-Indian war, which resulted in victory for the Mughals. After capturing Bombay, the Mughals restored the commercial privileges of the British and returned the city.

Throughout the seventeenth century, the Europeans operated with the permission of the Indian rulers of that time, though the scope of their operations was very limited. However, the weakening of the Mughal empire in the early eighteenth century provided the opening the Europeans needed. With the loosening of the central authority, numerous independent states came into existence all over India. These states lacked unity and were continuously engaged in wars to expand or defend their territories. They often sought the help of well-trained British and French forces to support their war activities. The foreigners were always eager to help, as it gave them the perfect opportunity to further their territorial or political influence under the guise of helping the local Indian rulers. They desperately needed the political influence to protect their trade, which was threatened by the political uncertainty prevailing in India at that time.

The eighteenth century was marked by intense rivalry between the British and French, who skirmished over the control of trade. The British viewed the French as a serious threat to the rapidly growing power of its East India Company. In 1740, the French were defeated at the Battle of Wandiwash. The British finally prevailed over the French in 1751, winning a decisive battle in the southern city of Arcot and effectively putting an end to the French ambitions in India. The French, however, retained the colonies that it established in Pondicherry until it ceded them to independent India in 1950.

In 1756, five years after the British victory over the French, the Muslim ruler of Bengal, Siraj-ud-Daula, provided the British with a perfect opportunity to expand their power in eastern India. Perhaps not fully aware of British power and reach, he provoked a needless war by overrunning the British settlement in Calcutta and causing the death of about fifty Britons. The British army, led by Robert Clive, hero of the Arcot war with the French, defeated the forces of Siraj-ud-Daula in the Battle of Plassey. The British then installed their own nominee to govern Bengal. The significance of this victory in Bengal was enormous for the British because it was the first battle they won against Indian rulers. The battle marked the beginning of Britain's conquest of India.

By 1774, the British government had begun taking an active interest in the affairs of the East India Company. The Regulatory Act, approved by British Parliament, consolidated power in the hands of a newly created post of governor-general, who was directly accountable to the British government. With these changes, Calcutta emerged as the seat of power for the British, with authority over all British territories across India including, Bombay and Madras.

The first appointee to the position of governor-general was Warren Hastings. His rein lasted for about twelve years, during which he consolidated and maintained the British position in India. Although he neutralized the Marathas in the first Anglo-Maratha war in 1774, which took place on the west coast, he did not engage the Muslim rulers of Hyderabad and Mysore. At that time, the Nizams ruled Hyderabad, after declaring independence from the Mughals. Haider Ali, and later his son Tipu Sultan, were in control of the Mysore kingdom after displacing the Hindu king.

Lord Cornwallis replaced Warren Hastings as the governor-general in 1786. Cornwallis attempted to streamline administrative functions by introducing a new class of workers called the "civil servants," which were separate from Company officials. However, he did not allow Indians to serve in any capacity. This marked the beginning of a civil service staffed by British salaried officials. On the military front, he won a war against Tipu Sultan of Mysore, who had earlier attacked the British-protected Travancore kingdom in the south.

Lord Wellesley took over from Cornwallis in 1798 with a clear plan for expanding British power in India. He was responsible for creating the two-tiered British rule of India: direct and indirect. The indirect rulers consisted of Indian kings who signed an allegiance to Britain. In return, they were given security guarantees and allowed to function in a semiautonomous fashion. With this clever approach, the British were able to get control of almost all of India without much fuss or bloodshed. He then set out to conquer the three remaining kingdoms of the south: Hyderabad, Mysore, and Maratha.

Wellesley tamed the independent state of Hyderabad in 1800 by signing a treaty under which the British would ensure the security of the state, threatened by the powerful Mysore and Maratha kingdoms, in return for control. Hyderabad retained its semiautonomous status under the British until India's independence in 1947, when it merged with the Indian union.

Mysore was high on the list for the British, as its fearless ruler, Tipu Sultan, had posed a great military threat. Although the odds were clearly loaded against him, Tipu Sultan was determined to defeat the British on the battlefield and preserve his independence. In 1799, the British marched to the Seringapatam to take on Tipu Sultan's army. Tipu was killed defending the city. The British annexed half of the state and restored the other half to the heir of the dispossessed Hindu king.

The British then went on to remove one of the last hurdles in the form of Maratha resistance. The second Anglo-Martha war (1802–05) effectively destroyed Maratha power in central and northern India. The British defeated Scindia of Gwalior and took possession of Agra and Delhi. The British also downgraded the status of the Mughal emperor Shah Alam II to that of a nominal king. Soon the Rajput rulers of Jaipur, Udaipur, and Jodhpur also signed treaties with the British, accepting subsidiary status. There was only one serious rival left: the Sikh ruler Ranjit Singh in the northwest frontier.

The Sikhs had immensely benefited from the downfall of Mughal rulers. No longer on the defensive, they carved out a number of independent states in Punjab. It was Maharaja Ranjit Singh who united these states into a powerful Sikh kingdom. Ranjit Singh, who started off as a Sikh warlord, acquired Lahore in 1799 at the age of nineteen. He captured Amritsar in 1800 and Ludhiana in 1806, then extended his authority to Peshawar on the Indian-Afghan border. The British did not seek confrontation with Ranjit Singh but instead signed a treaty in 1809 that recognized Satlaj River as the border between the territories controlled by the British and Ranjit Singh.

By 1820, Ranjit Singh had consolidated his power over territories that included Punjab, Kashmir, and Multan. Popularly known as the Sher-e-Punjab (lion of Punjab), Ranjit Singh was popular among all his subjects, regardless of their religion. His rule was marked by complete freedom of expression and religious worship. What worried the British most was his strong military force, which was known for its professionalism. The British did not attempt to annex Punjab while Ranjit Singh was alive. But Ranjit Singh's death in 1839 provided the necessary opening, allowing the British to capture his territories.

Ranjit Singh's death set in motion a series of bloody succession battles. Sikh unity, which was the hallmark of Ranjit Singh's rule, was severely undermined. Four years after the death of Ranjit Singh, his six-year-old son, Dalip Singh, was proclaimed the king of Punjab. In the First Anglo-Sikh War, the Sikhs fought fiercely but lost control of Lahore, which had been Ranjit Singh's seat of power. The Sikhs were forced to cede some parts of Punjab and the mountain region of Kashmir. The British then sold the predominantly Muslim Kashmir to the highest bidder, who turned out to be the Hindu ruler Gulab Singh of the adjoining Jammu region. Thus the state of Jammu and Kashmir was born.

Following the Second Anglo-Sikh War in 1849, the child king, now eleven years old, was forced to relinquish his territories to the British. The British also took possession of the famed Kohinoor diamond, which was among Ranjit Singh's priceless possessions. The Kohinoor diamond was then presented to Queen Victoria of England.

Nineteenth-Century British Rule

By the beginning of the nineteenth century, virtually all of India was under British control, and the East India Company had begun to assert itself in the foreign land. As the ruling power of India, the company felt that it was within its rights and responsibilities to reform and modernize the country along Western lines. English was adopted as the official language of India in 1835, rather than Sanskrit or Persian. The brains behind this policy was Lord Macaulay, who had argued that such a policy would help create a new class of Indians molded by Western culture and ideas, thus paving the way for the country's development. This policy also came in handy for the company itself, which hired the English-speaking Indians to serve as clerks and assistants. There was also an increase in interference with Indian customs and traditions. The British were horrified by a Hindu custom called *sati*, which called for a widow to jump into her husband's funeral pyre and die as a symbol of her devotion and to help him achieve salvation. This custom was prohibited in 1829. Child marriages were banned in 1860.These actions received the active support of reformists like Raja Ram Mohan Roy, who relentlessly fought for the rights of women. Although the British did not try to impose Christianity on the Indians, they did establish the Church of England in India and allowed Christian missionaries unrestricted access in the country.

Under Lord Dalhousie, the modernization of India picked up steam with the introduction of railways, road networks, the telegraph, and the postal system. The first railway opened between Bombay and Thana in 1853. The first telegraph opened in 1851. Education got a push when new universities were established in Bombay, Calcutta, and Madras. Tea was introduced in India when British entrepreneurs began planting tea in the Assam region. Industrialization got a boost when the British government established jute mills in Calcutta in 1854. However, India's thriving cottage cotton industry was ruined by imports of British-made textiles, which began flooding the subcontinent in 1824.

Lord Dalhousie also used controversial measures to bring more territories under direct British rule. He enacted a new law under which a Hindu king could be succeeded only by his natural, or biological, male heir. In case the king did not leave a natural heir, the British would take direct control of the state upon his death. This method was used to annex a number of kingdoms, which were already client states of the British after relinquishing their control of power in return for security. The British also resorted to arbitrary dismissal of local kings on the grounds that they were either corrupt or inept.

Lord Dalhousie's new annexation policies did not go down well with India's ruling class, which felt that its existence was in danger. Social reforms and the spread of English had a similar effect on India's masses; they believed that their religion and culture were in danger. The government's modernization project was also viewed with fear and mistrust.

British policies also alienated the Indian soldiers of the East India Company army, who had formed the backbone of British military operations. The army consisted of Indian troops operating under the command of a small number of British officers. By 1857, the number of Hindu and Muslim Indian troops working for the British had swelled to about two hundred thousand men, divided into three regions: Calcutta, Bombay, and Madras. These troops were trained and equipped in Western style, and their loyalty to the British was never questioned. It was against this backdrop that Lord Canning, who replaced Lord Dalhousie as governor-general, initiated a series of ill-conceived actions that turned his loyal Indian soldiers against him.

One such action was the adoption of new rifles, called Enfield rifles, for the Indian army. There was nothing particularly contentious about the rifles, which were already being used in England. During early part of 1857, however, rumors spread that cartridges for the new rifles were greased with cow and pig fat. A military order directed the soldiers to bite open the cartridges before they could be loaded, which offended both the Hindu and Muslim soldiers. Hindus consider the cow to be sacred, and Muslims view pigs as unclean. These rumors ignited the already charged atmosphere, and the troops from Bengal rebelled in defense of their religion and social beliefs.

Ground zero of the rebellion, known later as India's First War of Independence, was the city of Meerut, about seventy kilometers from Delhi. In May 1857, the rebels took control of Meerut and then marched to Delhi, where they persuaded the deposed Mughal emperor Bahadur Shah III to resume his rule. To symbolize this event, the rebels hoisted the Mughal flag once again over the Red Fort, the seat of Mughal power. After the fall of Delhi, the mutiny spread across many northern and central Indian cities. In central India, one of the rebellion leaders was the widow of the former ruler of Jhansi, Lakshmi Bai. She fought on behalf of her adopted son, whom the British had refused to recognize as the legitimate ruler.

Fortunately for the British, the mutiny did not spread beyond northern India. The soldiers stationed in Madras and Bombay remained loyal. Many princely states, including Hyderabad and Rajasthan, supported the British, as did the Sikh forces of Punjab. The Sikhs, who suffered a great deal under Mughal rule, did not want to repeat the past. Although the situation was dire for the British, they slowly regrouped and managed to regain control.

By September 1857, the British had recaptured Delhi after a fierce fight. Kanpur and Lucknow were also finally recaptured. The retaking of Gwalior from the control of rebel leaders Rani of Jhansi and Tantia Topi signaled the end of the thirteen-month Indian uprising. Bahadur Shah III was convicted and sent to a prison in Burma, effectively ending the Mughal era in India's history.

The British Raj

The uprising of 1857 was a great shock for the British, and it sparked some fundamental changes to their controversial policies of past half century. The East India Company was dissolved, and its responsibilities were transferred to the British government. This marked the beginning of direct British rule of India from London: the birth of the British Raj. In 1877, Queen Victoria of Britain took the title of Empress of India.

To mollify the Indians, the British began reversing many of their earlier policies. Social reforms became a thing of the past, and the British shelved plans to modernize Indian society. There would be no more interference with Indian customs or religions. The previous annexation policies, which alienated the ruling class, were scrapped, replaced by new treaties that preserved the rule of Indian princes in return for their loyalty to the Crown. This policy gave rise to 542 princely states, which survived as semiautonomous regions until their absorption into the Indian Union in 1947. Together, these princely states accounted for 40 percent of India, and the rest was governed directly by the British.

There were several reforms on the administrative front as well. The Indian Civil Service, the forerunner to present-day Indian bureaucracy, was established in 1861. The goal was to increase the government's reach to every corner of the country. Legal reforms resulted in the establishment of Western-style high courts in Calcutta, Bombay, and Madras. The British also made efforts to include educated Indians in the decision-making process. They appointed Indian councilors to advise British officials, and established provincial councils with Indian members.

The uprising of 1857 also affected the daily lives of the British serving in India. Feeling less secure, British officers began voluntarily segregating themselves from the Indian masses by living in exclusive white-only enclaves. These small but modern enclaves, also known as *cantonments*, were built on the edges of cities and towns across the country.

Infrastructure development activities did not suffer from the uprising, and railway and road development continued at a rapid pace. Some of the changes implemented during nineteenth-century British rule had slowly begun to have a positive impact on the lives of many ordinary Indians, especially those in urban areas. Roads, railways, the postal service, and the telegraph all had a unifying effect on the country and yielded a new national identity. The English language began taking root, easing communication barriers between regions. The rapid spread of the telegraph and printing press paved the way for the creation of the national press, and the first daily newspaper in English launched in 1880. Growing political awareness and communication also began breaking down age-old barriers of caste, religion, and race.

However, on the economic front, it was the same old story, with the economic exploitation of India continuing. The newly developed infrastructure made trade and commerce easier than ever, but it benefited the British more than the Indians. Although India now had the necessary infrastructure to expand its industries, the British made no concerted effort to establish industries or encourage Indians to do so.

The British continued to view India as a cheap source of raw materials, and India exported huge amounts of raw cotton, jute, tea, and coffee to Britain. India also served as an enormous market for finished products, such as textiles and machinery made in British factories, which were imported into India without any import duty. No attempt was made to protect Indian handmade textiles or other local industries. The opening of the Suez Canal in 1869, which helped reduce the travel time between India and England from three months to only three weeks, helped the British and further damaged Indian economy. India soon emerged as the largest trading partner of Britain, although it did not realize any economic benefits from the one-sided relationship.

The Independence Movement: The Pre-Gandhi Era

Toward the end of the nineteenth century, Indians become increasingly aware of the heavy-handed rule of the British government. The rapid of growth of newspapers and communications led to increased political awareness, especially among the university-educated, English-speaking elite, who were concentrated in cities. Disenchantment with British rule took an organized form in 1885 with the formation of the Indian National Congress, or the Congress Party.

The brainchild of the Congress Party was not an Indian but a British national named Allan Octavian Home, a retired high-level official. At his initiative, Indian delegates met in Bombay and formed the Congress Party, with Calcutta-based Indian lawyer Womesh Bonnerje as its first president. The delegates consisted mainly of lawyers, journalists, and teachers. The Congress Party, which in later years became the voice for millions of Indians, had humble beginnings. At its inception it was not an active party; rather, it served as a debating society. It met infrequently, passed uncontroversial resolutions on civil rights, and pressed for increased participation of Indians in the decision-making process. The Congress initially adopted a moderate stance, seeking solutions within the British system. It did not ask for outright independence until much later, when British indifference to the Congress's aspirations alienated its members and turned the party into a mass movement.

The late 1800s also marked the beginning of a new social and religious awakening. The seeds of the social reform movement were sown in 1830 by a Bengali reformer named Raja Ram Mohan Roy, who fought vigorously against social evils tied to the Hindu religion. Another influential Hindu reform organization, the Arya Samaj, came into existence in 1875. Founded by Dayananda Saraswati, the Arya Samaj sought to rid Hindu society of social evils by drawing on the Vedas, the early Hindu sacred religious scriptures. The last great reform movement of the nineteenth century was the Ramakrishna Mission, founded by spiritual genius Swami Vivekananda, who based the movement on the teachings on his guru, Ramakrishna Paramahamsa. In his short life of thirty-nine years, Vivekananda made a lasting impression on his countrymen. His representation of Hinduism at the first World Parliament of Religions in Chicago in 1893 won him admirers both in India and abroad. The cumulative work of these reformers made Indians feel proud again about their own culture and history and inspired a new generation of freedom fighters, including Mahatma Gandhi.

The Congress Party, riding on popular sentiments against the unpopular British rule, had emerged as a national-level political organization by 1900. It had both moderate and extremist factions within its ranks. The moderate faction, led by Gopal Krishna Gokhale, the early mentor of Mahatma Gandhi, believed in the process of dialogue and petitioned for more political representation for ordinary Indians. At that time, the concept of independence had not fully evolved in the minds of Indian leaders. The extremist faction, led by Maratha politician Bal Gangadhar Tilak, advocated civil action and revolution to overthrow British rule. Impatient with the slow pace of the nationalist movement and determined to expand its scope, Tilak used Hindu religious festivals as a means for mobilization. This led to the public celebration of many Indian festivals, including the famous Ganpati festival, which is prevalent even today in many parts of Maharashtra. Tilak also broke new ground in the independence movement when he said, "Swaraj (self-rule) is my birth right, and I shall have it," which became an inspiration for many Indians. For the first time, *swaraj* entered the lexicon of the popular movement against British, and the Congress Party, which had begun as a party of elite citizens, slowly started attracting people from all walks of life.

Despite its secular outlook, the Congress Party was dominated by the majority of the Hindu community. This did not go down well with Indian Muslims, who became uneasy and apprehensive about the party's ability to protect their interests. Unlike Hindus, Muslims were slow to take advantage of education in English and therefore were poorly represented in government jobs and other professions. The Hindu reform movement also had the opposite effect on Muslims, who felt that their religion was threatened by reforms including a ban on cow slaughter and religious conversions. In 1906, these factors led to the creation of a new party called the Muslim League, whose objective was to ensure the religious, economic, and political rights of Indian Muslims. In 1909, the Muslim League managed to win major concessions from the British, which included separate electoral constituencies for Muslims and special consideration for government jobs. In 1913, the Muslim League joined hands with the Congress Party against British rule.

The first major action against British rule was resistance to the partition of the Bengal presidency by Viceroy Lord Curzon. The ill-conceived partition plan, implemented in 1905, divided Bengal on religious lines into Muslim-majority East Bengal and Hindu-majority West Bengal. Congress leaders perceived this move as a desperate effort by the British to divide the people of India along religious lines and weaken the Congress-led independence movement. Indian leaders did not buy into the British argument that the partition would improve the administrative efficiency of an otherwise unwieldy region. The response of the Congress Party was swift and widespread; party leaders called on Indians to openly defy the government and boycott British-made textiles and other products.

The British response was equally forceful. Peaceful protests were broken up, the leaders detained without trial or due legal process. When these drastic actions failed to stop the protests, the British relented and partially revoked the partition of Bengal. The government also introduced further constitutional reforms in the form of 1909 India Council Act, which allotted Indians more seats in the legislative bodies and reserved separate electoral constituencies for Muslims.

As an additional goodwill gesture toward the Indian subjects, the British arranged a royal trip by King George V to India in 1911. King George V was the third British royal ruler of India after Queen Victoria and King Edward VII. During his trip, he announced the shifting of India's capital from Calcutta to Delhi.

The years following King George V's visit to India were relatively peaceful but quite eventful. In 1913, Rabindranath Tagore won the Nobel Prize in Literature, becoming the first Asian to win this honor. The British Crown knighted him in 1915. The year 1913 also marked the beginning of the Indian film industry, with the screening of the first full-length silent feature film *Raja Harishchandra* by Dhundiraj Govind Phalke also known as Dadasaheb Phalke.

When the First World War broke out in 1914, India, along with the other British colonies and dominions including Australia, Canada, and South Africa, were dragged into the largely European war. Contrary to the initial fears of the British, there was no Indian revolt during the war. Instead, there was an unprecedented outpouring of support and goodwill for the war effort, including support from Congress and Muslim leaders. Over a million Indian soldiers fought in the war, and about sixty thousand of them gave their lives. Britain later constructed a monument in New Delhi, now known as the India Gate, to commemorate the dead Indian soldiers of World War I and the Afghan wars.

In return for their sacrifices and material support during the war, Indians hoped to gain more political freedom as well as other benefits enjoyed by British colonies such as Australia and Canada. The quid pro quo, although not explicitly stated, was clearly implied. Between the late 1800s and early 1900s, both Australia and Canada became dominion, or self-governing, states, while retaining ties to the British Crown. Indians were hoping for a similar deal.

The next set of political reforms launched by the British, though sweeping in nature, fell short of Indians' expectations. The Government of India Act of 1919 called for the gradual introduction of self-governing institutions in India, expanded legislative bodies, and widened the franchise considerably. At the provincial level, departments such as agriculture, health, and education were brought under Indian control, while finance, taxation, and other important responsibilities were left in the hands of the British. Indians were permitted to enter the civil service and become officers in the army.

The goodwill generated by these reforms evaporated quickly when the government implemented the controversial Rowlatt Act, which gave British officials sweeping powers to curb free press, detain political activists without trial, and arrest any individual suspected of sedition without a warrant. This act was passed despite objections from the Indian members of the Imperial legislative council. In protest, the Congress Party called for a general strike and a nationwide cessation of work. Both Hindus and Muslims actively participated in the protest. During this time, Mohandas Karamchand Gandhi formally entered the Indian political scene.

The Independence Movement: The Gandhi Era

Mohandas Karamchand Gandhi was born in Porbander, in the present state of Gujarat, on October 2, 1869. He grew up in nearby Rajkot, where his father served as prime minister to the local ruler. Gandhi lost his father before he could finish his schooling. At age thirteen, he was married to Kasturba, who was even younger.

In 1888 Gandhi left India to pursue a law degree in Britain. He obtained his law degree from University College, London, and was admitted to the British bar in 1891. He returned to India in 1891 and attempted to establish a law practice in Bombay, without much success. Two years later, Gandhi accepted a job offer from an Indian businessman in South Africa to work as a legal adviser. He arrived in Durban in 1893. From Durban, he wanted to travel to Johannesburg on a business trip. Gandhi booked a first-class train ticket and boarded the train, but he was ordered out of the first-class compartment due to his skin color. He spent a cold night in a waiting room at the Pietermaritzburg railway station. His encounter with racism made him realize the plight of Indians who had been living in South Africa without political rights. Rather than going back to India, Gandhi decided to stay on in Natal and organize the Indian community to fight for their rights. At that time, there were many Indians working in sugar plantations in South Africa.

In 1894, at the age of twenty-five, Gandhi founded the Natal Indian Congress and launched his long struggle against the South African government. Initially he based his campaign on passive resistance to and noncooperation with the regime. Later he coined a new term, *satyagraha* (truth and firmness), to signify his philosophy of nonviolent resistance. In 1907, he launched a major campaign against new laws requiring mandatory registration of Asians. Thousands of Indians joined his nonviolent civil disobedience movement. After a long and arduous campaign, Gandhi finally managed to win concessions from the South African regime. The government met many of his demands in 1914, including the recognition of Indian marriages and the abolition of the poll tax. His work in South Africa complete, Gandhi bid farewell to his followers and returned to India in 1915, at the age of forty-six.

Upon his return, Gandhi was deeply moved by the poverty and sufferings of his countrymen. On the advice of his political mentor and Congress Party leader Gokhale, Gandhi went on an extensive tour of India to gain an understanding of its diverse cultures and see firsthand the state of the country under British rule.

In 1919, Gandhi formally joined the independence movement by organizing a major nonviolent resistance effort against the Rowlatt Act. Inspired by his example, millions of ordinary Indians joined the Congress movement. One place of protest was Jallianwala Bagh, in the Punjabi city of Amritsar, where over twenty thousand people gathered on April 13, 1919, to protest the arrest of local Congress leaders. The location was an open area enclosed on three sides, with an exit on the fourth side. The crowd was unaware of the last minute ban imposed on such protests in Amritsar. In a well-planned and gruesome act, General Dyer, the military commander of that area, ordered his troops to fire on the unarmed and unsuspecting crowd, killing 379 people and injuring many more. The troops deliberately closed the only exit route out of the open area to maximize the casualties. The Jallianwala Bagh massacre was a major turning point in India's struggle for independence. The entire nation was outraged by this brutality. Following the lead of prominent Indians such as Rabindranath Tagore, who renounced the knighthood conferred by the British, many ordinary Indians abandoned their support for the British government and joined the independence movement.

In the period following the Jallianwala Bagh massacre, Gandhi took the reins of the Congress Party. The Congress Party was reorganized in 1920 and for the first time proclaimed swaraj (self-rule) its goal. Party membership was opened to anyone willing to pay a token fee. Under Gandhi's leadership, the Congress movement became national, supported by men and women from all religions, cultures, and social backgrounds. At the Calcutta session, Gandhi formally announced the start of a noncooperation movement and established very high standards. In Gandhi's view, there was no room for violence, and all protests had to be peaceful and adhere to principles of *ahimsa* (nonviolence). In the beginning, Gandhi's ideas and tactics seemed impractical to Congressmen and ordinary people alike. But soon the movement caught the imagination of Indians from all walks of life. Millions took to the streets to protest British rule. At Gandhi's urging, many Indians resigned from government service, withdrew their children from British-run schools, returned the honors and titles bestowed on them by the government, and began boycotting British-made goods.

Although the protests were largely successful, sporadic violence broke out in some parts of the country. A mob of agitators set fire to a police station at Chauri Chaura in 1922, causing the death of twenty-two Indian policemen working for the British establishment. Gandhi was deeply distressed by this incident and called off the successful campaign. When it came to nonviolence, he always walked the talk. He did not want the national freedom movement to degenerate into an orgy of violence against the British.

Gandhi was arrested in 1922, shortly after calling off the movement, and tried on the charge of conspiring to overthrow the government. He pleaded guilty to all the charges and began serving a six-year jail term; however, he was released after two years due to ill health. Upon his release, Gandhi took a break from the freedom movement and established an *ashram* (retreat) on the banks of the Sabarmati River in Ahmadabad, in present-day Gujarat. He focused his attention on reforms targeting socially disadvantaged people in Indian society, including the rural population and the untouchables.

In 1927, the British set up the Simon Commission to examine constitutional measures toward Indian self-rule, but they did not involve the Congress Party in the deliberations. At its historic Lahore session in 1929, the Congress Party responded by adopting a resolution to gain complete independence from the British; they named January 26, 1930, as their Independence Day.

In 1930, Gandhi emerged from his long seclusion and revived the independence movement by announcing a new campaign of civil disobedience. The immediate provocation for this announcement was a newly imposed tax on salt. Gandhi was determined to break the British monopoly on salt's production and sale. On March 12, he led a small group of followers on a three-week, four-hundred-kilometer march from his ashram in Ahmadabad to Dandi, on the coast of Gujarat. At Dandi, in April 1930, he and his thousands of followers broke the salt law by making their own salt from seawater. The British responded by arresting Gandhi and thousands of his followers. In November 1930, while Gandhi was in jail, the First Round Table Conference was held in London, without representation from the Congress Party. The same year, Gandhi was named "Man of the Year" by *Time Magazine*.[57]

After Gandhi was released in 1931, he negotiated a pact with the British known as the Gandhi-Irwin Pact, under which the government released all political prisoners. In return, Gandhi suspended the civil disobedience movement and agreed to participate in the Second Round Table Conference in London, which would focus on the future of India. Gandhi was the sole representative of the Congress Party. The negotiations proved inconclusive, so Gandhi returned to India and resumed the civil disobedience movement in January 1932. He was once again arrested and imprisoned without trial.

While in jail, Gandhi undertook an epic "fast unto death" to protest the British government's decision to grant separate electorates to Hindu untouchables. He believed the decision was a retrograde measure meant to produce permanent divisions within Hindu society. By undertaking the fast, Gandhi earned the hostility of the leader of the lower classes, Dr. B. R. Ambedkar, who vehemently argued for separate electorates for the downtrodden. Ambedkar, born to a poor, untouchable family, spent his life fighting against caste discrimination. Though Gandhi and Ambedkar shared the view that caste discrimination should be abolished, they had fundamentally different views on how to accomplish that goal. Gandhi wanted to abolish caste discrimination but keep the untouchables within the Hindu fold, while Ambedkar wanted the untouchables to leave Hinduism and create their own identity. Gandhi's fast provoked great public support across India. A number of Hindu leaders met Ambedkar and urged him to reconsider his demands. Gandhi ended his six-day fast after the British government accepted the terms of the Poona Pact, a settlement between Gandhi and Ambedkar. This pact provided reserved seats in legislatures for the depressed classes, in return for relinquishing demand for separate electorates.

After his release from prison, Gandhi embarked on a nationwide tour to campaign against caste discrimination. His efforts garnered great enthusiasm from his countrymen and helped break the caste barriers within the Hindu community. In February 1933, he founded a weekly newspaper, *Harijan*, which was devoted to the needs of the oppressed. In September 1934, he announced his decision to retire from politics and focus his attention on the development of village industries. Gandhi was replaced by Jawaharlal Nehru as the leader of the Congress Party. Rather than returning to his earlier ashram on the Sabarmati River, Gandhi decided to move his residence to a small village in central India called Sevagram. From 1936 until his death in 1948, Gandhi kept Sevagram as his headquarters.

The 1930s also saw the advancement of Indians in various fields, such as sports, science, and literature. The Indian field hockey team won its first gold medal at the 1932 Olympics. Indian scientist Sir C. V. Raman won the Nobel Prize in Physics in 1930.

By 1935, Britain's hold on India had weakened. The daily protests and acts of civil disobedience had taken a toll on governance. Trade was also severely affected due to the boycott of British-made goods. But the British were not ready to leave the country for good. Instead, the British parliament passed new legislation in 1935 that made the most sweeping concessions yet. Although the British kept control of the federal government, the reins of the eleven provinces were handed over to elected Indian representatives. The legislation also contained provisions for safeguarding the interests of religious minorities through separate electorates. In the elections that followed the constitutional changes in 1937, the Congress Party emerged victorious in seven of the eleven provinces, and the Muslim League faired poorly. Mohammad Ali Jinnah, the leader of the Muslim League, tried unsuccessfully to form a coalition government in some of the provinces. When his request was denied, he began to play up the Muslim fear of being dominated by a Hindu majority. Although the idea of a separate Muslim state had been floated in the early 1930s, it gained traction only in the late 1930s. Jinnah persuaded the Muslim League to pass a resolution in Lahore demanding the division of India into two separate states along religious lines. More and more ordinary Muslims began joining the Muslim League, which increasingly claimed to be the voice of Indian Muslims. This claim was rejected by the Congress Party, which saw itself as a national secular party representing all religions and castes. Undeterred, Jinnah continued to equate Congress Party rule as Hindu rule.

Meanwhile, not everything was going well within the Congress Party. In 1938, Subhas Chandra Bose was elected as the new party president. He was a fierce leader and believed that Gandhi's tactics of nonviolence would never be enough to secure independence. He advocated violent resistance and asked the Congress Party to pass a resolution that would give the British government an ultimatum: hand over power within six months or face a revolt. Bose's rigid stand attracted much opposition within the Congress Party, which was built on Gandhi's principles of nonviolence. Therefore, Bose resigned as president, formed an independent group called the Forward Block, and continued to call for complete and immediate independence. He was placed under house arrest but escaped to Japan in 1941, where he enlisted Japanese and German support to fight the British in India. Bose formed the Indian National Army (INA) in 1943, which fought with British troops in northeastern India. However, with the surrender of Japan to Allied forces in 1945, the INA's operations ceased. Though it is widely believed that Bose died in a plane crash in 1945, his death is still controversial in India.

When World War II broke out in 1939, the British government unilaterally declared India's participation in the war without consulting

Indian leaders. While the Muslim League supported the war efforts, the Congress Party opposed the move and withdrew from the provincial government. The Congress Party demanded complete independence for India as a precondition for supporting the war. The British offered to gradually extend dominion status after the war ended, but talks remained deadlocked and inconclusive.

In August 1942, Gandhi launched a major movement called Quit India, which called on the British to leave India immediately or face nationwide civil disobedience. The British responded forcefully by imprisoning the top brass of the Congress Party—then banning the Congress Party altogether. Large-scale protests and demonstrations broke out across the country, and the government resorted to mass arrests to control the situation. The entire Congress Party leadership was cut off from the rest of the world for the next few years. Gandhi suffered two personal blows when his wife, Kasturba, and his personal secretary, Mahadev Desai, died while he was in detention. Gandhi was allowed to attend his wife's funeral but promptly returned back to prison. In 1944, when Gandhi was seventy-five, the British set him free due to his failing health; they feared that his dying in prison would fuel greater unrest in the country.

Perhaps the biggest beneficiary of the disorder and confusion following the launch of the Quit India movement was Mohammad Ali Jinnah and his Muslim League. The full-scale detention of Congress Party leaders left the field open for Jinnah, who took advantage of the situation to consolidate his power. By supporting the British and vigorously campaigning against the Congress Party during wartime, Jinnah earned the goodwill of the British establishment. The ranks of the party soon swelled, and the Muslim League started flexing its political muscle by reiterating its demand for the creation of a separate state called Pakistan in the areas where the Muslims were the majority.

In some ways, World War II was a blessing in disguise for the Indian independence movement. Although it was part of the winning coalition, Britain faced enormous military and economic challenges both at home and abroad. In 1945, the political landscape of Britain changed dramatically when Prime Minister Winston Churchill suffered an electoral defeat by the Labor Party, led by Clement Attlee. Under Prime Minister Attlee, the decolonization of the British Empire went into high gear.

By early 1946, all political prisoners were released, and the British had begun discussions with the Congress Party to develop a strategy for transferring power to India. Mohammad Ali Jinnah, who was opposed to sharing power with the Congress Party, renewed his demand for an independent Muslim nation by carving out the Muslim majority regions. Gandhi vehemently opposed the division of the country and tried to persuade Jinnah to give up his demand. When the talks failed, Jinnah called for "direct action" by Muslims to achieve their goal. As a result, communal violence broke out in many parts of the country, and more than five thousand people lost their lives.

Fearing that any further delay in reaching a political settlement would lead to civil war and anarchy, Congress Party leaders agreed to the partition of the country. The British, now in a hurry to leave India, also threw their weight behind the proposal. The only dissenting voice came from Gandhi, who continued to argue against the partition of the country for which he had fought for over a quarter century.

At midnight on August 15, 1947, India became an independent nation. Jawaharlal Nehru, a close confidante of Mahatma Gandhi, was sworn in as India's first prime minister. In his famous inaugural speech, Nehru declared, "At the stroke of midnight when world sleeps, India will awake to life and freedom."[58] Gandhi, the architect of the independence movement, did not participate in the celebrations. He chose to spend his day fasting and praying in Calcutta.

As per the settlement negotiated by the new British Viceroy Lord Mountbatten, British India was divided into two independent nations: India and Pakistan. Pakistan consisted of the Muslim-majority regions. The princely states, which had retained some level of autonomy under British rule, were released from British control and asked to merge with either India or Pakistan. The provinces of Punjab and Bengal, which had mixed populations, were divided between the two nations.

The partition of the Punjab province along religious lines set into motion one of the largest migrations in history. Over fifteen million people poured across the newly created boundaries between India and Pakistan to settle in the country of their choice. Savage communal riots broke out in Punjab, and over half a million people are believed to have lost their lives. The newly formed governments were ill-equipped to handle such a gigantic crisis, and it took nearly six weeks to restore normalcy. In contrast to the violent partition of Punjab, the division of Bengal was carried out relatively peacefully. This was mainly due to the efforts of Gandhi, who had camped out in Calcutta to prevent bloodshed.

Within six months of gaining independence, India suffered an enormous tragedy: on January 30, 1948, while on his way to an evening prayer meeting in New Delhi, Gandhi was fatally shot at point-blank range. He was seventy-nine years old. His assassin was a Hindu who disagreed with his ideology and was enraged with his support for the Muslims.

Gandhi's death was a tremendous blow to the new nation, which was still grappling with the effects of partition. Millions of people poured into the streets of Delhi to follow Gandhi's funeral caravan. It was a personal loss for Prime Minister Nehru, who had been Gandhi's close associate for many years. In his radio address to the nation, Nehru summed up the feeling of his fellow citizens: "The light has gone out of our lives and there is darkness everywhere. But the light that shone in this country was no ordinary light. For a thousand years that light will be seen in this country and world will see it."[59] Albert Einstein remarked, "Generations to come, it may be, will scarce believe that such a one as this ever in flesh and blood walked upon this earth."[60]

Gandhi's success in achieving independence for India through a nonviolent mass movement made him one of the most remarkable leaders of all time. When it came to nonviolence, he always walked the talk. India's independence movement served as a catalyst for similar movements around the world, ultimately leading to the disintegration of the British Empire. American civil rights leader Martin Luther King

Jr. applied Gandhi's principle of nonviolent struggle to fight racial inequality in America. "Jesus gave us the strategy of nonviolence and Gandhi gave us the tactic," King said. "We may ignore Gandhi at our own risk."[61]

Post-Independent India: The Nehru Era

India gained independence from British colonial rule on August 15, 1947. British India was partitioned along religious lines into the Hindu-majority state of India and the Muslim-majority state of Pakistan. Then there was the question of the areas not governed directly by the British: the princely states, about 562 of them, that had maintained their autonomy under a treaty with the British. The outgoing British government urged them to join either India or Pakistan. While most opted for India and some opted for Pakistan, three states—Juganadh, Hyderabad, and Kashmir—joined neither, desiring to maintain their independence. The Muslim ruler of Juganadh wanted to join Pakistan, but eventually joined India. Hyderabad was under Muslim rulers, the Nizams, whose subjects were predominantly Hindu. India expected the state to join its union because it was situated in the middle of the country and had a Hindu majority, but the Nizams refused to bow to India's wishes. After months of fruitless negotiations, India's interior minister, Sardar Patel, ordered military action in 1948, putting an end to Hyderabad's ambitions and bringing the state into India's fold.

Kashmir, on the border between India and Pakistan, was the only state whose status was yet to be determined. Although overwhelmingly a Muslim state, Kashmir was ruled by a Hindu leader, Hari Singh. When he delayed his decision on which country to join, Pakistan launched an attack on Kashmir using tribal forces. Faced with the possibility of losing his entire kingdom, including the capital city of Srinagar, Hari Singh finally acceded to India and appealed for military help. After a fierce fight between Indian troops and Pakistani fighters, the Union Nations intervened at India's request and brokered a ceasefire agreement that left two-thirds of Kashmir in India's control and the rest with Pakistani control. Since then, Kashmir has remained a major source of friction between India and Pakistan.

In 1950, India adopted a new constitution, largely modeled after the British constitution. It guaranteed equal rights to all citizens and allowed for universal franchise, marking the beginning of the world's largest democracy. The population of India at that time was about 320 million, roughly the current population of United States. Women and men were given equal voting rights. Although overwhelmingly a Hindu state, India declared itself a secular state, consistent with the vision of Mahatma Gandhi. Dr. Rajendra Prasad became the first president of India and held the post until 1962.

When the first countrywide elections were held in 1952, the Congress Party, led by Prime Minister Nehru, won the overwhelming majority of seats in the Lok Sabha (lower house), capturing 364 of 499 seats.[62] Nehru went on to win the next two general elections in 1957 and 1962. The Nehru administration made a number of decisions that impacted the economic future of the country. Nehru was a strong advocate of a mixed-economy approach, which took the best elements from both capitalism and communism. A new planning commission was set up to coordinate economic activities in the public sector. Massive investments were made in basic industries, such as steel, heavy machinery, and power plants. Nehru's rapid industrialization paid off, and in a short time, India joined the ranks of the top ten industrialized nations in the world.

The Nehru administration also introduced far-reaching social reforms. The Untouchability Act of 1955 promised stiff penalties for discrimination on the basis of caste, color, or race. A comprehensive affirmative action program was launched, under which preferential treatment was given to the depressed classes in university admissions and public sector jobs. The Hindu Marriage Act of 1955 gave Hindu women the right to divorce, a concept that was foreign to Indian society until then. The minimum age for marriage was raised to eighteen.[63]

The Hindu Succession Act recognized the property rights of female children. The reorganization of Indian states along linguistic lines led to the creation of new states and the redrawing of existing states' borders. The French government ceded its territories, including Pondicherry, to India in 1956. However, the Portuguese government refused to cede its territories. Brushing aside American opposition, Nehru ordered military action and brought the Portuguese territories of Goa, Daman, and Diu under Indian control. Throughout his tenure, Nehru tried to cultivate friendly relations with India's neighboring countries, including China. His famous quote was: "The only alternative to coexistence is co-destruction."[64]

Nehru broke new ground in international diplomacy by cofounding the Non-Aligned Movement (NAM), which provided an option for countries that were not interested in being part of the American or Soviet block during the cold war. However, by the late 1950s, a territorial dispute with China threatened to disrupt the peace between the nations. China's invasion of Tibet occurred at approximately the same time. Although Nehru did not condemn the Chinese crackdown on Tibet, his eventual decision to grant asylum to the fleeing Tibetan spiritual leader the Dalai Lama was not well-received by the Chinese government. Bowing to domestic pressure, the Nehru government adopted a policy under which army patrols were sent to the disputed territories, provoking a response from the Chinese military. In 1962, China prevailed in the brief war with the ill-prepared, ill-equipped Indian army. The war ended when China unilaterally announced a cease-fire after occupying parts of the disputed territories.

In 1964, seventy-four-year-old Nehru died in office, after leading India for seventeen years. He is remembered as the architect of modern India and the most popular political figure after Mahatma Gandhi. Lal Bahadur Shastri, a senior member of Nehru's cabinet, succeeded him. During Shastri's brief tenure, India fought a border war with Pakistan over the disputed region of Kashmir. The war ended when the Soviet Union intervened and brokered a U.N.-sponsored cease-fire agreement. In January 1966, within hours of signing the agreement in Tashkent, Shastri died of a massive heart attack.

The Indira Gandhi Era

After Shastri's death, the ruling Congress Party leaders chose Indira Gandhi, daughter of Nehru, as the new premier. In electing Indira, the party ignored the claim of a senior party leader, Morarji Desai, on the grounds that he lacked national appeal and was ill-suited to lead the party in the general elections. Indira Gandhi thus became the second female prime minister in the world, after Sirimavo Bandaranaike of Sri Lanka. Indira Gandhi (no relation to Mahatma Gandhi) got her name from her politician husband Feroze Gandhi, who had died in 1960.

In the fourth general elections, held in 1967, the Congress Party secured only 284 seats in the 545-member Lok Sabha (lower house), compared with 361 seats in 1962. Also, for the first time, the party lost control of several states, including West Bengal and Madras. There were several reasons for the decline in support for the Congress Party. The party entered the general elections for the first time without its charismatic leader, Jawaharlal Nehru. The monsoons of 1965 and 1966 caused hardships nationwide. The nation also faced an economic crisis in 1966, forcing the government to devalue the rupee[65] under pressure from the United States and the International Monetary Fund, a move that was unpopular with the electorate.

Amid declining popular support, Indira Gandhi implemented a slew of populist measures, including the nationalization of the country's fourteen largest private banks and implementation of a ceiling on personal income, private property, and corporate profits. Differences over her policies led to the splitting of the Congress Party into two, with Indira Gandhi as leader the Congress-R Party faction. She traveled throughout the country to mobilize support. Campaigning fiercely on the slogan of "*garibi hatao*" (banish poverty), she won a dramatic victory in the fifth general election in March 1971, garnering 352 of 545 seats in the Lok Sabha. The rival Congress Party was trounced beyond recognition, winning only sixteen seats.

Just after her reelection in 1971, Indira Gandhi's attention was drawn to a crisis in neighboring Pakistan. In December 1970, civil war broke out in Pakistan when the ruling military establishment refused to hand over power to a democratically elected political party based in East Pakistan. As a result, large-scale demonstrations and street protests had broken out in East Pakistan. The ensuing Pakistani army crackdown led to the fleeing of millions of East Pakistani refugees into neighboring India. Over ten million refugees are believed to have fled the conflict zone, putting a considerable strain on India's resources. India responded by providing arms training and diplomatic support to East Pakistani rebels as they defended themselves from Pakistani army attacks. Full-scale war broke out between India and Pakistan, the third war since independence, when Pakistan bombed Indian airfields on December 3, 1971. The Indian government declared a state of emergency and began counterattacking Pakistani positions. The Indian army quickly prevailed, and the war ended when over ninety thousand Pakistani troops surrendered to the Indian army in Dhaka.[66] East Pakistan was liberated, and a new nation, Bangladesh, was born.

Indira's deft handling of the war helped her win admirers both within and outside India. By the early 1970s, she had firmly established herself as India's indisputable leader. "India is Indira" became the new slogan. However, the country experienced a severe drought in 1971 and 1972, leading to serious food shortages. The decision of the Organization of Petroleum Exporting Countries (OPEC) to increase oil prices led to high inflation and increased unemployment. India's decision to conduct its first nuclear test in May 1974 did not help matters, drawing worldwide condemnation, including sanctions from Canada.[67]

Discontent and disillusionment with Indira's premiership started to grow across the country. There were numerous strikes, including a major strike by railroad employees. Amid social unrest and rapid economic deterioration, Indira Gandhi received a personal jolt in 1975 when the Allahabad High Court invalidated her 1971 election after finding her guilty of violating electoral laws. Indira Gandhi maintained her innocence and refused to resign, prompting nationwide protests by her detractors. On June 25, 1975, she declared a national emergency on.

Her immediate provocation was a fiery speech by Jayaprakash Narayan, a popular socialist leader, in which he had asked the military and police not to take orders from what he described as an unconstitutional and immoral government. That night, Indira Gandhi suspended civil rights and ordered the arrest of almost all of the opposition parties' leaders. The press came under strict censorship as well. In all, over one hundred thousand people were detained without trial during the emergency. This period also saw the political rise of Indira Gandhi's youngest son, Sanjay Gandhi, who became a chief proponent of the emergency rule. Although India registered significant economic and industrial growth, it came at the cost of civil rights and individual freedom. Sanjay Gandhi, who at times functioned as de-facto prime minister, generated severe criticism for his role in pushing forward several controversial schemes, including the forced sterilization of poor people to control country's population and the eviction of slum dwellers in cities like Delhi, in the name of beautification. In January 1977, Indira Gandhi lifted the emergency rule and called for general elections in March. She also ordered the release of all her opponents from prison.

With the elections two months away, opposition parties came together under the banner of the Janata Party (people's party), led by Jayaprakash Narayan. Riding on the anti-Indira, anti-emergency wave, the new coalition secured a clear majority in the Lok Sabha. The Congress Party tally dropped from 352 to 154, and Indira Gandhi lost her own seat in the parliament.

Morarji Desai, who was deputy prime minister under Indira Gandhi, became India's fourth prime minister. Incidentally, his government was India's first non-Congress Party government since independence. Desai wasted no time and restored democracy and freedom to the country. But from the very beginning, his government was paralyzed by the factionalism and disparate ideologies of the constituent parties. The coalition was a marriage of convenience, bound only by their common dislike of Indira. Once the common enemy disappeared, things went south. The Janata Party had plenty of stalwarts, including Vajpayee as foreign minister and L. K. Advani as minister of information and broadcasting, but that was not enough to save the government. After two years of squabbling, the Janata Party coalition collapsed under its own weight and was replaced by an interim government led by Charan Singh. In the fresh elections held in January 1980, Indira Gandhi, campaigning on the failures of the Janata Party, returned to power with a comfortable majority. During the run-up to the elections, the Congress Party again split with Indira's group, renamed now as Congress-I ("I" for "Indira").

In June 1980, just a few months after returning to power, Indira Gandhi was struck by a personal tragedy when her younger son and heir apparent, Sanjay Gandhi, was killed when an airplane that he was piloting crashed. She persuaded her elder son, Rajiv Gandhi, also an airline pilot, to join her political party. Rajiv joined reluctantly, and in 1981 he won a seat in the parliament from Amethi, Sanjay's constituency.

Soon, Indira faced problems on several fronts. Her political support in the south, once considered bastion for her party, was eroding. Three of the four southern states fell into the hands of opposition parties. The most critical among them was the state of Andhra Pradesh, where a movie-star-turned-politician, N. T. Rama Rao, formed a new political party; within eighteen months, he unseated Indira's ruling Congress Party. In Assam, the native people started a violent agitation against Bengali immigrants. But the worst of the conflicts was brewing in the northern state of Punjab, where the Sikh separatist movement was gaining traction.

Punjab, whose politics was traditionally dominated by the Akali Dal Party, was one of the few states where the Congress Party was unable to develop a significant political base. In order to break the stronghold of the Akali Dal, some elements in the Congress Party encouraged Jarnail Singh Bhindranwale, a young Sikh leader, to build a separate Sikh organization. The goal was to weaken the Akali Dal by siphoning off some of the Sikh votes. However, Bhindranwale had other ideas. After initially agreeing with the Congress Party, he suddenly turned the tables by demanding a new independent Sikh state to be known as Khalistan.

The separatist movement turned violent when his followers targeted anyone opposed to their ideology. All mainstream political parties were completely marginalized, and hundreds of innocent people, especially those belonging to the minority Hindu community, lost their lives in random acts of violence. By May 1984, Bhindranwale and his followers had taken complete control of the Sikh Golden Temple, the holiest shrine of the Sikh faith, converting it into a haven for terrorists. The writ of the government did not run any more. Against this backdrop, Indira Gandhi decided to take the militants head-on. In June 1984, she sent the Indian army into the Golden Temple to flush out the militants.

The operation, code-named Operation Blue Star, pitted the men of the Indian army against the militants inside the Golden Temple and resulted in thousands of deaths on both sides within the temple premises. Bhindranwale was killed along with his followers, and the government managed to take control of the shrine. But the Indian army could not prevent the damage to some of the shrine's buildings. The desecration of the shrine enraged Sikhs worldwide. On October 31, 1984, four months after launching the military action, Indira Gandhi was assassinated in her official residence in New Delhi by her own Sikh body guards, in retaliation for storming the Golden Temple.[68]

The country was rocked by violence for the next week. Mobs targeted innocent Sikhs, and over one thousand were killed before the army could restore order. Within twelve hours of Indira Gandhi's death, President Zail Singh swore in her surviving son, Rajiv Gandhi, as the new prime minister. Rajiv Gandhi also became the president of the Congress Party.

The Rajiv Gandhi Era

Rajiv Gandhi succeeded Indira Gandhi, continuing the Nehru-Gandhi dynastic rule. At age forty, he was the youngest prime minister of India. He won the respect of the nation for handling the aftermath of his mother's assassination with great poise and dignity. But his infamous remark, "When a big tree falls, the earth below shakes," which he made to rationalize the rioting following Indira's death, drew sharp criticism. About a month after Indira's assassination, tragedy struck India again when the central Indian city of Bhopal, a densely populated city of nine hundred thousand inhabitants, experienced the world's worst industrial disaster to date.

On the night of December 23, 1984, about forty tons of highly poisonous methyl isocyanate gas leaked from a pesticide factory owned by Union Carbide (currently owned by Dow Chemical). Over two thousand people died immediately, and thousands were maimed for life. After a five-year court battle, the Indian government and Union Carbide struck a deal: Union Carbide would pay a paltry $470 million,[69] and the government would drop all criminal charges against the company. The settlement was denounced by the disaster's survivors and the victims' families as a sell-out by the Indian government. The government defended its actions by saying that the deal would avoid a longer legal fight.

Meanwhile, the new prime minister was eager to get a fresh mandate from the people, mainly to legitimize his government. The eighth general election was held toward the end of December 1984. Gandhi proved to be a tireless and effective campaigner. He promised to end the culture of corruption in the ruling Congress Party and attempted to breathe new life into the organization by bringing in new faces. Riding on the sympathy wave brought about by his mother's death, the Congress Party won by a landslide, winning an unprecedented 415 seats of the 517 seats contested. The sympathy wave was so strong that many stalwarts belonging to opposition parties were swept up by it. In March 1985, Rajiv's Congress Party went on to win eight of the eleven state assembly elections, once again giving the Congress Party complete control of national affairs.

Rajiv Gandhi wasted little time and began to address the nation's most critical and urgent problems. The young prime minister enjoyed tremendous goodwill from the people of India, who had optimism and hope for the future of the country. His first act was to pass a historic antidefection law in January 1985, which made it difficult for a parliament member elected on one party ticket to defect to another party. Although the move was ostensibly to end the culture of corruption and bribery that lured the members into switching parties, the main reason was to discourage Congressmen from defecting. There was no immediate threat, but Rajiv did not want to take any chances. Indians appreciated his anticorruption drive, which earned him the nickname "Mr. Clean."

As expected, the Punjab problem was on the top of his agenda. Violence in Punjab had increased dramatically in retaliation for the anti-Sikh riots following Indira Gandhi's assassination. Some high-profile Congress Party leaders, such as Lalit Makhan and Arjan Das, were gunned down. On June 11, 1985, India witnessed its worst form of terrorism when an Air India Boeing 747 passenger jet, en route from Toronto to London with a stopover in Montreal, exploded in midair off the coast of Ireland, killing all 329 passengers. The bomb was apparently planted in retaliation for the anti-Sikh riots in Delhi. After a twenty-year investigation, a Canadian court acquitted[70] two of the accused, to the utter dismay of the victims' relatives.

Amid continuing violence and bloodshed, Rajiv Gandhi ordered the release of most of the political leaders belonging to Punjab's Akali Dal Party. He initiated new talks with Sikh leaders to find a political solution to the vexing Punjab problem. The talks resulted in the signing of an accord between Rajiv Gandhi and Sikh leader Sant Longowal on July 24, 1985. Known as the Rajiv-Longowal Accord, the agreement guaranteed to fulfill many of the demands put forward by Sikh leaders over the years. Less than a month after signing the accord, Sant Longowal was shot dead in his native village as he was addressing a public meeting. Undeterred by the development, the government called for elections for the Punjab state assembly in September 1985, and Akali Dal emerged victorious. Surjit Singh Barnala became the new chief minister.

Rajiv Gandhi's government also embarked on modernizing the country. Foreign investment was encouraged, some restrictions on imports were removed, and business controls were loosened. Although the reforms were limited in scope compared to the 1991 reforms initiated by the Narasimha Rao government, they were nevertheless significant. The prime minister took personal interest in revamping the telecommunications and computer sectors. There were some successes on the foreign policy front as well. South Asians came together for the first time to form the South Asian Association for Regional Cooperation (SAARC) in December 1985. All of these factors contributed to Rajiv Gandhi's soaring popularity during the first half of his premiership.

But as Rajiv Gandhi entered the second half of his premiership, things began to go downhill, though he was not entirely to blame. Despite the installation of a democratically elected government in Punjab, the peace accord that he had signed with Sikh leaders began to unravel, and terrorist violence continued unabated. By May 1987, it was back to square one in Punjab, when the Barnala government was dismissed and presidential rule imposed. Rajiv Gandhi's efforts to end the civil war in Sri Lanka by brokering a peace deal between the Sri Lankan government and the Tamil separatists also ended in failure, as both parties reneged on the terms of the peace accord and resumed fighting. The Indian Peace Keeping Force (IPKF), which was sent by Rajiv Gandhi's government to enforce the peace accord, was embroiled in a guerilla war with Tamil Tigers, the very people it wanted to protect. Thousands of casualties later, the Indian government had enough and withdrew from Sri Lanka in 1990.

But the issue that weakened Rajiv Gandhi's government most was the Bofors issue. In 1986, India spent $1.4 billion on artillery pieces[71] from a Swedish manufacturer, A. B. Bofors. After a year, a Swedish radio report claimed that Bofors had bribed Indian politicians and key defense officials to win the deal. Rajiv Gandhi expressed outrage at the accusations and maintained that no kickbacks had been paid to anyone. But the continued press coverage of the Bofors issue and allegations that somehow the prime minister and his friends were connected with the scandal damaged Rajiv Gandhi's reputation as an honest politician. Apart from public opinion, trouble was brewing for Rajiv within his own cabinet. Before the Bofors scandal became a major issue, defense minister V. P. Singh was forced to resign after Rajiv Gandhi stymied his attempts to investigate another scandal involving the purchase of submarines from West Germany. The Bofors scandal provided V. P. Singh fresh ammunition to attack Rajiv Gandhi. He criticized the government's failure to root out party corruption. Singh quit the Congress Party in 1987 and became a rallying point for non-Congress parties, who were eager to dislodge the Rajiv Gandhi government. Singh's relentless campaign against "corruption in high places" rapidly eroded the Rajiv Gandhi's popularity. In the 1989 general elections, Rajiv Gandhi's party received a severe drubbing from the electorate.

India Under V. P. Singh

The 1989 general election was remarkable in many ways, most notably because it was the first time in independent India's history that an election resulted in a hung parliament. No party even came close to the 263 parliamentary seats required to form a government. Rajiv Gandhi's Congress Party won 196 seats of the 505 it contested, a loss of 204 seats from its previous tally of 400-plus seats.

The Janata Dal Party, a new party led by ousted defense minister V. P. Singh, came in second with 143 seats, riding on the anticorruption platform. But the real winner was the Hindu-nationalist Bharatiya Janata Party (BJP), which increased its tally from 2 seats in 1984 to 85 seats in 1989. The BJP made the construction of a temple for Lord Ram at the disputed site in Ayodhya their central campaign issue.

In the absence of a clear winner, the onus of forming a government fell on V. P. Singh, the star of the 1989 elections. He wasted little time and allied himself with three other regional parties to form a new political entity, the National Front. He formed a government with the outside support of other parties, marking the beginning of the era of coalition governments. The 1989 elections saw the emergence of a number of new political parties, which wielded varying amounts of political influence in Indian states. India's political landscape underwent a permanent transformation, and since 1989 all the governments formed at the federal level have been minority governments, coalitions, or both.

When V. P. Singh took over the government reins, expectations were very high. He was widely regarded for his personal integrity and unblemished political career. In August 1990, Singh hastily announced that his government would expand the affirmative action program by reserving an additional 27 percent of federal government jobs for the so-called other backward class (OBC) community. Recommendations for such an action were made by the one-man Mandal Commission in 1980 but were largely ignored by successive governments. Singh retrieved the report from the archives and implemented the measure with little or no consultation with opposition parties. Singh's announcement led to massive protests across northern India. Dozens of youth belonging to the upper castes, fearful of lost job opportunities, resorted to self-immolation to dramatize their opposition to the expansion of the affirmative action program.

By implementing the Mandal Commission's recommendations, Singh wanted to kill two birds in one shot. By doling out privileges to the OBC community, he wanted to create a vote bank for his new Janata Dal Party. Besides, such a move would divide Hindu votes along caste lines and weaken the Hindu-nationalist BJP, whose strategy was to consolidate Hindu votes across various castes. The BJP was understandably taken aback by the new development and decided to retaliate. To trump Singh's new social justice platform and unify Hindus around a common cause, BJP president L. K. Advani announced that he would undertake a *Rath Yatra* (chariot ride) from Somnath to Ayodhya, where he would lead Hindu activists in the construction of a new temple for Lord Ram at the disputed site. As his chariot journey progressed, riots broke out between Hindus and Muslims throughout the country. With religious tensions reaching a boiling point and law and order weakening, Singh's government finally had enough. They arrested Advani at Samastipur, Bihar, thus stopping the progress of his chariot journey to Ayodhya. The BJP retaliated swiftly by withdrawing support for Singh's government on October 23, 1990.

Subsequently, Singh lost a parliamentary vote of confidence in November 2007 and resigned, bringing to an end his eleven-month-old minority government. During Singh's brief tenure, the separatist movement in the Kashmir valley received a fillip when he was forced to set free five terrorists to secure the release of the kidnapped daughter of India's home minister,[72] Mufti Mohammed Syed. On Bofors, his major campaign issue, Singh's government was unable to come up with any further evidence.

After Singh's exit, the ruling Janata Dal Party fell apart. Dissident leader and veteran politician Chandrasekhar formed a new party called Janata Dal (Socialist), and with the support of Rajiv Gandhi's Congress Party, he became the new prime minister. But the bonhomie did not last too long. Chandrasekhar's government fell within four months, after the Congress Party withdrew its support. With no political party or coalition in a position to form a government, the parliament was dissolved, and fresh elections were scheduled for May 1991—within two years of previous elections. With the second non-Congress Party experiment since independence failing miserably, Rajiv Gandhi, now forty-six, was clearly on a comeback trail. The 1991 elections were marred by sectarian violence between Hindus and Muslims, and the election proved to be the most violent in Indian history. On May 21, 1991, halfway through the election process, tragedy struck when Rajiv Gandhi was assassinated during a political campaign in the town of Sriperumbudur, thirty miles from the southern city of Chennai. The assassin was a female Tamil suicide bomber affiliated with the LTTE militant group, which fought for a separate homeland for the Tamils of Sri Lanka. It was a revenge attack for Rajiv Gandhi's decision as premier in 1987 to send troops to Sri Lanka to disarm Tamil separatists.

The Rao Premiership

Riding on the sympathy wave generated by Rajiv Gandhi's assassination, the Congress Party improved its tally from 197 to 227 but still lacked the numbers needed to form a government. The BJP also improved its tally, from 80 to 120, helped by their campaign for the Ram

Temple. Despite a fractured verdict, no party wanted to go through another election, so the Congress Party and its allies were allowed to form a minority government. The Congress Party initially turned to Rajiv Gandhi's widow, Sonia, to assume party leadership, but she refused. The leadership then fell to senior Congress Party leader P. V. Narasimha Rao, who had retired from politics before the 1991 elections to pursue his literary interests. When Rao was sworn in as India's ninth prime minister on June 21, 1991, India was facing its worst economic situation[73] in decades.

Fiscal indiscipline and political instability by successive governments ruined India's creditworthiness and plunged it into the worst balance-of-payments crisis in the nation's history. The outbreak of the First Gulf War added to India's economic woes. Oil prices went through the roof, causing inflation to increase to 14 percent. Foreign exchange remittances by expatriate Indians all but evaporated. By mid-1991, India's bankruptcy seemed imminent. In light of the economic situation prevailing in the country, Rao appointed renowned economist and technocrat Dr. Manmohan Singh[74] as his finance minister.

Together Rao and Singh gave impetus to the policies of globalization, liberalization, and privatization. The government dismantled the "License Raj," a term used to describe the vast and complex set of regulations that forced private businesses to get government approval for nearly any decision. The government also opened India to foreign direct investment (FDI), despite opposition from India's powerful industrial houses. The results of these economic reforms were spectacular. By the end of 1991, the economy showed signs of recovery. The FDI increased from a paltry $100 a year to $2 billion by 1995. The growth rate of the economy increased from less than 1 percent in 1991 to 7 percent by 1995. The inflation rate came down to a single digit. The foreign exchange reserves also started being replenished at a steady rate. Despite these successes, Rao and Singh continued to face criticism from the reforms' detractors, which included powerful vested interests and politicians belonging to various political parties. Many viewed the abandonment of the socialist economic model as a betrayal of Nehru's legacy, as well as the principles of self-reliance espoused by Mahatma Gandhi.

Amid good news on the economic front, a huge financial scandal involving stock markets and the banking system broke out in April 1992, causing despair for thousands of individual investors. Government investigators found that several major banks had illegally conspired to lend hundreds of millions of dollars in unsecured loans to stock speculators. The man at the center of the scandal was Harshad Mehta, a celebrated stockbroker with the Bombay Stock Exchange (BSE). Mehta started his career as a dispatch clerk in a major insurance company and later became a stockbroker. He'd made waves in the stock market by buying stocks aggressively since early 1990. By the second half of 1991, he'd become the darling of the business media, who gave him the title "Big Bull" for starting a "bull run" on the stock market. However, nobody had any idea where Mehta was getting the money to finance his stock purchases. All hell broke loose when a journalist discovered that he was dipping illegally into the country's banking system to finance his purchases. After the discovery, the stock market collapsed by eight hundred points, or 20 percent, causing an estimated loss of $1 billion[75] for Indian investors.

The government acted swiftly, arresting "Big Bull" and banishing him from the stock market. Also, heads of several banks were either forced to resign or sent to prison for their involvement in the scandal. But the damage was already done. The scandal shook the confidence of domestic and overseas investors in India's burgeoning financial system.

Close on the heels of the financial scandal, the Rao government faced a new political crisis when the Vishwa Hindu Parishad (VHP), a Hindu organization spearheading the movement for Ram Temple, vowed that it would perform a religious ceremony symbolizing the start of construction of a new temple at the site of the sixteenth-century mosque in Ayodhya. Hindus believe that the mosque was built on a sacred site, the very spot where the Hindu mythological god Ram was born. The mosque was the focus of Hindu-Muslim hostilities for over a decade. Although it was no longer used for prayers, Muslims were unwilling to relinquish control of the mosque. The Rao administration believed that courts should decide the matter. Armed with the Supreme Court's order that the mosque should be protected from demolition, the government sought and obtained pledges from the Hindu organizations that the proposed religious ceremony would not in disturb the mosque and that the court decision would be obeyed. On December 6, 1992, before the religious ceremony for the proposed temple could start, a screaming mob of two hundred thousand Hindu activists broke through the police cordons and demolished the mosque in a period of about six hours, using sledgehammers and their bare hands.[76] The destruction plunged India into a major political and religious crisis.

The mosque demolition sparked nationwide Hindu-Muslim riots, leaving over two thousand dead. Calling the demolition a matter of shame and a concern for all Indians, Rao responded by dismissing the Uttar Pradesh state government headed by the BJP for its failure to protect the mosque. But Rao drew severe criticism for failing to foresee the demolition despite the warning signs. Within months, India's financial capital Mumbai (then Bombay) was hit by a series of coordinated bomb blasts set off by timing devices, which killed 250 people and injured over a thousand. The Bombay stock exchange, one of the oldest in Asia, was severely damaged. These attacks were apparently masterminded by Dawood Ibrahim, a local don of the organized crime syndicate, in retaliation for the destruction of the mosque.

In June 1993, Prime Minister Rao's image was further tarnished when Harshad Meta, the stockbroker under indictment in the multibillion-dollar securities scam, stunned the nation by alleging, without any independent corroboration, that he had personally delivered suitcases containing ten million rupees in cash in political donations to Rao at his official residence[77] on November 4, 1991. Rao vehemently denied the charges and produced evidence to support his alibi that he was not at home when Mehta allegedly delivered the money. But the fact that it had taken over seventy-two hours for the prime minister's office to offer its version of events greatly weakened Rao's position within his party and the parliament.

Prime Minister Rao's success in bringing changes to India's economic policies is well-known and well-documented. What is not widely known is that his administration was able to end separatist violence in Punjab state and initiate a reconciliation process in the troubled Kashmir region. Bringing peace to Punjab was not a small achievement. Punjab was under the firm grip of Sikh separatists, who were campaigning for an independent nation of Khalistan. Attempts to negotiate with the militants did not yield results. The people of Punjab were caught between the violence of the terrorists and the repressive measures of the security forces. Within six months of taking office, Rao appointed K. P. S. Gill, a tough, no-nonsense cop, as the new police chief of Punjab state to spearhead counterinsurgency operations. Gill's efficient, no-holds-barred campaign against separatists brought the violence down considerably, restoring Punjab's peace and prosperity.

In the 1996 general elections, the Congress Party, led by Prime Minister Rao, suffered its worst electoral defeat since independence, despite orchestrating one of the greatest economic turnarounds in history. There were several reasons for the ruling party's poor performance. The destruction of the mosque and the revival of Hindu nationalism severely weakened the party base. The various corruption scandals that broke out during Rao's premiership alienated urban and middle-class voters. Rao's lack of charisma and weak campaign performance did not help matters. As soon as Rao left office, he faced a flurry of corruption charges and was unceremoniously removed from party leadership. In September 2000, Rao achieved the dubious distinction of being the first Indian prime minister to be convicted of criminal conspiracy and corruption for bribing four lawmakers to vote in favor of his government during the 1993 no-confidence motion. He was later acquitted on appeal and never had to serve any prison time.

All things considered, however, Rao's premiership was one of the most successful in the history of independent India. He not only brought stability at a time when the country was going through turmoil, but he also was able to free the nation from economic woes once and for all. Rao had several firsts. He was the first South Indian to become India's prime minister. He was also the first person outside Nehru-Gandhi family to become the leader of Congress Party.

Post-Rao India

The May 1996 general elections, like those in 1989 and 1991, once again resulted in a fractured verdict. None of the political parties was in a position to form a government on its own. The BJP, which had emerged as the single-largest party with 194 seats, took a gamble and formed a new government with party stalwart Atal Bihari Vajpayee as the new prime minister—despite the fact that it did not have the numbers needed to prove a majority in the parliament. Almost every other political party, wary of BJP's Hindu-nationalist agenda, refused to back the party in the parliament. Vajpayee was forced to resign after thirteen days, bringing an end to his government.

Vajpayee was succeeded by Deve Gowda, who led a fragile fourteen-party United Front coalition with outside support from the Congress Party. The Gowda government fell after less than a year, when the Congress Party withdrew its support in March 1997. After weeks of political turmoil, the Congress Party supported the candidacy of outgoing foreign minister Inder Kumar Gujral. Like Gowda, Gujral headed a coalition of parties with outside support from the Congress Party. He led the nation in its fiftieth year of independence from British rule in August 1997. However, Gujral's government met the same fate as Gowda's; the Congress Party withdrew its support in November 1997. The fall of the fourth government in eighteen months deepened India's political turmoil and economic uncertainty. The pace of economic reform slowed considerably, and many major decisions, such as opening key sectors like insurance to foreign competition and disinvesting loss-making public enterprises, were kept on the back burner. This drove India's three most influential business groups to make an unusual collective appeal to the politicians, urging them to bring an end to the political drama and start governing.

India Under BJP Rule

Fresh general elections were conducted in March 1998. The BJP and its allies improved their tally to 252 seats in the 539-member upper house, but they were still about 20 seats short of an absolute majority. This time, however, the BJP learned from its earlier mistakes and abandoned its radical Hindu-nationalist agenda in order to secure support from some key regional parties, including the AIADMK of Tamil Nadu and the Trinamul Congress of West Bengal. In March 1998, the BJP-led coalition government took office, with Vajpayee as prime minister—finally ending two years of political uncertainty. The post-election period also marked the formal election of Sonia Gandhi, the Italian-born widow of assassinated premier Rajiv Gandhi, as the new president of the Congress Party.

Within two months of taking office, the Vajpayee government stunned the world by conducting a series of underground nuclear tests, India's first tests in more than two decades. To be sure, ending India's twenty-five-year-old nuclear moratorium was part of the BJP's election manifesto; but no one expected Vajpayee to move with such speed and urgency. The nuclear tests enjoyed widespread support in India but provoked universal condemnation from the international community. After failing to dissuade Pakistan from conducting tit-for-tat nuclear tests, President Clinton angrily imposed economic sanctions[78] on both India and Pakistan. The economic sanctions hurt India's fragile economy, and the prices of vegetables and other essential items shot up. As a result, the ruling BJP suffered major setbacks in the November 1998 state elections in its strongholds of Rajasthan and Delhi, where the Congress Party swept to power.

The BJP government, which derived its strength from Hindu-nationalists, drew sharp criticism for its failure to stop violence against India's Christian minority. For years, the BJP and other Hindu parties had been harshly critical of the activities of Indian Christian missionaries, claiming that they had forcefully converted poor Hindu tribal people into Christianity through bribes and intimidation. The situation took an ugly turn when a Hindu mob of about fifty people attacked and burnt alive an Australian missionary and his two young sons while they were sleeping in their vehicle in a remote tribal village in the eastern state of Orissa. After this gruesome incident, the Indian government came under tremendous pressure from Western diplomats and allies within the ruling coalition to stop the attacks, which had tarnished India's secular credentials. The attacks against Christian churches and schools finally dwindled by the beginning of March 1999.

From its inception, the Vajpayee government relied on the support of several smaller and regional parties, who held narrow political agendas as conditions for their support. In April 1999, the AIADMK Party, a key regional party from the southern state of Tamil Nadu that was headed by a powerful and mercurial actress, Jayalalitha Jayaram, summarily withdrew its support, plunging the country into yet another political mess. The drama ended when the president dissolved the parliament and asked Prime Minister Vajpayee to continue in a caretaker capacity until after midterm elections in October/November 1999.

During his brief period of power, Prime Minister Vajpayee tried in earnest to improve relations with India's neighbor and archrival, Pakistan. Relations had worsened after the nuclear tests, and there was a surge in the exchange of artillery fire along the Line of Control (LOC) in Kashmir. To diffuse tensions, Vajpayee took a historic bus trip to Lahore in February 1999, becoming the first Indian prime minister in a decade to visit Pakistan. First Vajpayee and then Pakistani premier Nawaz Sharif signed a peace pact, under which both sides agreed to intensify efforts to resolve the vexing Kashmir issue, which had been a bone of contention for decades. After the peace deal, people on both sides of the border thought the worst was over; they believed the countries had entered a new chapter in their relationship. Little did they realize that the Pakistani army, headed by General Pervez Musharraf, was not on board with the idea of rapprochement with India and was actively plotting to scuttle the peace process. The Pakistani army decided to strike when India was politically tumultuous. In May 1999, the Indian military discovered that hundreds of Pakistani army-backed Islamic guerillas and irregular forces had crossed over to the Indian side of Kashmir and seized a strategic peak overlooking the mountainous region of Kargil. Apparently, the guerillas sneaked onto the Indian side under the cover of artillery fire from the Pakistani army. This act was considered Pakistan's first direct violation of the LOC in several decades.

Amid the escalating crisis along the Kashmir border, India rallied behind the lame-duck Prime Minister Vajpayee. He responded forcefully, ordering relentless air attacks on guerilla positions in Indian-administered Kashmir with jet fighters and helicopter gunships. India relied primarily on air power because of the terrain's inaccessibility. It managed to seize Tiger Hill, a strategic peak, from the guerillas' control by early July. Around that time, international diplomacy gained traction when President Bill Clinton, alarmed by the conflict between two new nuclear powers, asked Pakistan to unconditionally withdraw its irregular forces and Islamic guerillas from Indian territories. Pakistan complied, and the conflict ended by the second week of July. In all, over 1,500 soldiers from both sides lost their lives in the eight weeks of conflict.

India's military victory over Pakistan in the Kargil conflict enhanced the popularity of Prime Minister Vajpayee. In the general elections held in September 1999, the ruling BJP-led National Democratic Alliance, consisting of twenty-four parties, secured a comfortable majority in the parliament, with 293 of the 543 seats. Vajpayee also became the first incumbent prime minister to be voted back into power since 1971. The Kargil military victory, coupled with the smart new alliances the BJP had worked out with state-level parties, worked to the BJP's advantage this time. On the other hand, the Congress Party, which had hoped to make a comeback, once again suffered a humiliating defeat.

On December 24, 1999, a week before the arrival of the new millennium, India witnessed one of the most audacious hijackings in its history. An Indian Airlines Airbus on a routine flight from Kathmandu, Nepal, to New Delhi, with 190 people on board, was hijacked in midair by a group of five Kashmiri militants, armed with grenades, pistols, and knives. Militant groups had been waging bloody insurgency for nearly a decade, demanding an end to Indian rule of the Himalayan region of Kashmir. The plane was stuck on the tarmac of the Kandahar airport for one week as the Indian government began the arduous task of negotiating with the hijackers; they had help from Afghanistan's Taliban regime, with which India did not have a diplomatic relationship. The hijacking drama, which began on Christmas Eve, finally ended on New Year's Eve. India agreed to release three hard-core militants, including Pakistani Muslim cleric Maulana Masood Azhar and Britain-born Omar Sheik, who had been held in Indian prisons since 1994 on terrorism and kidnapping charges. Omar Sheik was later convicted and sentenced to death for murdering *Wall Street Journal* reporter Daniel Pearl in January 2002. India's millennium celebrations, overshadowed by the hijacking, were more subdued than in many other parts of the world.

In January 2001, a huge earthquake measuring 7.9 on the Richter scale[79] devastated the Kutch district in the western Indian state of Gujarat. In all, nearly twenty thousand people lost their lives, two hundred thousand people were injured, and one million homes were destroyed. The damage totaled $4.5 billion, making the earthquake the most intense and devastating India had suffered in almost half a century. The town of Bhuj and surrounding villages, best known as the sites where the Oscar-nominated Indian movie *Lagaan* was shot six months before the quake, bore the full brunt of the quake and were completely destroyed. But the horrific news that nearly four hundred schoolchildren and their teachers were buried alive under the rubble of collapsed buildings in Anjar stunned the nation and galvanized people around the world to begin a massive humanitarian relief effort. The damage was so widespread that it took nearly a year for the region to regain some semblance of normalcy.

In July 2001, the Vajpayee government launched yet another peace initiative with Pakistan by inviting Pakistani leader General Musharraf to summit-level talks to discuss all the contentious issues between the nations. This historic peace summit, held near the fabled Taj Mahal in Agra, ended in complete failure[80] after neither side could transcend its stated position on the Kashmir dispute.

In December 2001, the Indian parliament building in Delhi faced a bloody suicide attack by militants with guns and hand grenades, resulting in fourteen deaths. Fortunately, no lawmakers were injured. There was a similar attack on the Kashmir assembly in Srinagar in October 2001, resulting in thirty-eight deaths. It was clear that the Kashmir separatists were targeting India's democratic institutions. The brazen attack on the Indian parliament enraged India's political leadership, and they accused Pakistan's Inter Services Intelligence (ISI) Agency of backing the terrorist groups responsible for the attacks. India made categorical demands that Pakistan must crack down on terrorism and hand over twenty men India suspected of terrorist activities.

When Pakistan refused to do so, India downgraded its diplomatic relationship with Pakistan and imposed sanctions, including a ban on Pakistani overflights. Amid mounting fears of a looming war between the world's newest nuclear neighbors, both sides mobilized hundreds of thousands of troops along the common border. All the major Western countries, including Britain and the United States, urged their citizens and diplomats to leave India and Pakistan.

In April 2003, Prime Minister Vajpayee finally relented and said that dialogue was the only way to resolve the Kashmir issue and bring peace to the region. In a public speech delivered in Srinagar in Indian-controlled Kashmir, he offered a hand of friendship[81] to Pakistan and agreed to hold talks on the status of Kashmir, provided that Pakistan would stop cross-border terrorism and rein in the militants operating from its soil.

Vajpayee's speech swiftly launched a series of diplomatic initiatives by both sides. In November 2003, Pakistan declared a cease-fire in Kashmir, which was reciprocated by India. This effectively brought an end to the border skirmishes across the LOC, much to the relief of people in the border areas. India and Pakistan also resumed direct flights on January 1, 2005, after a two-year ban.

In January 2004, two years after nearly going to war, Prime Minister Vajpayee and General Musharraf shook hands for the first time at a regional summit. Both sides agreed to launch a series of confidence-building measures (CBMs) to improve relations. Pakistan pledged to forbid terrorists to operate from its soil and implicitly agreed to abandon its military support for the fourteen-year-long separatist insurgency in the Kashmir Valley. In return, India agreed to start a comprehensive dialogue on all issues, including the half-century-old Kashmir issue.

On the domestic front, Prime Minister Vajpayee's attempts to find an amicable solution to the vexing Ram Temple issue, which polarized the country along religious lines, yielded no results, and the situation remained tense throughout his term. In February 2002, the western state of Gujarat witnessed communal riots after an express train carrying 1,500 Hindu activists was set on fire in Godhra,[82] allegedly by Muslims, resulting in fifty-nine deaths.

As news about the attack on Hindus spread throughout the state, vengeful mobs took to the streets and started attacking innocent Muslims of all walks of life. The communal violence continued unabated in Gujarat for the next three months, claiming over a thousand lives, mostly Muslims. Ironically, Gujarat is the home state of Mahatma Gandhi, apostle of peace and nonviolence. There were widespread allegations by witnesses and survivors that the state government, headed by the Hindu-nationalist BJP, the same party that ruled at the federal level, had turned a blind eye to the attacks against the Muslims. India's National Human Rights Commission (NHRC) censured[83] the state government for its comprehensive failure to control the bloodshed.

The violence finally abated by early May after the federal government beefed up security in the state and replaced some key officials, including the police commissioner. In addition to the massive loss of lives, over one hundred thousand survivors became refugees in their own country. The situation was so acute that the government had to set up over a hundred refugee camps. The Gujarat communal riots, considered among the worst in India since the partition riots of 1947, caused irreparable damage to India's democratic and secular credentials and will forever remain a black mark on Prime Minister Vajpayee's otherwise successful six-year rule.

On the economic front, the Vajpayee government deserves a lot of credit for taking a number of bold steps to encourage foreign investment and trade. Within months of taking office in 1998, Vajpayee launched a multibillion-dollar road project[84] to link India's four biggest cities: Delhi, Mumbai, Chennai, and Kolkota. Nearly 3,750 miles of highway were built during Vajpayee's term in office. It is considered one of the most ambitious infrastructure projects since independence. The GDP grew at a healthy rate of 6–7 percent during Vajpayee's tenure. His period was also marked by India's emergence as a global IT powerhouse and a premier outsourcing destination for companies around the world.

Recent Events

Riding on the economic boom and optimistic mood prevailing in the country, the ruling BJP scored impressive victories in the state assembly elections held in late 2003, which were widely seen as a dry run for the parliamentary elections in 2004. The BJP wanted to repeat their performance at the national level and called for an early parliamentary election. Its hopes for returning to power were based on three favorable factors: the booming economy, the soaring popularity of Prime Minister Vajpayee, and India's successful peace talks with Pakistan. To that end, the BJP waged a slick election campaign with the slogan "India Shining" to highlight the administration's achievements of the past six years. Most opinion polls and political pundits predicted the return of Vajpayee as prime minister. But in a stunning reversal of political fortunes, the ruling BJP-led alliance was defeated in the general elections by the opposition Congress Party-led alliance.

There were several reasons for the ruling party's defeat. Voters, especially the poor and rural population, which had yet to experience the economic boom, did not buy into the "India Shining" argument.[85] Voting patterns reflected anger in India's villages. They were angry at the ruling party's failure to fulfill their basic needs, including clean water, power, quality healthcare, and education. Furthermore, the Gujarat communal carnage of 2002 alienated the Muslims, who make up 12 percent of India's population.

The victorious Congress Party chose Dr. Manmohan Singh, the former finance minister credited with launching the groundbreaking economic reforms in 1991, as the new prime minister. Singh's election was historic because he was the first non-Hindu and the first person from the minority Sikh community to occupy India's premiership. Singh formed a center-left coalition known as the United Progressive Alliance (UPA), consisting of fifteen parties supported by the communist parties.

The defeat of the reform-friendly Vajpayee government and its allies stunned domestic businessmen and foreign investors alike. During the election season, the Congress Party had been very critical of Vajpayee's economic policies, for political rather than ideological reasons. Immediately after taking office, Singh assured the nation that the economic reforms would continue but that the emphasis would change. To drive home the point, the new government coined a new phrase: reform with a human face. The new ruling UPA alliance agreed on a common minimum program[86] (CMP), which aimed to spread rural prosperity and make the reforms work for ordinary Indians. In 2006, India launched one of the country's most ambitious efforts to tackle rural poverty. Under the National Rural Guarantee Scheme, one member from each of India's sixty million rural households is guaranteed one hundred days of work each year. The plan made sense because 70 percent of Indians live in villages.

On the foreign policy front, Prime Minister Manmohan Singh moved quickly to continue the peace process with Pakistan. In April 2005, a new bus service was launched between Srinagar (Indian Kashmir) and Muzaffarabad (Pakistani Kashmir), reuniting ordinary Kashmiri families after nearly sixty years of separation. Singh also tried in earnest to forge strategic ties with the United States, and in President Bush he found a willing partner. The nuclear deal with the United States is considered to be one of the Singh government's major foreign policy achievements. Under the agreement, energy-hungry India will get access to U.S. civil nuclear fuel and technology for the first time in thirty years, in return for opening its civilian nuclear facilities for inspection. This deal is significant because India hadn't signed the nuclear Non-Proliferation Treaty (NPT), calling it discriminatory. The nuclear deal received overwhelming bipartisan support in the U.S. Congress, with the House of Representatives approving the bill by 359–68 and the Senate by 85–12 margins.[87]

In December 2006, President Bush signed legislation permitting civilian nuclear cooperation with India. But the deal suffered due to sharp differences over India's right to conduct nuclear tests and reprocess spent fuel. India wanted complete freedom to process all of its spent fuel, while the United States argued that material it provides must not be used for military purposes. In a major concession, the United States agreed to let India reprocess spent nuclear fuel under safeguards by the International Atomic Energy Agency (IAEA). That paved way for the finalization of the nuclear deal in August 2007.

Key Things to Know About Indian History:

- India has had continuous civilization since 2500 BC. The Indus Valley Civilization is the first known Indian civilization; it existed at the same time as the ancient civilizations of Egypt and Sumer. It declined around 1500 BC, due to either floods or Aryan invasion.
- The Aryans, nomadic tribes from central Asia, started infiltrating into the Indian subcontinent around 1500 BC. They brought with them new sets of religious beliefs and traditions, which later evolved into the Hindu religion.
- Buddhism was founded by Siddhartha Gautama (563–483 BC) in response to discontent with various aspects of Hinduism based on the Vedas.
- Ancient India consisted of a number of kingdoms with fluctuating boundaries. The Greek conqueror Alexander the Great invaded India in 327 BC.

- Chandragupta Maurya established the Mauryan empire in 321 BC. The Mauryan empire reached its zenith under Emperor Ashoka (304–232 BC), who made Buddhism India's official religion.
- In the fourth and fifth centuries AD, the Gupta dynasty reigned over northern India. The Gupta period is considered the golden age of Indian history. Southern India charted its own course and was ruled by different Hindu empires, including the Cholas, Pandyas, and Cheras.
- After the fall of the Gupta empire in the 500s, India split into a number of small kingdoms.
- The Islamic conquest of the Indian subcontinent began in the seventh century AD. Mahmud of Ghazni attacked India seventeen times between 1001 and 1027 and ransacked many cities.
- By the 1200s, most of northern India was under Muslim control. The period between AD 1206 and 1526 is known as the Delhi Sultanate period. For more than three hundred years, five dynasties ruled from Delhi.
- Babur, a descendent of Genghiz Khan and Timur, defeated the rulers of Delhi and founded the Mughal empire (*Mughal* comes from the Persian word *Mogul*, meaning "Mongol"). The Mughal dynasty remained a dominant force in India for the next two hundred years.
- Babur's grandson Akbar, who ruled India for nearly fifty years (1556–1605), is considered the greatest of all Mughal rulers.
- The Vijayanagara Hindu empire, founded in 1336, remained a major force in southern India until its military defeat in 1565. By the seventeenth century, large areas of southern India had come under Muslim rule.
- Lured by the spice trade and encouraged by the discovery of sea routes, the Europeans—Portuguese, French, Dutch, and British—started arriving in India in the early 1660s.
- By the 1850s, the British had gained political control of most of present-day India, Pakistan, Sri Lanka, and Bangladesh. In 1877, Queen Victoria of England became the Empress of India, and India thus became a British colony.

- In 1920, Mohandas Gandhi (known as Mahatma, or "great soul") became the leader of the mass movement against British colonial rule. His doctrine of nonviolent protest and noncooperation to achieve political goals has made him one of the most influential leaders of the twentieth century.
- After a prolonged struggle, India won its independence from Britain in 1947 with Jawaharlal Nehru as prime minister. Political tensions between Hindus and Muslims led the British to partition British India into two separate states: India, with a Hindu majority, and Pakistan, with a Muslim majority.

Chapter 4: Polity

India, the world's largest democracy, is a secular, democratic republic with a parliamentary system of government that is modeled after the British parliamentary system. The central or federal government is the seat of power in India. The president is the head of state, and the prime minister is the head of the government. This is different from the U.S. system, in which the president is the head of both state and government. In India, the president, like the queen in the United Kingdom, has a largely ceremonial role, whereas the prime minister has the real executive power.

The president is elected not directly by the people but by an electoral college consisting of elected members of parliament and the state legislatures. A vice president is elected in a similar fashion. However, a vice president doesn't automatically become president following the president's death or removal from office. The prime minister is the leader of the party or coalition of parties that has the largest number of parliamentary seats. He or she heads a council of ministers drawn from the members of parliament. The appointment of ministers (equivalent to secretaries in the United States) is the prime minister's prerogative.

India is made up of twenty-eight states and seven union territories.[88] The state government system closely resembles that of the federal government. At the state level, the governor is the ceremonial head and the chief minister wields the executive power. The union territories are administered by the president of India through appointed officials.

India's polity is shaped by its constitution, which came into force on January 26, 1950.

The Indian constitution guarantees equal rights to all citizens and prohibits discrimination based on race, sex, caste (social class), religion, or place of birth.

The Indian parliament (equivalent to the U.S. Congress) is the chief law-making body at the federal level. It consists of two houses, the 543-member Lok Sabha (house of people) and the 250-member Rajya Sabha (council of states). Members of the Lok Sabha are elected directly by the people on the basis of universal suffrage. Indians who are at least eighteen years old are eligible to vote. Each Lok Sabha is formed for a five-year term, after which it is automatically dissolved and new elections are held. Rajya Sabha members are elected not by the people but by state legislatures. Members serve six-year terms, and a third of its members retire every second year. Rajya Sabha members generally review but do not veto legislation.

India has six national parties and a plethora of state-level political parties. The Indian National Congress (INC), or the Congress Party; the Bharatiya Janata Party (BJP), or Indian People's Party; the Communist Party of India (CPI); and the Communist Party of India-Marxist (CPI-M) are the major national parties. State-level parties include the DMK (Tamil Nadu state), Telugu Desam (Andhra Pradesh state), Shiv Sena (Maharashtra), and Akali Dal (Punjab).

For nearly four decades since independence, the Congress Party, which has its roots in the freedom struggle against British colonial role, dominated the Indian political stage at both national and state levels. The party ruled uninterrupted for thirty years beginning in 1947 but briefly lost power in 1977 to a coalition of non-Congress parties in the aftermath of a highly controversial period of emergency rule imposed by Prime Minister Indira Gandhi. The party again bounced back to power in 1980 and ruled until 1989.

Toward the end of the 1980s, the centrist-Congress Party dominance was challenged by the emergence of the right-wing BJP and a plethora of regional and caste-based political parties. The 1989 general election was a watershed movement in Indian electoral history, as it marked the polarization of the nation along religious and caste lines. The Congress Party, led by Rajiv Gandhi, failed to secure a majority in the parliament and was replaced by a coalition of parties known as National Front, led by Prime Minister V. P. Singh. However, Singh's governing coalition fell apart in 1991 and was replaced by the Congress Party, led by Prime Minister Narasimha Rao. In the 1996 general election, the Congress Party suffered its worst-ever electoral performance. After two years of political uncertainty, the right-leaning National Democratic Alliance (NDA), led by the BJP, finally gained power and ruled the nation from 1998 to 2004.

India has now firmly reached an era of coalition governments. No political party has won a national election outright since 1984. The currently ruling United Progressive Alliance (UPA) is a coalition of the Congress Party and fourteen small regional parties. It is headed by Sonia Gandhi, the Italian-born widow of the former prime minister Rajiv Gandhi. Following the upset victory for the alliance in the 2004 general election, Sonia Gandhi declined the post of prime minister and instead nominated party stalwart and former finance minister Manmohan Singh, who became India's first-ever non-Hindu prime minister.[89]

The Indian election process is a mammoth exercise. For starters, India has more than a billion people and 671 million registered voters.[90] The general election is usually held over a period of three weeks, mainly to deploy hundreds of thousands of security personnel to maintain peace and ensure the election's fairness. The 2004 general election saw the largest nationwide deployment of e-voting technology in the world. Nearly 380 million Indians (56 percent of registered voters) cast their ballots in seven hundred thousand polling stations. By comparison, over 122 million people (61 percent of registered voters) voted in the 2004 U.S. presidential election.

Unlike U.S. presidential elections, which are dominated by issues such as abortion rights, gun control, environmental issues, and taxes, Indian elections are largely fought on bread-and-butter issues including unemployment, poverty, price increases, water and power shortages, and corruption. There is also a great urban/rural divide between voters. More people vote in the countryside than in the cities, and therefore rural issues dominate elections. Caste, religion, and regionalism play a huge role in the selection of candidates by political parties.

Political Parties

Indian National Congress

The Indian National Congress (the Congress Party) has ruled India for forty-seven of the sixty years since the country's independence from Britain. For the majority of that time, thirty-eight years, the country's prime minister was a member of the Nehru-Gandhi dynasty (Jawaharlal Nehru, his daughter Indira Gandhi, and her son Rajiv Gandhi). As the Congress Party's fortunes waned after the assassination of Rajiv Gandhi in 1991, party leaders convinced his Italian-born widow, Sonia Gandhi, to take the reins of the party. Sonia Gandhi led the party back to power as the head of the current coalition government in the 2004 general election. She is the unchallenged leader in the Congress Party today.

Bharatiya Janata Party (BJP)

The right-leaning BJP, associated with Hindu nationalist groups, has enjoyed tremendous success in national politics since the early 1990s. Riding the wave of Hindu nationalism, the BJP increased its tally in the parliament from 2 seats in 1984 to an impressive 182 seats in 1999. The BJP-led National Democratic Alliance (NDA) ruled the nation from 1998 to 2004 under the leadership of Atal Bihari Vajpayee.

Left Front and Regional Parties

India's communist parties hold about 10 percent of the seats in the Lok Sabha. Although they are recognized as national parties, they derive their strength mainly from two states: West Bengal and Kerala. India is also home to dozens of parties with regional orientation. Since the 1989 general elections, the national parties taken together have been rapidly losing ground to regional and caste-based parties, in terms of both the total number of seats won and the share of the votes.

Key Things to Know About Indian Polity:

- India is a secular, democratic republic with a British-style parliamentary system of government. India, with a billon people and 670 million registered voters, is the world's largest democracy.
- The president is the head of the state, and his or her duties are largely ceremonial. The Indian president is elected by an electoral college consisting of members of both houses of parliament and legislative assemblies of the states.
- In India, the real executive power rests with the prime minister, who is the head of the government.
- The Indian parliament consists of the Lok Sabha (house of people) and the Rajya Sabha (council of states). Lok Sabha members are chosen by direct election on the basis of adult suffrage. They serve five-year terms.
- India has twenty-eight states and seven union territories. At the state level, the governor is the ceremonial head of the state, and the chief minister is the head of the government.
- The Congress Party has ruled India for forty-seven of the sixty years since the country's independence from Britain.
- The Congress Party's political fortunes suffered badly in the 1990s when it lost its support to emerging regional and caste-based parties.
- Since 1984, no party has won an absolute majority in the parliament. Instead, India has entered an era of coalition governments.

- India has rich democratic traditions. It has never had a military coup in its sixty years of existence as an independent country. The transfer of power has always been peaceful and orderly.
- India prides itself on being an inclusive democracy. The primarily Hindu India had three Muslim presidents and one Sikh president. The current prime minister of India is from the minority Sikh community, and India elected its first female president in 2007. India has already had a female prime minister, Indira Gandhi, one of the most powerful leaders the country has ever seen.

Chapter 5: Economy

India is the world's twelfth-largest economy in nominal terms and the fourth-largest (after the United States, China, and Japan) as measured by purchasing power parity (PPP). It is also the third-largest economy in Asia (in nominal terms) after Japan and China. India's economy has been growing at an average annual growth rate of 8.5–9 percent, making it one of the fastest growing major economies in the world.

Table 16: World Gross Domestic Product (GDP) Rankings (Nominal)

Ranking	Economy	Millions of U.S. Dollars
1	United States	13,811,200
2	Japan	4,376,705
3	Germany	3,297,233
4	China	3,280,053
5	United Kingdom	2,727,806
6	France	2,562,288
7	Italy	2,107,481
8	Spain	1,429,226
9	Canada	1,326,376
10	Brazil	1,314,170
11	Russian Federation	1,291,011
12	India	1,170,968

Source: World Bank

Table 17: World Gross Domestic Product (GDP) Rankings (PPP)

Ranking	Economy	Millions of International Dollars
1	United States	13,811,200
2	China	7,055,079
3	Japan	4,283,528
4	India	3,092,126
5	Germany	2,751,843
6	Russian Federation	2,088,207
7	United Kingdom	2,081,549
8	France	2,053,695
9	Brazil	1,833,601
10	Italy	1,780,135
11	Spain	1,372,717
12	Mexico	1,345,530

Source: World Bank

The Indian economy, propelled by growth in the services and manufacturing sectors and the appreciating rupee, crossed the trillion-dollar mark for the first time in 2007. However, India's large population results in a relatively low per capita income of $950 in nominal terms and $2,740 at PPP.[91] Therefore, India is considered a developing country and one of the poorest countries in the world. Services, industry, and agriculture account for 53 percent, 29 percent, and 18 percent of the GDP, respectively.[92] Agriculture is the livelihood of two-thirds of the population. Nearly 80 percent of the population lives on $2 or less a day.[93] However, India is home to a large and burgeoning middle class of three hundred million people, equivalent to the entire population of the United States.

India follows a mixed-economy model, with a semiregulated private sector and a large public sector controlled almost entirely by the government. From the time of independence in 1947 to 1991, the Indian government directed and controlled every sphere of economic activity within the country. Although the private sector existed in most areas of the economy, it was subjected to burdensome regulations and controls that stifled its growth. Domestic industries were protected from foreign competition through excessive tariffs and nontariff measures, making India one of the most closed economies in the world. Under this system, India achieved a large and diverse industrial base and self-sufficiency in food production. But the economy experienced slow growth and high inflation, faced large fiscal deficits, and often operated under a weak balance of payment conditions.

In 1991, India suffered a major economic meltdown due to a confluence of factors, including the collapse of the Soviet Union (a major trading partner and a key source of foreign aid), large budgetary deficits, a sharp rise in oil prices due to the war in the Persian Gulf, and a decline in foreign exchange reserves. India received emergency funds from the International Monetary Fund (IMF) and the World Bank, but they were conditional on India's making a greater commitment to economic reforms. Beginning in 1991, India pursued economic reforms that deregulated domestic industries, liberalized controls on foreign trade and investment regimes, and made significant changes to monetary and fiscal policies. The reforms moved India closer to a free-market enterprise system.

The market-oriented reforms have moved the Indian economy from its traditional growth rate of around 3.5 percent a year to a much higher growth rate. Between 1991 and 2005, the economy expanded by an annual average of 6 percent.[94]

In the past three years, growth has been even higher, at around 8 percent. Foreign direct and portfolio investment have risen significantly in recent years. Many U.S.-based companies, including Microsoft, IBM, Oracle, and Dell, have announced multibillion-dollar investments in India. The reforms have made India's products and services globally competitive, leading to the rapid expansion of two-way trade. More importantly, the economic growth has improved living standards in many parts of the country. The proportion of people living below the poverty line has declined significantly, from 36 percent in 1994 to 22 percent in 2005.

India's economic boom has been fueled by the services sector, led by exports of business services from IT and related sectors. By contrast, China's economic expansion has largely been built on export-oriented manufacturing, enabled by massive foreign investment. The rapid expansion of the IT and related services sector has had a positive impact on the broader Indian economy by generating substantial export earnings and tax revenue and by creating a significant number of high-paying jobs. The services sector now constitutes half of India's economic output with less than a third of its labor force. In 2006, the services sector grew at 11.2 percent, compared with just 2.7 percent for agriculture and 10.6 percent for industry.[95]

A byproduct of India's economic growth is the emergence of a burgeoning middle class, 250–300 million strong, with increasing purchasing power. Their insatiable appetite for consumer goods and services has fueled domestic, demand-led growth. As a result, the manufacturing sector has been witnessing a major revival in the past four years. The sector has grown from a 9.1 percent rate in 2005 to a record 12.3 percent in 2006. Compare this with the growth rate of 5.9 percent between 1996 and 2006.[96]

Many multinationals have also been stepping up their investment in India. Companies like Hyundai, Samsung, Motorola, Nokia, LG Electronics, Siemens, and Cummins have already established manufacturing facilities. Initially, these companies manufactured goods for the domestic market. Now, they are positioning India as an export hub by taking advantage of its abundant engineering talent and low-cost production capabilities.

But the benefits of economic reforms have not reached everyone, especially the urban poor and those living in rural areas. Although the services and manufacturing sectors have grown rapidly, there has been very little job creation. The IT and related services sector has thus far created merely two million jobs, mostly highly skilled, professional positions. The agricultural sector, which provides the livelihood for an overwhelming majority of the population, has experienced relatively slow growth for many years. Unimpressed and untouched by the reform program, the electorate, mainly from rural India, voted out the government of Prime Minister Vajpayee in a shocking upset in 2004. Its successor, the Congress Party-led coalition, vowed to recalibrate the reform program by renewing the emphasis on rural development and poverty alleviation programs. Subsequently, the government launched an ambitious rural employment program that would guarantee jobs for one member of each of India's sixty million rural households.

India's long-term economic expansion is constrained by antiquated infrastructure, cumbersome bureaucratic controls, rampant corruption, and a high fiscal deficit driven by loss-making public sector enterprises. As per some estimates, India needs about $380 billion in infrastructure investment in the next five to ten years.[97] The government is actively seeking foreign investment in power generation, ports, roads, railroads, petroleum exploration, and mining. So far, foreign investment in infrastructure has been very slow to take off. Ports have been opened up for competition, the modernization of airports is underway, and private sector participation in highway projects has been permitted.

However, electricity shortages are quite severe in India and are seriously hindering further economic progress. The privatization of public-sector enterprises is proceeding at a slow pace and has yet to gain traction.

Meanwhile, the federal government is continuing with the needed reform process, although at a slower pace. The good news is that the reform process has more or less become irreversible, and the gains appear to be permanent. All political parties, barring India's two major communist parties, agree on the need for reforms, and differences among them are minor and merely reflect political posturing. As the reform process enters the next phase, the government is coming under intense pressure from the international community to loosen remaining controls, such as the ban on foreign investment in the retail sector, and further open up the financial sector, in particular the insurance sector. The government has recently opened up the retail sector in a very limited way by permitting FDI of up to 51 percent in single-brand retailing.[98]

India's economy is booming and shows no signs of cooling. The outlook for India's services and manufacturing sectors remains buoyant. Rising wages and cheap credit are pushing the demand for both durable and nondurable consumer goods. With demand outpacing supply, Indian manufacturers are operating at near-full capacity. There is genuine concern that the economy is "overheated," as evidenced by rising inflation rates. So far, efforts by India's Reserve Bank (the equivalent of the Federal Reserve in the United States) to dampen inflationary pressures by increasing interest rates have not slowed economic growth. According to a study by Goldman Sachs, the Indian economy will grow at a rate of 5 percent or more until 2050, assuming the maintenance of pro-growth policies. India is also projected to become the third-largest economy in the word, behind China and the United States.[99]

Table 18: India, China Comparative Data

	India	India	China	China
	1990	2006	1990	2006
Population (millions)	850	1110	1135	1311
GDP ($ billions)	317.5	911.8	354.6	2645
GNI per capita (current US$)	390	820	320	2000
Merchandise trade (% of GDP)	13	32	33	67
Merchandise trade ($ billions)	41.3	291.8	117.0	1772.2

Source: World Bank Key Development Data and Statistics

India's Brief Economic History

India's economic history can be broadly divided into four periods: pre-colonial period, colonial period, "license raj" period, and post-reform period.

The Pre-Colonial Period

India in the pre-colonial period had a stable economy: self-sufficient agriculture, flourishing trade, and rich handicraft industries. Through the centuries, travelers to India described it as a land rich in gold, spices, textiles, and other valuables, and India became fabled for its wealth. This attracted European traders. The first European known to set foot in India was Portuguese explorer Vasco de Gama in 1498; he recognized that India's spices were valuable trade goods. Portuguese and Dutch traders were soon buying silk, cotton, indigo, grains, and spices cheaply in India to sell for great profits in Europe.

The Colonial Period

In 1600, Queen Elizabeth I granted a charter to a group of traders to create the British East India Company. The charter gave the Company a monopoly on Britain's sea trade with India. In 1858, India officially became a British colony, and Queen Victoria became the Empress of India. Colonial rule brought a uniform currency system, a modern legal system, a functioning bureaucracy, and a modern railway and telegraph network. India's overseas trade also grew rapidly during the second half of the nineteenth century. India supplied raw materials (jute, cotton, and tea) to Europe and absorbed large quantities of manufactured goods, which were admitted duty-free. In particular, India was a captive market for the Lancashire textile industry.

The import of textiles and clothing from British mills virtually destroyed the livelihoods of millions of India's hand-weavers, who were thrown out of work. For centuries, cotton spinning and weaving had been India's most important domestic industry. As part of his campaign for India's independence, Mahatma Gandhi called for a boycott of British-made goods, especially textiles, and encouraged Indians to use homespun and woven cotton clothes. Gandhi adopted the spinning wheel, or *chakra*, as his symbol to drive home the principle of self-sufficiency. His campaign was so successful that many mills in Lancashire and Blackburn had to close due to lack of demand.

Upon independence in 1947, India inherited an economy that was one of the poorest in the world, with a nonexistent industrial base and an agricultural sector that was unable to feed India's large population. India's economic woes were further exacerbated by the massive costs associated with the settlement of millions of refugees who crossed the border between the newly created states of India and Pakistan.

Independent India: The Pre-Reform Era or "License Raj"

Jawaharlal Nehru, the first prime minister of India and the chosen political heir of Mahatma Gandhi, formulated and oversaw the economic policies of independent India. Nehru opted for a mixed-economic model under which the public and private sector coexisted. He differed from his mentor Gandhi's ideal of an agrarian society. Instead, he wanted to make India economically self-reliant through a large-scale industrialization drive. Drawing heavily from Soviet-style central planning, India set up heavy industries, basic industries, and power plants, all in the public sector. Nehru preferred the steel sector to the textile sector to propel economic growth. He feared that modern textile mills would take employment away from the handloom sector. The government also took a number of steps to irrigate more land. Major irrigation dams were constructed to provide water for irrigation and power for industrialization. Nehru was a firm believer in state control of key economic sectors. As a result, many key sectors, such as mining and quarrying, financial institutions and insurance, power generation and distribution, civil aviation and railroads, and telecommunications were reserved for the public sector. But other sectors, including agriculture, retail and wholesale trade, road freight traffic, and the manufacture of consumer goods, were left in the private sector.

Although the Nehru administration emphasized the importance of the private sector to the overall health of the economy, it had taken several steps that impeded the free and rapid growth of private companies. Procedural delays, stifling bureaucratic controls and regulations, and small-scale sector reservations contributed to the slow growth of domestic industry.[100]

Licenses and permits were required to start a new company, produce a new product, or even expand the production capacity of existing products. The period between 1951 and 1991 came to be known as the "License Raj" (*Raj* in Hindi means "rule" or "reign"). Price controls imposed on many goods, ostensibly to protect customers, did not give manufacturers any incentive to expand capacity and therefore ended up perpetuating shortages. The government's efforts to encourage the growth of small and cottage sectors by imposing a lower rate of excise duty (a duty levied on manufactured products) further served to dampen the growth of medium and large scale industries. On the external front, India followed "import substitution" policies that promoted industrialization by shielding domestic companies from foreign competition through high tariffs on imported manufactured goods. India also discouraged exports by keeping its currency overvalued.

The automobile sector best exemplified India's ambivalence toward the private sector before 1991. Until the early 1980s, India had two automobile manufacturers, which produced two car models. One model, the "Ambassador," was based on the 1948 Morris Oxford; the other was the "Premier Padmini," based on the 1963 Fiat 1100 design. These two cars virtually ruled Indian roads for nearly four decades without any significant design change. High tariffs protected the companies from foreign imports, and the license and quota regimen prevented other domestic players from competing in this market. The government had a say in every aspect of product creation, from design and manufacturing to marketing. Production volumes and pricing, including dealer commissions, were decided not by market demand but by government bureaucrats. Therefore, the manufacturers had little or no incentive to change the product design or improve quality. In 1980, India produced roughly forty thousand cars per year for a population of seven hundred million people. The waiting period for automobile delivery ranged from five to ten years. The situation was no different for other products and services.

India's GDP growth rate stayed around 4 percent during Nehru's years in office (1947–64). Thereafter, growth stagnated. By the mid-1960s, India was facing tough economic times. In the aftermath of Chinese aggression in 1962, India was forced to increase its defense spending; this put an enormous burden on its already crumbling economy, which had been hurt by severe droughts. To make matters worse, the Indo-Pakistan war of 1965 led to the suspension of American aid to India. The resumption of aid was made conditional on the devaluation of India's currency and the liberalization of some of its restrictive trade policies. In response, the Indian government devalued[101] the rupee by 57.5 percent (from 4.75 rupees to $1, to 7.50 rupees to $1), a move that proved very unpopular with the Indian electorate during the 1967 general elections. In response to public criticism and disappointment, Prime Minister Indira Gandhi took a hard line against the World Bank and the West by moving India even further to the left, nationalizing all major banks, insurance companies, coal mines, and oil companies. Also, the government placed a ceiling on personal income, private property, and corporate profits. Indira's left-leaning economic policies were a big hit with the electorate, and she won a landslide victory in the 1971 general elections.

Within a couple of years, however, the economy was once again suffering due to the cumulative effect of various factors, including the enormous cost of the 1971 Indo-Pakistan war, a dramatic rise in world oil prices, and a decline in industrial output due to excessive bureaucratic controls. The Green Revolution brought some hope. India did not want a repetition of the 1943 Bengal Famine, in which an estimated three million people died of hunger. Food security was also a critical element. The ambitious Green Revolution sought to increase the yield by using seeds with improved genetics and better farming techniques. The results were dramatic, and India transformed itself from a hungry nation to an exporter of food grains.[102]

As the 1980s arrived, India's economic problems mounted. Losses at state-owned enterprises led to massive public deficits, and excessive government controls hampered economic growth. Prime Minister Rajiv Gandhi, who took over in 1984, brought some hope. He emphasized economic liberalization and pushed hard for the development of the technology sector. Rajiv slashed regulations, liberalized software imports, eased some restrictions on foreign equity, and launched a massive effort to improve the telecommunications network throughout India. At that time, India had two million telephones for a population of 750 million people. People had to wait 7–8 years to acquire a telephone connection. To increase telephone penetration and revamp the antiquated telephone system, India initiated the C-DOT[103] initiative, which ushered in India's first telecom revolution. Under this initiative, low-cost telecom systems were indigenously designed, and the equipment was sold to local entrepreneurs who set up manned public call offices (PCOs) in every corner of the country. Around 650,000 PCOs were set up all across India, allowing the average Indian easier and cheaper access to a telephone than ever before.

In 1986, Texas Instruments became the first multinational to set up an offshore development center in India. Pepsi also entered the Indian market, but only after it had agreed to some onerous conditions imposed by the government. Rajiv's liberalization efforts somewhat paid off, and India's GDP grew at 6 percent during his term (1984–99), after growing at 3–4 percent in India's first forty years of independence.

The Economic Crisis of 1991

India's journey of economic reforms began on an ominous note. The reforms were initiated in the middle of a balance-of-payments crisis that rocked the nation in the spring of 1991. The root cause was the macro-economic mismanagement throughout the 1980s that led to an unsustainably high fiscal deficit. A fiscal deficit is essentially the difference between what a government spends and what it earns through taxes and other means. In India, it was caused by excessive employment in the government sector, losses in state-run enterprises, the interest burden, mounting subsidies, and a rise in military spending. What do governments do when they face fiscal deficits? They simply borrow money from federal reserve banks (in India's case, the Reserve Bank of India) because the government has to carry out its regular business. When governments borrow large sums of money, this increases the supply of money, which then leads directly to a high inflation rate. That's what happened to India. The inflation was soaring above 16 percent. When inflation is that high, exports are bound to suffer because the comparative advantage (the ability to produce at a lower cost than others) is lost. In India's case, imports rose faster than exports, leading to high current account deficits. To finance the current account deficit, the government borrowed money that in turn made the problem of external indebtedness worse.

The First Gulf War in 1990 further exacerbated the already precarious foreign exchange reserves situation by sending oil prices through the roof and cutting off valuable foreign exchange remittances from Indian nationals working in the region. India's foreign exchange reserves dwindled to around $1 billion, barely enough to cover two weeks of imports. Without foreign exchange, governments can't pay the bills they owe other countries. The nation was on the brink of defaulting on its sovereign obligation—in other words, India was about to go bankrupt for the first time since gaining its independence.

The Indian government averted the crisis by obtaining emergency loans from the World Bank and International Monetary Fund (IMF), agreeing to ship forty-seven tons of gold to London as collateral. Further economic assistance was made contingent upon India undertaking a fundamental economic restructuring. Unlike his predecessors, Prime Minister Narasimha Rao agreed to reform, setting into motion one of the most comprehensive economic reforms of recent times. In his first speech as India's new leader, Rao struck pro-Western, pro-investment notes, a marked change from leaders of the past.[104]

For the first time, the Indian government acknowledged that the system of licensing and regulating industries ("License Raj") was no longer suitable for the country and required a complete overhaul. Rao appointed Dr. Manmohan Singh, a prominent economist and apolitical figure, as his new finance minister to spearhead his reforms program. Singh decided to take the bull by the horns. He tackled the fiscal problem by devaluing the rupee by 23 percent against the dollar, tightening the credit policy, and slashing subsidies.[105]

Currency devaluation is akin to having a sale or markdown of all of a country's goods and services. It is a quick way to reduce trade deficits and improve the balance-of-payment position. The price of domestic goods will decrease from the standpoint of an overseas customer, which will give a fillip to exports. By the same token, foreign goods become more expensive for domestic buyers, so imports will drop. India's exports picked up and its imports dropped after the initiation of the reforms. After tackling the macroeconomic crisis, Singh swiftly ended the "License Raj" by freeing private enterprise from the shackles of state regulation. He also began opening the economy to foreign trade and investment and laid the foundation for the ensuing economic boom. Deregulation, globalization, and privatization have become the new mantras of post-1991 India.

Summary of Economic Reforms[106]

Industrial Policy Reforms

The industrial sector underwent massive deregulation to bring in competition and increase efficiency. Prior to the reforms, eighteen industries were reserved solely for the public sector, including iron and steel, heavy plant and machinery, telecommunications, minerals, oil, mining, air transport, and electricity generation and distribution. Also, industries had to go through a cumbersome licensing process to invest in new ventures as well as expand existing capacity. As part of the reform process, the state monopoly was abolished and private companies were allowed to enter virtually all industries, with the exception of defense aircrafts and warships, atomic energy generation, and railway transport. Industrial licensing was also abolished in all but a few hazardous and environmentally sensitive industries. Now, companies are free to make their own investment and capacity decisions without securing government approval.

Recently, India has made significant revisions to its long-standing policy of reserving the production of certain items for the small-scale sector. Until now, large and medium units could manufacture such reserved items provided that they exported 50 percent or more of their production. Over the years, the number of items on the reserved list has increased to 836. Now, the government has reduced the list[107] to just 35.

Trade Policy Reforms

India followed a very restrictive trade policy in the pre-reform era, characterized by high tariffs and import restrictions, to protect domestic industry from foreign competition. The import of manufactured consumer goods was completely barred, resulting in a thriving market for smuggled foreign goods. The import of some capital goods, raw materials, and intermediates was allowed, but many items required import licenses. (In economic terms, *capital goods* are items used in the production of goods. The definition includes machinery and tools but doesn't include raw materials.) The import-licensing process was nontransparent and inefficient and was fraught with delays and corruption. As part of India's reforms, import licensing was completely abolished for capital goods and industrial raw materials in 1993. The import duties came down in a phased manner. In fiscal year 1991/1992, just before the start of its economic reforms, India's average tariff rate was almost 130 percent. For fiscal year 2006/2007, the tariff rate became 30 percent for most agricultural goods and 12.5 percent for most nonagricultural goods.[108]

Quantitative restrictions on imports of manufactured consumer goods were finally removed in 2001, as India began doing business under the WTO regime. India had little choice in this matter: the WTO agreements stipulate that a member country should not prohibit or restrict trade by imposing quotas, requiring licensing, or by any other means.

Foreign Direct Investment (FDI) Reforms

In the pre-reform era, India's attitude toward foreign investment was very cautious and unfriendly. Foreign companies were not allowed majority ownership, and their participation was limited to export-oriented or high-tech sectors. The situation is markedly different in the post-reform era. India now allows 100 percent foreign ownership in several industries and majority ownership in virtually all industries except banks, insurance companies, and airlines. The government also made the FDI procedures transparent and efficient by publishing a list of industries that are eligible for automatic approval of foreign equity.[109]

100 Percent Foreign Equity Is Permitted in the Following Sectors:

- Manufacturing (automobiles, auto parts, textiles and garments, food processing, chemicals and plastics, electronic hardware)
- Infrastructure (power, roads, ports, airports, petroleum refining)
- Knowledge (IT, healthcare, pharma and biotech)

- Resource-based (coal processing, mining, oil and natural gas exploration)
- Others (hotels and restaurants, agro-processing, real estate)

Majority Ownership Is Allowed in the Following Sectors:
Telecom (74 percent), single-brand retail (51 percent)

Minority Ownership Is Allowed in the Following Sectors:
Airlines (49 percent), insurance (26 percent), newspapers (26 percent)

The investments not eligible for automatic approval are routed through a newly established Foreign Investment Promotion Board (FIPB), which has earned a reputation for the speedy processing of requests. The new, liberal FDI policies have resulted in significant inflows of foreign investment in many economic sectors. In 1992, India also dismantled an eighteen-year-old law that banned large foreign companies from selling products under their internationally known trademarks and also ended a rule that blocked foreign companies from owning property in India.[110]

Financial Sector Reforms

Financial sector reforms affected the exchange rate system, tax system, banks, capital markets, and insurance sector. India made a transition from a discretionary, basket-pegged system to a market-driven exchange-rate system. The rupee was made convertible on the current account in 1994. Prior to the reforms, one had to get permission from government to procure foreign currency for any purpose, whether it be the import of raw material, travel abroad, or overseas education. The measures were put in place to avoid the sudden erosion of foreign reserves, which are essential for maintaining a trade balance and economic stability. Now that the forex reserves are increasing at a rapid pace, India doesn't need such restrictions.

In addition to current account convertibility, India is also actively mulling capital account convertibility (CAC), which, if implemented, will give Indians the freedom to convert local currency into foreign currency and vice versa for any purpose whatsoever. In other words, CAC implies complete mobility of capital across countries. India also initiated tax reforms intended to increase compliance by reducing marginal tax rates for both individuals and corporations. Currently, only a small fraction of India's population (thirty million out of one billion) pays income tax. In 2005, the government switched over from a complex, multiple-sales-tax system to a value-added tax (VAT) system.[111]

Prior to the reforms, India had twenty-seven public-sector banks that controlled 90 percent of all deposits, assets, and credit. They operated under strict government controls, with little incentive to improve services or profitability. They were required to direct 40 percent of their deposits to priority sectors that were identified by the government. In the post-reform era, public-sector banks were given considerable operational autonomy, and several controls were loosened. The government also deregulated interest rates in the banking system. The entry of both private-sector banks and foreign banks paved the way for an increase in competition in the banking sector. ICICI emerged as the nation's largest private-sector bank and the second-largest bank in India, with assets totaling $96 billion. Foreign banks, such as Standard Chartered, HSBC, Citibank, and ABN-AMRO, all have a presence in India now. Until 2005, India did not allow foreigners to own more than 49 percent of a bank. That limit has now increased to 74 percent. As a result of the competition, the asset share of public-sector banks came down from 90 percent in 1991 to 75 percent in 2004.

As part of India's reforms to the stock market, capital markets were opened for foreign institutional investors. India ended government authority to regulate the price of initial public offerings (IPOs). It also set up a market watchdog entity known as the Security and Exchange Board of India (SEBI) in 1992, along the lines of the Securities and Exchange Commission (SEC) in the United States. India also established the technologically advanced National Stock Exchange (NSE), which was conceived as a fully electronic trading platform. Within a few years, the NSE overtook the Bombay Stock Exchange (BSE) as the largest stock exchange in the country in terms of traded volume. The NSE is now one of the top ten stock exchanges in the world in terms of the number of daily transactions, or trading volume. But the BSE still maintains its position as the second-largest stock exchange after the NYSE based on the number of companies listed.

Indian firms are also allowed to raise funds from abroad through ADRs and GDRs. An American depository receipt (ADR) is a stock that trades in American stock exchanges but represents shares in a foreign corporation. ADRs are bought and sold in American markets like regular stocks. A global depositary receipt (GDR) is very similar to an ADR and gives access to two or more markets. Since the relaxation of rules, achieving a listing in the NYSE or NASDAQ has become a status symbol for many Indian companies.

Reforms in the insurance sector came much later, with passage of the landmark Insurance Regulatory and Development Authority (IRDA) Bill, which ended the state's monopoly. Until 1999, two state-run insurance companies, Life Insurance Corporation (LIC) and General Insurance Corporation (GIC), were the only insurance providers in India. Now, the insurance sector has been opened up to private investors, both domestic and overseas, but the foreign equity is capped at 26 percent.

Results of the Reforms

By any measure, India's reform process was a huge success. Fiscal stabilization measures brought down the central government's fiscal deficit, as a percent of GDP, from 8.3 percent in fiscal year 1990/1991 to 5.7 percent[112] by the end of 1992/1993. This was partially achieved by the necessary but politically unpopular reduction of export subsidies and fertilizer subsidies. The rate of inflation was reduced from 17 percent in August 2001 to 5.7 percent in 1995.[113]

The economy grew at an average of 6 percent in the decade following the reforms, placing India among the fastest-growing major economies of the 1990s. In reality, India achieved an annual average growth of

5.7 percent even in the 1980s, but it was fueled largely by external borrowings rather than sound macroeconomic policies.[114]

The past five years have been arguably the best ever for the Indian economy, with the GDP growth rate clocking in at over 8 percent[115] since 2003. China, which opened up its economy a decade before India did, has consistently maintained a growth rate of 8–10 percent in the past fifteen years. The per capita income has doubled since 2001.[116]

Rising incomes have helped to reduce poverty rates, which have fallen by nearly a third in both rural and urban areas. India has also witnessed a steady accumulation of foreign exchange reserves since 1991. The reserves rose from around $1 billion in June 1991, at the beginning of the reforms, to $43 billion by 2001, a decade after the reforms. In March 2008, they reached the $300 billion milestone.[117] India currently holds the third-largest stock of foreign reserves among emerging markets, after China and Russia.

The economic reforms have also restored international confidence in India's economy, which has been reflected in the dramatic increase in both FDI and foreign portfolio investments. In 1990, one year before the reforms, India attracted a paltry $100 million a year in FDI. As part of the reforms, India opened up many sectors for foreign investment, increased the limit on foreign ownership of firms, reduced red tape, and created "special economic zones" that provide world-class infrastructure to attract foreign investment. Now the FDI inflows are on a roll, and FDI averages $5–$6 billion annually. This number is likely to go up substantially in the next decade or so, since global companies like IBM, General Motors, and Suzuki have announced major investments in the country. The cumulative amount of FDI inflows from August 1991 to February 2008 stood at $75 billion. The numbers do not include the billions of dollars that have been coming into the stock and bond markets. Although this calls for celebration, India's FDI still pales in comparison with China, which routinely receives $50–$60 billion per year. Much of India's FDI is routed through Mauritius, an island in the Indian Ocean with 1.2 million people, because both nations have an agreement to avoid double taxation.[118]

India's exports got a boost with these economic reforms, which included a liberal trade policy and a new exchange rate regime. Within a few years, exports shot up by 20 percent, thanks to the software and business process outsourcing (BPO) sectors. India's remarkable growth, along with the booming stock market, has also attracted huge portfolio investments. Foreign institutional funds (FII) poured $10.7 billion into India's stock market in 2005.

India benefited from closer integration into the global economy in industries such as automotive, BPO, and IT. The software and outsourcing industries have created hundreds of thousands of high-paying jobs and billions in export revenues. Beyond numbers, consumers benefited from lower prices, better quality, and a wider selection of products and services.

What Needs To Be Done?

Without a question, the Indian economy has made real progress over the past sixteen years. But further liberalization will be required to sustain growth and reduce poverty rates. India needs to open up other sectors to foreign investment and global competition to replicate the success of the IT and outsourcing industries in the broader economy. Currently, foreign ownership is prohibited in agriculture and retailing and limited to minority stakes in banking, insurance, and news media.

Steps should also be taken to keep the fiscal deficit from getting out of control. Within a decade of reforms, the combined fiscal deficit for the federal and state governments had reached 10 percent, an unsustainable level. Moody's warned that very rapid growth would not be sustainable unless the fiscal situation was stabilized. There are signs that the Indian government is taking the fiscal deficit challenges seriously. A new law known as the Fiscal Responsibility and Budget Management Act (FRBMA), enacted in 2004, requires the government to reduce the fiscal deficit to no more than 3 percent of the GDP by March 31, 2009.[119]

India's economic reforms thus far have focused mainly on industrial and trade policies, much to the chagrin of the agricultural sector, which provides a livelihood for 60 percent of India's population. Despite a steady decline in its share of the GDP, agriculture plays a critical role in India's overall socioeconomic development. A recent World Bank report called for a highly productive, internationally competitive, and diversified agricultural sector.

The lack of adequate infrastructure has been a major handicap in developing the manufacturing sector. Infrastructure includes power, telecommunications, roads, ports, airports, and urban infrastructure. Companies operating in India must overcome erratic electricity supplies, poor roads, and gridlocked seaports and airports. These services are traditionally provided by public-sector monopolies but are increasingly being opened up to private investment, including foreign investment.

India has upgraded its roads, airports, and telecommunications network. But progress in the power sector remains troublesome, with energy shortages still causing frequent blackouts. India has the power generation capacity of 132 GW, the fifth-largest capacity in the world. Yet it faces an average energy shortfall of 10 percent and peak demand shortfall of 14 percent. India's electricity sector is in dire need of investment. An estimated $150 billion is required in the next five years to meet the growing demand.[120] Reforms involving the privatization of power generation and distribution have been undertaken, but the results have been far from spectacular.

India's public-sector reforms have been very slow and cautious. The privatization of the public sector needs to be accelerated to both improve efficiency and reduce the drain on the exchequer. The government's initial efforts to sell a minority stake in public-sector companies while retaining management control (an approach known as *disinvestment* instead of *privatization*) garnered partial success. India also desperately needs to revamp its inflexible and outdated labor policies. It needs to scrap a 1947 law (later revised in 1980) that requires any firm employing more than one hundred workers to seek government permission before firing employees. This law reduces productivity as well as India's competitiveness in exports. Many prominent economists, including Professor Kaushik Basu of Cornell University, have called on the government to implement flexibility in the labor markets to attract foreign capital, create jobs, and unleash higher growth.

Sector Analysis

India has been gradually transforming its economic base from agrarian to industrial and commercial. At the time of independence, agriculture accounted for 57 percent of the GDP; today, it accounts for only 18 percent. Services are the major source of economic growth, accounting for half of India's output with less than one quarter of its labor force. India leapfrogged from the agricultural phase to the services phase, bypassing the industrial phase.

Table 19: India: Sector Share in Real GDP (%)

	Agriculture	Industry	Services
1950–51	57.4	14.7	27.9
1979–80	37.9	24.4	37.7
1991–92	31.3	26.7	42.0
2002–03	22.1	27.1	50.8

Source: Asian Development Bank, India Economic Bulletin December 2003

The Agriculture Sector

Agriculture is one of India's most important economic sectors because nearly two-thirds of the population depend on agriculture for their livelihood. Farms cover about half of the country's land. India's arable land (land that can be used for growing crops) is the second largest in the world, second only to the United States, and its irrigated crop area is the largest in the world. India is among the top three global producers of a broad range of crops, including wheat, rice, pulses (chickpeas, pigeon peas, lentils, dry peas, etc.), cotton, peanuts, fruits, and vegetables. It is also the largest producer of milk and has one of the largest and fastest-growing poultry sectors.

India is a land of small farmers, most of whom own less than 2.5 acres. This is due in part to inheritance practices. Upon the death of a farmer, his land is divided among his sons, so with each generation the size of the farm decreases. Most farmers grow crops to feed their families, not for commercial purposes. Many farmers still use oxen to plow the land. There is no beef farming in India because many Indians, particularly Hindus, don't eat beef for religious reasons. Agricultural production faces occasional declines due to irregular monsoons and other climate problems.

At the time of independence, India did not produce enough food to meet its demands, and it became one of the leading recipients of American food aid shipments in the 1960s under the PL 480[121] program. Today, however, India is self-sufficient in food production mainly because of the government-sponsored agricultural program known as the Green Revolution. This program encouraged the use of high-yield wheat and rice varieties, fertilizers, pesticides; improved irrigation; and implemented supportive price policies. It was a huge success, resulting in a record grain output that transformed India from a starving nation into one of the leading agricultural producers in the world by the late 1970s.

The agricultural sector has seen a steady decline in terms of its contribution to GDP growth and its share of GDP. It was largely untouched by the first generation reforms and continues to be plagued by several structural weaknesses. More than two-thirds of the area under cultivation are not irrigated, and crop harvests are completely dependent on the annual monsoon rains. Also, yields of most major crops remain well below world standards. Complying with World Trade Organization (WTO) rules, India removed all quantitative barriers to agricultural imports in 2001 and reduced tariffs[122] on a number of commodities, including edible oils, pulses, and cotton. For other products, including fresh fruits and processed foods, India has chosen to protect domestic production by imposing high tariffs. India's 50 percent import tariff on apples is one of the highest in the world.

Despite slowing growth in farm output, India remains a substantial net agricultural exporter. The exports consist of tea, coffee, spices, fruits and nuts, tobacco, fish and meat products, rice, and soybean meal. Edible oils and pulses (chickpeas, pigeon peas, lentils, dry peas, etc.) account for the bulk of India's agricultural imports.

The Industry Sector

Industry accounts for 29 percent of India's GDP and 12 percent of its total labor force.[123] Manufacturing, a major constituent of the industry sector, accounts for nearly 17 percent of GDP, employing nearly thirty million people and contributing to two-thirds of exports.

At the time of independence, India was largely an agrarian economy with a nonexistent industrial base. India's first government, headed by Prime Minister Nehru, viewed industrialization as the engine of economic growth and a means to reduce unemployment. Since the private sector lacked the financial resources to set up large industries, the government stepped in and jump-started industrialization by setting up massive steel mills, fertilizer plants, cement and chemical plants, shipyards, ordnance factories, oil refineries, locomotive works, and large engineering and manufacturing enterprises, all in the public sector. As a result, India achieved a good measure of industrial self-efficiency within a few decades, emerging as the tenth most industrialized nation in the world.

India's primary industries are steel, textiles, petrochemicals, cement, fertilizers, transportation equipment, and mining. India is world's tenth-largest steel producer. The textile industry is the largest in the country, accounting for a third of India's exports. India has eighteen oil refineries, with a daily refining capacity of two million barrels. Sixteen of the refineries are state-owned, one is jointly owned, and one, Reliance Industries refinery, is privately owned. India's cement industry is the second largest in the world, after China, and its fertilizer industry is the third largest in the world. India is also a major exporter of a variety of heavy and light engineering goods. Apart from big industries, millions of Indian men and women work in home-based industries and small-scale sectors, producing a wide range of products including handwoven carpets and clothes, fireworks, matches, incense sticks, handicrafts, embroidered textiles, jewelry, and leather goods.

While the government nurtured public sector companies and channeled much of the country's resources into them, it implemented stringent industrial licensing policies that stifled the growth of private enterprises. Despite unflinching government support, many public-sector companies, plagued by high wages, low productivity, obsolete plants and machinery, outdated technology, lack of competition, and fiscal profligacy, started to bleed, which put an enormous strain on the state exchequer. Nearly 50 percent of the 237 state companies were operating at a loss in 1992. Stringent labor laws made it impossible to retrench workers from loss-making firms.

In 1991, as part of India's economic reforms, the government abolished the industrial licensing policies and opened nearly all sectors of the economy to private investment and competition. However, it kept the politically sensitive issue of privatization, or the strategic sale of loss-making public companies, outside the purview of its reforms program. This situation continued until 1999, when the government, faced with a growing fiscal deficit, announced its intention to gradually divest or privatize some public firms. In 2001, the government sold 51 percent of the stake in an aluminum company, Bharat Aluminum Company (BALCO), to Sterlite Industries. This was followed by the sale of 46 percent of the state-owned international telecom monopoly, VSNL, to the Tata Group. However, the ambitious divestment program came to a screeching halt after the 2004 federal elections, which strengthened the legislative power of socialist-leaning political parties who vehemently opposed the divestment program. Nevertheless, even partial privatization (or even talk of it) has improved productivity in many public-sector companies.

Although the public sector continues to underperform, the private sector, set free by the 1991 reforms, has truly transformed itself into a lean, mean fighting machine. In reality, it had no choice but to improve. In the post-liberalization era, India's great family-run private companies, which earlier had been protected by political connections and high tariffs, faced increased domestic and foreign competition and the threat of cheap Chinese imports. It is not that the government did not want to help address this threat; rather, India had to bow to the WTO mandate and remove quantitative restrictions on many import items. The private sector responded to the threats by cutting costs, revamping operations, improving products, and upgrading technologies. Not everyone succeeded; some companies had to close their operations, while others were gobbled up by multinational companies. In the end, however, India has welcomed the arrival of a vibrant private sector.

India's industrial growth since the 1991 reforms has been a mixed bag. The manufacturing sector grew by an impressive 9.5 percent annually during 1992–97, the period encompassing the first five years of reforms; a lackluster 3.3 percent annually during 1997–2002; and a robust 8.7 percent annually during 2002–07. Although the industry sector is free of stifling government controls, it continues to be hampered by poor infrastructure, restrictive labor laws, and bureaucratic red tape. In India, companies that employ more than one hundred workers need government approval to fire them.

However, during the past four years, the manufacturing sector has witnessed a major revival, and there are clear signs that the business cycle has turned. The sector has been averaging a 9 percent growth rate in the last four years (2004–08), with a record 11.3 percent in 2006–07. Two factors account for this surge: domestic demand and the phenomenal growth of FDI equity inflows. According to a study by the McKinsey Global Institute[124], aggregate Indian consumer spending could more than quadruple to $1.77 trillion from current levels by 2025 due to an expected ten-fold increase in the middle-class population and the three-fold jump in household income. Rising household incomes and low financing rates are bolstering demand for both consumer durables (refrigerators, washing machines, automobiles, etc.), and nondurables (clothing, footwear, paper products, etc.). The scorching pace of demand has prompted businesses—both large and small—to undertake massive capacity expansion, modernization, and diversification. Businesses are expanding not only to meet domestic demand but also to tap overseas markets—and cushion themselves from any future demand recession within India.

Many multinationals have also stepped up their investment in India. More than two-thirds of foreign investment in recent years has gone into manufacturing, not services. Buoyed by the recent success, the Federation of Indian Chambers of Commerce and Industry (FICCI) has set an aggressive target of increasing the share of manufacturing in India's GDP from its current level of 17 percent to 25 percent by 2015.

Is India an emerging manufacturing superpower? Perhaps. Can it give China a run for its money in manufacturing? Not likely in the near future. Here are the cold facts. India is still a minnow in the global manufacturing scene. In 2005, the net output of India's manufacturing amounted to only $115 billion, compared to China's $750 billion and $1,500 billion in the United States. India's manufacturing exports were 6 percent of GDP ($37 billion), compared with 35 percent for China ($712 billion). Industry contributes to merely 29 percent of India's GDP; in China it contributes to nearly 50 percent.

China continues to grow from strength to strength and is unlikely to cede any ground in manufacturing. It has inserted itself into the supply chains of almost every manufacturing company in the developed world—in many cases, China *is* the supply chain. Analysts credit four factors for China's spectacular rise as a manufacturing giant: high domestic savings rate, world-class infrastructure, high intake of FDI, and low-cost labor. India comes up short in the first three factors: the national savings rate is lower, its infrastructure is vastly underdeveloped, and its FDI of $5–$6 billion per year pales in comparison to the $50–$60 billion China attracts year after year. With the exception of telecommunications, all other infrastructure-related expenses are quite high in India as compared to China.

Like China, however, India can count on its huge population base to provide the low-cost labor needed for manufacturing. The fact that developed countries will continue to rely on developing countries to fill their manufacturing needs bodes well for countries like China and India. Although China is in the driver's seat as far as manufacturing is concerned, its "one-child" rule is likely to result in fewer young workers available for factory jobs. This may provide an opening for India, which is expected to have nearly 70 percent of its population (913 million people) in the fifteen to sixty-four age group by 2020, providing a large pool of factory workers.[125]

Already there are signs that global companies are taking a serious look at India. Companies like Hyundai, Samsung, Motorola, Nokia, LG Electronics, Siemens, and Cummins have already set up manufacturing facilities. Many more multinationals have plans to start operations in the next five to ten years. Initially, these companies manufactured goods in India with the goal of selling products to India's burgeoning middle-class consumers. The tariffs for manufactured goods were so high that they could not bring products from overseas and sell them in India. These companies are now realizing that they can make India an export hub by taking advantage of India's low-cost production capabilities. LG wants to export India-made home appliances by 2009. Hyundai exports the India-made Santro sedan to other countries.

Many automotive companies have also started sourcing components from India; for example, Sundram Fasteners is General Motors's principal supplier of radiator caps. India also offers abundant engineering and technical talent; every year it produces 350,000–400,000 engineers, second only to China. The Indian government expects the manufacturing sector to witness an annual growth rate of 12 percent, creating 1.6 million new jobs every year.

While global companies are arriving in India in droves, some major domestic players are flexing their muscles on the global scene. Indian companies spent over $10 billion to buy foreign firms in 2006. With the economy booming, many domestic companies are now in a strong financial position in terms of cash flow and profitability. K. M. Birla's Hindalco acquired the world's largest producer of rolled aluminum products, Novelis, for $6 billion. Tata Steel bought Corus to become the fifth-largest steel producer. Mittal Steel, based in London but run by Indian businessmen L. N. Mittal, took over the world's largest steelmaker, Arcelor. Indian companies large and small, after making their mark domestically, are now reaching overseas to tap new markets and acquire new technologies.

The Services Sector

The services sector has been at the forefront of India's rapidly growing economy, with its share in the GDP growing from 43 percent in 1991, at the beginning of the reforms, to 53 percent in 2007. In contrast, the service sector has lagged behind China's manufacturing sector. From 1990 to 2004, the services sector as a percentage of China's GDP increased modestly, from 34 percent to 39 percent. Services cover a wide range of activities, including wholesale/retail trade, banking and finance, real estate, hotels/restaurants, transportation, communication, and business services. The business services sector includes information technology (IT) and business process outsourcing (BPO).

Table 20: 2007 GDP Breakdown by Sector

	India	China	United States
Services	53 percent	40 percent	78 percent
Industrial	29 percent	49 percent	21 percent
Agriculture	18 percent	11 percent	1 percent

Source: CIA The World Factbook

India's services sector has caught the world's attention for its stellar growth and development. While the overall economy is growing at 8 to 10 percent annually, the services sector has been growing in double digits for the past few years. Service exports have grown from a meager $9 billion in 1997 to $75 billion in 2006. India's share of worldwide service exports is expected to go up from its current 2.7 percent to 6 percent by 2012. The services boom is expected to continue, as India has emerged as a global services hub.

India's IT/BPO sector has witnessed exponential growth in the last few years. As a percentage of GDP, the contribution of the technology sector has gone up from 0.3 percent in 1991 to 5.5 percent by 2008.[126] The United States and the United Kingdom remained the two largest export markets for IT/BPO services, accounting for 61 percent and 18 percent respectively in 2007. Banking, financial services, and insurance (BFSI) remains the largest vertical market for Indian IT/BPO exports, accounting for 40 percent of the exports, followed by high-technology and telecom verticals at 20 percent.

India's Foreign Trade

The gradual opening up of the economy since 1991 has resulted in a substantial increase in India's foreign trade. India now accounts for 2.4 percent of world merchandise share, signaling its arrival on the global scene.[127]

Merchandise trade (exports and imports), as a percentage of GDP, increased from 14.6 percent in 1991 to 22.5 percent in 2001, and further to 32.6 percent in 2006. Inspired by favorable foreign trade policies and improved competitiveness in domestic industry, India's exports have grown at a compound annual growth rate (CAGR) of 25 percent from 2004 to 2007, compared to 12.7 percent in the preceding three years. After nearly achieving the export target of $125 billion in 2006, India has now set an export target of $200 billion for fiscal year 2009. Today, domestic manufacturers have a far greater export-orientation than at any time since independence. Total merchandise exports and imports increased from $128 billion in 2003 to nearly $300 billion in 2006. These numbers still pale in comparison to trade numbers in China ($1.659 trillion) and the United States ($2.954 trillion). China's merchandise trade is about five times that of India, whereas the United States's merchandise trade is close to ten times that of India.

Table 21: World Trade: India/China/

United States (2006) $ Billions

	India	China	United States
Merchandise Exports	120.0	968.0	1,036.0
% World Total	1.0	8.0	8.6
Merchandise Imports	175.0	791.0	1,918
% World Total	1.4	6.4	15
Total Merchandise Trade ($ Billions)	295.0	1,659.0	2,954.0
Services Exports	75.0	91.0	397.0
Services Imports	63.0	100.0	308.0

Source: WTO

Top Indian exports include engineered goods, petroleum products, textiles and clothing, and gems and jewelry. India has also become a top exporter of software services and software workers. Top imports include crude oil, machinery, electronic goods, gold and silver, and chemicals and fertilizers. Crude oil accounts for a third of India's imports. India's top export partners in 2006 were the United States (17 percent), the United Arab Emirates (7.7 percent), and China (7.7 percent), whereas its import partners were China (8.7 percent), the United States (6 percent), and Germany (4.7 percent).

The United States and China are India's top two trading partners. Jewelry (cut and polished) and textiles account for half of India's exports to the United States. India imports engineering goods and machinery, precious stones and metals, optical and medical instruments, aircraft, and fertilizers from the United States. From a modest $5.6 billion in 1990, bilateral trade with the United States has increased to $41.6

billion in 2007, an eight-fold increase in seventeen years. Currently, India enjoys a modest $7 billion trade surplus. Similarly, trade with China has increased from a paltry $250 million in 1991 to $20 billion in 2006. With trade growing at nearly 50 percent, China is expected to surpass the United States as India's largest trading partner within a couple of years. It should be noted that India is still a minor player as far as its trade with the United States is considered. Consider this. In 2007, bilateral trade between the United States and China trade stood at $387 billion, with China enjoying a $256 billion surplus. (China exports $321 billion in goods from the United States and imports $65 billion in goods from the United States.)

Table 22: 2007 Merchandise Trade with the United States ($ Billions)

	India	China
Exports	24.0	321.5
Imports	17.6	65.2
Total Bilateral Trade	41.6	386.7
Trade Surplus	6.4	256.3

Source: U.S. Census Bureau, Foreign Trade Statistics

Selective Sector Deep-Dive

The Steel Sector

India is one of the world's top producers of iron and steel. Before the liberalization of the economy in 1992, the steel industry was highly regulated, and licenses were required for the production and sale of steel. Large-scale production licenses were granted only to the government-owned Steel Authority of India Limited (SAIL) and the privately owned Tata Steel. The lack of competition, combined with the fact that the largest player was government-owned, resulted in an extremely unproductive industry. The price of steel was administered and protected by high import duties. After India's economic reforms, steel prices began to decline as a result of the entry of many new players, a reduction in import duties, and worldwide overcapacity in steel production.

Globally, the steel industry is consolidating rapidly, driven by the need to reduce costs and meet substantial demand from the fast-expanding economies of India and China. What drives demand for steel? Steel is important for automobiles, with an average mid-sized automobile containing one thousand pounds of corrosion-resistant steel (valued at $400). Automakers such as Ford and General Motors each buy five million tons of steel. Steel is a tricky area for governments. For instance, the United States protects its steel industry by using tariffs that prevent the dumping of cheap steel from foreign countries. Automakers hate that because it deprives them of low-cost steel. In fact, in 2006, the top six U.S. automakers joined forces to call on the U.S. International Trade Commission to end thirteen years of tariffs on imported steel. Having a domestic, low-cost steel industry is a definite plus for the automotive industry.

Some Indian companies are at the forefront of global steel consolidation trends. Indian steelmaker Tata Steel made headlines when it acquired Anglo-Dutch steel company Corus for $11.3 billion, outbidding a Brazilian rival, CSN; this acquisition created the fifth-largest steel company in the world. It is a classic case of a small fish swallowing a big fish: Corus was the ninth-largest steel producer in the world, with an output of 18.2 million tons, whereas Tata Steel was fifty-sixth on the list, with an output of 5.3 million tons. The chairman of Tata Steel, Ratan Tata, called the acquisition a "moment of great fulfillment for all in India."[128]

Tata Steel is also exploring a joint venture with the world's second-largest steelmaker, Nippon of Japan, to jointly produce the alloy for automakers and other companies. Essar Group, an Indian conglomerate whose interests span energy, telecom, and shipping, acquired U.S.-based Minnesota Steel and Canada-based Algoma. In 2006, Indian business tycoon Lakshmi Mittal of Mittal Steel acquired rival steelmaker Arcelor for $41 billion, creating the world's largest steel company as measured by revenues.

The Automotive Sector

India's automobile Industry has witnessed tremendous growth in recent years and has emerged as one of the key sectors of India's economy. Carlos Ghosn, chief executive of alliance partners Renault and Nissan, called India one of the fastest-growing markets in the world. India is predicted to become the world's third-largest car market behind China and the United States by 2030. Consider this. India currently has a vehicle ownership of 8 per thousand. That number is expected to reach 140 per thousand by 2030. What that means is that the number of vehicles sold will jump from the current rate of two million per year to twenty million per year by 2030.[129]

What are the key drivers for the explosive growth in India's automotive industry? For starters, India's booming economy and rising income levels have boosted the spending power of more than three hundred million middle-class families, who are the core of those buying cars. Even rising fuel prices and high interest rates have not dampened the spirit of the customers, mostly first-time buyers. Driving through India's gridlocked cities can be a grueling and hazardous experience, but millions of "newly" rich Indians are willing to take the plunge.

Historical Perspective

The Indian passenger car industry has gone through three different phases since independence: the Ambassador era, the Maruti era, and the reforms era. The Ambassador era, which lasted until 1983, was dominated by a single domestic carmaker, Hindustan Motors, which produced and sold just one car model called the Ambassador, which was based on an antiquated 1940s Morris Oxford. A combination of high tariffs and a ban on foreign investment and imports shielded the company from global competition. Furthermore, the government controlled the supply side by fixing production volumes on a yearly basis with little regard to actual demand in the marketplace. The result was that the demand always exceeded the supply, and customers had to endure years of waiting before their vehicle was delivered. Due to the lack of competition, the carmaker had little or no incentive to upgrade products and improve operational efficiency, and the Ambassador, or India's Model-T, ruled the roads unchallenged until 1983.

Apart from Hindustan Motors, there was another player, Premier Automobiles, which had modest sales volumes and operated under the same conditions. In 1981, India's automobile production stood at 149,000 vehicles for a population of 673 million people.[130]

The Maruti era began in 1983 when the Indian government allowed Suzuki Motors of Japan to take a minority stake in a joint venture (JV) with a newly formed, Indian government-owned enterprise called Maruti Udyog to produce small passenger cars for the Indian market. Maruti was the brainchild of Sanjay Gandhi, son of then prime minister Indira Gandhi, who had the vision of bringing affordable cars to the Indian masses. Toward the end of 1983, the Maruti Udyog/ Suzuki JV started rolling out its flagship car, the Maruti 800, which was based on Suzuki's 1960s technology. The Maruti 800, also called "the people's car," was a huge hit with Indian middle-class families and quickly gained market share, accounting for 80 percent of all passenger cars produced in India. The new competition forced the other two incumbents to make changes to their models. Maruti's entry was the first step in the liberalization of a sector that had been heavily regulated since independence.

India's full-blown economic liberalization program, which started in 1991, had a dramatic impact on the automotive sector. The first major step was the de-licensing of the passenger car sector in 1993, which led to the entry of several global players into the market through JVs and subsidiaries. The pace of the reforms continued throughout the decade, with the government opening up the sector to FDI, removing qualitative restrictions on imports, and finally permitting 100 percent foreign ownership in 2002.

Today, competition in the car market is very stiff, with all major global automakers boosting their presence with new investments. Major automakers have announced a number of greenfield and brownfield projects, which add up to billions of dollars in India. Of all the global carmakers operating in India, Hyundai Motors has had the most success. Within nine years of rolling out its first vehicle from an assembly plant in the southern city of Chennai, Hyundai produced its 1.5 millionth car in 2007, becoming the fastest-growing automaker in India. Hyundai plans to add a second plant to bring its capacity to six hundred thousand units by 2007.

Amid increased competition, the position of Maruti Udyog (which until recently accounted for the bulk of car sales) has become less dominant, with its market share falling from 80 to 60 percent. The sector also saw the entry of yet another domestic player, Tata Motors, which decided to diversify into the passenger car market in 2001 after its truck and commercial vehicle business plummeted due to lack of demand. Tata's success was dramatic; its flagship car, the Tata Indica, has become one of the best-selling cars in India.

In addition to the passenger car market, India also has strong commercial vehicle and two-wheeler markets. India produces about half a million commercial vehicles and nine million two-wheelers a year. The commercial vehicles segment is dominated by Tata, Ashok Leyland, Eicher Motors, and Mahindra and Mahindra, whereas the two-wheeler sector is dominated by Hero Honda, Bajaj, TVS, and Yamaha. India is the second-largest two-wheeler market in the world.

Table 23: Indian Automobile Domestic Sales Trends (# of Vehicles)

	2002–03	2007–08
Passenger Vehicles	707,198	1,547,985
Commercial Vehicles	190,682	486,817
Three-Wheelers	231,529	364,703
Two-Wheelers	4,812,126	7,248,589
Grand Total	5,941,535	9,648,094

Source: Society of Indian Automobile Manufacturers

Importance to Economy

The automobile sector is one of the key sectors of India's economy in terms of growth and employment. The sector forms 5 percent of economic output, but it is poised to account for 10 percent of India's GDP by 2016. Currently, the Indian automotive industry provides employment to ten million people, and the Indian government is eyeing a whopping twenty-five million automotive jobs by 2016 due to relatively low automation in Indian plants as compared to the countries in the West.[131]

With the stakes so high, the Indian government is putting its weight behind the industry by relaxing tax laws, reducing excise duties, and rolling out the red carpet to foreign automakers to encourage them to set up plants in the country. A number of high-profile auto executives, including Richard Wagoner of General Motors, Carlos Ghosn of Renault-Nissan, and Norbert Reithofer of BMW, visited the country in recent years to explore growth opportunities. Compare this situation with the shrinking workforce of the ailing U.S. domestic automakers, who have laid off a third of their workers since 2003.

India as Automotive Export Hub

India is fast becoming a low-cost manufacturing base for automotive companies around the world. For instance, Hyundai Motors is positioning India as a global export hub for compact cars by exporting the Indian-made Santro sedan to overseas markets. Even domestic carmaker Maruti Udyog, controlled by Suzuki, is aggressively looking at exporting vehicles from India. In all, passenger car exports from India went up from seventy-two thousand units to two hundred thousand units in the past five years.[132]

Most automakers and component suppliers in developed countries are struggling due to their high cost structure, which is driven by high wages, employee healthcare costs, pension costs, costly recalls, lawsuits, ever-increasing environmental and safety standards, high commodity prices, and the need to upgrade technology and features to keep pace with customer expectations in a crowded marketplace. The bad news is that the companies cannot pass on their cost increases to the customers due to stiff competition from newer players who do not have the same legacy costs. Consider this. For each vehicle it makes, General Motors spends on average $1,635 for active employee and retiree healthcare costs, compared to $215 for Toyota Motor. The Big 3 American carmakers spend more than $10 billion per year on healthcare costs, and General Motors and Ford have $100 billion accumulated healthcare liability. In fact, General Motors was the largest private provider of healthcare in the United States in 2005, spending $5.3 billion to cover 1.1 million people. Ford spends $1,100 per vehicle on healthcare—more than the amount spent on steel. The net effect of all this is a cumulative loss to the tune of $60 billion for the Big 3 American automakers since 2000.

With their survival at stake, most American and European automakers are increasingly sourcing automotive components from low-cost countries like India and China. The global market for outsourced automotive components is expected to reach $375 billion by 2015, and India has the potential to capture $25–$30 billion.[133] General Motors is expected to source auto components worth $1 billion from India within five years.[134]

Many U.S.-based auto suppliers are also opening facilities in India to take advantage of the low-cost labor and high market potential. The struggling parts-maker Visteon, the former Ford Motor parts division that was spun off in 2000, opened a software engineering center and aims to have 50 percent of its engineering workforce in low-cost countries by 2008. With demand soaring, cities like Chennai, Pune, Delhi, and Nashik are positioning themselves as major automotive centers. Of all the cities, Chennai, also known as the "Detroit of India," has the edge due to its well-developed infrastructure and presence of parts suppliers, despite its well-known water and power shortages.

While India's automotive sector is booming, China's is booming even stronger. Twenty years ago, China had no auto industry. Now, with sales of over seven million new vehicles a year, China has just overtaken Japan and is now the second-largest market in the world, after the United States, which has sales of 16.5 million vehicles a year.[135]

In China, like in India, the growing middle class is fueling the demand. The other factor is the growing road network. China, which had no national road network until the late 1990s, currently has fifty thousand kilometers of highways and plans to add twenty-five thousand kilometers more. The Chinese auto sector is highly regulated. Foreign automakers can invest only in JVs. They have to source components from local suppliers, and high tariffs shield the market from imports.

Key Developments in India's Automotive Sector:

- Renault is ramping up Indian production plans and signed a JV with India's Mahindra and Mahindra. It plans to build fifty thousand entry-level Logan sedans a year from Mahindra's Nashik facility.
- Daimler is planning a second plant in India to produce S-Class, E-Class, and C-Class Mercedes-Benz cars for the Indian market. It already has a plant in Pune that makes two thousand cars a month.

- Luxury carmaker BMW (worldwide sales: $63 billion) is building its first India assembly plant in Chennai to produce 3 Series and 5 Series vehicles. Why is the world's most profitable carmaker rushing to India? It wants to position itself as a high-end player in the growing luxury segment. Shipping cars into India is prohibitively expensive since the Indian government imposes a high import duty. Therefore, it makes more economic sense for companies like BMW to build cars in India.

- Ford Motor employs about two thousand people in its assembly plant near Chennai to produce Ikon cars (annual sales: forty-five thousand units), designed specifically for the Indian market. Ford also maintains 1,800 IT and service personnel in India to support the company's IT and business activities around the world.

- General Motors is setting up a new assembly plant in Pune, doubling its production to nearly a quarter million cars a year.

- Meanwhile, the Indian government completely exited from the auto business by selling most of its stake in Maruti Udyog to its JV partner, Suzuki. Suzuki currently owns a 54.2 percent stake in Maruti Udyog. Life Insurance Corporation (LIC), the country's biggest insurer, is the second-largest shareholder in the company, with a 12.5 percent share.

- India's Tata Motors (NYSE: TTM) unveiled an ambitious plan to launch the world's cheapest car for as little as $2,500, a move intended to lure millions of India's two-wheeler owners who wish to upgrade to the next level. Currently, Tata Motors has a market share of 16 percent in the passenger car market. Renault responded by announcing plans for its own $3,000 car.[136]

The Airline Sector: The Sky Is the Limit

It's official: India is now the fastest-growing aviation market in the world. India's aviation sector is experiencing 25 percent annual growth, spurred by a red-hot economy and rising incomes among the country's three-hundred-million-strong[137] middle class. The Airbus Global Market Forecast[138] has predicted that India will see annual passenger traffic growth of 7.7 percent until 2025, well above the world average of 4.8 percent and China's average of 7.2 percent. Currently, airlines carry around 60 million passengers a year in India, as compared to 658 million[139] carried by U.S. domestic airlines. With India's current high growth, passenger traffic is expected to reach 100 million by 2010 and 200 million by 2020, mainly driven by urban middle-class consumers.

Until the economic liberalization of the 1990s, India had just two state-owned airlines catering to domestic and international traffic. In 1994, the government initiated an open-sky policy that formally ended the state monopoly on Indian skies and allowed private operators to provide service. FDI up to a 49 percent equity stake was allowed, but no foreign airlines could hold equity in a domestic airline.[140]

Within a few years, several private airlines entered the liberalized aviation business and gradually started taking market share from the state airlines. Today, private airlines dominate Indian skies with a 75 percent market share. Jet Airways emerged as the biggest airline, with an estimated 46 percent market share, beating its rival, state-run Indian Airlines, which currently is at a 25 percent market share.[141]

With the arrival of several budget airlines, air travel in India has suddenly become very affordable, and Indians are traveling by air more than ever before. But even with all the growth in the aviation sector, only a fraction of Indians can afford to travel by air. Indian Railways, which runs seven thousand passenger trains a day, forms the backbone of India's passenger traffic network, carrying over thirteen million people[142] a day. But the rail industry is steadily losing business to the budget airlines, which are luring the high-end luxury rail customers with low prices.

Lured by India's rapid growth in international traffic, many foreign airlines are also expanding their services. Qatar Airlines is launching flights to New York and Washington from six Indian cities via Doha. American Airlines is running nonstop daily flights from Chicago to Delhi, and Continental is running nonstop flights between Delhi and Newark, New Jersey.

India's fledgling airline industry has already been seeing some signs of consolidation in recent years. Facing a relentless onslaught from the private carriers, the struggling state-run airlines, Air India and Indian, are poised to merge, despite protests from their employees. After months of negotiations, India's largest private airline, Jet Airways, acquired another private carrier, Air Sahara, further boosting its dominance of domestic operations.

The booming aviation sector has made India one of the most attractive markets for the aircraft industry. Hundreds of new aircraft are being ordered each year. Over 135 aircraft have been added in the last two years alone. The current fleet strength of 300–320 aircraft is expected to reach 500–550 aircraft by 2010. Aircraft manufacturer Airbus estimates that India will need 1,100 aircraft over the next twenty years. India's airlines have already placed orders for four hundred aircraft[143] worth about $30 billion. The booming aviation industries of India and China are vital to the long-term profitability and survivability of aircraft manufacturers like Boeing and Airbus.

An international air show at the Yelahanka air base in Bangalore in February 2007 attracted more than five hundred companies, including Lockheed Martin, British Aerospace, Dassault, and Boeing. The U.S. military aircraft industry is showing a lot of interest in the Indian market since the relationship between the countries is on the upswing. India plans to buy 126 fighter jets for its air force to replace its Soviet-made MIG-21s.

So far, Boeing appears to be way ahead of its rival Airbus in securing firm orders from India's airlines. The city of Seattle celebrated when state-owned Air India placed an order[144] for 68 planes, including the new 787 Dreamliners, for a whopping $11.6 billion; the purchase was described in the media as one of the single largest in Boeing's history. The fuel-efficient Dreamliner aircraft is expected to be the mainstay of the international services offered by Indian carriers, which have been steadily losing market share to the foreign airlines.

Spearheading the Boeing campaign is Indian-born Boeing sales executive Dinesh Keskar, who is credited with Boeing's dominance of the Indian market. Boeing also won a thirty-plane order from Jet Airways, India's largest private airline, and a ten-plane order from SpiceJet.

Airbus is also wooing India with its new A380 superjumbo planes. It already received an order for ten planes from Kingfisher Airlines, which plans to use it for nonstop flights between India and the United States. Airbus also received another order for a fleet of one hundred A-320 planes from Delhi-based IndiGo Airlines.

The rapid growth of the aviation sector has put an enormous strain on India's outdated and overcrowded airports, which are undergoing a complete makeover to cope with the demand. India's civil aviation ministry estimates that the industry needs $40 billion in the next ten years to upgrade airports, runways, antiquated ground-handling equipment, and air traffic control systems to handle higher traffic volumes. To encourage foreign investments, the government is allowing 100 percent foreign equity in greenfield airport projects.

Many airports, including thirty-five smaller airports, are being upgraded at breakneck speed. The Mumbai and Delhi airports, the largest Indian airports, were privatized recently. Today, the Delhi airport handles twenty million passengers a year, as compared to eighty-five million passengers handled by the world's busiest airport, Atlanta, or seventy-six million passengers handled by Chicago O'Hare. But Delhi is gearing up to handle one hundred million passengers by 2030.

Two greenfield airports have recently opened in the southern cities of Bangalore and Hyderabad, known for their burgeoning IT offshoring business. The new Hyderabad airport is a public-private joint venture between GMR Group (63 percent equity), Malaysia Airports Holdings Berhad (11 percent equity), and both the state government of Andhra Pradesh and the Airports Authority of India (13 percent equity each). The new Bangalore airport is also a public-private venture.[145] Investments are pouring into other areas as well. Airbus is planning a $1 billion investment in the next ten years for setting up a Maintenance, Repair, and Overhaul (MRO) center.

The Mobile Telephone Sector

India is the fastest-growing mobile telephone market in the world, expanding at the rate of six million new subscribers a month and adding more mobile subscribers per month than China. With more than 270 million connections, India's telecommunications network is the third largest in the world and the second largest among the emerging economies of Asia. Between March and December 2007, India added 68 million new subscribers,[146] taking the wireless subscriber base to 233 million. By 2010, India is expected to have five hundred million mobile phones as handsets and calling plans become more affordable in a country of 1.1 billion people.

India's telecom sector has gone through different phases. The government had a complete monopoly over all telecom services from 1947 to 1994. In the 1990s, the sector benefited from the general opening up of the Indian economy. A new National Telecom Policy (NTP) was launched, kicking off an era of partial deregulation. Fixed-line services, with the exception of long-distance services, and wireless services were opened up to the private sector. Later, the government also opened up the long-distance service and entered the lucrative wireless market. In March 2007, the government increased the limit of FDI in the telecom sector from 49 percent to 74 percent.

Today, India's state operators, BSNL and MTNL, control 90 percent of the fixed-line services market. Both GSM (Global System for Mobile Communications) and CDMA (Code Division Multiple Access) cellular systems are offered in India, with GSM accounting for three-fourths of all subscriptions. Airtel, Vodafone-Hutch, and Idea Cellular dominate the GSM space, while Reliance and Tata Indicom dominate the CDMA space. Bharti Airtel, with a 24 percent market share, is India's leading private cellular provider,[147] with a subscription base of fifty-seven million. One of the earliest entries into the cellular market, Bharti took eleven years to reach twenty million subscribers, then doubled the number in just thirteen months. It plans to spend $8 billion by 2010 to keep its leading position. Reliance is India's second-largest mobile services provider, followed by state-owned BSNL (Bharat Sanchar Nigam Limited).

Global mobile leader Vodafone of the United Kingdom bought a 67 percent controlling stake[148] in Hutchison Essar for $11.1 billion. The phenomenal growth in the cellular phone market has opened up opportunities for handset-makers around the world. The world's largest mobile manufacturer, Nokia, is ramping up its mobile handset manufacturing plant in Chennai with a four-year investment commitment of $150 million. India is the third-largest market for Finland-based Nokia in terms of volumes. In 2006, Nokia shipped twenty-five million handsets from its Chennai plant. As the markets in developed countries are becoming increasingly saturated, many other players, such as LG, Samsung, Sony Ericsson, and Motorola, are also competing in the Indian market. Many companies are opening factories in India to avoid import duties. Motorola and Sony Ericsson are planning to open manufacturing plants in India.

Thus far, the phenomenal growth in the mobile sector is mainly driven by urban consumption; in the coming years, however, the boom is likely to be sustained by the growth in rural teledensity. Even today, the total number of telephone connections, fixed and cellular combined, stands at only 211 million in a country of 1.1 billion; this means that the telecommunications sector offers huge growth potential for companies and investors alike.

The Pharma Sector

If you are among those who thought the worst was over in offshoring, think again. Pharma offshoring may be the next big thing, after IT offshoring. Although India's pharma sector doesn't hog the limelight as does the IT sector, it is nevertheless a very important sector that is quietly undergoing a revolution of its own.

For starters, India boasts one of the largest pharma sectors in the world, serving the needs of its vast population of 1.1 billion people. The sector meets domestic demand by manufacturing basic and advanced drugs at affordable prices. The sector is highly fragmented with 250 companies, including five state-owned enterprises that control 70 percent of the market. The sector has estimated revenues of $4.5 billion[149] and is growing at the rate of 8–9 percent a year. Until 2005, India's pharma sector thrived due to the Indian Patent Act of 1970, which protected process patents, but not product patents, for drugs. A number of drug companies entered the market to exploit this government-engineered loophole, which was intended to bring drugs as cheaply as possible to the Indian masses. In essence, domestic companies were allowed to produce a generic version of any patented drug, often developed through painstaking and costly research and clinical trials, without paying any royalty, as long as they used a manufacturing process that was different from the process used by the patent-holder. With no R & D costs to recover, Indian drug companies were able to produce drugs at a fraction of the price charged by their Western counterparts. Unable to protect their IP in developing countries like India, many global drug companies largely stayed away.

In 2005, the Indian parliament approved a controversial bill[150] that introduced a product patent regime for food, chemicals, and drugs. The government did not have too much choice in this matter because India was required to provide product patents in accordance with its obligation under the Trade-Related Intellectual Property Rights (TRIPS) agreement of the World Trade Organization. This new law effectively banned Indian companies from producing cheap generic drugs without paying royalties to the patent-holders.

The passage of the new patents bill, which accepted the global patent regime, has made India a very attractive location for the offshoring of new drug discovery and clinical trials.

The pharma sector, like the IT sector, is benefiting from the huge pool of highly skilled scientific and technical personnel available at a fraction of the usual cost. U.S. drug-maker Eli Lilly is outsourcing a range of clinical data management services[151] to India's Tata Consultancy Services. Eli Lilly cited three reasons for offshoring clinical data to India beyond the cost savings: gaining access to a global talent pool, increasing resource flexibility and scalability, and maintaining a global workflow that is operational twenty-four hours a day.

The other significant cost savings come from clinical trials (testing of new drugs on humans), which account for 50 to 60 percent of the cost of developing new drugs in the United States and Europe. Consider this. In 2006, Pfizer, the world's largest drug-maker, had to abruptly pull the plug on the company's most promising experimental drug for heart disease, torcetrapib, after clinical trials showed that it actually caused an increase in deaths and heart problems; its $1 billion investment turned into a complete loss.[152] The point is, not only are clinical trials expensive, but their results are far from guaranteed.

Also, with the increased awareness of the risks associated with new drug testing, the pool of patients available for clinical trials in developed countries is shrinking rapidly. That's why drug companies are increasingly moving clinical trials to densely populated developing nations like India, where they can find a huge pool of patient recruits at a fraction of the cost. According to Frost and Sullivan[153], India's huge patient population, genetically distinct groups, large number of hospital beds, 221 medical colleges, and skilled English-speaking researchers are the factors behind India's recent success as a hotspot for clinical trials. McKinsey predicts the Indian clinical trials market size will be $1.5 billion by 2010. Today, all the major drug-makers, including Novo Nordisk, Aventis, Novartis, GlaxoSmithKline, Eli Lilly, and Pfizer, conduct clinical drug trials in India.

Among the other new developments in the pharma sector is the emergence of Indian drug companies in the global marketplace. Ranbaxy, which entered the U.S. drug market in 1995 and operates through its Florida-based subsidiary Ranbaxy Pharmaceuticals Inc (RPI), is aiming to push its sales in the United States, the world's largest drug market, from $350 million today to $5 billion by 2012. It joined the ranks of the top ten generic drug manufacturers in the world, with presence in twenty-three of the twenty-five biggest drug markets. Generic drugs are the same as brand-name products but are dispensed under their generic chemical name.

Although a relatively small player in the global market, with annual revenues of $1.2 billion, Ranbaxy has become a thorn in U.S. drug giant Pfizer's side[154] by aggressively challenging its patents in U.S. courts for a variety of blockbuster drugs. Pfizer, the world's largest drug company, with $50 billion annual sales and $14 billion profits, has seen several of its drugs coming out of patents and is trying aggressively to keep its remaining patents intact. Companies like Ranbaxy challenge the patents because they want to get the exclusive rights to produce drugs alongside the patent-holder for a limited period, typically six months, before the drug can be copied freely—at which time the prices will drop. Companies typically can't make much money selling only the generic versions of drugs whose patents have already expired.

Some Indian firms are also actively engaged in manufacturing affordable drugs for poor HIV/AIDS patients throughout the world. Ranbaxy won approval from the U.S. Food and Drug Administration for an antiretroviral (ARV) drug[155] under the U.S. President's Emergency Plan for AIDS relief. ARVs can delay the onset of AIDS by protecting the immune system from attack. As per the plan, ARV drugs will be manufactured in Ranbaxy's plant in India.

The Energy Sector

The energy sector is turning out to be the Achilles' heel for India's red-hot economy. India needs to maintain an 8–9 percent GDP growth rate for the next twenty-five years to meet its goal of eradicating poverty and improving the quality of life. To sustain high growth levels, India needs to increase its energy supplies by 3–5 times the current levels. According to a report[156] released by KPMG, the energy sector needs investments to the tune of $120–$150 billion to keep pace with current demand.

India is now the world's fifth-largest energy consumer and is projected to become its third-largest consumer by 2030, behind the United States and China. India's per capita energy consumption of 491 kilograms of oil equivalent[157] is very low compared to 7,893 in the United States and 1,316 in China. That means the average Indian consumes eighteen times less energy than the average American. Coal accounts for 55 percent of all energy consumption, whereas petroleum and natural gas account for 31 percent and 7 percent respectively.

India is heavily dependent on coal for its energy needs. Coal-based thermal plants account for 53 percent[158] of India's electricity generation, whereas hydroelectric plants account for 25 percent. Most countries use coal to produce electricity because it is a low-cost energy source. The United States uses coal to produce 50 percent of its electricity, whereas France uses nuclear power to produce 77 percent of its electricity. India has fourteen nuclear reactors in commercial operation and nine under construction. Nuclear power supplies about 3 percent of India's electricity. By 2050, that number is expected to grow to 25 percent.

India has large coal reserves, estimated at ninety-six billion tons, or 10 percent of the world's total. India is currently the third-largest coal-producing country[159] in the world behind the United States and China. Despite having large coal reserves, India lags behind in domestic production mainly due to the fact that coal mining, essentially a state-owned monopoly, is plagued by inefficiencies and corruption. In contrast, privately owned U.S. companies mine over one billion tons of coal a year, almost three times India's output.

India currently imports 72 percent of its crude oil requirements, spending over $68 billion[160] in 2007–08 due to a relentless increase in international prices. India's crude oil import dependency is likely to increase to 90 percent by 2025[161] from the current level of 72 percent. In 2006, India was the world's sixth-greatest oil consumer[162] (after the United States, China, Japan, Russia, and Germany), accounting for about 3.1 percent of the world's total annual petroleum consumption. India's proven oil reserves are currently estimated at about 5.7 billion barrels, or about 0.5 percent of the world's total.[163]

Most of these reserves lie offshore near Mumbai and onshore in Assam state. In 1974, India discovered an offshore oil field called Bombay High, located 160 kilometers off the coast of Mumbai city. Bombay High now accounts for 30–40 percent of India's domestic oil production and fulfills 14 percent of India's oil requirements.

Perhaps the greatest infrastructure challenge India faces is meeting the demand for electricity. Given the current pace of economic growth, the country must add about 78 gigawatts of power generation capacity[164] by 2012 to today's capacity of 132 gigawatts.

The Indian power sector is characterized by nearly bankrupt state electricity boards (SEBs), low tariffs for farmers and domestic consumers, excessively high tariffs for industrial consumers, and high levels of transmission and distribution losses resulting from widespread theft. Government-owned utilities dominate the industry. Electricity in India reaches about 80 percent of the country. The country faces an average electricity shortage of 10 percent and a peak shortage of 14 percent.[165] As a result, electricity blackouts are common. Although the government has loosened limitations on foreign investment in the power sector, not many foreign investors have showed any interest.

The Retail Sector

India's highly fragmented $350 billion retail industry[166] is dominated by small, family-run stores. With thirteen million retail outlets, the unorganized retail sector provides employment to over eighteen million people, the largest employment provider after agriculture. The organized retail sector, which currently has only a 3 percent market share, is gaining traction and emerging as the fastest-growing sector of the economy. A. T. Kearney's Global Retail Development Index for 2007[167] indicates that in all, India's retail sector is expected to grow from $350 billion to $635 billion by 2015. The organized retail sector is expected to grow at a compound annual growth rate (CAGR) of 40 percent, from $8 billion to $22 billion, by 2010.

What is driving this phenomenal growth? The key drivers include the following: growing middle-class families; a rise in disposable incomes, spurred by a booming economy; rapidly changing lifestyles; growing consumerism, especially among young middle-class Indians; and the availability of better products in the marketplace. A recent McKinsey Global Institute study projected that India's middle class will grow to 583 million[168] by 2025, almost double the current population of the United States.

For generations, Indians have bought food and groceries from street vendors and crowded open markets known as *bazaars*, which allowed them to bargain and get the best value for their money. Now, with the evolution of dual-income families in the cities, people are not necessarily looking for the best price; instead, they are focusing on convenience, product choices, and better quality. Many tier-one cities in India have witnessed the growth of malls, supermarkets, and hypermarkets to cater to the growing needs of middle-class families. Several domestic corporate powerhouses are seriously contemplating entry into the retail space.

The first major domestic player to enter the retail sector is Reliance, which entered the food-retailing sector by opening eleven stores in the southern city of Hyderabad. Reliance, whose businesses range from petroleum refining to the power industry, has set an ambitious goal of achieving sales from its food retailing business to the tune of $25 billion[169] by 2011. Reliance plans to bring high-quality fresh foods to customers at affordable prices. This makes sense; in India, 40 percent of vegetables and fruits perish before they reach the markets. Reliance's latest plans have set off alarm bells within the trading community, which fears extensive job losses.

Reliance is not alone in entering the retail space. Bharti, which had great success in the telecom sector, is planning to enter the retail sector[170] by joining hands with U.S. retail giant Wal-Mart. As per current FDI policy, the stores will be wholly owned by Bharti, which will also manage the front-end of business including branding and advertising; Wal-Mart will provide expertise in creating and managing an efficient supply chain. The joint venture plans to invest $2.5 billion by 2015 and open stores across the country, providing employment for sixty thousand people.

All the leading retailers around the world, including Wal-Mart, Tesco, and Carrefour, are attempting to enter India's retail sector. While other emerging economies like Brazil, China, and Mexico allow FDI in the retail sector, India still restricts the operation of foreign multiple-brand retail stores, limiting them to cash-and-carry or franchise operations. Until India relaxes its rules, global giants like Wal-Mart, the world's number-one retailer, will have to be content with playing the role of back-end operator for domestic players. France's Carrefour, the world's second-largest retailer, has decided to postpone its plans to enter India, citing not-so-clear FDI policies. As per local media reports, Carrefour was in talks with Indian companies, including the Wadia Group. In February 2006, the Indian government took some baby steps toward opening the retail sector by permitting FDI in "single-brand" retail up to 51 percent.

Key Things to Remember About the Indian Economy:

- India has the world's twelfth-largest economy, and the third largest in Asia behind Japan and China, with total GDP of around $1 trillion.
- India's large population base of 1.1 billion people results in a relatively low per capita income of $950. (Comparative numbers include $46,040 for the United States and $2,360 for China.) Nearly 80 percent of the population lives on $2 or less a day.
- India is home to a large and burgeoning middle class of three hundred million people, equivalent to the entire population of the United States.
- From the time of its independence in 1947 to 1991, India was largely a closed economy, with high tariffs and strict controls on foreign investment. Stifling government controls and regulations constrained the growth and profitability of domestic industries. As a result, India's economy grew at an anemic rate of 3.5 percent between 1950 and 1980.
- The economic reforms launched in 1991 in the wake of a severe fiscal and balance-of-payment crisis moved India closer to a free-market enterprise system. Liberalization, deregulation, globalization, and privatization have become the new buzzwords in post-1991 India.

- The reforms deregulated domestic industries, liberalized controls on foreign trade and investment regimes, and made significant changes to monetary and fiscal policies. As a result, the Indian economy has been growing at an average annual growth rate of 8.5–9 percent, making it one of the fastest-growing major economies in the world.

- While China's economic boom has been fueled by the manufacturing sector, India's economic boom has been fueled by the services sector. India's celebrated software and outsourcing industries have created hundreds of thousands of high-paying jobs and billions in export revenues.

- India's automobile, aviation, and mobile phone industries have also witnessed tremendous growth in recent years, spurred by a red-hot economy and the rising incomes of the country's middle class. Although the economic reforms have helped bring down poverty, the benefits have not reached everyone, especially the urban poor and those living in rural areas.

- India's economic growth is constrained by inadequate infrastructure, cumbersome bureaucratic controls, and rampant corruption. There are also fears that high growth will trigger inflationary pressures and that India will sacrifice growth to keep inflation in check.

- Despite the challenges, India is likely to remain a key destination for foreign investors in the twenty-first century due to its enormous market size and potential, its skilled labor force, and low costs.

Chapter 6: Outsourcing Industry

Information technology (IT) behemoth IBM conducted its 2006 annual financial analyst meeting in Bangalore, India. Why is this significant? Because it is perhaps the first time that such a meeting was held outside the United States. The meeting was attended by IBM CEO Sam Palmisano, along with fifty of his top executives and over fifty Wall Street analysts. The event was webcast across the globe, covering over three hundred thousand IBM employees. But that's not the real story. Amidst great fanfare, Palmisano announced that IBM would invest $6 billion dollars in India over the next three years, the largest investment[171] by any international company in India to date. "India is at the epicenter of the flat world," said IBM's vice president for business development in India and China.[172]

IBM is not the only company that is bullish on India. Microsoft, Intel, and Cisco together pumped over $3.8 billion dollars into India in 2005. Many analysts are calling these investments a validation of India's capabilities in the area of IT. So why is everybody rushing to India? The simple answer is the availability of a large pool of highly skilled, English-speaking software professionals at low cost. By some estimates, India will have a pool of twenty million college graduates and one of the largest pools of computer scientists and technology professionals in the world by the end of the decade. Entry-level Indian software engineers typically make $5,000–$7,000 a year, roughly one tenth of what their Western counterparts earn but a decent wage in a country with an average per capita annual income of $950. The wage arbitrage is the main reason why global companies are ramping up their headcount in India. For instance, IBM's headcount in India increased from four hundred in 1995 to four thousand in 2000 and now stands at around forty thousand.

If past results are any indication, it is safe to assume that these investments will pay off within a short time. Microsoft is already reaping huge benefits from its past investments in India. A Microsoft development center based in Hyderabad played a key role in developing some of the new features for its newly released Vista operating system. Many U.S. companies have established tech centers in India to take advantage of the greater availability and lower cost of Indian engineers. The availability of cheap software professionals is only part of the reason why companies are investing in India. As India, helped by its booming economy, has become an attractive market in its own right, many multinationals are looking to take advantage of its vast potential market for growth.

Investments from global companies aside, the export-oriented domestic IT industry is growing at a phenomenal rate, as more and more American and European corporations are outsourcing their business activities to India. Fueled by external demand, India's IT exports are expected to reach $40 billion in 2008 and $80 billion by 2010.[173] To put this number in perspective, one needs to look at India's software export revenues in 1992, which stood at about $100 million. As a proportion of national GDP, the revenue of the Indian technology sector has grown from 1.2 percent in 1998 to an estimated 5 percent in fiscal year 2008. Companies around the world are slashing their payrolls in the United States and Europe and tapping Indian IT professionals to do everything from coding simple software applications to developing enterprise-wide business solutions.

In addition to software development, India also has attained a dominant position in the business process outsourcing (BPO) sector. This includes call centers, technical support services, and transaction processing for leading companies in banking, insurance, financial services, healthcare forms processing, and others. If China is the world's factory floor, India is now the world's back office. Although not as ubiquitous as Chinese-made toys, apparel, and other items found in neighborhood Wal-Mart stores, India's invisible hand is nevertheless present in a number of day-to-day transactions.

Four companies—Tata Consultancy Services, Infosys, Wipro, and Satyam—dominate the export-oriented domestic IT company landscape. The Indian IT companies are competing with big names in the IT services industry, such as EDS, Accenture, and IBM Global Services, on a range of services, including software application development, data warehousing, CRM, ERP, SCM package implementation, and technology infrastructure services.

The IT boom has managed to increase the living standards of millions of people by bringing in high-quality jobs. The sector has been a catalyst of India's growth and has had a significant impact on the broader Indian economy by generating substantial export earnings and tax revenues. The IT/BPO industry employs nearly two million people and represents the India's best hope for achieving economic prosperity in the twenty-first century. The new mantra from India is, "We don't need financial aid; we need work for our work-hungry software professionals."

India's IT expertise is earning recognition around the world. It is one of the few sectors where India's dominance is complete. An unbeatable mix of first-mover advantage, low costs, and deep technical and English-language skills has catapulted India to become one of the top destinations for offshoring services. Over the past decade, the IT boom cities of Bangalore and Hyderabad have figured prominently in the itineraries of several visiting heads of state. Wen Jiabao (China), Vladimir Putin (Russia), Gerhard Schroder (Germany), Tony Blair (the United Kingdom), and Calderon Hinojosa (Mexico) have all visited Bangalore. But no U.S. president or vice president has ever visited Bangalore out of fear of the potential political backlash they would face at home from opponents of outsourcing.

India's recent success as the world's number-one offshoring destination has been underpinned by the availability of a large number of low-cost, highly skilled workers. But as the supply of workers tightens and the wages rise, its advantages relative to other countries could erode. Demand for workers is boosting labor rates in the IT/BPO sector by 15 percent annually, threatening profit margins. The industry is currently facing attrition levels as high as 25–40 percent as demand for trained talent is outpacing supply.

Despite these challenges, the Indian IT industry is maturing, and the future looks bright. Global spending on IT services grew 11 percent in 2007 to $751 billion and is showing no signs of cooling down. Indian outsourcers grew revenues 38 percent in 2007, accounting for 4.1 percent of global revenue.[174]

Key Things to Know About India's IT Industry:[175]

- India's software export revenues were $100 million in 1992. In 2008, the combined export revenues of IT services, BPO, and engineering services are expected to reach $40 billion.
- The IT industry provides direct employment to two million people; IT exports account for 1.6 million jobs, or 80 percent of all IT jobs.
- The United States (61 percent) and the United Kingdom (18 percent) are the top two export markets for the Indian IT industry. Exports to continental Europe (12 percent) are also on the rise.
- The banking, financial services, and insurance (BFSI) sector (40 percent) forms the largest vertical market for Indian IT/BPO exports, followed by hi-tech/telecom (19 percent), manufacturing (15 percent), and retail (8 percent).
- India's domestic IT spending is increasing at a rapid pace. In 2008, it is expected to reach $23 billion, growing at over 40 percent over the previous year.

Table 24: NASSCOM's Top Twenty IT Exporters from India (2005–06)

Rank	Company	Rank	Company
1	TCS	11	Polaris
2	Infosys	12	Hexaware
3	Wipro	13	Mastek
4	Satyam	14	MphasiS
5	HCL	15	Siemens Information
6	Patni	16	Genpact
7	I-Flex	17	i-Gate
8	Tech Mahindra	18	Flextronics Software
9	Perot Systems (TSI Ltd)	19	NIIT
10	L & T Infotech	20	Covansys

Source: NASSCOM; Companies with Corporate Headquarters Inside India

Table 25: India's IT Industry: Financial Overview ($ Billions)

	2004	2008 (Estimated)
IT Services Exports	7.3	23.1
BPO Exports	3.1	10.9
Engineering Services, R & D	2.5	6.3
Total IT Exports	12.9	40.3
Domestic IT/BPO	3.8	11.7
Domestic Hardware	5.0	11.5
Total Domestic IT	8.8	23.2

Source: NASSCOM

A Brief History of India's Emergence as an IT Superpower

India was under British colonial rule for over two hundred years. After gaining independence in 1947, India adopted protectionist policies that discouraged foreign trade and investment.

In 1973, India passed a draconian Foreign Exchange Regulation Act, which stipulated that a foreign company could operate in India only with minority equity not exceeding 40 percent. Many overseas companies, including IBM and Coca-Cola, exited the Indian market rather than submit to the government's wishes. IBM's exit from India resulted in a void in the computer industry, which local players were eager to fill.

In the mid-1970s, Mumbai-based Tata Consultancy Services (TCS) pioneered the practice of exporting talented Indian programmers to developed countries (a practice disparagingly known as "body shopping") as an alternative to developing software in India. The initial batch of Indian programmers consisted of computer graduates from the world-renowned Indian Institute of Technology, whose graduates were eager to go to the United States and pursue the American dream due to a lack of job opportunities at home. Meanwhile, India maintained its hostile policies toward foreign investment through the 1970s and mid-1980s. Import tariffs on computer hardware and software were maintained at over 100 percent, and the computer industry never really took off—despite the presence of a large number of Indian programmers working overseas. There was little or no incentive for the overseas Indian programmers to return to India, and most people stayed in United States. This led to "brain drain."

The seeds for India's modern-day computer revolution were sown by Prime Minister Rajiv Gandhi, who took over the reins of the country in 1984. Rajiv, who was only forty years old when he became prime minister, unveiled a new computer policy that called for the substantial reduction of import tariffs on hardware and software. The policy also allowed foreign companies to set up wholly-owned units in India. Encouraged by these developments and lured by the prospect of finding cheap programmers, Texas Instruments started operations in India in 1985. Domestic firms that had been in the "body-shopping" business also started setting up software development centers in India to cater to the needs of multinational companies. This period saw the emergence of Bangalore as the hub of India's software activities. Bangalore was the natural choice due its relatively pleasant climate, cheap real estate (when compared with Mumbai), and the presence of talented and cheap computer programmers. India's IT industry got a further boost in 1991 when Prime Minister P. V. Narasimha Rao launched a series of economic reforms that opened India's doors to foreign trade and investment.

Then came the Y2K boom, which changed the face of India's software industry. Y2K, or millennium bug, hit global headlines in the mid-1990s. It was feared that computers could potentially stop working or produce erroneous results because they stored years as only two digits. As the decade progressed, nervous companies and organizations around the world undertook the arduous task of identifying and correcting computer systems to make them Y2K compliant. Facing an acute shortage of qualified software professionals at home, many American companies began looking for cheap programmers overseas. India, with its abundant supply of computer programmers, got the lion's share of Y2K-related work. Soon, planeloads of Indian programmers belonging to Indian consulting companies like TCS started arriving in the United States. The U.S. government enabled the entry of these professionals by introducing the liberal H-1 and L-1 visa regimes. In all, Indian companies earned $2 billion in cumulative export revenues from 1996 to 1999 from Y2K-related work.

At midnight on January 1, 2000, governments and organizations around the world sighed in relief as the computer systems moved into the new year without a hitch. But the real winner was India. The success of Y2K-related engagements helped establish India as the number-one location for cheap and talented programmers. When the Y2K glitch vanished, many Indian programmers stayed in the United States to take advantage of the soaring demand for IT professionals during the dot-com boom of the late 1990s, creating a large Indian community in the Silicon Valley.

Meanwhile, offshore Indian companies stepped up their offerings to attract new projects from multinational corporations. They pioneered what is now known as the "global offshore delivery model." Until the late 1990s, the majority of software projects were executed in the form of onsite services (or "body-shopping") at the client site. The advent of the Internet and a cheap telecommunications network made geographies irrelevant. This enabled Indian companies to execute projects from remote locations at lower costs. Outsourcing contracts worth billions of dollars started pouring into India, marking the birth of a new offshoring industry. In the post-dot-com crash of 2000 (when the NASDAQ lost 10 percent of its value in just one day), more and more American companies joined the offshoring bandwagon to cut costs and get better value for their money. Today, a significant chunk of Fortune 500 companies outsource work to India either through third-party vendors or through captive Indian operations.

Factors that Made India an IT Superpower

Software development is a very labor-intensive activity, and the critical raw material needed is a highly skilled workforce. India's comparative advantage is the availability of a huge pool of highly skilled, English-speaking workers at low cost. India may not have the crude oil reserves of Saudi Arabia, but it certainly has plenty of human resources. Currently, over two million people are working in the IT/BPO segment. Besides first-mover advantage, there are several factors that made India an IT superpower.

Young Workforce

For starters, India is the second most populous country in the world, with a population of over one billion people. India's population is exploding; within a few decades it is expected to surpass China as the most populous country. India's population has a median age of twenty-five. That means that nearly half of the population (or five hundred million people) is under the age of twenty-five. In comparison, the United States and China, with a median population age of thirty-seven and thirty-four, respectively, are older than India.[176]

Highly Acclaimed Higher Education System

Even though India's primary education system is in appalling shape, its higher education system is in relatively good shape, and India is clearly reaping the benefits from its past investments. India's three hundred universities and fifteen thousand colleges produce around 2.5 million graduates each year. As per some estimates, India produces 350,000–400,000 engineering graduates a year, twice the number produced by the United States.

The Indian Institute of Technology (IIT) system is India's top engineering school system, consisting of seven autonomous institutes located in various parts of the country. The admissions criterion is arguably the toughest in the world. Each year, about three hundred thousand people take an entrance exam, and only the top 1–1.5 percent is accepted. While eight applicants compete for one seat at Harvard and MIT, about seventy-five applicants battle for one seat in the IITs. Mirroring the IIT system is the Indian Institute of Management (IIM) system, India's premier business school system.

Both IITs and IIMs are owned and financed by the federal government. Many top companies in the United States are packed with IIT and IIM graduates. In addition to IITs and IIMs, India also has a large number of educational and training institutes such as the National Institute of Technology (NIT) that enjoy a good reputation. India's education system places a strong emphasis on science and mathematics, resulting in a large number of science and engineering graduates and creating a huge pipeline for IT jobs. Also, higher education is relatively affordable in India, especially in the government-run institutes. For instance, the MBA program at IIM costs about $7,500 a year. Compared that to $44,000 a year in a top business school in the United States.[177]

English-Language Proficiency

Which country has the largest number of English speakers? Until a decade ago, it was the United States. Now it is probably India. About a quarter of India's population has some ability to converse in English. That translates to about 250 million people, which is more than the 215 million English-speaking people of the United States or four times the population of the entire United Kingdom.

The English language, a legacy of colonial rule, continues to enjoy the status of an associate official language along with Hindi. India's main advantage over China in the IT sector results from the large English-speaking population. With China going all-out to make its youth proficient in English, India's dominance in the IT sector is likely to be contested in the near future.

Enviable Cost Advantage

Perhaps the biggest comparative advantage India has is the cost advantage. The starting salaries for IT engineers range from $5,000–$7,000 per year, compared to $50,000–$70,000 for a U.S.-based professional. Although these salaries are low by U.S. or European standards, they are very attractive in a county where the per capita annual income hovers around $950.

The story is even more compelling for low-end jobs such as call centers, data entry, accounting, and other back-office services. At around $1 an hour (less than one-fifth of the U.S. minimum wage) versus $10 an hour in the United States, the savings can be potentially enormous for Western companies that outsource to India. A call-center worker in the U.S. makes about $30,000 a year, while a mid-level call-center manager in India makes about $7,000 a year.

Time-Difference Advantage

India has an eight- to twelve-hour time zone difference with respect to the United States due to its unique geographic location. When it is daytime in India, it is nighttime in the United States, and vice versa.

The time-difference advantage has played a huge role in the phenomenal growth of India's outsourcing industry. Consider this. A U.S.-based company can technically work around the clock by stationing part of its workforce in India. At the end of the work shift, work can be transferred to offshore employees, who will complete the tasks while the United States sleeps. U.S. companies are using India-based call centers to provide twenty-four-hour customer service to its customers at an affordable cost.

Quality Advantage

Conventional wisdom says that quality suffers when costs are reduced. But not in India's case. The Capability Maturity Model (CMM),[178] the most respected measure of quality in the IT world, was developed by the Software Engineering Institute at Carnegie Mellon University in Pittsburgh, Pennsylvania. It is basically a software-development approach to attaining high quality. Level 5 is the highest rating that a software company can attain. More than half of the world's CMM Level 5 companies are based in India.

In addition, a large number of software vendors and BPO companies adhere to ISO 9000 and Six Sigma standards. Many companies are outsourcing to India with quality in mind, not just cost cutting. Cisco's Scheinman summed it up very well: "We came to India for the costs, we stayed for the quality, and we're now investing for the innovation."[179]

Friendly Government Policies

Although India's enviable software sector owes its existence to a small group of visionary private entrepreneurs, the government continues to play a huge role in its continued development. The reason for government involvement is simple. The software industry will soon account for 7 percent of GDP and is therefore a top-priority sector for the government. When Bill Gates, John Chambers, or any other top business leaders visit India, they routinely get an audience with the prime minister, which signifies the level of commitment and importance the government accords to the industry. Contrast that with the months of waiting that CEOs of U.S. companies endure to meet their own president. IT is on India's national agenda, and India is among the few countries in the world to have an independent department of IT within the federal government. India launched a national IT task force in the late 1990s to promote the industry in the country.

In 2000, India became only the twelfth country in the world to adopt a cyber law[180] regime, which made digital signatures legal for the first time and gave extra power to the police to combat cyber crimes. Starting in early 1991, the government began setting up Software Technology Parks (STPs), which offer state-of-the-art infrastructure and incentives to encourage export-oriented software development activities.

Lastly, the prominent role being played by India's IT association, the National Association of Software and Service Companies (NASSCOM), in India's success cannot be overestimated. With over a thousand Indian IT companies as members, NASSCOM has emerged as the voice of India's IT industry, and it closely interacts with the government in formulating national IT policies.

Indian Diaspora in the United States

Asian Indians make up less than 1 percent of the U.S. population. Yet they account for 26 percent of the United States's tech start-up companies founded by immigrants in the Silicon Valley. According to the U.S. Census Bureau, Asian Indians have the highest average income of any racial group. The Indian immigrants in the United States, especially the highly successful entrepreneurs, venture capitalists, and computer professionals, have played a huge role in promoting India as an attractive IT outsourcing destination.

Indian entrepreneurs are increasingly leveraging nonprofit networking groups such as Indus Entrepreneurs (TiE) for inspiration and money. The aim of TiE is to nurture entrepreneurs from South Asia, and it is now the world's largest not-for-profit organization for entrepreneurs.

The U.S. Outsourcing Debate

America is not new to outsourcing. First it was manufacturing; now it is services. Just as the United States created China's manufacturing boom, it has also created the IT and back-office outsourcing boom in India. The postwar years saw the relocation of manufacturing jobs from developed to low-wage developing countries, usually in Asia and the Far East, in areas such as light engineering, shoes, and apparel. Companies like Nike and Adidas are pioneers in this style of operation. Intel and Texas Instruments followed the strategy of assembling chips in wholly-owned subsidiaries in China, Malaysia, and Hong Kong.

The idea was to relegate mundane, low-skilled manufacturing work to low-wage locations while utilizing labor back home for highly skilled work like design, marketing, and project management. As a result, the GDP of developed nations such as the United States underwent a profound change from the manufacturing sector to the services sector.

In the 1990s, Western companies realized that back-office operations could be done anywhere in the world. The combination of cheap computers, the Internet, and a cheap high-speed telecommunications network has enabled Western companies to outsource work that once belonged to American workers to far-off places like India. White-collar jobs ranging from low-end call-center jobs to high-end software programming, design, and R & D jobs are being shipped to India at a steady rate.

Proponents maintain that offshoring is necessary because America and Europe do not produce enough engineers to meet their demand, and companies are forced to outsource to keep themselves afloat in this highly competitive global economy. They contend that the cost savings realized by offshoring could help companies hire more people at home. Sean Randolph, president and CEO of the Bay Area Economic Forum, rejects the notion that offshoring is a "zero-sum game" in which a job created in India is a job lost in America.[181] Steve Ballmer of Microsoft feels that outsourcing to India will benefit the United States in the long run.[182] He calls India Microsoft's second home, where the company employs the largest number of people after the United States. Opponents argue that offshoring will not only lead to job losses but also result in the drying-up of homegrown talent.

The U.S. political debate, which traditionally revolves around abortion, guns, and gay marriage, has seen the emergence of yet another polarizing issue: job losses due to outsourcing. Democrats generally take the side of U.S. workers, while Republicans support businesses' right to outsource. During the 2004 presidential campaign, Democrats threatened to impose tax penalties on companies that move jobs overseas. However, after Senator John Kerry's defeat, the issue of outsourcing lost traction.

As offshoring continues unabated, many Americans wonder what the future holds for them. Is this a temporary phenomenon, or something so big that it will eventually result in a decline in living standards? What kind of jobs can displaced workers hope to get, and at what pay? Can offshoring be stopped? Unfortunately, there are no easy answers for members of the American middle class, who bear the brunt of offshoring. It is not possible to legislate how a company spends its money. America must adjust to new realities. Offshoring makes too much business sense for companies to simply eliminate it, and many companies regard it as a routine business practice. Displaced workers may have to update their skills and possibly relocate to areas where demand is high. Author and *New York Times* columnist Tom Friedman counsels his own daughters to study harder to avoid losing their jobs to countries like India.[183] His advice should be considered against the backdrop of a recent federal study that found that 40 percent of U.S. high school seniors failed to perform at the most basic level on national math and science tests.[184]

So what has been the Bush administration's position on this issue? Gregory Mankiw, the chairperson of the White House Council of Economic Advisors, came under fire in 2004 when he publicly stated that outsourcing is a long-term plus for the economy. He was later forced to retract that statement. The Bush administration opposes the use of tariffs and tax penalties to discourage outsourcing. Even

Alan Greenspan supported this position, cautioning that protectionist measures will make matters worse. He hoped that the United States would be able to replace the lost jobs with new jobs, as it had done in the past. President Bush, on a visit to Hyderabad, remarked,[185] "We won't fear competition, we welcome competition." He added that he favors pro-growth policies such as low taxes and less regulation.

Despite the noninterventionist stance of the Bush administration, opposition to outsourcing is bound to grow as India expands its offerings from low-end coding and call-center jobs to more sophisticated jobs such as designing cars for U.S. automakers and conducting research for Wall Street firms. Alan S. Blinder, a former vice chairman of the Federal Reserve and economic adviser to President Bill Clinton, described outsourcing as a "third Industrial Revolution"; he estimates that outsourcing threatens as many as thirty to forty million jobs in the United States. "We have so far barely seen the tip of the offshoring iceberg, the eventual dimensions of which may be staggering," he wrote in *Foreign Affairs*.[186]

New Trends in Offshoring

Moving Up in the Value Chain, Moving into New Areas

Indian programmers and BPO personnel were initially deployed at the low end of the value chain, undertaking tasks such as writing simple computer code, performing data entry, and managing U.S. customers through call centers. That trend is changing very fast, and India is no longer a programming country. Downplaying their expertise in low-end coding jobs, the Big 4 Indian software companies—Infosys, Wipro, TCS, and Satyam—are turning their attention to high-end, high-margin areas such as system integration, application development, and high-end IT consulting, areas that were traditionally dominated by the likes of IBM, Accenture, Deloitte, Bearing Point, and Capgemini. The BPO space has also undergone a dramatic change.

Growing Indian Domestic Markets

The Indian outsourcing market thus far has been driven mainly by exports, but there are signs that the domestic market for IT services is also heating up, especially since the GDP growth rate is constantly clocking in at over 8 percent. Driven by investment across various sectors and increased spending by small and medium businesses, the domestic IT sector grew 22 percent in 2006, making it the fastest-growing market in the Asia-Pacific region.

While Indian outsourcing companies like Infosys are pursuing lucrative contracts abroad, global players like IBM are harnessing opportunities in Indian domestic markets. Recently, IBM won a major domestic IT contract worth $800 million over ten years from India's fifth-largest wireless operator, Idea Cellular. This is on top of the $750 million contract IBM won in 2004 from another mobile operator, Bharti Airtel.

The shape of the burgeoning Indian retail industry, worth $350 billion a year, is being transformed from unorganized family-run stores to Western-style malls and modern shopping formats. It is expected to spend $1 billion on IT services like enterprise resource planning (ERP) systems by 2010, versus the $250 million currently being spent, as per the report released by Springboard Research, an IT market research body.

Deepening Presence in Non-U.S. Markets

Indian IT offshoring companies, which still derive 60 percent of their business from the bread-and-butter U.S. market, are trying to reduce their dependency on the core market and are moving aggressively to expand their footprint in the $400 billion Western Europe IT market. Since European companies are relatively conservative and favor local vendors, Indian companies are shedding their "Indian" image and positioning themselves as truly "global" companies. For instance, Infosys has 2,500 employees based in Europe. Wipro has announced plans to increase its already strong 2,000 U.K. headcount by 500, and Satyam has been operating an IT development center in Budapest,

Hungary, since 2004. Wipro also has development centers in Brazil, China, Mexico, and Canada.

Responding to the Democrats' political outcry that they are taking jobs away from the United States, some Indian companies have begun hiring U.S.-based software engineers. Wipro has announced plans to open a software development center[187] in Atlanta, which will create over five hundred jobs, with three more facilities planned for Georgia, Texas, and Virginia.

To put the number in perspective, today only 2.5 percent of Wipro's workforce is non-Indian, and the company wants to push that to 10 percent in a few years. TCS, which has one thousand American employees on its payroll, plans to hire an additional two thousand Americans in the coming years. Though these actions will no doubt increase their cost structure, the companies will benefit from being able to bid for high-value services that may require local talent and expertise.

Problem Areas for India

The question on everybody's mind is whether India's advantages in IT are sustainable. Some recent studies indicated that it will be years before India's number-one status is seriously contested. The reason is that many Indian companies have become integrated into the business processes of their Western clients. Switching costs for these U.S. companies will be too great. The problem with the offshoring business is not a lack of demand but too much demand. Offshoring has now evolved into a long-term strategy for companies and has become a permanent fixture in business planning; demand is unlikely to slow down in the near future. The bigger question is whether India has the means and resources to meet the demand for its services.

Manpower Crunch and the Erosion of the Price Advantage

The offshoring business is growing at such a breakneck pace that IT companies around India are facing a shortage of qualified professionals. NASSCOM estimates that the offshoring business will reach $80 billion by 2010, which is still 10 percent of the potential market. The Big 3 Software companies, TCS, Infosys, and Wipro, are planning to hire a combined one hundred thousand new software professionals this year, as their businesses continue to grow at 30 percent annually. More hiring is expected from IBM, Accenture, Microsoft, and scores of other multinationals who plan to ship a chunk of their worldwide operations to India. Infosys founder Narayana Murthy called the manpower shortage the most serious problem faced by the industry.

So why is workforce availability such a big problem for India, which churns out 350,000–400,000 engineers and 2.5 million other graduates each year? The simple answer has to do with the quality of available people. Only 10 percent of graduates are believed to be "employable." For instance, Infosys gets one million applications a year but finds only a fraction of the applicants qualified. Thousands of new educational entities, including engineering colleges and software training institutes, have cropped up across the country to address the shortage of professionals. But due to the lack of qualified teachers and infrastructure a relaxing of admissions criteria, the quality of students graduating is not that great. Even those who are technically qualified often lack the basic skills required to succeed as software professionals, including communication, presentation, and language.

Recruitment is a problem, but retention is an even bigger problem. Young programmers are hopping jobs frequently in search of better pay, nicer work environments, and more opportunities to work on the hottest new technologies. Current attrition rates at blue-chip companies stand at 11–13 percent and are much higher for other lesser-known companies. The NASSCOM-Hewitt Total Rewards Study[188] concluded that many companies in the IT-enabled services sector are seeing a 100 percent attrition rate, whereas the IT sector is seeing a 75 percent attrition rate. Another study[189] revealed that more than 75 percent of IT professionals have been with their current employer for less than two years.

As a direct consequence of the manpower crunch, the industry is already seeing steady upward movement in wages at the rate of 15–

30 percent annually. Some analysts wonder if this trend will make India uncompetitive in the global market, as companies will pass on increasing labor costs to their U.S. customers. The erosion of India's cost advantage is the single-biggest threat posed by the industry; it provides an opening for other developing countries, those who were relegated to the sidelines as India grabbed a huge chunk of the market in the past decade. Ironically, some Indian players are opening up development centers in neighboring China, where software labor costs are lower than they are in India.

As the wage gap between top Indian professionals and their Western counterparts continue to narrow, more and more U.S.-based Indian software engineers with advanced degrees are seizing these unprecedented opportunities and returning home to work in India. The media is calling this new trend a "reverse drain," as opposed to "brain drain," a term used to describe the exodus of highly qualified individuals from India to Western countries. It is estimated that over sixty thousand Indian professionals have returned to Bangalore in recent years. In addition to an increase in wages, India's export-driven IT companies are also seeing an erosion in margins, due to the strengthening of the rupee against the dollar. As per Infosys, every 1 percent of appreciation impacts margins by 30–40 basis points.

Infrastructure Woes

A lack of infrastructure is another challenge faced by companies operating in India. Power outages are common in every city and state, and there is a severe lack of potable water. India's labor costs are comparable to those of China, but infrastructure costs could eat into profits. Due to the lack of an uninterrupted power supply, every company is required to maintain power backup systems and people to manage them. If you believe the government, however, help is on the way. The Indian government has made infrastructure development a top priority and has launched several projects in the private-public domain, but it will take years before tangible improvements can be seen on the ground.

Data Security Issues, Quality Issues

India-based call centers came under increased scrutiny after the media widely reported incidents of data theft. Three employees of a Bangalore-based company were arrested for allegedly stealing money to the tune of $350,000 from the bank account of a client based in New York.[190]

In addition, some U.S. companies have stopped outsourcing computer help-desk work to a prominent Indian outsourcer, citing slips in quality and customer dissatisfaction. In response, NASSCOM announced the formation of a self-regulatory body to address data security issues and assure overseas clients that India is a safe place to do business. In addition, a nationwide register of IT employees has been launched, including information such as employee photographs, fingerprints, and employment histories.

Threat from Other Countries

India's dramatic success in the IT/BPO sector has prompted other developing counties to follow its model. India's neighbors Sri Lanka and Pakistan offer advantages similar to India's, including low labor costs, widespread use of English, and similar education systems; they, too, are joining the IT bandwagon. But due to a relatively low population base and concerns about security, these nations are unlikely to pose any immediate threat to India.

Perhaps the only country that can pose a serious threat in the long run is none other than China. China, like India, has an enormous population base. However, due to the lack of English-language skills, rampant piracy, and concerns about protection for intellectual property, the offshoring business has not taken off as expected. China has a long way to go before becoming a potential alternative to India, but it has the necessary fundamentals to emerge as a preeminent destination for offshore IT services. For starters, China has a strong, educated workforce, world-class infrastructure, and government backing to push an aggressive IT offshoring agenda. China also has deep pockets, receiving $50 billion a year in foreign investment; India receives less than $6 billion a year. India currently owns anywhere between 60–80 percent of the U.S. offshoring market. But business leaders like Infosys cofounder Nandan Nilekani are cautioning Indian companies against being complacent about IT leadership.

Many Indian companies, attracted by the domestic Chinese market, are trying to establish a foothold in China. Infosys, which made headlines when it invested $65 million to open centers in Shanghai and Hangzhou, is planning to hire two thousand Chinese software professionals to compete in the Chinese domestic market. The Chinese are not sitting idle, either. Huawei, a leading Chinese networking equipment manufacturer, has set up a facility in Bangalore to tap Indian software talent and learn the tricks of the trade in India's Silicon Valley.

Some Ways the Offshore Outsourcing Landscape Is Changing[191]

The first wave of offshoring began in the early 1990s when American corporations, faced with shortages in skilled workers, sent low-end back-office software development work to India. Indian companies were viewed as nothing more than software "sweatshops." By the late 1990s, the offshoring phenomenon entered its next phase. Companies realized that they could cut costs by outsourcing to India mundane tasks such as answering customer enquiries, manning computer helpdesks, chasing credit card debts, and performing services like payroll processing, forms processing, and medical transcription.

Now offshoring has entered a new and decisive phase. Increasingly, Western white-collar jobs in hitherto unthinkable fields such as equity research, journalism, investment banking, aircraft design, pharmaceutical research, and radiography have begun to move to India at a steady pace. The new mantra has become something like, "If you don't outsource, your competitor will do it and reap cost benefits and undermine your competitive position. Therefore, you better do it."

Drug Research Outsourcing

Pharmaceutical giants Pfizer, GlaxoSmithKline, and AstraZeneca are outsourcing drug research and patient trials to India to shave costs. Eli Lilly and Novo Nordisk have outsourced some of their clinical data management services[192] to TCS. Eli Lilly is relying on India's Nicholas Piramal to convert its patented molecule into a commercial drug.[193]

Radiology Outsourcing / Offshore Radiology Services[194]

American hospitals facing a shortage of radiologists are utilizing teleradiology services offered by Indian companies like Telerad.[195] Indian doctors interpret the radiological images (x-rays, CT scans, MRIs) of American patients sent electronically and provide a preliminary diagnosis and summary report to hospitals at a fraction of the cost. Due to the time-difference advantage, Indian radiologists working their regular morning shift can cover the night shifts of American hospitals.

Aircraft Design Outsourcing / Engineering Process Outsourcing (EPO)

Aircraft manufacturers Boeing and Airbus are using hundreds of Indian engineers and software professionals for challenging tasks such as building systems to prevent airborne collisions and writing software code for next-generation cockpits. Gone are the days when Indian workers were involved only in low-end tasks such as digitizing old hand drawings. Airbus used Infosys to design part of the wing of its new A380 aircraft. India is poised to become the hub of EPO. The size of the Indian EPO market is expected to reach $30 billion annually by year 2015, from the current size of a little over $3 billion.[196]

Wall Street Outsourcing

Multinational companies have long taken advantage of India's low-cost, high-skilled talent for software development tasks. Now it's Wall Street's turn to join the outsourcing bandwagon. Wall Street firms are increasingly hiring India-based analysts to research American stocks, analyze company balance sheets, and develop sophisticated financial models, jobs that commonly pay six-figure salaries on Wall Street.

Medical Treatment Outsourcing / Medical Tourism[197]

Faced with soaring healthcare bills and a shortage of specialist physicians, a growing number of foreign patients, both insured and uninsured, are heading to India for medical, dental, and cosmetic treatments. Healthcare costs are prohibitively expensive in the United States, and patients in Canada and Britain must endure long and frustrating waiting periods for treatment in their socialized healthcare systems. India found an opening here. Private hospitals like Apollo are offering a range of treatments in their state-of-the-art medical facilities at around a tenth of the price of comparable treatments in the United States and Britain.

As if a 90 percent reduction in treatment costs is not enough motivation for foreign patients, Indian hospitals are partnering with travel agencies and tour operators to send their foreign patients to exotic vacation spots after their treatments. For instance, Sahaj Dental Clinic has a partnership with Exotique Expeditions, a Delhi-based travel management company specializing in dental tourism. You can get your root canal procedure done for $100–$200 and then visit the Taj Mahal before heading home. India's medical tourism export revenues are projected to reach $2 billion by 2012.

Media Outsourcing[198]

Wall Street news from Bangalore! This will make Lou Dobbs cringe. Maybe one day he will report from Bangalore. News agency Reuters is employing Bangalore-based financial journalists to broaden its coverage of American companies without incurring crippling costs. Many American newspapers, facing severe cost pressures and a rapid decline in readership, are looking to outsource many of their key functions to India. Ohio newspaper the *Columbus Dispatch* has outsourced its advertising design to Affinity Express in Pune, India; and the Knight Ridder Group is considering outsourcing its copyediting to India. Even the BBC has jumped in. It recently signed a ten-year, $170 million deal with Xansa, based in Chennai, to outsource its finance and accounting functions.

Tutoring Outsourcing

India is now at the forefront of the lucrative online tutoring market, which is potentially worth $12 billion annually.[199]Companies like Bangalore-based Tutorvista.com are offering tutoring in math, English, and science for as little as $2.50 an hour (or $100 per month for unlimited hours), less than the price of a latte at Starbucks. Online tutoring is enabled by a technology known as Voice over Internet Protocol (VoIP), which allows the student and tutor to talk naturally with headphone and microphone by using their personal computers. Both student and tutor share an online virtual "whiteboard" where they work out problems and do activities.[200]

Legal Outsourcing[201]

Why pay an American lawyer $250 an hour when you can get the same work done by an India-based lawyer for $50 an hour or less? Welcome to the world of legal outsourcing, one of the newest growth areas. Forrester Research predicts that the offshore legal services market will grow to over $4 billion by 2015 and that more than seventy-nine thousand U.S. legal jobs will be offshored.[202] Mindcrest, an Indian legal process outsourcer (LPO) in operation since 2001, has its roster filled with 460 lawyers who perform everything from mundane document preparation and review to contract management for its Fortune 1000 clients.

Key Domestic Players

India's export-oriented domestic IT and BPO landscape is dotted with close to three thousand companies, both big and small, catering to the needs of nearly all Fortune 500 corporations and hundreds of mid-sized companies around the world. The domestic industry has achieved a whopping average annual growth rate of 40 percent, as diverse businesses from the United States and Europe have outsourced IT functions and back-office tasks to take advantage of low-cost, high-skilled workers.

The Big 4 companies, TCS, Infosys, Wipro, and Satyam, have rapidly evolved into established global players, a fact that all recent surveys confirm. The third annual Forbes Asia Fabulous 50 List featured the top four companies among the top fifty Asian companies based on criteria such as long-term profitability, sales and earnings growth, stock price appreciation, and projected earnings. The latest 2008 Global Outsourcing 100,compiled by the International Association of Outsourcing Professionals (IAOP), featured five Indian firms: Infosys (ranked 3), TCS (6), Wipro (7), Genpact (9), and Tech Mahindra (10) are among the top ten.

Table 26[203]: 2008 Global Outsourcing One Hundred: Featured Indian Companies

Rank	Company	Rank	Company
3	Infosys	36	Cambridge
6	Tata Consultancy Services	40	ITC Infotech
7	Wipro	42	KPIT Cummins
9	Genpact	46	Patni
10	Tech Mahindra	53	Zensar
11	HCL Technology	54	MindTree
16	Mastek	56	MphasiS
19	WNS Global Services	62	Aditya Birla Minacs
22	Hexaware	73	Firstsource Solutions
26	ExlService	84	vCustomer
28	24/7 Customer		

Source: International Association of Outsourcing Professionals

It is true that the combined annual revenue of India's IT giants is significantly less than their global peers like Accenture or EDS. But the market capitalization numbers tell a different story. The combined market value of India's four IT giants is 5.5 times their combined annual revenues, as against less then 2 times for their global peers. The market capitalization numbers assume importance in deals like mergers and acquisitions. An acquiring company is expected to pay a premium over the market value to buy control of another company. The point is that the big Indian firms have substantially grown in value and will be very expensive to acquire. For instance, if IBM wants to acquire Infosys, it has to shell out a minimum of $26 billion, plus a premium.

Table 27: India's Big Four Versus Global IT Companies

Company	Revenue ($ Billions)	Employees	Market Cap ($ Billions)	Market Cap/ Revenue Ratio
TCS	4.3	89,419	27.6	6.4
Infosys	4.2	91,187	25.9	6.1
Wipro	4.3	82,122	20.1	4.4
Satyam	1.9	51,000	9.2	4.8
Big 4 Total	15.0	313,728	82.8	5.5
Accenture	23.3	170,000	23.7	1.0
EDS	22.3	139,500	12.3	0.6
IBM	101.0	386,588	178.0	1.8

Source: Yahoo! Finance, May 29, 2008; TCS Data from Forbes

Infosys

Infosys Technologies, based in Bangalore, is one of India's leading and most widely admired IT services export companies. The company provides a broad range of back-office business services, including custom software application development, systems integration, IT consulting, business process management, and engineering. Established in 1981, Infosys grew at a snail's pace during its first decade, finishing 1991 with revenues of $4 million. With the liberalization of the Indian economy in the 1990s, the company's export-oriented business grew rapidly, capitalizing on the explosive demand for IT outsourcing from Western companies seeking to cut costs and improve operational efficiency.

The company is one of the pioneers of the global delivery model for IT services outsourcing, which has helped corporations cut costs, deliver value, and become globally competitive by leveraging the workforce from low-cost countries. Infosys grew at a compound annual growth rate (CAGR) of 70 percent in the 1990s and 40 percent in the five-year period 2003–07. In 1999, Infosys became the first Indian company to be listed on the NASDAQ. The company currently has a market capitalization of $26 billion, more than the combined market value of Ford Motor and General Motors.

Key Things to Know About Infosys:

- Infosys was established in 1981 with a capital of $250 (in the current exchange rate) by seven engineers led by N. R. Narayana Murthy and Nandan Nilekani.
- Fueled by the global demand for IT outsourcing services and helped by India's economic liberalization policies, Infosys revenues grew exponentially from about $4 million in 1991 to $4 billion in 2008.
- Infosys derives its revenues from its more than five hundred global clients. Twenty-four of its clients contribute $50 million each. It derives 90 percent of its revenues from the United States and Europe. India contributes to only 1 percent of its revenues.
- In 1998, Infosys employed 2,605 workers. Today, ten years later, Infosys employee base stands at 92,187 (a thirty-five-fold increase). Infosys is one of the hardest companies to get into. It receives close to 1 million job applications each year accepts just 2.3 percent.

- The Infosys workforce is amazingly young, with 86 percent of its employees under thirty and 99 percent under forty.

Table 28: Infosys Summary

Year	Employees	Revenue ($ Millions)	Net Income ($ Millions)
1996	1,172	27	7
2000	5,389	203	61
2004	25,634	1,063	270
2008	91,187	4,176	1,155

Source: Infosys Annual Statements, SEC Filings

Tata Consultancy Services (TCS)

Tata Consultancy Services (TCS) is India's oldest software services company and the only one not based in Bangalore. Established in Mumbai in 1968, the same year Intel was founded, TCS offers a broad range of services, comprising software application development, consulting, BPO, and engineering. TCS is part of India's venerable $55 billion Tata Group, whose interests range from steel and automobile manufacturing to energy and chemical production. Like Infosys, TCS benefited as American and European companies began outsourcing service jobs to India to cut costs. Fueled by a record number of client wins in the past decade, TCS ramped up its workforce from under ten thousand in 1996 to ninety thousand in 2007. It has now become a force that is taking on global firms like IBM, Accenture, and EDS. TCS has been very successful in setting up near-shore development centers to capture business from companies that may be risk-averse to offshoring to India. TCS now has operations in more than forty countries, and it counts seven of the Fortune Top Ten companies among its clients.

Key Things to Know About TCS:

- TCS is a leading provider of IT consulting and outsourcing services. It is Asia's largest IT services company in revenues and profits.
- TCS is considered the crown jewel of the Tata Group, one of India's largest and most respected business conglomerates with annual revenues in excess of $55 billion and market capitalization of $64 billion.
- TCS's profits immensely helped the Tata Group's finances. TCS, Tata Steel, and Tata Motors account for 75 percent of the Tata group's revenues and profits.
- In 2003, TCS became the first of the Indian outsourcers to cross the $1 billion revenue mark. Four years later, TCS's revenues quadrupled to reach $4 billion in March 2007. The American market accounts for 62 percent of TCS's revenues.[204]
- TCS serves clients in almost all business verticals, including banking, insurance, financial services, manufacturing, energy and utilities, retail and consumer goods, transportation, telecom, healthcare, life sciences, media, and entertainment.

Wipro

Wipro is India's third-largest software services exporter, behind TCS and Infosys. The company originated as a maker of vegetable oil; Wipro stands for Western India Vegetable Products Limited. In the 1970s and 1980s, the company diversified into many areas, including lighting, soaps, and computers, before settling on IT services as its core business. Today, Wipro is a $4.3 billion IT services behemoth, providing a comprehensive range of IT services, software solutions, BPO services, IT consulting, and R & D services to companies around the world.

In 1999, Wipro became the first IT services provider in the world to achieve SEI-CMM Level 5, the highest level of quality certification. SEI-CMM is widely accepted in the software industry as a standard for measuring the maturity and effectiveness of software processes. Although software services still account for the largest percentage of

Wipro's revenue, the company has also become the world's largest independent provider of R & D services for companies. Wipro's R & D services division works with nine of the top ten telecom companies, six of the top ten mobile phone manufacturers, and with all of the top semiconductor and computer companies.

Key Things to Know About Wipro:

- Wipro was founded in 1945 as a vegetable oil company. After the founder's death in 1966, his son, Azim Premji, an electrical engineering graduate from Stanford University, diversified the business and built the company into a global IT outsourcing giant.

- Wipro is largely a family-owned business like Tata and Reliance. Azim Premji owns about 80 percent of Wipro's stock, valued at $12.7 billion, making him one of the richest people in the world.[205] Wipro's ADS started trading on the New York Stock Exchange in 2000.

- In 2001, Wipro became the first IT services company in the world to achieve SEI-CMM Level 5, the highest level of quality certification.[206]

- Wipro is the world's largest third-party R & D provider, with clients from telecom, semiconductor, and computer companies. Wipro is also India's leading offshore BPO provider.

- Although Wipro is largely dependent on mature markets like the United States and Europe, it is diversifying the geographic mix of its business. It has big expansion plans for China and Latin America.

Global Companies with a Presence in India

Many multinational companies, taking their cue from offshoring pioneers like Texas Instruments, Motorola, British Airways, American Express, and General Electric, have set up captive product development centers, back-office centers, and R & D facilities in India during the past decade. They are using India-based centers to fuel next-generation products for their parent companies. Microsoft and Oracle are among the top software companies with a significant presence in India.

The Microsoft India Development Center (MIDC) in Hyderabad is the company's largest product development center outside its headquarters in Redmond, Washington. The MIDC is touted as the company's strategic center of innovation and incubation. It has already filed 180 patents in the past three years and has created products that impact millions of its customers worldwide. Oracle, world's largest enterprise software company, has two development centers in India that contribute to core software development across the entire Oracle product family. Companies like Microsoft and Oracle are expanding their footprint in India to lower their software development costs and leverage India's world-class software development skill base.

Semiconductor-maker Advanced Micro Devices (AMD) is expanding its R & D center in Hyderabad and aims to focus on intellectual property creation in the areas of next-generation consumer electronics, graphics capabilities, and microprocessors. But India also holds great promise as a domestic market for these companies. Today, India is Oracle's fourth-largest market in the Asia Pacific area, up from its standing several years ago as tenth largest.

In addition to software firms, high-end IT consulting firms like IBM, Accenture, and EDS are aggressively moving into India to establish low-cost offshore services delivery capabilities and improve their competition against Indian outsourcing giants TCS, Infosys, and Wipro. While some have taken the organic route, others have relied on acquisitions to boost their presence in India. French IT services giant Capgemini's buyout of Kanbay and EDS's acquisition of a majority stake in MphasiS has helped the two companies boost their service delivery from India.

Global investment is also starting to pour into India's fledgling telecom and IT manufacturing sectors. SemIndia is teaming up with AMD to set up a $3 billion semiconductor fabrication plant, the first of its kind, near Hyderabad. India wants to replicate the success of Taiwan and China in this area and grab a slice of the $226 billion global chip market.[207]Networking giant Cisco announced a major investment initiative totaling $1 billion, its largest investment outside the United

States in scope and size. Finnish mobile handset-maker Nokia has invested $200 million to set up its first handset manufacturing plant in India.

Although the presence of foreign firms in India is on the rise, there are growing signs that some firms are scaling back on captive BPO centers[208] in favor of third-party service providers, due to spiraling costs and high attrition rates. British Airways spun off its Indian BPO (now known as WNS Holdings) in 2002, and General Electric divested its back-office captive GECIS (now known as Genpact) to U.S. private equity firms Oak Hill and General Atlantic Partners[209] in 2004.

Dell

Dell's India operations mainly consist of customer contact centers (offshore call centers), which provide technical support to its customers based in the United States, Europe, the Middle East, and Africa. It currently employs thirteen thousand people in India and is expected to increase that number to twenty thousand. The company is also a big player in India's commercial market with its server and storage business. With the Indian PC market poised to grow at a rapid rate, Dell has set up a manufacturing facility at Sriperumbudur, near Chennai, to manufacture PCs, laptops, and computer peripherals for the domestic market.

Accenture

Global management consultant and outsourcing company Accenture has significantly ramped up its presence in India since setting up its first Indian delivery center in 2001 to lower costs and compete with offshoring companies in their own backyard. The company's headcount in India is expected to reach thirty-five thousand[210] by fiscal year 2008. Accenture considers India the crown jewel of its global delivery network, which serves clients around the world through a variety of technology and service offerings.

Intel

Intel, the world's largest chip manufacturer, employs three thousand engineers and software professionals in its India Development Center (IDC) in Bangalore, considered its largest nonmanufacturing site outside the United States. In 2005, Intel announced that it would invest more than $1 billion in India over five years to expand R & D and sales operations.

Motorola

Motorola, a Fortune 100 global communications leader, has developed India as a global hub for cutting-edge R & D work. It currently employs three thousand software engineers in its Bangalore and Hyderabad R & D centers. Motorola recently inaugurated a $43 million mobile phone plant near Chennai, in an attempt to boost its market share in one of the world's fastest-growing mobile markets, currently dominated by Nokia, LG, and Samsung.

Microsoft Corp.

Microsoft, which began its Indian operations in 1990, has expanded rapidly, employing more than five thousand people across six business units. In 2005, Bill Gates announced a $1.7 billion investment in India, focusing on innovating in and for India.

The MIDC in Hyderabad is the second-largest development center outside the United States facility in Redmond. The MIDC, which currently employs 1,400 engineers and software professionals, has played a critical role in Microsoft's global product development initiatives and future product innovations.[211]

Cisco

Cisco, the leading supplier of networking equipment for the Internet, has recently selected India as the site for the Cisco Globalization Center, aimed at driving the company's worldwide expansion. The company also announced that it is moving 20 percent of its top global executives to India.

Cisco first established an R & D facility in India in 1998 as an extension of its global R & D center based in San Jose. Cisco plans to invest $1.2 billion in India within the next six years and double its headcount to six thousand employees during that same period.

Hewlett-Packard

Hewlett-Packard (HP), which began its operations in India in 1988, is now the leader in India's burgeoning PC market, with a 15 percent market share. HP has two manufacturing sites, Bangalore and Pantnagar, and a laboratory in Bangalore.

With the PC market expected to grow at an annual rate of 25 percent for the next decade or so, India is emerging as the key battleground for global computer-makers like HP, Lenovo, Dell, and Acer.

IBM

International Business Machines Corporation (IBM), or "Big Blue," is India's largest foreign employer, with an employee base of 53,000 people, a total that represents 15 percent of its global workforce of 356,000 people.[212]

IBM has hired thousands of engineers and software engineers (at the rate of a thousand new employees a month) since unveiling its three-year, $6 billion investment plan in 2007 to set up new research facilities and expand its outsourcing centers in India. IBM is rapidly expanding in India to fend off competition from low-cost Indian IT services providers like Infosys, TCS, and Wipro, who are increasingly grabbing business from its worldwide technology consulting business. It also wants to capitalize on opportunities in the fast-growing domestic Indian market. In 2004, IBM acquired Daksh, an Indian BPO and call-center vendor, to build operational capabilities in India.

General Electric

A majority of businesses of General Electric (GE), a $170 billion, U.S.-based conglomerate, have a presence in India. The John F. Welch Technology Center (JFWTC), inaugurated in Bangalore in September 2000, houses state-of-the-art laboratories and facilities to conduct R & D for GE businesses worldwide. The center's employee base has grown from 275 in 2000 to close to 3,000 employees today.

The Bangalore R & D center is among the four GE centers of excellence, with the other three in Niskayuna, New York; Shanghai, China; and Munich, Germany.[213]

Electronic Data Systems (EDS)

Electronic Data Systems (EDS), a $20+ billion technology services industry leader, presently has a fully owned subsidiary in India with operations in Chennai and Gurgaon. In 2006, EDS acquired a majority stake in the Bangalore-based offshore IT services provider MphasiS, boosting its headcount in India from three thousand to fourteen thousand. The move was intended to bolster its global talent pool in software development and IT outsourcing and establish low-cost offshore services delivery capability. It plans to further ramp up its headcount to between twenty-five thousand and thirty thousand by 2008.

Adobe

Publishing software-maker Adobe, whose PDF file format is the de facto standard for secure electronic document exchange, established its India operations in 1998 with a state-of-the-art facility at Noida, near New Delhi. Adobe's India center played a key role in the development of products like PageMaker and Acrobat Readers, used in mobile devices. The company currently employs six thousand people in India.

Adobe's India operations will likely get a further boost with the appointment of India-born Shantanu Narayen as president and CEO in December 2007.

Oracle Corporation[214]

Oracle has a significant presence in India, with two development centers in Bangalore and Hyderabad and sales and marketing offices in six other cities. The Bangalore center began its operations in 1994, and the Hyderabad center opened four years later. Oracle is among the first multinational companies to establish core software development operations in India to support its global product development strategy. The company's Indian headcount is expected to reach ten thousand in the near future.

India is Oracle's fourth-largest market in the Asia Pacific area in terms of revenue, up from tenth-largest a few years ago. The company has made investments to the tune of $2 billion since 2001 and bought a majority stake in i-flex, the Indian banking software company.

IT Boom Towns of India

When Silicon.com recently assembled a panel of experts, consisting of the world's most respected CIOs, entrepreneurs, and tech writers, to put together a list of the world's Top Twenty Tech Hotspots for 2008, the panel picked four Indian cities—Bangalore, Chennai, Pune, and Hyderabad—as four of most innovative and influential locations for technology development. The Silicon Valley (the Santa Clara Valley, to the southeast of San Francisco) is still the hottest of all the Tech Hotspots, but its reign is increasingly being challenged by Bangalore, number two on the list.

Table 29: 2008 World's Top Twenty Tech Hotspots

1	Silicon Valley	8	Tel Aviv	15	Moscow
2	Bangalore	9	Seoul	16	Hong Kong
3	London	10	Beijing	17	Hyderabad
4	Tokyo	11	Chennai	18	New York
5	Boston	12	Pune	19	Sydney
6	Cambridge	13	Singapore	20	Shenzhen
7	Shanghai	14	Helsinki		

Source: Silicon.com

At present, close to 90 percent of India's IT workforce is based in top cities like Bangalore, Hyderabad, and Chennai. Just about every major technology company in the world has operations in one of these cities. Their main attraction is the availability of a large pool of IT workers. Consider this. Four Indian states, Andhra Pradesh, Tamil Nadu, Karnataka, and Maharashtra, account for 763 engineering colleges (or 60 percent of all of India's engineering institutions), providing admission to a quarter million engineering students each year.[215]

Table 30: India's Engineering Schools

State	Major City	# of Schools	Annual Intake	% Total
Andhra Pradesh	Hyderabad	236	82,970	19
Tamil Nadu	Chennai	254	80,217	18
Maharashtra	Mumbai, Pune	155	48,250	11
Karnataka	Bangalore	118	46,375	11
India Total		1346	439,689	100

Source: All India Council for Technical Education (AICTE)

But as the top cities run out of space and frustration grows at congestion, high costs of living, and increasing wages, many companies are turning to tier-two cities like Pune, Kolkota, Gurgaon, Jaipur, and Coimbatore to expand operations. Pune, India's eighth-largest city, located 120 kilometers from Mumbai, is now home to dozens of IT companies. Kolkota, once written off as a dying city, is witnessing a major economic rejuvenation due to the rapid development of the IT industry, spurred by the investment-friendly policies of its state government. A burgeoning BPO industry has made Gurgaon, a satellite town of New Delhi, the call-center and BPO capital of India.

Bangalore

Bangalore, widely known as India's Silicon Valley, is at the center of India's IT boom. All major technology companies, including Indian giants Infosys and Wipro, have operations in Bangalore. The city's population has grown rapidly, from 2.8 million in 1990, when the hi-tech boom began, to 5.6 million today, making it Asia's fastest-growing city.

The city's swift and sensational transformation from a sleepy city sought after by pensioners into a bustling IT center has taken a heavy toll on its already creaking infrastructure. Traffic gridlock has become the norm, pollution has increased, the cost of living has skyrocketed, and city development has become chaotic. The city's long-awaited new international airport has recently become operational, bringing some hope to travelers. Bangalore's preeminent position is under threat due to the rising costs of labor and real estate and cheap alternatives in other cities like Chennai and Hyderabad. With an average room rate running at 13,341 rupees per night (over $300), Bangalore is among the world's five most expensive cities[216] in terms of hotel rates, after Moscow, New York City, Dubai, and Paris. At present, however, Bangalore is arguably the most happening place on earth.

Key Things to Know About Bangalore:

- Bangalore is the undisputed IT capital of Asia, with nearly 1,500 companies employing nearly half a million software professionals and engineers. Tens of thousands of new jobs are being created in Bangalore each year.

- Bangalore's main attraction is the high density of low-cost, highly skilled, English-speaking IT workers. Office space in Bangalore is dominated by foreign multinationals.
- With an estimated population of 5.6 million, Bangalore is one of India's most populous cities. The city's population is expected to reach 10 million by 2015.
- Bangalore also has the highest average income in India, and it is the favorite offshore destination in the Asia Pacific area, according to a study by Interactive Data Corporation.[217]
- Long before the IT boom, Bangalore was known as India's premier center for defense and space research due its moderate weather and reputable educational institutions.
- Electronic City is Bangalore's hi-tech hub, home to IT giants like Infosys, Wipro, Hewlett-Packard, and Satyam.
- In addition to software development, Bangalore is also a major hub for engineering and high-end R & D in sectors like biotechnology, pharmaceuticals, electronics, and automobiles. A large number of American companies have their engineering and development centers in Bangalore.
- The city was officially renamed Bengalaru by the state government in 2006, joining the list of other cities like Bombay (now Mumbai), Calcutta (now Kolkota), and Madras (now Chennai) that reverted to their pre-colonial names. But most people still call it Bangalore.
- Bangalore faces several challenges, including overcrowding, gridlocked roads, pollution, and high cost of living.

Hyderabad

Hyderabad, a sprawling four-hundred-year-old southern Indian metropolis in Andhra Pradesh state with a population of 5.5 million people, became a major hub for software and IT in the 1990s, second only to Bangalore. Hyderabad Information Technology Engineering Consultancy City (HITEC City), a major technology township that was inaugurated in 1998, is at the center of the city's IT boom. In 2004, Gartner, in its report "IT Outsourcing to India—Analysis of Cities,"[218] rated Hyderabad high on account of its improving infrastructure and the availability of a highly skilled workforce.

Key Things to Know About Hyderabad:

- Nicknamed "Cyberbad," the historic city of Hyderabad is regarded as the second most prominent technology hot spot of India, after Bangalore.
- Located at the gateway between northern and southern India, Hyderabad is a melting pot of different cultures, religions, and ethnic groups.
- Hyderabad is home to Microsoft's biggest campus outside the United States. Satyam, the Indian IT giant, has major operations in the city.
- The city has been selected as the site for a new $3 billion AMD-backed semiconductor manufacturing facility known as Fab City.
- Besides the IT industry, the city is emerging as a biotechnology and pharmaceutical hub. Hyderabad's Genome Valley is India's first biotech hub that provides state-of-the-art infrastructure for biotech companies.

Chennai

Chennai (formerly Madras) is the state capital of Tamil Nadu, the fourth-larges2t city in India, and India's second-biggest exporter of IT services. Compared to Bangalore, it offers better physical infrastructure and a low-cost advantage. Chennai's IT industry consists of over a thousand companies, employing around 150,000 IT professionals. Attracted by tax benefits, relatively cheap skilled labor, and infrastructure advantages, many global companies, including prominent automakers and telecom giants, have set up manufacturing facilities in and around Chennai.

Chapter 7: Foreign Relations

India has followed a largely independent foreign policy since gaining its independence from Britain sixty years ago. The architect of India's foreign policy was Prime Minister Jawaharlal Nehru, who emerged as one of the most influential global leaders and statesmen of his time. India attained its freedom in 1947, toward the end of World War II and at the beginning of the cold war, which polarized the world in western and eastern blocks. Nehru, an idealist, did not want to align India with any particular block; instead, he wanted to cultivate relations with all the countries of the world. Nehru's vision led him to create the Non-Aligned Movement[219] in 1961. Nehru's efforts in the international arena enhanced India's prestige and visibility, especially in the developing world.

The Nehru era, which lasted seventeen years, was marked by a war with Pakistan over Kashmir, peace overtures to China throughout the 1950s, and a brief border war with China in the early 1960s. Other highlights of the Nehru era include a special relationship that India cultivated with the Soviet Union, which remains strong even today. This relationship was mainly driven by economic and security imperatives. At the time of independence, India's economic needs were enormous. With generous help from the Soviet Union, India built a massive industrial base from scratch.

India also maintained good relations with the United States during the Nehru era, although military relations did not take off. Unlike neighboring Pakistan, India refused to become part of the Western strategy of isolating the Soviet Union. The United States helped India economically and helped launch its nuclear power plants under President Eisenhower's Atoms for Peace Initiative.[220]

The border war with China in 1962 was a major turning point in India's foreign policy. China easily prevailed over the ill-equipped and underprepared Indian army. Nehru had just brokered his numerous peace deals with China and did not feel it was necessary to substantially enhance military capability. In the aftermath of the China war debacle, India began to beef up its armed forces. Since military help from the United States and the West was not forthcoming, India leaned heavily on the Soviet Union to procure military hardware for its armed forces. This eventually pushed India firmly into the Soviet camp, even though it did not wholly embrace or subscribe to Soviet ideology. Ironically, democratic India found it easier to work with communist Soviet Union than with democratic America, mainly because Soviet help came without any strings attached. Similarly, democratic America found a more suitable ally in military-ruled Pakistan than in democratic India, which was bent upon charting its own independent foreign policy. By the end of the 1960s, cold war politics slowly crept in to southern Asia. The Soviet Union sided with India, while the United States sided with Pakistan.

Nehru's death in 1964 marked an end of an era for India's foreign policy. Nehru was devastated by India's humiliation at the hands of the Chinese military. It was a personal blow because he had invested a lot of time cultivating a relationship with China. After all, India was the first noncommunist country to recognize China, and Nehru vigorously supported China's early entry into the United Nations fold.

Prime Minister Lal Bahadur Shastri replaced Nehru, and during his brief tenure, Pakistan made an unsuccessful attempt to wrest control of Kashmir from India. Perhaps Pakistan was testing the resolve of India's new political leadership. Pakistan was surprised when Shastri responded forcefully by opening another front in Punjab and bringing the Pakistani city of Lahore under mortar fire. The war ended when the leaders of India and Pakistan signed a cease-fire agreement brokered by the Soviet Union in Tashkent (in modern Uzbekistan). Before the ink dried on the agreement, Shastri died of a heart attack, plunging India into a political crisis.

Nehru's daughter Indira Gandhi took over the reins of the country in 1966. Indira guided India's foreign policy for the next eighteen years, with the exception of two years when she was out of power. In 1971, India won a major war against archrival Pakistan, leading to the creation of a new nation, Bangladesh, in the erstwhile region of East Pakistan. Indira Gandhi also tried to increase India's profile internationally by taking forceful positions against apartheid in South Africa and Israel's occupation of Palestinian territories. In 1974, India refused to play South Africa in the final of the Davis Cup tennis tournament to protest against its apartheid policies, handing it a walkover victory.[221]

India also extended its support to the Palestinian cause and became the first nation to allow Yasser Arafat's Palestinian Liberation Organization (PLO) to open an office in New Delhi. India's anti-Israel stance was part of an effort to ensure uninterrupted oil supplies from the Middle East and curb Pakistan's influence in the region. It should be noted that India recognized the state of Israel in 1950 but did not establish full diplomatic relations until 1992.

In 1974, India upped the ante by conducting its first-ever nuclear test at Pokhran, becoming the first nation outside the five permanent members of the United Nations Security Council to conduct a nuclear test. Why was this significant? India was the first country to propose a global ban on all nuclear testing in 1954. Also, it flew in the face of the nuclear Non-Proliferation Treaty (NPT), which came into effect in 1970. Only three states refused to sign or ratify the treaty: India, Pakistan, and Israel. So, legally speaking, India did not violate any international laws by going nuclear. India considers the NPT a discriminatory measure and ineffective in achieving global nuclear disarmament. India had other reasons to go nuclear. Throughout the 1960s, India's neighbor and rival China made considerable progress in developing nuclear weapons. China conducted its first nuclear test in 1964 and followed up with forty-three additional nuclear tests, including its first hydrogen bomb, in 1967.[222]

At the outset, it appeared that the West did not mind China conducting its tests. Instead, China was rewarded. Nixon was eager to extend a hand of friendship to China, and the People's Republic of China got a further boost when it got its permanent membership in the coveted U.N. Security Council. Perhaps the thinking was that a nuclear test by India would enhance its prestige and visibility in the world and also serve as a deterrent against future attacks from China. If that was indeed the intention, Indira did not show it. Indira code-named the nuclear project "The Smiling Buddha," and to signify her peaceful intentions, the nuclear blasts coincided with a holiday marking the birthday of Gautama Buddha, founder of Buddhism.

India's decision to test the nuclear bomb attracted worldwide condemnation, as it dealt a blow to the new NPT regime. Canada reacted angrily by cutting off any further nuclear cooperation with India. Canada's reaction was predictable because India's nuclear test had used plutonium produced in the Canadian-supplied CIRUS research reactor. Reaction from Pakistan was equally forceful.[223] Then Pakistani prime minister Bhutto said, "If India builds the bomb, we will eat grass or leaves, we go hungry. But we will get one of our own."[224] True to his words, Bhutto jump-started Pakistan's nuclear program in 1976 in direct reaction to India's program. India, for its part, declared a unilateral moratorium on further tests.

Throughout the 1980s, India deftly steered clear of cold war hostilities by maintaining good relations with both the United States and Soviet blocks. To underscore this point, one has to look at India's participation in the Summer Olympics. India did not follow the West-led sixty-four-nation boycott of the 1980 Moscow Olympics in protest against the Soviet invasion of Afghanistan. (In return, India was rewarded with a gold medal in field hockey, since none of the medal-winning nations from the 1976 Olympics participated.) Subsequently, India did not follow its ally the Soviet Union's call to boycott the 1984 Los Angeles Olympics. India also kept its nonalignment credentials intact by conducting a Non-Alignment Movement (NAM) summit in 1983, attended by none other than Cuban leader Fidel Castro. Rajiv Gandhi, who succeeded Indira Gandhi as prime minister in 1984, tried to cultivate a friendly relationship with the United States without antagonizing the Soviet Union. Rajiv Gandhi visited the Reagan White House twice during his five-year tenure. But he visited Moscow twice as many times to keep the Soviet friendship intact.[225]

Meanwhile, a profound transformation in global power equations was taking place, starting with the reunification of Germany brought about by the fall of the Berlin Wall and culminating with the dissolution of the mighty Soviet Union. India was forced to review its foreign policy due to the harsh realities of the times. During the first Persian Gulf War of 1991, India did the unthinkable. It briefly allowed refueling facilities for the U.S. military transport aircraft traveling to and from the Persian Gulf, in direct contradiction of its official neutral stance. All hell broke loose when the mainstream media got wind of this operation, and the government had to back down under pressure from the major political parties.

India, under Prime Minister P. V. Narasimha Rao, launched a slew of new foreign policy initiatives during the early to mid-1990s. India refined its exclusive relationship with Russia by replacing the 1971 Treaty of Friendship with a new diluted treaty, which did not include any security clauses. In 1992, India finally established diplomatic relations with Israel. It did not make sense for India to maintain its traditional opposition toward Israel at a time when both Israeli and Palestinian leaders were engaged in peace talks. Today, Israel has emerged as the one of the biggest suppliers of military hardware to India. The two-way trade between the nations now stands at $3.3 billion.[226]

India also embarked on a new "Look East"[227] initiative, which brought it closer to the ASEAN nations. The move was intended to gain market access and counter China's growing political and military influence in the region. Today, this initiative is paying rich dividends for India, which has become a "full dialogue partner" of ASEAN. In June 2007, India and Thailand agreed to conclude a landmark free-trade agreement (FTA) by 2010. Prime Minister Surayud Chulanont called India Thailand's new major market and a key engine of the rising Asian economy.[228]

After the Narasimha Rao administration, it was Prime Minister Vajpayee who had a profound effect on India's foreign policy. Vajpayee, who belonged to the nationalist Bharatiya Janata Party (BJP), started with a bang by ordering nuclear tests in May 1998, within three months of assuming office. The immediate provocation was the test-firing of a 1,500-kilometer-range, India-specific, intermediate-range ballistic missile by Pakistan. The nuclear tests confirmed India as a major power in the world, one that the world could no longer ignore. Although India faced the wrath of the international community, the nuclear tests helped kick-start a strategic dialogue between India and the United States.

Why did the United States engage India in a strategic dialogue? The main reason was the burgeoning trade relationship between the countries, which doubled from $7 billion in 1993 to $14 billion in 2000, making the United States India's largest trading partner.[229] The United States also realized that the nuclear genie was out of the bottle and there was nothing to be done about it.

Prime Minister Manmohan Singh, who took office in 2004, has built on the foreign policy successes of the 1990s and 2000s. The past five years or so have been arguably the best years for India in terms of foreign policy. It was able to forge a close relationship with the United States without antagonizing its traditional ally, Russia. New Delhi has been working to improve relations not only with the United States but also with other major power centers, including Europe, Japan, China, and the nations of southeast Asia. China has decided to put contentious issues on the back burner to pursue peace initiatives with India. Trade between the nations is growing at breakneck speed. Even ties with Pakistan are improving. Pakistan is increasingly unable or unwilling to support the jihadi groups operating on Indian-controlled Kashmir. This bodes well for continued peace in the region.

India's relations with other nations of southern Asia are also on the mend. Leaders of the twenty-two-year-old regional grouping South Asian Association of Regional Cooperation (SAARC), who met in Delhi as part of a regional summit in April 2007, agreed to create a South Asian Free Trade Area (SAFTA) by 2012. The group currently consists of eight members: India, Pakistan, Bangladesh, Sri Lanka, Nepal, Bhutan, Maldives, and Afghanistan.

Everyone from Australia to Germany, Mexico to Japan is courting India, and India is increasingly flexing its muscles on the international scene. India's goal of attaining a permanent seat in the United Nations Security Council remains elusive. Ironically, it is India's new friend Washington who is opposing such a move. When Kofi Annan retired as U.N. secretary general, India tried unsuccessfully to get its candidate Shashi Tharoor elected. Once again, Washington thwarted India's move and instead supported Ban Ki-moon's candidacy.[230] Likewise, India will probably have to wait a few more decades before it is considered for membership in the elite G-8 group of industrialized nations. The G-8 countries include the United States, Britain, Canada, France, Germany, Italy, Japan, and Russia.

India-United States Relations

India is the world's largest democracy, and the United States is the world's oldest and most powerful democracy. Yet the relationship between these two democracies was, until recently, marked by indifference and deep mistrust.

Mark Tully (BBC Delhi bureau chief) and Zareer Masani (BBC) wrote the following in their 1988 book, *India: Forty Years of Independence*:

One of the ironies of forty years of independence is that the United States has come to see the world's largest democracy as a crypto-communist state, as little more than a Soviet satellite. The opposite is true; India follows its own way of life. Indian values are American, not Soviet values.

They further added:

Recently, there have been signs of a break in the clouds of misunderstanding which have darkened the relationship between the U.S. and India. If the clouds are to lift altogether, there must be greater understanding of India in America.

Mark Tully's wishes seem to be coming true now. The clouds that darkened the relationship between India and the United States are slowly lifting. Relations are on the upswing, and there is even talk of forging a strategic relationship.

Historical Perspective

During the 1950s, India enjoyed good relations with the United States. Prime Minister Nehru visited the United States in 1949 to meet with President Truman. He also met with Eisenhower, who was then the president of Columbia University. Nehru again visited Washington in 1956, this time to meet President Eisenhower. The United States provided liberal economic assistance to India. It jump-started India's nuclear energy program by building a nuclear reactor under the *Atoms for Peace* program. It also provided India with nuclear fuel and trained Indian scientists and engineers at U.S. laboratories.

The 1950s also marked the beginning of a military relationship with the United States and India's neighbor and rival Pakistan. Unlike India, which spurned the United States's offer to join its cold war alliance against the Soviet Union, Pakistan joined the U.S.-led cold war alliance aimed at curbing Soviet influence. As a result, the United States began supplying arms to Pakistan with assurances to Nehru that the arms would not be used against India. In 1959, President Eisenhower made his first trip to India, the first-ever visit by a U.S. president. The trip lasted about four days and was part of Eisenhower's nineteen-day, eleven-nation peace tour.

India faired well under President Kennedy, who continued the policies of providing generous economic assistance to India. Kennedy appointed his personal friend John Kenneth Galbraith as ambassador to India and also took the lead in organizing financial support for India's third five-year development plan. Nehru visited Washington in 1961, and Kennedy sent his wife, Jacqueline Kennedy, to India in 1961. It was the first visit of a First Lady to India. Jackie Kennedy stayed for two days at the home of Prime Minister Nehru and his daughter, Indira Gandhi.

As relations continued to grow, the Pakistani factor emerged when Kennedy decided to deliver twelve F-104 fighter jets to Pakistan, overruling objections from India. Another point of disagreement was India's annexation of the Portuguese territories of Goa. Goa had been under Portuguese rule since 1510. Even after the British left India, Portugal was dragging its feet, unwilling to surrender its territories to India. After years of fruitless negotiations, India launched a military attack and assimilated Goa into the Indian union. The United States opposed the military action because Portugal was a NATO ally. The United States condemned India's actions in the U.N. Security Council as a violation of U.N. charter.

In 1962, when border skirmishes between India and China erupted into a full-scale war, Nehru appealed to Washington for help. The United States responded by providing limited military assistance. In 1965, when India and Pakistan went to war over Kashmir, the United States refused to back India and cut off military aid to both sides. The United States continued its nonmilitary financial aid to India, however. It helped India usher in the Green Revolution, contributed to the food aid program, and provided assistance in setting up the famed Indian Institute of Technology.

But starting in the 1970s, relations began to decline at a rapid pace, first due to war with Pakistan and later due to India's first nuclear test. When civil war broke out in erstwhile East Pakistan (present-day Bangladesh), leading to the exodus of millions of refugees into India, Prime Minister Indira Gandhi urged President Nixon to cease supplying arms to Pakistan and persuade its leaders to take steps to end the civil war, which was straining India's economy. But Indira's pleas fell on deaf ears. President Nixon and his advisor Henry Kissinger continued to support the failed Pakistani military policy of suppressing the civil war with brute force.

After being snubbed by Washington, Indira Gandhi signed a twenty-year treaty of friendship with the Soviet Union, further steering India away from the United States and its allies. Later, when full-scale war broke out between India and Pakistan, the United States and China joined hands and proposed an anti-India cease-fire agreement in the U.N. Security Council, which was promptly vetoed by the Soviet Union. In an unprecedented and ill-conceived move, the Nixon administration dispatched its seventh fleet[231] to the Bay of Bengal in the midst of the war, hoping to intimidate India and save Pakistan from further humiliation. With these actions, Washington pushed India firmly into the Soviet fold.

Nixon and Kissinger maintained a tough posture toward India for the remainder of their term in office. It was only after President Carter took office in 1976 that hopes were raised about a possible rapprochement. Around the same time, India had its own regime change. Indira Gandhi lost the elections and was replaced by eighty-year-old Morarji Desai of the Janata Party, the first non-Congress Party government to assume power. President Carter wasted little time and made a highly successful trip to India in 1978, becoming only the third U.S. president to set foot on Indian soil.[232]

However, in 1980, Jimmy Carter lost his reelection bid to Ronald Reagan; the Morarji Desai government fell apart, and Indira Gandhi assumed power once again. Around the same time, Soviet forces invaded Afghanistan, and the Reagan administration started a proxy war to dislodge them by using irregular forces based in Pakistan. Pakistan received generous military and financial aid to the tune of $3 billion over the next five years from the United States, which threatened India's security. In providing this aid, the Reagan administration deliberately overlooked the fact that Pakistan was ruled by military ruler General

Zia-ul-Haq, who had just deposed and hastily hanged Pakistan's democratically elected leader.

Although upset with the military ties between the United States and Pakistan, which resulted in an arms race in the region, India realized the futility of maintaining its hostile posture toward the United States. Indira Gandhi visited the United States in 1982, her first trip since her visit to the Nixon White House in 1971. During Indira's visit, a previous dispute over nuclear fuel was amicably resolved; the Reagan administration allowed France to supply low-enriched uranium fuel for an American-built nuclear power plant at Tarapur, near Bombay.[233]

Rajiv Gandhi, who succeeded Indira Gandhi after her assassination in 1984, visited Reagan's White House twice in his five-year tenure. Rajiv's first visit in 1985 resulted in the entry of Texas Instruments into Bangalore, thus laying the foundation for a future IT revolution. By 1988, India had taken more steps to end its economic isolation by allowing Pepsi to set up operations in India. In total, U.S. investment in India reached a modest $1 billion by 1989. Cooperation also began to grow in military technology and defense matters when the United States agreed to provide technology for India's light combat vehicle program and F-5 fighter jets. The U.S. also began to develop an appreciation for India's role as a force of stabilization in southern Asia.

Despite this bonhomie, serious differences remained over nuclear arms and Pakistan. Washington continued to insist that New Delhi should sign the NPT and roll back or freeze its nuclear weapons program. India rejected it on the grounds that the NPT discriminated against nonnuclear states and instead campaigned for universal disarmament. New Delhi was angry at the United States for not cutting off military aid to Pakistan despite the overwhelming evidence about Pakistan's covert nuclear program. India was also upset at Washington's unwillingness to place Pakistan on its list of nations that sponsor terrorism for its support of terrorist activities in Punjab and Kashmir.

The end of the cold war and the collapse of the Soviet Union helped unshackle the relationship between the United States and India. India's decision to end its economic isolation by easing restrictions on foreign trade and foreign direct investment (FDI) further enhanced its economic relations with the West. By the mid-1990s, the United States emerged as India's largest trading partner and a major source of investment and technology. For the first time, the Clinton administration also identified India as one of the ten emerging markets in the world.[234]

Prime Minister Rao, the architect of India's economic reforms, made an uneventful visit to the United States in May 1994. Unlucky for Rao and India, the visit occurred on the same day that Jackie Kennedy passed away, and there was little or no press coverage of Rao's visit. Nevertheless, Rao was given the honor of addressing the U.S. Congress.[235]

Rao's visit opened the floodgates for several high-level visits from the United States, including visits from Defense Secretary William Perry, Commerce Secretary Ron Brown, and Treasury Secretary Robert Rubin. Perry's visit culminated in a landmark agreement on military cooperation. During Ron Brown's visit, U.S. companies pledged $7 billion in investments in communications, healthcare, insurance, finance, and automotive sectors. In March 1995, First Lady Hillary Clinton toured India as part of a goodwill tour to southern Asia, only the second such visit after Jackie Kennedy's visit to India in 1961.

Just when relations seemed to be reaching new heights, India's surprise decision to conduct nuclear tests in 1998 infuriated the United States, as it flew in the face of the Comprehensive Test Ban Treaty (CTBT) that Washington was pushing with other countries. Clinton worked hard on the phones to prevent Pakistan from conducting its own copycat nuclear tests by offering billions of dollars in aid and even F-16s as inducement. But Clinton's efforts failed, and Pakistan conducted its own tests two weeks later. Clinton slammed Pakistan for not showing restraint.

In response, the United States imposed stiff economic sanctions first on India and later on Pakistan, blocked World Bank loans, halted all military cooperation, and persuaded Japan, India's largest aid provider, to follow suit. The Clinton administration was embarrassed by the fact that the CIA did not have a clue about the impending nuclear tests.

It took a few years for the dust to settle on the nuclear tests. Both sides were eager to take the relationship forward and not let the nuclear fallout impact their relationship. As a result of the nuclear tests, the United States was finally taking India seriously. President Clinton deployed his deputy secretary of state, Strobe Talbott, to conduct a strategic dialogue with India to bring the relationship back on track. Talbott's partner on the Indian side was influential foreign minister Jaswant Singh. They met fourteen times in seven countries on three continents in the most intense set of exchanges the nations had ever undertaken.[236]

The talks did not lead to any immediate results. The United States did not get India's signature on the CTBT, nor did India succeed in getting the economic sanctions lifted. But what the talks did do was lay a foundation for a solid understanding between the nations on security issues.

In February 1999, President Clinton welcomed the successful Lahore summit meeting between the prime ministers of India and Pakistan and offered help in promoting peace in the region. But the India-Pakistani bonhomie did not last long. President Clinton was forced to intervene when Pakistan precipitated military conflict with India in May 1999 by seizing strategic heights near Kargil on the Indian side of the Line of Control (LOC) in Kashmir.

During the initial months of the conflict, the United States did not intervene; it merely asked both sides to show restraint. As the conflict progressed, disturbing information arose about Pakistan's possible use of nuclear weapons against India. By July 1999, the tide turned in India's favor, with its troops taking back the strategic Tiger Hills. Facing an imminent rout and worldwide condemnation for his foolhardy military adventure, then Pakistani prime minister Nawaz Sharif appealed for President Clinton's help to engineer a face-saving formula. Pakistan suffered an even bigger blow when China, Pakistan's staunch ally in the region, asked it to respect the LOC and take steps to diffuse the situation.

Prime Minister Nawaz Sharif flew into Washington on a Pakistan International Airlines (PIA) flight and stayed at Blair House (a presidential guesthouse opposite the West Wing of the White House).[237] The day was July 4, 1999, America's Independence Day. Normally, no business is transacted on this day. But President Clinton agreed to meet Sharif on the condition that Pakistan would immediately and unconditionally withdraw its troops, paving the way for a cease-fire. Initially, Sharif tried to convince Clinton to mediate in Kashmir as a quid pro quo for any concessions from the Pakistani side, but Clinton dismissed the idea as preposterous. Sharif agreed to a joint statement saying that he would take immediate steps for the restoration of the LOC. As a minor concession to Sharif, President Clinton agreed to take a personal interest in future bilateral talks between India and Pakistan.

The Kargil conflict and the positive role played by President Clinton changed India's perception of the United States. India was pleased at the definite tilt in the U.S. position vis-à-vis the Kashmir issue in its favor. There was jubilation in India, as it was able to get a cease-fire agreement on its terms. The Kargil conflict went a long way toward establishing trust between India and the United States.

Finally, in March 2000, the long-awaited presidential visit took place when President Clinton made his first trip to India in the last year of his presidency. He did not let his impending lame-duck status affect the trip. India rolled out the red carpet for him, and the trip lasted five days. He spent five days in India, but only five hours in Pakistan.

Incidentally, this was the first presidential trip in twenty-two years, following the 1978 trip of fellow Democrat President Carter. The trip by any account was a huge success. President Clinton and Prime Minister Vajpayee signed a vision statement, giving a major boost to the new relationship. But Clinton's description of Kashmir as the most dangerous place on earth did not go down well with his hosts. At the state banquet in Clinton's honor, President K. R. Narayanan (the presidency in India is largely a ceremonial position) chastised President

Clinton for making alarmist statements, which he said could increase tension in the region.[238]

Clinton's visit to India was immediately followed by Prime Minister Vajpayee's state visit to Washington in September 2000, two months before the presidential election. At a glittering banquet for the visiting Indian leader, Clinton hailed his country's new partnership with India. It was the largest state dinner hosted by President Clinton in his eight years in office.[239] In all, there were seven hundred guests, including many from the influential Indian American community such as Hotmail founder Sabeer Bhatia, former tennis star Vijay Amritraj, and Indian American astronaut Kalpana Chawla. First Lady Hillary Clinton interrupted her campaign for the U.S. Senate to attend the event. Even some Hollywood stars, such as Goldie Hawn and Chevy Chase, were invited. During his visit, Vajpayee was also given the honor of addressing the U.S. Congress.

By the time Clinton left office in January 2001, relations had matured so much that the disagreements over nuclear tests seemed like a distant memory. But the economic sanctions imposed on India in the wake of the tests were still in place. There was a general consensus on both sides that a new era in the Indo-U.S. relationship had finally begun.

When George W. Bush took office in 2001, the likelihood of India appearing on his foreign policy radar screen appeared very remote. After all, he was a Republican, and India traditionally fared better under Democratic presidents than Republican. Nobody expected George W. Bush to start where Clinton left off with regard to relations with India. But the Bush administration had other ideas about India. It was envisioning a strategic relationship with India as a counterweight to China's growing influence in the world. The U.S.-China relationship was already tense by then.

The Chinese were very upset when a U.S. missile mistakenly hit the Chinese embassy in Belgrade during the Kosovo campaign in May 1999. Upon taking office, President Bush further alienated China by pledging to take a tough line with China on arms sales to Taiwan. The final straw was the spy plane incident that occurred in April 2001. The Bush administration was infuriated when Chinese fighter jets intercepted a U.S. Navy EP-3 spy plane claiming to be on a routine surveillance mission.

The incident with the spy plane further bolstered arguments within the Bush administration that the United States should actively engage like-minded countries to strategically contain China. India fit the bill because it too viewed China as a strategic adversary. But New Delhi had little desire to overtly side with the United States against China, preferring to take a middle-ground approach that suited its security needs. For instance, India opposed the United States's move to censure China at a recent meeting of the United Nations Human Rights Commission. At the same time, India was more accommodating to Washington's National Missile Defense (NMD) plans than were America's traditional allies.

In August 2001, the Bush administration was preparing to lift the nuclear test-related sanctions imposed on India to pave the way for enhanced military and economic cooperation and stronger political dialogue between the countries. There was also the realization that the time was ripe for accepting India as an unofficial nuclear power, as it was not possible to put the nuclear genie back in the bottle. But the administration was not prepared to lift sanctions on Pakistan since it was under military rule.

In the aftermath of the 9/11 attacks, the foreign policy priorities of the Bush administration underwent major changes. The containment of China was no longer a priority, but containing the Taliban and Al Qaida was. Pakistan's role as a major supporter of the Taliban regime came under increased scrutiny. Pakistan was one of only three countries that had officially recognized the ruling Taliban regime in Afghanistan. Within days of the 9/11 attacks, the Bush administration had put extraordinary pressure on President Musharraf to find those responsible for the terrorist attacks, bring them to justice, and assist with a potential attack on Taliban targets. President Musharraf quickly got on board by severing his links with the Taliban regime and declaring Pakistan's unstinted cooperation in the flight against terrorism. Overnight, Pakistan became a front-line state in Bush's global war on terror. To the utter chagrin of India, Pakistan was back in the saddle as the most important ally of the United States in southern Asia. With that, India's importance to the United States somewhat waned. India's attempt to expand the definition of the global war on terror to include terrorist activities in the Kashmir region did not pan out due to opposition from Pakistan.

Within ten days of the 9/11 attacks, the United States lifted its nuclear program-related sanctions against India and Pakistan. In October 2001, Colin Powell traveled to India and Pakistan to shore up support for the U.S. military campaign against the Taliban. Amid concerns that the United States was turning a blind eye to Pakistan's terrorist activities in Kashmir as quid pro quo for Pakistan's cooperation in the war of terror in Afghanistan, Powell issued a strong statement condemning terrorist attacks by Islamic militants in Indian-controlled Kashmir. He also sought to assure India that it was not being marginalized and that the American-led fight against terrorism encompassed all forms of terrorism worldwide, including those faced by India. To further mollify India, Powell extended President Bush's invitation to Prime Minister Vajpayee to visit Washington.

In December 2001, three months after the 9/11 attacks and just two months after the start of the U.S.-led campaign against Afghanistan, tensions between India and Pakistan escalated rapidly in the aftermath of a terrorist attack on the Indian parliament. Thirteen people, including the attackers, were killed in a forty-five-minute battle with security forces outside the parliament building. India's home minister described the attacks as the most audacious and alarming act of terrorism in two decades of Pakistan-sponsored terrorism in India. He blamed the suicide attacks on two Pakistan-based terrorist groups and accused Pakistan's intelligence agency (ISI) of complicity. Pakistan's initial reactions of sorrow and condemnation did little to mollify New Delhi or to stem rising tensions.

The terrorist attack on the Indian parliament has drawn strong condemnation from the United States. Secretary of State Colin Powell interrupted his Christmas holiday to urge both countries to exercise restraint as the war of words escalated. Despite calls from the United States to show restraint, India and Pakistan began to build up their military forces along the border for a possible showdown. On January 11, 2002, India's army chief, General S. Padmanabhan, announced that Indian military forces were totally mobilized and awaiting the green light from political leaders.

At Washington's insistence, Pakistan took a few tentative steps to address India's concerns. On January 12, 2002, President Musharraf delivered his much-awaited, hour-long, nationally telecast address, in which he pledged to crack down on militants operating on Pakistani soil. He then banned the two terrorist organizations that were blamed for the terrorist raid in New Delhi, but ruled out handing over their leaders to India.

While the United States was quick to welcome Musharraf's pledge, India remained deeply skeptical and rebuffed any resumption of talks until Pakistan stopped the acts of terrorism and dismantled terrorist training camps. In the meantime, troop deployment continued along the border. Emotions were running high, and only the smallest spark was needed to initiate a major conflict. That spark came in the form of a militant attack on May 14, 2002. This time, the militants stormed a Kashmir army camp and killed thirty people. Yet again, the tension created by the latest attack pushed India and Pakistan to the brink of war. Prime Minister Vajpayee, under considerable domestic pressure, visited the front lines in Kashmir and delivered a message to the military men that "the time has come for a decisive battle, and we will have a sure victory in this battle."[240]

That chilling message launched a flurry of diplomatic activities in Washington. On May 31, 2002, the U.S. State Department issued a voluntary evacuation order for nonessential embassy and consulate personnel and dependents in India, citing the growing risk of conflict between India and Pakistan. Other governments immediately followed suit.

Both Secretary of Defense Donald Rumsfeld and Deputy Secretary of State Richard Armitage traveled to New Delhi and Islamabad in early June 2002 to diffuse the situation. Armitage announced a Pakistani pledge to renounce cross-border infiltration into Indian Kashmir. Washington played a pivotal role in lowering the temperatures in southern Asia. The United States was concerned that Kashmir could become a recruiting ground for anti-American Islamic extremists.

In the run-up to the U.S. invasion of Iraq in early 2003, India kept a low profile, primarily because it did not want to jeopardize its burgeoning relationship with the United States. Behind the scenes, India was worried about the possible adverse affects of the war on its economy and the three million Indian workers who had made the Persian Gulf their home. India traditionally had a good relationship with Saddam Hussein's regime in Iraq. India was a big importer of Iraqi oil and participated in the U.N.-sponsored oil-for-food program. Hussein supported India's stand on Kashmir, one of the few Islamic countries to do so, and in 2000 he leased two oil fields to India's state-owned Oil and Natural Gas Commission (ONGC).

President George Bush telephoned the Indian prime minister shortly after the first strikes had begun on Baghdad. In a muted reaction, Prime Minister Vajpayee expressed the hope that "military action would be concluded at the earliest"[241] and conveyed India's willingness to provide humanitarian assistance to Iraq. Even as the U.S.-led coalition forces were closing in on Baghdad in April 2003, the Indian parliament unanimously passed a largely symbolic resolution deploring the U.S. invasion and calling on coalition forces to withdraw. This reflected the general antiwar mood prevailing in the country at that time.

Even as the war was progressing, the United States was drawing up its plans for its postwar occupation force. India came under increasing pressure from the Bush administration to provide seventeen thousand troops to serve in the Kurdish region.[242] Such a move would have made the number of Indian troops second only to the United States—larger than the troops provided by Britain, America's closest ally. For the next few weeks, it appeared that things were going the United States's way and that India would commit its troops to Iraq. A Pentagon team visited India to assist in planning the Indian deployment. India had begun consultations with Iraq's neighbors to gauge their reaction to a possible deployment of its troops in Iraq. Later in 2003, India finally dealt a sharp blow to America's postwar plans by politely turning down its request to send troops. The reason was simple. The invasion of Iraq was extremely unpopular in India, which, though predominantly Hindu, has the second-largest Muslim population after Indonesia. Besides, the presence of Indian troops in Iraq would have upset Muslim nations like Iran and Turkey.

Although disappointed by India's decision not to send troops, the Bush administration decided not to dwell on it and continued to focus on its long-term strategic relationship with India. In January 2004, President Bush and Prime Minister Vajpayee launched a new initiative called the Next Steps in Strategic Partnership (NSSP).[243]

Under this major initiative, the United States and India agreed to expand cooperation in three specific areas: civilian nuclear activities, civilian space programs, and high-technology trade. In addition, the two countries agreed to expand the dialogue on missile defense. In March 2004, Secretary of State Colin Powell visited India as part of a five-day tour through southern Asia. After his trip to India, Powell visited Pakistan and announced the intention of the United States to grant "major non-NATO ally" (MNNA) status to Pakistan.[244]

With that announcement, Pakistan joined the elite club of key American allies including Japan, Israel, and Australia. Pakistan is the fifth Muslim country to receive this designation. The others are Egypt, Jordan, Bahrain, and Kuwait. The United States typically gives its MNNAs greater access to defense technology and training. A week later, the Bush administration also lifted the sanctions on Pakistan that were imposed after the military coup led by General Musharraf in October 1999.

Pakistan was understandably jubilant. For the first time since the 1990s, it would have access to advanced weapons from the United States, which would give them a tactical advantage in any future wars with India. India was upset for the same reason. India was also unhappy with the way Secretary Powell had chosen to handle the situation, by keeping them in the dark about the impending announcement about Pakistan's new status. After all, he had been in Delhi only days earlier.

New Delhi's sharp reaction took the U.S. State Department slightly off guard. Secretary Powell immediately tried to contact India's foreign minister Yashwant Sinha to explain the United States's position, but he was kept on hold for a few days. Sinha's reaction was understandable because his government had taken pride in cultivating "special" relations with the United States. The opposition Congress Party called the U.S. decision on Pakistan "a public repudiation of India."[245]

When a new Congress-led government assumed office in India after the general election in May 2004, there was some concern in Washington that relations might somewhat cool off. U.S. Deputy Secretary of State Richard Armitage visited India in July 2004 to gain an understanding of the new government's policy toward Washington. He was assured that India would maintain its close relationship with the United States.

Meanwhile, in March 2005, within a year of bestowing the new ally status on Pakistan, President Bush authorized the sale of F-16 fighter jets to Pakistan. This reversed a fifteen-year-old policy that barred the sale of combat aircraft to Pakistan out of concern over its undeclared nuclear weapons program. This latest move was an attempt to further sweeten the pot for General Musharraf, who had committed troops in the search for Osama bin Laden. This time, President Bush kept India in the loop by informing the Indian prime minister of the F-16 sale to Pakistan. He even went a step further by announcing that the U.S. government would allow U.S. firms to compete for contracts to provide India with the next generation of combat aircraft, including upgraded F-16 and F-18 war planes.

When Prime Minister Manmohan Singh visited the United States in July 2005, the Bush administration rolled out the red carpet for him, and President Bush hosted a rare state dinner in honor of India's new leader. Incidentally, it was Bush's first state dinner since his reelection in 2004, and only his fifth since taking office. In his welcoming toast, Bush said, "India and the United States are separated by half a globe, yet today our two nations are closer than ever before."[246]

Unlike in the past, when a visit by an Indian prime minister received scant media attention, Dr. Manmohan Singh's visit received wide media coverage in the United States, signifying the arrival of India on the world scene. Mr. Singh's visit coincided with the completion of the Next Steps in Strategic Partnership (NSSP) initiative, which had been launched eighteen months earlier. In an address to a joint session of Congress, Mr. Singh said that India was a responsible nuclear power that would never be a source of proliferation of sensitive technologies. President Bush acknowledged India as a responsible state with nuclear technology but did not endorse its bid for a permanent seat in the U.N. Security Council. The United States currently supports only Japan's candidacy.

President Bush finally visited in March 2006, becoming the fifth president to visit India. Setting aside protocol, Prime Minister Manmohan Singh greeted Bush at a heavily guarded Delhi airport where Bush's Air Force One had landed. U.S. National Security adviser Stephen Hadley described President Bush's visit to India as a historic one intended to "broaden and deepen"[247] the relationship. The *New York Times* described Mr. Bush's three-day presidential trip as far more significant than former president Bill Clinton's five-day visit in 2000 for both strategic and economic reasons.

The trip centered on a civilian nuclear deal under which the United States would supply nuclear technology and fuel desperately needed by India to fuel its energy-starved and rapidly growing economy. Speaking at a joint press conference with Manmohan Singh, Bush labeled the Indo-U.S. nuclear accord "historic," and then argued that the accord was in America's national interest because the expansion of India's civilian nuclear capacity would lessen her dependence on imported energy sources and thereby lessen pressure on world oil and natural gas prices.

President Bush addressed[248] the people of India from the majestic setting of the sixteenth-century Purana Qila (Old Fort) in Delhi. In his address, Bush said that India in the twenty-first century is a natural partner of the United States. He also referred to Martin Luther King's famous words when he visited India in 1959. King said: " To other countries, I may go as a tourist, but to India, I come as a pilgrim."[249] Bush added, "I come to India as a friend." In his speech, Bush welcomed India's economic rise and strongly defended outsourcing as the reality of a global economy.

The theme throughout his visit was that the United States should welcome rather than fear competition from India, and that the United States should focus on India as a new market for American-made products and services. But he reminded India of its responsibilities, including lifting caps on foreign investment, lowering tariffs, and opening markets to American goods.

But in order to secure a nuclear deal with the United States, India had to toe the U.S. line on Iran's nuclear program. While India maintained that it would not bow to outside pressure from the United States on the Iran issue, it was clear that abstaining or voting against the resolution before the board would have jeopardized U.S. Congress support for the U.S.-India nuclear deal. Therefore, India decided to bite the bullet. In two crucial votes at the Governors' Board of the International Atomic Energy Agency (IAEA), in 2005 and 2006, India voted against Iran. The first time was to condemn Iran for not meeting its obligations under the Non-Proliferation Treaty (NPT); the second time was to report Iran's file to the U.N. Security Council. Iran had expected stronger backing at the IAEA, especially from India. After the vote, Iran singled out India for criticism for siding with the West.

The Indian government also drew severe domestic criticism, especially from the political parties belonging to the left, for its willingness to abandon the independence of Indian foreign policy for the sake of strengthening its strategic partnership with the United States.

Burgeoning Trade Ties

Bilateral trade between the countries currently stands at $41.6 billion, an eight-fold increase in seventeen years. In 2006, Frank Lavin, the under secretary for international trade, led a trade mission to India to explore new investment opportunities and develop partnerships with local companies. It was the biggest trade mission from the United States to any country in the world, bringing over 250 American firms to India.

U.S. Commerce Secretary Carlos Gutierrez visited India in February 2007 to push American exports. With the economy roaring ahead with an 8 percent growth rate, foreign investors are showing a keen interest in entering the Indian market. Not to be left behind, several U.S. states are eyeing business opportunities in India. Governors from Virginia and Iowa headed trade missions to India, and governors from Minnesota, Utah, and California are likely to follow suit.

Without a doubt, India offers a number of business opportunities. But results for foreign investors are far from guaranteed. David Mulford, the U.S. ambassador to India, cautioned American investors not to expect instant results. "India is not a journey for the faint hearted, or for those who expect overnight success," he remarked[250]. "You will need a strategy—a long term view—patience, and persistence. But one of the world's great markets is here."

Although bilateral trade between India and the United States is growing at breakneck speed, the countries are at loggerheads at the World Trade Organization's multilateral trade negotiations. The Doha round of talks, named after the Qatari capital where the talks started in 2001, aims to increase world trade and help fight poverty. But the talks failed last year after leading developed and developing countries failed to agree over issues that were important to them. Developing countries like India and Brazil are pushing developed nations to reduce farm subsidies and allow more agricultural imports, while rich nations are pressing developing nations to reduce import duties and open their markets to farm and manufactured goods.

After four years of negotiations, progress has been slow, and none of the key players are willing to make enough concessions to bring the talks to a conclusion. Both Brazil and India have drawn sharp criticism from the United States and the European Union for refusing to yield ground on providing market access. In the absence of a comprehensive multilateral trade deal, India and other major countries are moving ahead with bilateral trade pacts with countries around the world. India is considering signing free trade agreements (FTAs) with ASEAN, Singapore, the Gulf Cooperation Council, and Thailand.

Anatomy of the India-U.S. Nuclear Deal

What Is It?

Under the deal, energy-hungry India has access to U.S. civil nuclear technology and fuel, even though it has not signed the NPT. In return, India pledged to open its civilian nuclear facilities to outside inspection. But its nuclear weapons sites remain off-limits.

Why Is India Keen on This Deal?

The nuclear deal ends India's three decades of nuclear isolation and gives its nuclear power plants access to U.S. technology and equipment. India is keen to secure alternative fuels to feed its fast-growing economy, and the nuclear option is attractive. Nuclear power currently supplies only 3 percent of its electricity. By 2050, nuclear power is expected to provide 25 percent. India currently has fourteen reactors in commercial operation and is building nine more.

Why Is This Deal Unique?

The deal is unique because it reverses decades of U.S. nonproliferation policies. It would carve out an India-specific exception to laws that forbid the transfer of nuclear technology to countries that have not signed the NPT.

When Was the Deal Struck?

The deal was signed during President Bush's visit to India in March 2006. The U.S. Senate voted eighty-five to twelve in favor of the legislation in December 2006. The proposal received bipartisan support in the U.S. Congress, and President Bush signed it into law.

What Were the Key Differences that Slowed the Talks?

A crucial sticking point was over a clause stipulating that the United States would withdraw fuel and equipment if India breached its unilateral moratorium on nuclear tests. India opposed the clause on the grounds that a nuclear test by its neighbors China or Pakistan could compel it to resume tests. Another key area of difference was over the reprocessing of spent fuel. India wanted complete freedom to process spent fuel, whereas the United States insisted that the fuel not be used for military purposes. The third disagreement was over India's close relationship with Iran. Washington wanted New Delhi to support its policy of isolating Iran.

Why Was the U.S. Government Pushing for This Deal?

The United States wanted to create a broad strategic relationship with India, an emerging economic and military power. It also saw the deal as a way to accelerate India's rise as a counterweight to China. Nicholas Burns, who was until recently the administration's point person for the nuclear deal, called the agreement one of the most important foreign policy initiatives of the last few decades. The deal also had strong backing from U.S. companies, who are aiming for twenty-seven thousand new jobs for the U.S. nuclear industry alone as a result of the agreement. The U.S.-India Business Council has welcomed the U.S. Senate's approval of the U.S.-India nuclear deal, saying that it will lay the foundation for major trade and investment opportunities in India for U.S. companies.

This deal should also be seen in the context of growing India-U.S. cooperation in the energy sector. Legislation on enhancing cooperation was introduced in the U.S. Congress in February 2007. Titled the

"United States-India Energy Security Cooperation Act of 2007," the bill urges the United States to cooperate with India to address common energy challenges to ensure future global energy security.

What Do Critics of the Deal Say?

Critics of this deal say that it could boost India's nuclear arsenal. Arms control experts warn that the deal will weaken global nuclear nonproliferation efforts and send the wrong message to countries like Iran and North Korea, whose nuclear ambitions the United States vehemently opposes. However, the deal received support from Mohamed ElBaradei, the director of the IAEA, who called India an important partner in the nonproliferation regime. At home, the Indian government faced criticism that the deal will compromise its nuclear independence. India's communist parties, who oppose closer ties with the United States, fear that the deal will make India a subordinate ally of the United States.

What Are the Next Steps of the Deal?

The Nuclear Suppliers Group (NSG), an assembly of nations that export nuclear material, has recently approved the deal. President George W. Bush signed the nuclear deal into law in October 2008 after it was approved by the U.S. Congress. India must separate its military and civilian nuclear infrastructure and bring civilian facilities under U.N. inspections.

Indo-U.S. Relations: Closing Thoughts

U.S.-India relations have come a long way since the days of Nixon/Kissinger, when there was a definite U.S. tilt toward Pakistan at India's expense. Although relations did not take off until the early 1990s, they never reached a breaking point. It is not very hard to understand why relations are improving at a breathtaking pace. India shares many of the United States's values. Both are both multiethnic, multilingual, multireligious societies with increasingly converging interests on the world's most important issues. The United States admires India because of its impeccable democratic credentials and the nonviolent way it won its independence.

Until the early 1990s, India did not have anything substantial to offer and therefore did not figure in American strategic thinking. India's main grievance with the United States was that its arming of Pakistan fueled the arms race in southern Asia. The United States was unhappy with India because it did not take its side in the cold war, did not adhere to the NPT or CTBT, and pursued an independent foreign policy that was often at odds with its own foreign policy. The United States wanted India to cap its nuclear program, which India resisted. The United States did not understand the terrorism battle India went through in the 1980s and 1990s. It did not rein in Pakistani military regimes, which were openly supporting the terrorist activities within India. Until 9/11, the United States considered terrorism a bilateral issue between India and Pakistan.

The end of cold war hostilities and the opening of the Indian economy to foreign trade introduced unprecedented opportunities for the U.S. government and businesses alike. The bilateral relationship is now in its best shape in decades. Nicholas Burns, the U.S. under secretary of state for political affairs in the Bush administration, hailed current ties as the strongest relationship the two countries have enjoyed since India's independence in 1947.

For the United States, a strategic relationship with a major democracy like India, which is strategically located between the Middle East and China, has become a necessary element of its foreign policy. The United States is keen to partner with India due to its vast economic and military potential. Only India has the scale and depth to serve as a counterweight to China's rising ambitions.

The military ties between the nations, which did not exist prior to the 1990s, are also on the upswing, including, among other things, the regular staging of joint military exercises. Recently, two U.S. warships, the USS Kitty Hawk and USS Nimitz, along with several other warships, participated in joint naval exercises with India, Japan, Australia, and Singapore in the Bay of Bengal. U.S. companies like

Lockheed Martin and Boeing are sniffing out opportunities resulting from the increased defense cooperation between the countries.

So far there were only five state visits by U.S. presidents to India: Eisenhower, Nixon, Carter, Clinton, and Bush. After Carter's trip, it took twenty-two years for the next U.S. president to set foot on Indian soil. Both Bill Clinton and George W. Bush visited India in their second terms.

India-Russia Relations

India's relationship with Russia (the previous Soviet Union) has been cordial and consistent for the past fifty years. Analysts routinely describe the relationship as an all-weather relationship, akin to China's relationship with Pakistan.

India's relations with the Soviet Union began to take off after Joseph Stalin's death in 1953. The Soviet Union was attempting to broaden its international reach and cultivate relationships with the newly independent nations of Asia and Africa in order to wean them away from American influence. Indian Prime Minister Nehru made his first trip to the Soviet Union in 1955, and Nikita Khrushchev reciprocated later that year. To the delight of the Indian hosts, Khrushchev endorsed India's position on Kashmir for the first time.

Initially, it was a purely an economic relationship. Post-independence, India desperately needed financial aid and technology from other countries to build its industrial base. As India shopped around for aid, it quickly realized that the help from Western powers was either too little or, when it arrived, was weighted down with strings attached. For instance, in return for financial aid, the United States expected India to take its side in the cold war with the Soviet Union. There was also a reluctance to transfer the latest technology to a third-world country like India. Against this backdrop, India began to cultivate an economic relationship with the Soviet Union in the mid-1950s. India was attracted by the Soviet Union's "no strings attached" financial aid and technology transfer programs. There was no insistence on setting up military bases in India. India had to neither adhere to the Soviet communist ideology nor endorse its cold war policies. All that was expected from India was that it would not take America's side in the cold war and it would avoid any harsh criticism of Soviet policies.

The Soviet Union helped India set up its major steel plant at Bhilai and other world-renowned public sector enterprises like Bharat Heavy Electricals Limited (BHEL), Hindustan Aeronautics Limited (HAL), and numerous other companies.

Starting in the 1960s, the economic relations soon turned into a solid military relationship. In the aftermath of its military defeat at the hands of the Chinese in the border war of 1962, India had begun bolstering its long-neglected armed forces, and the Soviet Union was eager to help. It gave India the latest military hardware. It did not demand immediate payment, and the military hardware was sold against deferred currency payments, keeping in mind India's fragile foreign reserves position at that time. A liberal technology transfer regime and licensing allowed India to manufacture weaponry on its soil. It turned out to be a mutually beneficial business relationship between a reliable supplier and a reliable customer, a relationship that continues even today.

The rapid growth in the Soviet Union's relationship with India further soured its relationship with China. Soon, financial aid to India surpassed the aid provided to China. The Soviet Union also agreed to transfer MIG-21 fighter aircraft technology to India after denying it to China. However, the Soviet Union took a neutral position in the Indo-China border dispute of 1962.

No less significant was the India-Soviet Union friendship at international forums. The Soviet Union provided yeoman services to India by supporting it at the United Nations on every single issue to date (similar to the United States's support for Israel). Today, Russia fully supports India's position vis-à-vis Pakistan on the Kashmir issue and supports its right to have nuclear weapons outside the NPT regime. The Soviet Union also played a constructive role during the India-Pakistan War of 1965 by arranging a cease-fire.

In August 1971, months before India's intervention in the civil war in eastern Pakistan, Prime Minister Indira Gandhi signed a twenty-year Treaty of Peace, Friendship, and Cooperation with the Soviets, which included some security clauses. This treaty helped India in several ways. It acted as a deterrent to any fresh Chinese aggression at a time when its armed forces were busy engaging the Pakistani military during the Bangladesh Liberation War. Military shipments from the Soviet Union came in handy in India's war against Pakistan in 1971. When the seventh American fleet arrived in the Bay of Bengal in support of Pakistan, the Soviet Union promptly dispatched its Pacific fleet in support of India.

Later in the 1970s, the Soviet Union emerged as India's largest trading partner. A number of high-level visits between the leaders of both countries took place during that time, including the state visit of Soviet leader Leonid Brezhnev. The cooperation also extended to the space arena. The Soviet Union helped India launch its own satellites. In 1984, Rakesh Sharma of the Indian Air Force became the first Indian cosmonaut by spending eight days aboard the Soviet space station Salyut 7.

When the Soviet Union invaded Afghanistan in 1979, India's reaction was muted and subdued. But soon India began to feel the negative impact of the invasion. The Reagan administration started shipping billions of dollars in arms to neighboring Pakistan in order to dislodge the Soviets, setting off an arms race in southern Asia. To keep pace with Pakistan's latest military hardware, which included state-of-the-art F-16s, India had to procure military hardware; once again there was no alternative to the Soviet Union.

When the Soviet Union disintegrated in the early 1990s, both sides struggled to redefine their relationship. After Prime Minister Rao's visit to Moscow in July 1994, Russia restored the sale of cryogenic engines and space technology to India despite the threat of sanctions by Washington.

Why does the Indo-Russian relationship remain strong? There are several reasons. At a mundane level, the arms trade drives it. Consider this. A recent Congressional study found that India was the leading buyer of conventional arms among developing nations in 2005, with purchases to the tune of $5.4 billion. Needless to say, India is a very attractive arms market. During the cold war, the Soviet Union, due to its close relationship with India, enjoyed a near-monopoly as India's central arms supplier. Even today, close to 80 percent of Indian military hardware is based on Russian design, and India is critically dependent on Russian arms and spare parts.

Now Russia is facing stiff competition from other nations, including France and the United States, that are eager to tap into India's lucrative arms market. Russia is currently bidding to sell 120 MIG-35 fighter plans to Delhi. So far, New Delhi has not committed to the deal. But India doesn't want to upset its old friend Russia. Therefore, in February 2007, India inked a $1.6 billion deal with Russia to supply forty Sukhoi-30 MKI fighters.

In addition, Russia and India are rapidly deepening their cooperation in the energy sector. India urgently needs to secure energy suppliers to feed its red-hot economy, as it has relatively few energy sources of its own. That's where Russia, the largest gas exporter in the world, wants to step in. Europe is totally dependent on gas imported from Russia. India is not yet dependent, but it is keen to source more oil and gas from Russia. It is actively trying to secure a stake in Russia's oil and gas field developments. The Indian prime minister recently remarked that energy was at the core of the future Indo-Russian relationship.

Russia is already actively engaged in India's civilian nuclear sector. It is building two nuclear reactors in Tamil Nadu state and is now offering four more reactors. Unlike the United States, Russia is relatively easy to deal with when it comes to nuclear trade. It doesn't ask too many questions and doesn't play the role of the world's nuclear police.

Despite the talk of greater cooperation, bilateral trade between the nations stands at only $2 billion a year, which is a fraction of India's trade with the United States or China. Even more bad news is that it is entirely driven by defense purchases. Until recently, Russia was the largest economy outside the WTO. But recently, Russia and the United

States announced a deal that will pave the way for Russia's formal entry into the WTO. Once that happens, bilateral trade between India and Russia is expected rise considerably.

There is yet another factor that is driving the Indo-Russian relationship. It is the "C" factor, or the China factor. Both Russia and India are wary of China's status as an emerging economic and military power. Both are making a conscious effort to build good relations with China while at the same time closely watching its moves. When China successfully tested its satellite-destroying space weapons, India and Russia reacted cautiously by calling for a weapons-free outer space.

Russia, China, and India are equally worried about the global dominance of the United States. In 1998, then Russian prime minister Yevgeny Primakov even floated the idea of creating a strategic triangle with India and China as a counterweight to the growing American influence.[251] Although dismissed as a nonstarter at that time, such an alliance is becoming a real possibility now, with Sino-Russia relations growing deeper and Indo-Sino relations being normalized. Recently, foreign ministers of India, China, and Russia met in New Delhi to discuss matters of mutual interest in a tripartite format, the second such meeting in two years.

With so much at stake, it is no coincidence that Indian Prime Minister Manmohan Singh broke the protocol and personally received President Putin at the Delhi airport when he made his fourth trip to India in 2007. On the eve of Putin's visit, BBC News jokingly referred to PUTIN as a short form for "Planes, Uranium, Tanks, Infrastructure, and Nuclear Power" to signify President Putin's agenda during the trip.[252]Putin was spearheading Russia's efforts to defend its position as India's main arms supplier amid increased competition.

Russia has reason to worry, as India has recently signed a new strategic partnership with the United States. The United States is eager to sell nuclear reactors once the recently signed landmark Indo-U.S. civilian nuclear energy deal goes through. So India is in the enviable position of being courted by both a superpower and a former superpower.

Perhaps one thing that is lacking in the Indo-Russian relationship is the complete absence of people-to-people contacts. The main impediments are language and cultural differences. But the government-to-government ties continue to remain strong, driven by agreement among India's various political parties that it is vital to maintain strong relations with Russia.

India-China Relations

If India were to name two enemies, two nations will top the list: Pakistan and China. It did not start that way with China. Until the late 1950s, the nations enjoyed cordial relations, mainly due to the efforts of India's first prime minister, Nehru.

When the People's Republic of China (PRC) was formed in 1949, India became only the second noncommunist country after Burma to recognize it. At a time when the United States and other Western countries considered China a pariah, Nehru came to its rescue by forcefully arguing against isolating one of the world's largest nations. He advocated the PRC's early entry into the U.N. Security Council.

In 1954, India and China signed five principles of coexistence and a number of high-level visits took place. Chinese leader Zhou Enlai visited India in July 1954, followed by Nehru's visit to China in October 1954. Zhou again visited India in 1956. Relations between the nations became tense in 1959 when India decided to grant asylum to Tibetan spiritual leader the Dalai Lama, who escaped Lhasa after the Chinese invasion of Tibet.

The same year, territorial disputes came to the fore when China laid claim to forty thousand square miles of India's territory in the Ladakh region. The Indo-China border on the eastern side was defined in 1914, during India's British rule. China did not accept the legality of the border, referred to as the McMahon Line. Talks aimed at resolving the border dispute ended in a deadlock. Later, when India realized that China had built a road passing through its territories, it moved its security forces into the disputed area, marking the beginning of the border clashes.

The border clashes escalated into full-scale war when Chinese forces attacked Indian posts on October 20, 1962 and prevailed over the ill-prepared, ill-equipped Indian army. A month later, after occupying some strategic points in the Ladakh region, China declared a unilateral cease-fire and withdrew behind a newly established Line of Control.

After the border war of 1962, relations went into a chill for the next two decades. To counter China, India began cultivating a military relationship with the Soviet Union. For its part, China upgraded its relationship with India's archrival Pakistan and backed it openly during the 1965 and 1971 wars with India. In 1964, India was rattled when China conducted its first nuclear test within the January 1967 deadline set up by the NPT. As a result, China was inducted into the nuclear club. India responded by conducting its first nuclear test in 1974, but it missed the NPT deadline.

Throughout the 1970s, both sides kept diplomatic contacts to a minimum but did not cut off relations altogether. Toward the late 1970s, both sides renewed efforts to repair the troubled relationship. Indian foreign minister Vajpayee visited China in 1979, a visit that was reciprocated by Chinese foreign minister Huang Hua in 1981. India and China held several rounds of border negotiations between 1981 and 1987. Although no real progress was made, the negotiations helped reduce the tensions, paving the way for Prime Minister Rajiv Gandhi's landmark visit to China in 1988. It was the first such visit in thirty-four years by an Indian prime minister since Nehru's 1954 visit.[253]

After Rajiv Gandhi's visit, India and China agreed to bury the hatchet and broaden their bilateral ties. They decided to put the border dispute on the back burner and forge ahead with cooperation in areas where there was no disagreement. Border trade resumed in 1992, and new consulates opened in Mumbai and Shanghai. China softened its stand vis-à-vis Kashmir by favoring a negotiated settlement between India and Pakistan. Unlike in the past, China adopted a position favorable to India during the Kargil War of 1999.

In 1998, relations received a minor setback when India conducted a new round of nuclear testing, twenty-four years after its first tests. In a letter to Bill Clinton justifying the test, Prime Minister Vajpayee cited China as a security threat to India.[254] Fortunately, the damage was soon contained and did not adversely affect the relations.

In 2002, Chinese airlines made their first flight from Beijing to New Delhi, formally establishing a direct air link between the neighbors.[255] In 2003, China officially recognized Sikhim as part of India. There have been several high-level contacts in recent years. Chinese Premier Wen Jiabao visited India in 2005, and President Hu Jintao in 2006. Both nations celebrated 2006 as the Year of Friendship, signifying the upswing in their relationship.

India and China, the world's fastest-growing economies and the most populous nations, are making a conscious effort to improve their trade relationship. Bilateral trade quadrupled from $5 billion in 2002 to $20 billion in 2006 and is expected to touch $40 billion by 2010. Trade between the two nations has grown at over 30 percent annually since 1999.

What can India possibly export to a country that is considered the factory of the world? The simple answer is raw materials. Over 50 percent of India exports consist of iron ore and other raw materials to feed China's booming housing and construction sector. Chinese exports to India are fairly well-diversified and include manufactured items as well as technology products. Currently, Beijing enjoys a substantial trade surplus.

Meanwhile, many Indian companies are taking advantage of the trade bonhomie between the nations and setting up operations in China. They are attracted by China's high-quality infrastructure, investor-friendly policies, and low-cost structure, similar to that of India. In addition, they want to tap into China's huge domestic market as well as other Asian markets. Larsen and Toubro, India's top engineering and construction company, has a significant presence in China. All the major Indian IT players, including Infosys, Wipro, TCS, and Satyam, are growing in China by leaps and bounds. The latest entry is i-flex solutions, a provider of IT solutions for the banking sector, which has set up operations in Shanghai to tap into opportunities that the banking sector provides. In all, around 150 Indian companies are operating in China. Likewise, some Chinese companies are setting up operations in India. For instance, Huawei Technologies, a Shenzhen-based telecom-equipment company, runs a software center in Bangalore that employs 1,150 Indian engineers.

Despite growing business and trade links, several areas of disagreement and mistrust remain. For India, the memories of the 1962 war still remain; the wounds have never really healed. However, there will probably be no repetition of 1962, for two reasons. First, both countries have the world's biggest militaries, China with 2.3 million personnel and India with 1.3 million. Second, the increase in trade acts as a deterrent to any possible war.

India continues to be suspicious of China's assistance to Pakistan's nuclear and missile programs, which is now an established fact. Disputes along its 2,175 miles of shared border remain unresolved. During a visit to India by President Hu Jintao, the two sides agreed to resolve the border issues. However, progress has been slow. China formally recognized the border state of Sikhim as part of India.[256]

India is also suspicious of the burgeoning ties between China and African nations, with whom India has traditionally maintained strong relations. In November 2006, China hosted leaders of more than forty African countries for a summit meeting on trade and investment.[257] China's goal is to secure Africa's natural resources like oil, iron ore, and copper for its booming economy, in return for liberal economic assistance and help in building Africa's infrastructure. These moves are paying off in a big way for China. Angola has replaced Saudi Arabia as China's largest foreign source of oil. Sudan, which is shunned by the United States and its allies for its role in the civil war in Darfur, exports $1 billion of crude to China. The two-way trade between China and Africa has grown to $40 billion, a ten-fold increase since 1995, and Africa is emerging as a growing market for Chinese goods. China also launched a communications satellite for Nigeria, a major oil producer, and signed a satellite contract with another big oil supplier, Venezuela.

India is trying to make up lost ground by engaging Africa in a substantive way. Indian foreign minister Pranab Mukherjee recently visited Ethiopia, Africa's second most populous country, to boost trade ties.

China is upset that India bars its companies from participating in some sectors, such as ports and telecommunications, due to security concerns. China is also pressing for market economy status from India. China was admitted into the WTO as a nonmarket economy and will remain so until 2016. It was given an option of getting market economy status from individual countries, and so far around sixty nations have recognized China as a market economy. But India, the United States, Japan, and the European Union have so far refused to do so because China gives huge subsidies to the domestic manufacturing industry.

China also remains wary about growing Indo-U.S. relations, which it views as an attempt to contain its influence. In response, Indian foreign minister Pranab Mukherjee clarified that India doesn't believe in containing any country, whether large or small. Prime Minister Manmohan Singh echoed Mukherjee's statement and said that the world's two most populous countries should be friends despite the bitter past.

Many analysts refer to the presence of the Dalai Lama in India as the major obstacle in the relations. In reality, the Dalai Lama is not a factor. China considers Tibet to be an indispensable part of China and will not negotiate with the Dalai Lama until he recognizes this fact. China wants the Dalai Lama to abandon his demand for any kind of Tibetan independence. Although India hosts the Dalai Lama and his one hundred thousand followers in Dharamsala in Himachal Pradesh, it recognizes Tibet as an integral part of China. But the fact that the Tibetan government-in-exile exists in India still annoys China.

India-Pakistan Relations

Pakistan was formed by carving out the Muslim-majority regions of British India at the end of colonial rule in 1947. Democracy did not take root in Pakistan like it did in India. The Pakistani military has played an influential role in mainstream politics throughout Pakistan's history, with military presidents ruling from 1958–71, 1977–88, and 1999–2008.

At the time of independence, Pakistan consisted of two parts, West and East Pakistan, which were separated by more than one thousand miles of India's territory. Although both regions were predominantly Muslim, their ethnic makeup was different. West Pakistan consisted of Punjabi, Sindhi, and Pashtun groups, while East Pakistan consisted of the Bengali ethnicity. Since independence, the people of East Pakistan (present-day Bangladesh) were treated as second-class citizens and were politically marginalized by West Pakistanis. The breaking point came in the early 1970s. In the general elections, the Awami League, an East Pakistani political party, scored a victory over the Pakistan People's Party, a major political party based in West Pakistan.

The Awami League was led by Sheikh Mujibur Rahman, while the Pakistan People's Party was led by Zulfikar Ali Bhutto. Despite the election victory, the Pakistani military refused to handover power to the Awami League, triggering mass protests and civil disobedience. The military responded by launching a countrywide crackdown that led to hundreds of civilian deaths. The conflict soon escalated into guerilla warfare between the Pakistani military and the East Pakistani freedom fighters. Over ten million people fled to neighboring India to escape the Pakistani military crackdown. India, under Prime Minister Indira Gandhi, supported the freedom struggle and provided diplomatic and material support to the East Pakistani freedom fighters, known as Mukti Bahini. The Indian army formally joined the war against the Pakistani army on December 3, 1971, and fought on the side of the East Pakistani rebels. The war ended within two weeks when the Pakistani army surrendered to the Indian army, with nearly ninety-three thousand soldiers taken as prisoners of war. The new nation of Bangladesh was born in the erstwhile East Pakistani region. Pakistani ruler General Yahya Khan resigned in disgrace and handed over power to Zulfikar Ali Bhutto, who became president and the first civilian martial law administrator.

Under Bhutto, Pakistan adopted a new constitution and parliamentary democracy. Bhutto served as prime minister from 1973 to 1977. In the 1977 general elections, Bhutto's party scored a major victory, but allegations of widespread election fraud led to general unrest in the country. His regime came to an end when he was deposed by then army chief General Zia-ul-Haq in a bloodless coup on July 5, 1977. He was later executed by the army after being convicted of authorizing the killing of his political opponent.

General Zia ruled Pakistan for the next eleven years. He imposed martial law and introduced strict Islamic law. The Soviet invasion of Afghanistan came as a blessing in disguise for General Zia. Pakistan emerged as a front-line state in the U.S.-led insurgency aimed at dislodging Soviets from Afghanistan. For his role, the military dictator was rewarded by President Reagan, who pumped in billions of dollars of military and economic aid, overruling objections from India.

The year 1987 will go down as a major year in global nuclear proliferation. It was in this year that Pakistani nuclear scientist A. Q. Khan revealed to the world that Pakistan had manufactured a nuclear bomb. He later retracted his statement, but the damage was already done. This disclosure forced India to review its nuclear options, leading to the 1998 nuclear tests. U.S. intelligence reports also concluded that Pakistan had enriched uranium to weapons-grade levels. The Bush administration swung into action in 1990. It terminated economic and military aid to Pakistan after President Bush could no longer certify under the Pressler Amendment[258] that Pakistan did not possess a nuclear device. Interestingly, in 1986, President Reagan had certified to Congress that Pakistan did not possess a nuclear device, thus enabling the passage of a six-year, $4 billion aid package. Bush's move reflected the U.S. government's waning interest in Pakistan after the withdrawal of Soviet troops from Afghanistan.

Zia's rule ended in 1988 when his military transport aircraft, a C-130, exploded mysteriously in midair, killing all passengers on board, including his top commanders; the U.S. ambassador to Pakistan, Arnold Raphael; and a U.S. brigadier general. Democracy returned to Pakistan in 1988 when Benazir Bhutto, the daughter of executed prime minister Zulfikar Ali Bhutto, won a general election and became the country's first female prime minister. The return of democracy to Pakistan provided a rare opportunity for both nations to improve relations. Prime Minister Rajiv Gandhi attended a regional summit in Islamabad in 1988 and established personal rapport with Benazir Bhutto.

As always with India-Pakistan relations, the bonhomie did not last too long. Bhutto initially supported the 1972 Simla Accord, which provided a bilateral mechanism to resolve issues and improve ties, but was forced to back away from that position after being pressured by the army. In Pakistan, the military wields the real power. A separatist movement in Indian-controlled Kashmir, with the active support of the Pakistani military, also threatened to renew tensions.

About halfway through her five-year tenure, the army dismissed Benazir Bhutto from power on charges of corruption and incompetence; she was replaced by Nawaz Sharif in 1990. He, too, was dismissed in 1993, and fresh elections were called; Benazir Bhutto's party once again emerged victorious. Benazir was once again dismissed in 1996 on allegations of corruption, and Nawaz Sharif was brought back to power. Benazir was later convicted on corruption charges and was exiled.

Under Nawaz Sharif, Pakistan conducted its first-ever nuclear tests in 1998, breaking India's self-imposed moratorium. In the aftermath of the tests, the Indian government finally engaged Pakistan in an effort to reduce the level of violence in the Kashmir Valley. In February 1999, Prime Minister Vajpayee broke the ice by traveling to Pakistan, amid much fanfare and world media attention. Vajpayee and Pakistani premier Nawaz Sharif signed the historic Lahore declaration, under which both sides pledged to intensify efforts to resolve their issues peacefully, including the core issue of Kashmir. During Vajpayee's visit, a controversy erupted when the three chiefs of the Pakistani armed forces, including then army chief Pervez Musharraf, broke the protocol and refused to greet the visiting Indian leader.

Before the ink dried on the Lahore declaration, the Pakistani army, which had opposed any rapprochement with India, tried to scuttle the peace process by initiating a mini-war on the border in May 1999. Irregular forces crossed over to the Indian-controlled Kashmir region of Kargil and seized a sensitive point overlooking a highway linking the cities of Srinagar and Leh. After three months of conflict and a sustained air campaign, India managed to recover all its territories. The conflict weakened Nawaz Sharif's position considerably, and he was overthrown by then army chief General Pervez Musharraf in 1999 in a bloodless coup. Nawaz Sharif was later exiled to Saudi Arabia, thus becoming the second prime minister after Benazir Bhutto to be kept out of the country by the military.

General Musharraf declared himself president of Pakistan in 2001, in addition to being its army chief. In July 2001, India launched yet another peace initiative with Pakistan. After shunning him for two years, the Indian government finally accorded legitimacy to Pakistani military leader Pervez Musharraf by inviting him for peace talks. In a symbolic gesture aimed at reducing tensions between the nations, Musharraf became the first Pakistani leader to visit the Mahatma Gandhi memorial in New Delhi, considered a routine stop for foreign dignitaries but not so for the Pakistanis. The peace summit, which was held near the fabled Taj Mahal in Agra, ended in complete failure over a disagreement over Kashmir. Besides failing to achieve any forward movement on Kashmir, both sides were unable to agree on the joint statement describing the talks.

Post-9/11, Pakistan reluctantly decided to support America's global war on terror, and Taliban forces in neighboring Afghanistan were defeated by coalition forces. The Bush administration rewarded Pakistan by lifting the nuclear-related sanctions. While Pakistan was cooperating with the United States in its war on terrorism against the Taliban, it continued its policy of supporting terrorist activities in Indian-held Kashmir.

In December 2001, two months after the 9/11 attacks, relations between India and Pakistan reached a new low when India blamed

Pakistani-based militant groups for carrying out suicide attacks against its parliament building in New Delhi. Facing domestic pressure, India downgraded its relations with Pakistan and began massing its troops along the border to pressure Pakistan to stop supporting terrorist activities in Kashmir and elsewhere. Pakistan responded by amassing its own troops along the border.

The eighteen-month standoff between the nations ended when Prime Minister Vajpayee offered a hand of friendship to Pakistan. Vajpayee called the peace effort the last in his lifetime, as his previous two attempts to bring peace to the region were sabotaged by the Pakistani military. A cease-fire came into effect along the informal border dividing Indian-administered and Pakistani-administered Kashmir in November 2003. India and Pakistan also agreed to resume direct air links from January 1 after a two-year ban. The bonhomie continued when the Indian cricket team toured[259] Pakistan in March 2004 after a gap of fifteen years.

After the fall of the Vajpayee government in May 2004, a new Indian government, led by Prime Minister Manmohan Singh, continued the momentum of the peace talks. General Musharraf visited New Delhi in March 2005 to watch a cricket match. In a joint news conference, the leaders of India and Pakistan made a significant announcement that the peace process was irreversible.

In 2005, after months of negotiations, India and Pakistan launched a landmark bus service linking the towns of Srinagar (Indian Kashmir) and Muzaffarabad (Pakistan Kashmir), thus reuniting families who had been divided after bus service was halted as a result of the First Kashmir War of 1947. There has been a vast improvement in relations, and India and Pakistan are also trying to improve their trade ties. Bilateral trade crossed the $1.5 billion mark during fiscal year 2006. But Pakistan is holding off on granting most-favored nation status to India, saying that the Kashmir dispute must be resolved before it will allow free trade with India. Both sides have lifted travel restrictions for diplomats. Efforts are underway to reopen consulates in Mumbai and Karachi, which were shut down in 1992.

Anatomy of the Kashmir Issue

Relations between India and Pakistan have been tense for the past sixty years of their existence as independent countries. The main cause of conflict is the status of the Kashmir region. Both India and Pakistan claim the whole region and fought two major wars, in 1947 and 1965, over the territory. There have been a number of diplomatic initiatives, but none have born fruit. Kashmir remains one of the most militarized zones in the world.

Kashmir was part of the Sikh empire until 1846. After the death of Sikh leader Maharaja Ranjit Singh in 1839, his empire weakened considerably, inviting attacks from the British. In 1846, the British defeated the Sikhs and captured Kashmir but decided not to control it. Instead, the region was sold to Gulab Singh of neighboring Jammu for 7.5 million rupees (roughly $200,000 at today's exchange rate). Thus, the Kashmir Valley, which has a nearly 80 percent Muslim population, came under the control of a Hindu king, and a new state of Jammu and Kashmir was born.

After Gulab Singh's death, Ranbir Singh (1857–85), Pratap Singh (1885–1925), and Hari Singh (1925–49) ruled in succession. Starting in 1931, Maharaja Hari Singh faced a mass uprising against his rule from the majority Muslim community led by Sheikh Abdullah, who campaigned for freedom from Hindu Maharaja rule.

In 1947, Britain granted India freedom from colonial rule. The Indian subcontinent was partitioned into Hindu-dominated India and the newly created Muslim state of Pakistan. The Britain also indirectly controlled more than five hundred princely states within India. Under the partition plan, the rulers of the princely states were encouraged to join either India or Pakistan; most of them joined India. But the status of the princely state of Kashmir remained unsettled. India expected Kashmir to join its union because it was ruled by a Hindu king, while Pakistan expected it to join its union because the majority of its subjects were Muslim. However, the king of Kashmir joined neither country and kept postponing his decision.

In October 1947, Pakistani irregular forces invaded Kashmir to take it by force. Facing imminent defeat, Maharaja Hari Singh signed an instrument of accession to India. Officially, Kashmir became part of India in October 1947. Armed with the document of accession, India sent its military to protect its new territory.

While the fighting was going on, India approached the United Nations to complain about Pakistani aggression by invoking Articles 34 and 35 of the U.N. charter.[260] A U.N.-brokered cease-fire came into effect on January 1, 1949. A demarcation line was formalized later that year, which left two-thirds of Kashmir under India's control and one-third under the Pakistan's control. A U.N. military observer group was established to supervise the cease-fire line in Kashmir. The United Nations passed a resolution that the state's status should be determined at a future date through a free and fair plebiscite. As a prerequisite, the resolution required the aggressor (Pakistan) to withdraw its troops from Kashmir. Pakistan refused, so India backed away from conducting the plebiscite.

Though the stalemate continued, both sides got down to the task of governing their portions of Kashmir. Pakistan renamed its portion Azad Kashmir (Free Kashmir), implying that the part occupied by India was not free. India did not make any attempt to wholly assimilate Kashmir into its union, although it had the legal basis to do so. Instead, Sheikh Abdullah, the rebel Muslim leader who had earlier opposed the rule of Maharaja Hari Singh, was made the head of Indian Kashmir. India also passed Article 370 of the constitution in 1949, which gave special status to the state of Jammu and Kashmir. India limited its jurisdiction to defense, foreign affairs, and communications matters. Even today, people from the rest of the India are not allowed to purchase land in Kashmir.

In 1953, Sheikh Abdullah was removed from power and put in detention after he started advocating Kashmir's secession from India. Bakshi Ghulam Mohammad became Kashmir's prime minister. In 1956, Jammu and Kashmir, India's only Muslim-majority state, was proclaimed a state within the Indian union, somewhat diluting the autonomy that had earlier been granted to Kashmir. Meanwhile, China entered the Kashmir fray in the 1960s. It occupied 37,000 square kilometers of the northeast Ladakh region of Kashmir, an area called Aksai Chin. In 1963, Pakistan ceded 5,180 square kilometers of its Kashmir territory to China.

In August 1965, Pakistan made yet another unsuccessful attempt to secure control of Indian-controlled Kashmir. Pakistani-backed army infiltrators crossed the cease-fire line, India counterattacked, and a full-scale war broke out. Alarmed by these developments, the Soviet Union brokered a cease-fire agreement under which both sides agreed to restore the status quo and resolve their differences through negotiations.

In 1971, another war broke out between India and Pakistan, which led to the liberation of Bangladesh. Although not a Kashmir-centric war, the war ended up with several engagements in Kashmir as well. The Indian army, which fought alongside the Bangladeshi secessionists, inflicted a crushing defeat on the Pakistan military.

Postwar negotiations between Indian prime minister Indira Gandhi and Pakistani leader Zulfikar Ali Bhutto took place in Simla, India, in 1972. They reached an agreement under which India would release its prisoners of war and return the territory it captured in the war. All Pakistan had to do was respect the previously drawn cease-fire line in Kashmir and agree to settle differences through peaceful bilateral negotiations. Apparently, Bhutto verbally agreed to convert the actual cease-fire line into an international border as a final settlement to the Kashmir issue, but he did not want it to be entered into the agreement; he risked facing political backlash since Pakistan had already lost a substantial portion of its territory in the war. Hindsight is 20/20. It is now clear that India missed a golden opportunity to resolve the Kashmir issue once and for all by securing a final settlement with Pakistan. After the war, the cease-fire line was renamed the Line of Control (LOC).

In 1974, India signed a fresh agreement with rebel Kashmiri leader Sheikh Abdullah, paving way for his election as the new chief minister of the state. When Sheikh Abdullah died in 1982, his son Farooq

Abdullah became the chief minister. In the 1987 state elections, Farooq Abdullah was reelected, trouncing his chief rival, the Muslim United Front (MUF), amid allegations of election irregularities and rigging. The MUF consisted of Islamic organizations sympathetic to the cause of the Kashmir separatists. Protests over the election results turned into massive anti-India demonstrations throughout the Kashmir Valley, creating a law and order nightmare for India. Emboldened by the support it was receiving both within and outside Kashmir (primarily Pakistani), militants kidnapped none other than the daughter of the home minister (equivalent to the secretary of homeland security in the United States) and released her only after the government caved in to the demand to release separatist leaders who were jailed in India.

Beginning in 1990, much of the state plunged into secessionist violence. Farooq Abdullah, under pressure from both the Indian government and militants, finally had enough. He resigned in 1990, bringing the state under direct federal rule. As India struggled to contain the violence, Pakistan took advantage of the moment to fish in the troubled waters. By the mid-1990s, thousands of Kashmiri youth had crossed over to Pakistan for arms training. Foreign militant groups such as Lashkar-e-Toiba (LeT) and Harkat-ul-Mujahedin joined indigenous groups such as Hizb to fight Indian security forces. However, the original separatist groups including, JKLF, decided to shun violence and fight Indian rule politically. An umbrella political group called the All Parties Hurriyat (Freedom) Conference came into existence in 1994, becoming the voice of the moderate wing.

The proliferation of Islamic militant separatist groups into Kashmir led to the exodus of thousands of Hindu Kashmiri families (also known as "Hindu Pandits") into other parts of India. Even today, over three hundred thousand Kashmiri Pandit (Hindu Brahmin) families continue to languish in refugee camps in Jammu, Delhi, and other states.[261]

Amid continued violence and confusion, elections were held for the Kashmiri assembly in 1996. This time, the elections were widely acknowledged as fair, though not entirely free due to militants' call for a boycott. Once again, Farooq Abdullah won, but the people of Kashmir felt let down by the government's failure in dealing with their economic problems and the endemic corruption in public institutions. Militants continued to press for either complete independence or a merger with Pakistan. Throughout the 1990s, Kashmir was stuck in a cycle of unrest, demonstrations, militant attacks, and armed suppression by Indian security forces. India continued its diplomatic offensive and charged Pakistan with providing active support for the Kashmiri insurgency. It lobbied Washington and its allies for help in reining in Pakistan but received only lukewarm support.

The Indian government's decision to engage Pakistan in an effort to reduce the level of violence in the Kashmir Valley bore fruit when leaders from both sides signed the landmark Lahore Declaration in 1999. Under this agreement, both countries pledged to peacefully resolve all their issues, including the core issue of Kashmir, through a bilateral dialogue mechanism. But the Pakistani army leadership was opposed to any rapprochement with India. They tried to scuttle the accord by seizing some territory in Indian-controlled Kashmir through a covert operation. After months of fighting, India was able to recover the territories. The Kargil conflict and the military coup in Pakistan dealt a serious blow to finding a solution to the Kashmir issue.

As the millennium approached, India's Kashmir woes continued. On December 24, 1999, a week before the dawn of the new millennium, Kashmiri militants hijacked an Indian Airlines plane carrying 178 passengers from Kathmandu, Nepal, to New Delhi. The hijacking drama ended on December 31 when the Indian government released several militants, including Pakistani cleric Maulana Masood Azhar and Omar Sheik, in exchange for the hostages. The dramatic success of the hijacking effort further emboldened the militants, who escalated their violence in the Kashmir Valley. In response, India adopted a two-pronged approach. In addition to beefing up security, the government also decided to open negotiations with separatist leaders based in the Kashmir Valley.

In a goodwill gesture, India declared a unilateral cease-fire during the Muslim holy month of Ramadan in November 2000. Although the cease-fire was widely welcomed, the peace process did not gain traction; separatist leaders refused to negotiate with the Indian government until it convened trilateral talks with Pakistan. However, India agreed to talk to Pakistan only if it stopped cross-border terrorism. Meanwhile, in July 2000, the Indian Kashmir assembly passed a resolution urging India to restore autonomy to a pre-1953 level, with India's jurisdiction restricted to defense, foreign affairs, and communications. The Indian government promptly shot down the resolution.

In July 2001, India launched yet another peace initiative with Pakistan. The peace summit, which was held in Agra, ended in complete failure because of disagreement over Kashmir. In the months immediately following the 9/11 attacks, India and Pakistan's relationship reached a new low when India accused Pakistani-based militants of carrying out suicide attacks on its parliament. Facing domestic pressure, India downgraded its relations with Pakistan and began massing its troops along the border to pressure Pakistan to stop supporting terrorist activities inside Kashmir. Relations were normalized after eighteen months when General Musharraf finally relented and promised to act against the Pakistani-based groups who were fomenting trouble in Indian-controlled Kashmir.

In 2002, fresh elections for the state assembly were held in Indian-controlled Kashmir. Defying militant threats, around 50 percent of the electorate participated in the polls. The Indian government tried unsuccessfully to persuade the moderate separatist group APHC to participate. Their nonparticipation robbed the elections of legitimacy. Nevertheless, the elections were universally acclaimed as fair and free.

India was clearly buoyed by the elections. There was a great deal of violence during the run-up to the elections. The ruling party, which had held power for over two decades, was voted out, and a new coalition took over. In April 2005, after months of talks, India and Pakistan launched a landmark bus service across the cease-fire line dividing

Kashmir, reuniting families who had been separated by the conflict for over sixty years.

Kashmir: What Is the End Game?

Since 1990, when the separatist movement took a violent turn, an estimated forty thousand people have been killed in Kashmir. Separatist guerrillas, supported by Pakistan, have waged a consistent campaign against Indian forces. By some estimates, over four hundred thousand Indian troops are stationed in Kashmir in an effort to restore normalcy. The dispute over the state of Kashmir is ongoing, but discussions and confidence-building measures have led to decreased tensions since 2002.

India claims the whole territory of Kashmir, including those territories controlled by Pakistan and China. India has the legal basis to do so. It points to the instrument of accession signed by the Kashmiri ruler in 1947. Pakistan, which rejects the legality of accession, also claims the entirety of Kashmir, minus the areas controlled by China. The separatists want either independence or to become part of Pakistan. Both India and Pakistan reject the option of Kashmir becoming an independent nation.

Pakistani leaders continue to harp on self-determination by the Kashmiri people through a plebiscite. Pakistan's political and military establishment has made the liberation of Kashmir, India's only Muslim-majority state, a national cause. India is against internationalizing the issue, preferring to resolve the issue through bilateral dialogue. Indian diplomats accuse Pakistan of internationalizing the issue in violation of the 1972 Simla Accord. India maintains that the Kashmiri people's participation in assembly elections is a clear demonstration of their willingness to be a part of democratic India. Pakistan insists that a U.N.-supervised plebiscite is the only way to determine Kashmir's future.

India will probably never give up Kashmir; it's a matter of principle. Kashmir, the only Muslim-majority state of predominantly Hindu India, bolsters India's secular credentials. But India will probably accept the current LOC as the final solution, with some minor adjustments.

Prime ministers Vajpayee and Manmohan Singh made sincere efforts to engage the separatist leaders in finding a solution. The talks floundered over separatist demands that Pakistan should be included in the talks. India refused trilateral talks because of Pakistan's support for the Kashmiri insurgency.

Recent years have seen a thaw in India-Pakistan relations vis-à-vis Kashmir. Pakistan has softened its tough stance by showing a willingness to set aside its long-standing plebiscite demand. General Musharraf floated a four-point formula for a settlement of the Kashmir dispute, involving the demilitarization of Kashmir, autonomy for the region, a joint supervisory mechanism, and easy movement of people and goods across the border. India is still mulling over this formula. India for its part agreed to hold a composite dialogue with Pakistan, with Kashmir as one of the items on the agenda, backing down from its previous refusal to talk to Pakistan. Violence levels in Kashmir level have reduced considerably.

One might wonder why the stakes are so high on the Kashmir issue in the eyes of the international community. The simple fact is that the two nations have fought three major wars over the territory. One side (Pakistan) has been using terrorism as a weapon to force the other side (India) into submission. Both recently acquired nuclear arms and have a proven system of delivery. One side (India) declared a no-first-use nuclear policy, but the other side (Pakistan) doesn't give any such guarantees. Although no side is foolish enough to use nuclear arms in a future engagement, real worries remain over accidental use. President Clinton called Kashmir the most dangerous place on earth.

India is eager to end its enmity with Pakistan. There is a consensus in India that continuing animosity for Pakistan is not in the country's best interests. Nearly a quarter of India's armed forces are tied up in Kashmir. For India, the ongoing conflict with Pakistan deprives it of respect and moral standing in the world. Kashmir is a huge drain on its treasury. To add insult to injury, Indians cannot even visit Kashmir safely.

There are many possible solutions to the Kashmir issue. Converting the current LOC into an international border is one possibility, something that India, but not Pakistan, would probably agree to. Other solutions include integrating the regions of Jammu and Ladakh with India and making the rest of Kashmir an independent state, jointly administered by India and Pakistan. It is no secret that the people of Jammu and Ladakh want to stay with India. Militant activity is concentrated in the Kashmir Valley. After many years of unrest, there are definite signs that India is making headway in bringing law and order to the Kashmir Valley. In the post-9/11 era, Pakistan is finding it increasingly difficult to continue supporting the militants in Kashmir. India's goal is to stabilize the security situation and make enough political concessions to the separatist groups to bring them back into the Indian fold, thus ending the conflict. Until a solution to Kashmir is found, both nations will remain stuck in the current spiral of enmity and mistrust.

The Siachen Conflict

The Indian and Pakistani armies have been fighting a war since 1984 on the Siachen Glacier, located in the eastern Karakoram Range in the Himalayas. Siachen, the world's largest nonpolar glacier, is 78 kilometers long and situated at an altitude of 5,400 meters above sea level. The temperatures routinely hover around −60°C.

Prior to 1984, neither India nor Pakistan had any permanent presence on the glacier. There was no official demarcation of the area; the glacier was deemed inhospitable and had little strategic value. Trouble started brewing when Pakistan allowed mountaineering expeditions to climb high peaks on the glacier in the early 1980s. To reinforce its claim over the area, Pakistan issued official permits for the expeditions. Soon, alarm bells went off in New Delhi. India launched a preemptive attack in 1984 and captured two-thirds of the glacier in an operation code-named Operation Meghdoot. Pakistan quickly responded with troop deployments of its own. Since then, both armies have been locked in a fierce battle over control of the glacier, and the Siachen Glacier has become the world's highest battleground.

Currently, the Indian army controls the heights and therefore has the tactical advantage of high attitude. Siachen's inhospitable terrain has taken a heavy toll on the men and resources on both sides. More soldiers die from the extreme temperatures than from enemy fire. It is estimated that an average of one Pakistani soldier is killed every fourth day, while one Indian soldier is killed every other day. Since there is no road access to the peaks, India has faced a logistical nightmare in supplying its forward positions; it utilizes helicopters to provide supplies to its troops. Logistics comprise a big chunk of the $1 million a day that India spends to keep the peaks. Neither side wants to back off, fearing that the other side will gain a strategic advantage.

A cease-fire arrangement has been in place on the glacier since November 2003 as part of peace talks between India and Pakistan. A number of talks took place, but so far there has been no breakthrough. Pakistan wants both sides to restore the status quo and pull back to the positions they held more than twenty years ago. President Pervez Musharraf is believed to have privately assured Indian leadership that Pakistan would not seize the glacier if India decided to vacate. India agrees in principle but insists that any withdrawal must be preceded by marking the current positions.

Indian leaders routinely make morale-boosting trips to the Siachen Glacier. During one such visit in 2005, Prime Minister Manmohan Singh wanted the Himalayan glacier in Kashmir to become a "peace mountain" between India and Pakistan.[262] So far, Singh's wish remains a pipe dream. The Siachen, which translates to "place of roses," has not lived up to its name and continues to be the world's highest, bloodiest, and costliest battleground.

India-Sri Lanka Relations

Sri Lanka, a tiny Island nation of twenty-one million people, is dominated by the ethnic Sinhalese population. Most Sinhalese are Buddhists. The nation is also home to a million Indian Tamils, who are predominantly Hindus or Christians.[263]

The Sri Lankan people are believed to be migrants from India who settled the island in the fifth or sixth century BC. In the fourteenth century, a South Indian dynasty seized power in the north and established a Tamil kingdom. The Portuguese arrived in 1505, marking the beginning of European involvement. By 1815, the British had won control over the whole island, which was then known as Ceylon. The British brought Tamil laborers from southern India to work on tea, coffee, and coconut plantations. Ceylon gained independence from British rule in 1948. In 1972, Ceylon changed its name to Sri Lanka.

For the past three decades, Sri Lanka has been embroiled in a civil war, which has taken the lives of thousands of people. The civil war has its roots in the rise of Sinhalese nationalism, which swept through the country in the 1950s. Following decades of social and economic discrimination by successive Sinhalese-dominated governments, the Tamil minority began pressing for an independent homeland in the Tamil-dominated northern and eastern regions of the country.

By the late 1970s, the Tamil struggle had degenerated into guerilla warfare led by the Liberation Tigers of Tamil Eelam (LTTE), a Tamil-separatist group that draws its cadres from economically deprived Tamil agricultural workers and unemployed urban youth. The Tamil separatist movement has many sympathizers in the southern Indian state of Tamil Nadu, which is home to nearly sixty million Tamil-speaking people.

Over the years, the Indian Tamils provided arms, training, and sanctuary to the Sri Lanka-based Tamil rebels, much to the chagrin of the Sri Lankan government. In 1987, the Sri Lankan army launched an all-out offensive against the rebels. The government imposed an economic blockade on the Tamil-dominated Jaffna region, causing considerable hardship for the civilian population. The Indian government came under intense domestic pressure to intervene and protect the Tamils.

In May 1987, the Indian government sent a ship convoy of a thousand tons of relief supplies to the Jaffna area on humanitarian grounds, but the ships were intercepted and sent back by the Sri Lankan navy. Angered by Sri Lanka's actions, India violated Sri Lankan airspace and air-dropped twenty-five tons of food and supplies. Although the move was popular among Indian Tamils, the Sri Lankan government condemned the action as a blatant violation of its territorial integrity and sovereignty. As relations between the nations deteriorated, India tried hard to find a political solution acceptable to both the Sri Lankan government and the Tamil rebels. These efforts culminated in a peace accord signed in July 1987 by the governments of India and Sri Lanka.

Under the terms of the accord, the Sri Lankan government agreed to make several concessions to its Tamil minority, including granting greater autonomy to the Tamil-dominated areas and recognizing Tamil as one of the country's official languages. In return, the Tamils agreed to disarm and join the political process. The Indian government took it upon itself to disarm the Tamil rebels. It agreed to send fifteen thousand troops (later increased to forty thousand), known as the Indian Peace-Keeping Force (IPKF), to enforce the terms of the accord. The peace deal was hailed as one of the biggest diplomatic breakthroughs of the decade. But as time went by, opposition to the peace accord grew stronger. The Sri Lankan government faced a growing backlash from its Sinhalese population for making concessions to the Tamils. The Tamil rebels were upset that the accord did not fulfill its goal of securing an independent nation for Tamils. The rebels defied India's attempts to disarm them, and soon the IPKF was drawn into an open confrontation with the Tamil rebels to enforce peace.

After three years of fruitless confrontation with the Tamil rebels, the Indian government finally withdrew its troops from Sri Lanka in 1990. Rajiv Gandhi drew severe criticism for putting Indian troops in harm's way in Sri Lanka. After the withdrawal, Sri Lanka sunk back into violence, which continues today. Rajiv Gandhi himself paid a heavy price when a Tamil suicide bomber assassinated him in 1991 in revenge for sending Indian peace-keeping troops who ended up fighting the rebels. The LTTE also assassinated Sri Lankan president Premadasa in 1993. President Kumaratunga came to power with a pledge to restore peace back to the island nation. She opened peace talks with the LTTE in 1994, but the talks collapsed. The violence continued unabated.

In 2000, Norway stepped in and expressed its willingness to act as an intermediary between the LTTE and the government. Norway's peace initiative resulted in a permanent cease-fire agreement in 2002, perhaps the first major step toward ending the conflict. Following the agreement, road and air links to the Tamil-dominated Jaffna region were restored. The government lifted the ban on the Tamil Tigers, and both sides exchanged prisoners of war. In a significant step, the rebels dropped their demand for an independent state.

India-Middle East Relations

Predominantly Hindu India has always strived to maintain close relations with the Muslim states of the Middle East. India adopted an aggressive pro-Arab stance during the Arab-Israeli wars of 1967 and 1973. India was the first country to recognize the Palestinian Liberation Organization (PLO) and did not maintain diplomatic relations with Israel until 1992. Under Nehru, India maintained a close relationship with Egypt, and both countries played an active role in the formation of the nonaligned movement.

In 2007, King Abdullah of Saudi Arabia visited New Delhi as a guest of honor at India's Republic Day parade, marking the first visit of a Saudi king in more than fifty years. Why is India aggressively courting Saudi Arabia? There are several strategic reasons.

India depends heavily on Middle Eastern nations for its oil imports. It is now the fourth-largest importer of Saudi oil after China, the United States, and China. Although India imports oil from all the major Gulf states including Iran, Iraq, and Kuwait, it is increasingly relying on Saudi Arabia for its rapidly growing energy needs. Recently, relations between India and Iran were strained due to India's vote against Iran at the International Atomic Energy Agency (IAEA). India needs Saudi oil as a hedge against a possible disruption in supplies from Iran.

India also needs an ally in the Muslim world to blunt Pakistan's propaganda on the Kashmir issue, on which many Gulf states have adopted a neutral stance. Despite being home to the second-largest Muslim population in the world, India has not been granted membership in the influential Organization of Islamic Conference (OIC), largely due to opposition from Pakistan. Saudi Arabia is now supporting India's request for observer status in the OIC.

The Indian government also needs Saudi help to facilitate the travel of Indian Muslims to the holy sites of Mecca and Medina. Lastly, there are an estimated five million Indians working in the region, making India the largest source of migrant workers to the oil-rich Gulf nations.[264] Indians in the Gulf work mainly as contract laborers and send home more than $20 billion every year. Recently, India and Kuwait signed a landmark labor agreement to safeguard the rights of Indian workers.

Two-way trade between India and Arab nations, which currently stands at $24 billion, is expected to jump to $55 billion by 2010. India provides engineering services, manufactured goods, and workers to Gulf nations. It needs expertise from countries like Dubai to create world-class infrastructure to sustain its economic boom. India is also actively negotiating a free-trade agreement with the Gulf Cooperation Council.

India-Brazil Relations

Brazil is the largest and most populous country in Latin America (encompassing all of the Spanish or Portuguese-speaking nations south of the United States) and the fifth-largest in the world in both area and population. It has a population of 190 million. Brazil is a trillion-dollar economy with a per capita income five times greater than India's.

Brazil and India are part of the BRIC nations (a term coined by Goldman Sachs), consisting of Brazil, Russia, India, and China, which are projected to become the world's major economies by 2050. Each of the BRIC nations has a unique draw: Brazil as a raw material supplier, Russia as an energy superpower, India as a services superpower, and China as the world's top manufacturing hub.

There are definite signs that relations between India and Brazil are in high gear, with several high-level visits recently taking place. In 2006, Indian prime minister Manmohan Singh participated in the first-ever summit of India, Brazil, and South Africa (IBSA Trilateral Cooperation Forum) in Brazil's capital, Brasilia. The aim of this forum is to expand strategic and economic ties between these emerging regional powers.[265]

President Luiz Inacio Lula da Silva was the chief guest at India's 2004 Republic Day celebrations. In his latest trip in 2007, President Lula promised to maintain a special relationship with India. Both sides are consolidating ties in various sectors, including trade and energy. There is a convergence of views on international issues, whether it is the Doha Round of WTO trade negotiations or efforts to gain permanent a seat in the U.N. Security Council.

Brazil is India's largest trading partner in Latin America. Currently, bilateral trade stands at $2.5 billion, but it is expected to grow to $10 billion by 2010. Energy cooperation is set to grow with India's Oil and Natural Gas Commission (ONGC) acquiring a 15 percent stake in a Brazilian oil field. The ONGC also offered Brazil's state-run oil company, Petrobras, a stake in its refining ventures.

India has a lot to gain from its partnership with Brazil. Brazil's expertise in biofuels is acknowledged around the world. Brazil is the biggest producer and exporter of ethanol fuel and uses it extensively as fuel for automobiles. By some estimates, 80 percent of new cars sold in Brazil run on ethanol. India, which currently imports three-fourths of its crude oil requirements, is looking for cheaper and cleaner sources of energy to fuel its rapid growth. Brazil's expertise may come in handy.

The Indian economy, which is growing at a scorching pace, would benefit from Brazil's huge reservoirs of natural resources. Brazil and India are looking out for each other in the international arena. For instance, they are part of a G-4 group of nations that are pressing for permanent membership in the expanded U.N. Security Council. Both India and Brazil, acting as representatives of developing nations, are engaged in the tough Doha Round of trade talks with the United

States and the European Union. The talks reached an impasse over rich countries' refusal to cut farm subsidies and the developing world's reluctance to provide increased market access.

Key Things to Remember About Indian Foreign Policy:

- India has followed a largely independent foreign policy since its independence from Britain sixty years ago.
- During the cold war, India refused to align with either the American or Soviet block; rather, it cofounded the Non-Alignment Movement (NAM) to keep equal distance from both superpowers.
- A notable feature of India's foreign policy has been its strong advocacy of nuclear disarmament. India has refused to give up its nuclear option until all the countries in the world embrace its concept of universal nuclear disarmament in a phased manner.
- India is one of three countries, along with Pakistan and Israel, that haven't signed the Nuclear Non-Proliferation Treaty (NPT) or Comprehensive Test Ban Treaty (CTBT) on the grounds that they are discriminatory in nature.
- In the 1970s, India's relations with the United States soured after the Nixon administration openly sided with Pakistan during the 1971 war. India responded by signing a twenty-year friendship treaty with the Soviet Union.
- In the 1980s, India made a concerted effort to improve relations with the United States, while maintaining close ties with the Soviet Union.
- The end of the cold war and the demise of the Soviet Union forced India to reassess its foreign policy priorities. India has launched a slew of foreign policy initiatives, including establishing diplomatic relations with Israel and strengthening commercial ties with the United States and the West.
- The United States is keen to partner with India due to its vast economic and military potential. It recognizes that only India has the scale and depth to serve as a counterweight to the rising power of China.

- With India in the midst of a major economic expansion, many businesses in the United States view India as a lucrative market for American goods and also as a source of cheap white-collar labor.
- Relations between India and Pakistan, which have been locked in a bitter rivalry over Kashmir for the past six decades, continue to be tense. They are currently engaged in a "composite" dialogue process to normalize their relations.
- Relations between India and China, which went into a deep chill after a brief but bloody border conflict in 1962, have witnessed a gradual improvement since 1988. Bilateral trade quadrupled from $5 billion in 2002 to $20 billion in 2006 and is expected to reach $40 billion by 2010.
- Relations between India and Russia continue to be strong. Although bilateral trade between the nations is only a fraction of India's trade with the United States or China, Russia nonetheless remains India's largest supplier of military systems and spare parts.
- In recognition of India's growing stature as a major regional and world power, the European Union initiated summit-level talks with India in 2000, similar to its summit-level talks with the United States, Canada, Russia, Japan, and China.
- India's size, population, and geographic location, coupled with its growing military, economic, and technological power, will likely make it an important world power that could play a very important role in world affairs in the twenty-first century.

Chapter 8: Asian Indian Community

The United States is often called a nation of immigrants. More people migrate permanently to the United States than to any other nation in the world. In 2006, 12.5 percent of the U.S. population, or 37.5 million people, were foreign born.[266] Among the immigrants who have come to the United States are people from India. The U.S. Census Bureau defines *Indian Americans* as *Asian Indians* to avoid confusion with *American Indians*. The population of the Asian Indian community in the United States exploded from 1.68 million in 2000 to 2.48 million in 2006, a growth rate of 48 percent, the highest rate for any Asian community.[267] The Asian Indian community is now the second-largest Asian community after China.

Table 31: Asian Immigrant Population in the United States (in Millions)

	2000	2006
Chinese	2.3	3.1
Indian	1.68	2.5
Filipino	1.85	2.3
Korean	1.1	1.5
Vietnamese	1.12	1.47
Pakistani	0.15	0.21

Source: American Community Survey

Although Asian Indians have been living in the United States since the turn of the twentieth century, their real growth happened in the past fifteen to twenty years. A person can become a U.S. citizen by birth or through the naturalization process. Every year, thousands of foreign nationals become naturalized citizens of the United States. In 2007, a total of 660,477 people became naturalized citizens. Asian Indians, with 46,871 naturalizations, were the second largest group after Mexico.[268]

From its humble beginnings, the Asian Indian community has emerged as one of the most successful immigrant groups in America. The community has one of the highest average incomes in the country as per the U.S. Census Bureau. In 2006, the median family household income of Asian Indians was $78,315, the highest for any ethnic group in the country. More than two-thirds of adults have a bachelor's degree, and one-third have a graduate degree.[269] India also sends the highest number of students (83,833)[270]each year to universities across the United States to pursue advanced degrees in engineering, computer science, and business. High levels of education and command of English have enabled them to land lucrative jobs in various fields, including science and technology, software development, and medicine. In 2004, Indians accounted for 10 percent of doctoral degrees in science and engineering in the United States.[271] There are over four thousand faculty members teaching at various universities, including several Ivy League universities.[272]Over forty thousand Asian Indian medical doctors are practicing in the United States today.[273] Several Asian Indians have also become successful entrepreneurs. A Duke University study revealed that Indian immigrants founded more tech start-ups from 1995 to 2005 than immigrants from the next four largest sources combined, including the United Kingdom, China, Taiwan, and Japan. Of an estimated 7,300 U.S. tech start-ups founded by immigrants, 26 percent have Indian founders.[274] Sabeer Bhatia, who arrived in Silicon Valley from Bangalore with $250 in his pocket, went on to create the pioneering Hotmail e-mail system, which he sold to Microsoft for a cool $400 million. Also, Asian Indians virtually rule the hotel industry in the United States, accounting for 43 percent of all hotels and motels.[275]

Following in the footsteps of their successful parents and families, second-generation Asian Indians have also demonstrated a strong commitment to higher education. Nearly two-thirds of them have college degrees, and many are pursuing diverse professional interests. Asian Indian kids have dominated the Scripps National Spelling Bee Championship by winning six titles in the past ten years.[276] In 2005, all four of the top finishers were of Indian descent.

Table 32: Asian Indian Spelling Bee Champions

Year	Champion	Word
1985	Balu Natarajan	milieu
1999	Nupur Lala	logorrhea
2000	George Abraham Thampy	demarche
2002	Pratyush Buddiga	prospicience
2003	Sai R. Gunturi	pococurante
2005	Anurag Kashyap	appoggiatura
2008	Sameer Mishra	guerdon

Source: Scripps National Spelling Bee Web Site

Many Asian Indians are exerting political influence through campaign contributions and organization of fundraising events. Dr. Zach Zachariah, a cardiologist from Fort Lauderdale, has emerged as one of the leading fundraisers in the United States for the Republican Party. In June 2007, Senator Hillary Clinton raised $2 million from a fundraising event organized by a group known as "Indian Americans for Hillary," led by hotelier Sant Chatwal. In July 2007, Bill Clinton addressed a gathering of 14,000 members of the Telugu Association of North America (TANA), an association representing 250,000 people belonging to the Indian state of Andhra Pradesh. There are signs that Washington politicians are increasingly drawn toward the enviable money power of Asian Indians. The Congressional Caucus on India is the largest caucus in the U.S. Congress, with over 176 members: 115 Democrats and 61 Republicans.[277] The U.S. Senate India Caucus, which was launched in 2004, has thirty-two members, including Senator Hillary Clinton. Asian Indians are using their newfound leverage by pushing India's agenda on Capitol Hill. The U.S-India Political Action Committee (USIPAC), an Indian American political group, has played a key role in the successful passage of the India-U.S. nuclear deal in the U.S. Congress.

There has also been a steady increase in the number of Asian Indians seeking political office. Upendra Chivukula has been serving in the New Jersey General Assembly since 2002 as the representative of seventeenth legislative district. Republican Bobby Jindal was elected as governor of Louisiana in October 2007, becoming the first Asian Indian to lead a U.S. state—this despite the fact that only 1.4 percent of the 4.2 million people in Louisiana are of Asian origin.[278] Jindal is also the nation's youngest governor and the first nonwhite person to hold the state's post since Reconstruction.

Although the success of Asian Indians has been widely, the Indian government has been slow to recognize their potential. In 2003, the Indian government finally acted by passing a landmark bill to grant dual citizenship to some of the twenty million people of Indian origin living in other countries. The goal of this bill was to encourage investments from Indians living overseas and allow them to contribute to India's economic development. The dual citizens will not have voting rights in India but will have unhindered visa-free travel access to their homeland.

How is the incredible success of Asian Indians playing out at home? More Indians than ever want to come and settle in the United States to ensure a better future for themselves and their families. They are often inspired by the success stories they hear from their friends and families. Each day, hundreds of people, often braving sweltering heat and humidity, gather outside the four American consulate offices in India—Delhi, Mumbai, Chennai, and Kolkota—seeking American visas. For most Indians, an American visa is a one-way ticket to a better quality of life.

A Brief History of Indian Immigrants[279]

The first Indian immigrants to come to North America were agricultural workers from the Indian state of Punjab. The famine of 1899–1900 devastated Punjab's economy and forced the people to look for jobs outside their homeland. A few thousand Indian immigrant workers arrived in Canada and found jobs in lumber mills. The Indians were able to come to Canada because both India and Canada were British dominions and there were fewer travel restrictions. But as the number of immigrants swelled, local Canadian workers became uneasy because of the competition they faced from low-paid, hard-working Indians. The result was the passing of a law in 1909 that virtually ended immigration from India.

With the doors virtually closed in Canada, some Indians started arriving in the United States from the West Coast. The United States had plenty of jobs in the lumber and railroad industries, and there was plenty of land to farm in California. By the 1910s, the population of Indians in America reached about five thousand.

By the 1910s and 1920s, anti-immigrant sentiment was sweeping across the United States. In 1917, the U.S. Congress enacted a widely restrictive and discriminatory immigration law that barred immigration from several Asians countries, including India. It also barred all immigrants over the age of sixteen who were not literate. The U.S. Congress further tightened immigration laws in 1924 by introducing a national origin quota based on the number of immigrants living in the United States as of 1890. This in effect completely barred immigrants from Asia and allowed only white people to immigrate. The immigration laws of 1917 and 1924 virtually blocked all immigration from the Indian subcontinent. This situation continued for the next twenty years.

Indian immigrants finally got some relief in 1946, when President Truman signed into law the Lucent-Cellar Bill, which allowed citizenship rights for Indian immigrants in the United States. Indians could now own land, take part in elections, and even run for office. They were also allowed to bring their spouses and minor children to the United States. However, the bill restricted the number of immigrants from India to one hundred people per year. As a result, only six thousand people managed to immigrate to the United States from 1947 to 1964. Many of them were relatives of the first wave of immigrants.

The year 1965 was a watershed year for immigration reform in the United States. The Immigration and Naturalization Act of 1965 abolished the discriminatory national-origin-based immigration system of 1924 and replaced it with a quota and preference system. The act allowed for a total of 290,000 immigrants into the United States each year on a first-come, first-served basis. Each country was given a quota of twenty thousand, but spouses, parents, and minor children of U.S. citizens were not subject to any quotas. This act also provided preferential treatment to skilled workers who could meet the needs of the American economy.

The Immigration Act of 1965 resulted in a tremendous surge in immigration into the United States. The act set into motion a cycle of chain immigration whereby newly naturalized U.S. citizens could sponsor their family members and relatives back home to become citizens. The preferential treatment for skilled workers ensured that the best and brightest in the world could also migrate to the United States. By the early 1970s, thousands of the best-educated Indians were immigrating to the United States, lured by high-paying jobs and a better quality of life.

Also, opportunity came knocking for Indian doctors, as the United States was facing a severe shortage of trained doctors due to the enactment of the Medicare and Medicaid programs, which provide healthcare for elderly and poor Americans. Thousands of Indian doctors migrated from India to the United States between 1970 and 1980. Engineers, researchers, and other highly skilled people also entered the United

States during this period. Due to their skills and mastery of English, most Indian immigrants were able to find jobs within a short time. For the first time, South Asians have become a presence on the East Coast, especially in the New York City and New Jersey areas.

By the beginning of 1980, the Indian immigrant population in the United States had swelled to around 375,000. With the increase in numbers, there was also a gradual widening of class and status of the immigrants coming from India. Now, not everyone emigrating from India was highly educated or highly skilled. Many South Asians, including Indians, have taken up jobs as cab drivers, gas station attendants, and convenience store clerks. Some Indians, especially the Patels from Gujarat, have turned entrepreneurial by entering into the U.S. motel business. By 1990, thousands of the middle-class immigrants who had come to the United States from the Indian subcontinent had settled in urban areas.

The Immigration Act of 1990, signed by President George H. W. Bush (or Bush 41), further eased the restrictions on legal immigration into the United States. The act dramatically increased the total number of immigrants allowed into the country to seven hundred thousand annually. The act also retained preferential treatment for family reunification, while doubling employment-related immigration. The key part of this new act was the creation of a new nonimmigrant H-1B visa, which allowed U.S. companies to hire skilled workers from across the world. The H-1B program allowed a large number of Indians with degrees in computer science and engineering to come to the United States and pursue their American dream. The program also allowed hundreds of Indian students pursuing advanced degrees in American universities to take up employment in the United States after finishing their education. The immigration rules allowed H-1B visa holders to convert to permanent resident status before the end of their six-year visa term. Thus, most people who came on H-1B visas did not have to go back after their visas expired; rather, they became permanent residents of the United States. By 1997, the Indian American community became the third-largest Asian ethnic group in the United States after Chinese and Filipino Americans, displacing Japanese Americans.

Today, the Indian population is 2.5 million strong, including immigrants and the American-born, and is the second-largest Asian community in the United States after China.

According to media projections, the population of Indians in America could reach 4.5 million by 2010.[280] The community is not only growing but also maturing, with many people occupying preeminent positions in American society. It has been a remarkable transformation for a community that had fewer than ten thousand people in the mid-1960s.

Asian Indian Professionals

Doctors

There are around forty thousand[281] Asian Indian physicians in America, accounting for one in twenty doctors practicing medicine in the United States. Indian doctors make up the largest non-Caucasian segment of the American medical community. There are also over fifteen thousand Indian Americans and Indians in medical schools and residency programs around the country. These physicians have organized themselves through the American Association of Physicians of Indian Origin (AAPI), a powerful medical association second only to the American Medical Association (AMA).

The growing clout of the AAPI is evident from the fact that its annual conventions attract America's most influential politicians and administration officials. Some past speakers have included Bill Clinton, Bill Frist, Dick Gephardt, Newt Gingrich, and Condoleezza Rice.

**Table 33: Top Ten Countries Where U.S.
Physicians Received Medical Training**

Country	Doctors	Percentage
India	47,581	19.9
Philippines	20,861	8.7
Mexico	13,929	5.8
Pakistan	11,330	4.8
Dominican Republic	7,892	3.3
U.S.S.R.	6,039	2.5
Grenada	5,708	2.4
Egypt	5,202	2.2
Korea	4,982	2.1
Italy	4,978	2.1

Source: American Medical Association

Nurses

The migration of nurses from India may be the next big thing. With U.S. hospitals facing a critical nurse shortage, the U.S. Congress is calling for increased recruitment from countries like India and the Philippines. The American Hospital Association reported that it had 118,000 vacancies[282] for registered nurses in 2006, and the shortfall of nurses could increase to more than 800,000 by 2020.

For healthcare workers in India and the Philippines, the lure of working in the United States is hard to pass up. An average nurse in the Philippines earns around $2,000 a year, compared to $36,000 a year in the United States. Nurses in India earn even less. India graduates over thirty thousand nurses each year. Until recently, the opportunities for Indian nurses to work in the United States were very limited. Many American hospitals preferred nurses from countries like Ireland, Canada, and the Philippines. However, with the supply drying up from these countries, recruiters are now focusing on India. Training institutes and recruiting agencies are springing up across India to prepare nurses for lucrative American jobs. In order to qualify, foreign nurses must pass an exam conducted by the Commission on Graduates of Foreign Nursing Schools (CGFNS).

Although the doors are open to foreign-trained nurses, the immigration process is very long and cumbersome. Foreign nurses come to the United States using an H-1C visa, which is sponsored by a U.S. hospital or medical facility. There is a limit of five hundred H-1C visas per year.

Students

Each year, tens of thousands of foreign students arrive in the United States to pursue advanced degrees in colleges and universities. According to the Institute of International Education, the total number of international students in American colleges and universities in 2006 was 582,984. The United States does not have a cap on the number of foreign students it annually admits, and students accepted by American universities generally end up getting a visa. Foreign students contribute $13.5 billion to the U.S. economy through tuition and living expenses.[283] There are 83,833 Indian students currently enrolled in various U.S. educational institutions. Since 2001, India has remained the leading source of students coming to the United States, followed by China, Korea, Japan, and Taiwan.[284]

The majority of Indian students are enrolled in graduate programs. It is no exaggeration that some graduate engineering and computer programs in U.S. colleges and universities are kept afloat by the Indian and Chinese students. Graduate programs don't attract American students since they pay very little. But for foreign students, graduate programs provide a path for coming to the United States. Besides, graduate programs generally offer financial assistance, albeit a small amount, in the form of research assistantships and teaching assistantships. Most Indian students aspiring to come to the United States are from middle-class families, and they need some form of financial assistance to pursue their studies.

Most international students arrive on F-1 nonimmigrant student visas. This visa category is monitored by the federal government through an electronic database called the Student and Exchange Visitor Information System (SEVIS). Individuals on F-1 visas are exempt from paying Social Security and Medicare (FICA) taxes on their earned income. Also, an individual can bring his or her spouse on an F-2 visa. Minor children of the student visa holder can attend public schools in the United States. The student visa holders are generally required to return to their home countries after completing their studies. However, they are authorized to work legally in the United States for a period of twelve months under a program known as Optional Practical Training (OPT), which allows students to gain practical work experience. Many student visa holders on OPT convert into H-1B status before the end of the twelve-month training period. That allows them to work for an additional six years.

While they are in H-1B status, they can apply for permanent residency and a get a green card, a process that takes three to four years. Once an individual has been on a green card for five years, he or she is eligible to apply for U.S. citizenship. In short, an individual who enters the United States on a student visa can stay on to become a citizen. It is a long and arduous process, but most people make it. Typically, it takes ten to twelve years to transition from a student visa to U.S. citizenship. Of course, there are no guarantees.

Indian Technology Workers

Many professionals come to the United States each year on an H-1B nonimmigrant temporary worker visa. The H-1B visa, which was launched in 1990, allows American companies to employ foreign professionals with hard-to-find technical skills for a period of six years. At the end of that period, the foreign workers must obtain permanent residency status or return home. In fiscal year 2003, nearly 40 percent of H-1B petitions were approved for workers in computer-related occupations.[285] An overwhelming number of H-1B visas are issued to engineers and computer professionals from India.

When the H-1B program was launched in 1990, the U.S. Congress set an initial quota of 65,000 visas per year. The quota was subsequently revised to 115,000 per year due to a growing shortage of high-tech workers brought about by the Internet boom and the Y2K issue. But even that increase proved inadequate. Responding to the pleas of the high-tech industry, the U.S. Congress substantially increased the H-1B visas from 115,000 to 195,000 from fiscal year 2001 to 2003. The bill had bipartisan support in Congress. Soon came the bursting of the dot-com bubble, and NASDAQ lost 78 percent of its value. Most of the developed world went into a recession, and there was a sharp rise in the unemployment rate of U.S. high-tech workers. This led to renewed calls from opponents of the H-1B program to cut the number of visas issued to foreign workers. Congress finally relented and reduced the number of H-1B visas from 195,000 to the original level of 65,000, starting in fiscal year 2004. However, Congress set aside an additional 20,000 work visas for foreign students graduating from U.S. schools.

Table 34: H-1B Visa Recipient by Country (New and Renewal Visas) Fiscal Year 2003

Country	# Visas	Percentage
India	79,166	36.5
China	20,063	9.2
Canada	11,160	5.1
Philippines	10,454	4.8
Total	217,340	100

Source: U.S. Department of Homeland Security, Office of Immigration Statistics

Microsoft Chairman Bill Gates, an ardent supporter of the program, has recently called on the U.S. Congress to raise the cap on skilled-worker visas.[286]About one-third of Microsoft workers based in the United States are foreign-origin workers with work visas or permanent resident cards (green cards). It is no surprise that Microsoft views the

H-1B program as critical to its continued success. Testifying before a Senate committee in March 2007, Gates argued that the United States should not shut its doors on the best and brightest when the country needs them most. He pointed to the fact that Microsoft has not been able to fill about three thousand technical jobs in the United States due to a shortage of skilled workers. Companies like Intel and Oracle also voiced their opposition to the reduction of work visas and argued that the H-1B program helps the U.S. economy by allowing companies to hire needed foreign workers.

Despite widespread support from leaders in the high-tech industry, the H-1B program has its detractors. American high-tech workers and labor groups vociferously oppose the program, which they consider a direct threat to their job security. They blame the program for depressing wages in the high-tech industry and discouraging American students from pursuing high-tech careers. These opponents reject the notion that there is a serious shortage of high-tech workers in the United States and fault the high-tech industry for not exhausting the local talent before looking overseas. Although federal law requires companies to pay H-1B workers the same as American workers for comparable work, a recent study confirmed that H-1B workers make 33 percent less than their American counterparts.[287]

Recently, the detractors of the H-1B program got a shot in the arm when a U.S. government review of the program discovered that Indian software companies, not U.S. companies, were the primary beneficiaries of the program. In fiscal year 2006, seven of the top ten companies that received H-1B workers were Indian companies, with Infosys and Wipro leading the pack. In response, two top U.S. lawmakers, Republican senator Charles Grassley and Democratic senator Richard Durbin, have asked the Indian software companies to disclose details about their workforce and their use of H-1B visas.

What does the future look like for the H-1B program? Going by the recent trends on the number of H-1B petitions filed on behalf of foreign workers, the program is not in any kind of imminent danger. The U.S. Citizenship and Immigration Service (USCIS) announced that it had received more than 150,000 applications for the 65,000 H-1B visas available for fiscal year 2008 on the very first day that filing was permitted. Clearly, foreign workers continue to be sought after by U.S. employers. This may be bad news for American workers, who are already reeling from the continuous loss of their jobs through outsourcing.

Asian Indians in the American Hotel Industry[288]

Fact 1:

Indians constitute less than 1 percent of America's population. However, they own about 43 percent of the forty-seven thousand hotels and motels in the United States.

Fact 2:

An overwhelming number of Indian hotel owners have the last name Patel.

The American hospitality industry, especially the economy hotel segment, is dominated by the Indian community. Most Indian hotel owners belong to the Patel community, a trading community with roots in the western Indian state of Gujarat. In America, the last name *Patel* has become so synonymous with hotels that some people even refer to hotels run by Patels as *Potels*. What is even more amazing is the fact that the Patel conquest of the American hotel industry did not begin until the early 1970s.

How did they do it? Patels, like others Asian Indians, began arriving in large numbers in the early 1970s after President Lyndon Johnson overhauled American immigration policy, making it easy for Asians to migrate. Many Indians also migrated from Uganda and other African nations due to political and racial tensions. For instance, over seventy thousand Indians were expelled from Uganda by Idi Amin in 1972. Some of them ended up resettling in the United States. The arriving Indians soon started looking for business opportunities around the country, and the timing could not have been better. America in the mid-1970s was hit hard by the Arab oil embargo. With fewer people taking driving vacations, the American hotel business was badly hurt, and hundreds of motels were up for sale. That's when the Patels stepped in, bought several hotels at rock-bottom prices, and began the arduous task of rebuilding them. Over the years, property values appreciated considerably, putting them in the driver's seat. Today, the market value of the hotel properties owned by Indians in the United States is around $38 billion.

Why were the Patels attracted to the hotel business? They viewed it as a safe investment that they could run without having much experience. Besides, it could provide employment for the entire family. How did they finance their ventures? Being conservative and frugal in nature, they bypassed the traditional banks and lending institutions and relied on their network of relatives and friends to borrow money.

The hotels run by the Patels are mostly budget or no-frills hotels. They offer limited or no food service. Also, Indian hoteliers prefer to stay in their own hotels to cut costs and closely control the operations. Today, Indian American hotel owners have emerged as a major force in the American hospitality industry. They are increasingly shedding their image as owners of budget hotels and are eyeing top-brand hotels. A recent study indicated that 40 percent of new applications for the Hilton Garden Inn and Homewood Suites are from Indians, compared with 10 percent five years ago.

Asian Indian Communities in the United States[289]

Asian Indian communities exist in every state in the United States. However, they are most heavily concentrated in five states: California, New York, New Jersey, Texas, and Illinois.

Among the urban areas, they have a large presence in New York, San Francisco-Oakland-San Jose, Chicago, Los Angeles, and Washington, D.C. In recent years, they have significantly increased their representation in states like Michigan, Pennsylvania, and Virginia.

Table 35: Asian Indian Population in the United States: State-Wise (2005)

State	Population
California	449,722
New York	336,423
New Jersey	228,250
Texas	175,608
Illinois	157,126
Florida	95,043
Georgia	79,169
Michigan	78,466
Virginia	77,208
Pennsylvania	75,159

Source: American Community Survey 2005

New Jersey

Asian Indians are the largest Asian ethnic group in the Garden State. Their population swelled from 169,180 in 2000 to 230,000 in 2005, a growth rate of about 35 percent. Edison Township has a large population of Asian Indians, accounting for 17 percent of one hundred thousand people. Asian Indian professionals, mostly engineers, computer professionals, and doctors, continue to flock to Edison Township due to its reputable schools and affordable housing. Many are employed in the high-tech, electronics, and pharmaceutical industries of Middlesex County. The Asian Indian community helped elect Jun Choi, son of Korean immigrants, as mayor of Edison, making him the first Asian mayor of a New Jersey city. Mayor Choi recently made an announcement that he would help build a cricket ground for Edison's South Asian community.

Jersey City's Indian community is fifteen thousand strong and growing rapidly. It is home to "India Square," a group of Indian restaurants and grocery stores that serves as a shopping district for the immigrant community. Each year, thousands of Indians converge in Jersey City's Indian neighborhood to celebrate the Hindu festival Navratri. As a sign of the Indian community's growing economic and political importance in Jersey City, Governor Corzine attended the Navratri festival in October 2007.

Jersey City witnessed racially and religiously motivated attacks against Indian Hindus in the late 1980s. A group of teenagers calling themselves "dot busters" carried out a series of vicious attacks, including the fatal beating of a thirty-year-old Indian banker in 1987. The "dot" refers to the decorative mark worn by Hindu Indian women on their forehead. Since then, the attacks have subsided, and life has become normal for the Indians.

Asian Indians continue to be the fastest-growing Asian group in New Jersey, a fact reflected in the increase in airline connections between Newark airport and major Indian cities. Continental Airlines has been operating nonstop flights between Newark and Delhi since 2005. It now plans to offer nonstop services to Mumbai as well.

New York

Asian Indians constitute the second-largest Asian group in New York City, second only to the Chinese. According to the Asian American Federation of New York, between 1990 and 2000, the Indian population jumped by 118 percent (from 94,590 to 206,228), far exceeding the city's overall 9 percent population increase.

Although Indians account for only around 1 percent of New York City's nineteen million people, they are nevertheless omnipresent. They are noticeable in all kinds of jobs, ranging from investment bankers and doctors to newsstand vendors and cab drivers. According to Schaller Consulting, of the 42,900 licensed taxi drivers eligible to drive taxicabs in New York City, 39 percent of them emigrated from South Asia.[290]

Table 36: Country of Birth: Taxi Drivers of New York City (2005)

Country	Percentage
United States	9
Foreign-born	91
Pakistan	14
Bangladesh	14
India	10
Other Countries	53

Source: NYC Taxicab Handbook, Schaller Consulting

New York City is one of the few places in the United States where an Indian can live like an Indian. An Indian can buy a newspaper from an Indian vendor, take a cab driven by an Indian driver, head to an Indian restaurant to have a sumptuous Indian meal, watch an Indian movie in a nearby movie theater, and on the way back pick up Indian groceries from a local Indian grocery store. New York City boasts several Indian restaurants from low-priced fast-food joints to high-priced restaurants. There are over a dozen Indian restaurants along a two-block stretch of Lexington Avenue between 27th and 29th Streets, also known as "Little India" or "Curry Hill."

Each year, the Indian community celebrates India's Independence Day by organizing an annual parade in Manhattan. The parade, considered the largest Indian Independence Day parade outside India, routinely attracts over a hundred thousand people, including Indian film stars, celebrities, and city officials like the New York City mayor. It is organized by the Federation of Indian Associations (FIA), an influential umbrella organization of three hundred thousand members mainly from the tri-state area of New York, New Jersey, and Connecticut.

As per the 2000 census, over 63 percent of Indians live in Queens, one of the five boroughs of New York City.[291] Within Queens, they are mainly concentrated in the neighborhood of Jackson Heights. Many prefer to stay in Jackson Heights because it is situated along the number 7 subway line, which provides access to midtown Manhattan in about twenty minutes. Jackson Height's 74th Street serves as a major shopping district for immigrants from South Asia, hosting dozens of Indian grocery, video, and jewelry stores. Seventy-fourth street has recently been renamed Kalpana Chawla Way, in honor of the Indian American astronaut who perished in the Columbia space shuttle disaster. In 2006, after several years of lobbying, the Jackson Heights city council recognized Diwali, the Hindu festival of lights, as an official city holiday.

Santa Clara County, California

The Asian Indian population in Santa Clara County, also known as "Silicon Valley," has been growing by leaps and bounds. The emergence of Silicon Valley as a Mecca for IT has created a sharp demand for computer professionals. Many Indian software professionals who came on temporary work visas have made Santa Clara County their home since the early 1990s. The arriving Indians were also attracted by the county's mild climate, which stays warm and dry for most of the year.

The Indian community is relatively new to Silicon Valley, with a third of them arriving after 2000 and three-quarters of them born in India. According to a *San Jose Mercury News* report, Indians have a median income of $116,240, which is 44 percent above the county's median income of $81,000. The median price of an Indian-owned home is around $860,000, compared with the county's price of $743,000. That means that Indians own the most valuable real estate in the county. What accounts for their success, especially in such a short period of time? The simple answer lies in their education levels. More than four in five Indian adults have at least a bachelor's degree. They possessed the right skills (in this case, software skills) at the right time (when the economy was booming). Indians are mainly concentrated in San Jose, the largest city in Santa Clara County. San Jose has the largest concentration of technology companies in the world, with more than 6,600 companies employing 250,000 people.

Chicago

Chicago's Asian Indian community accounts for about 1 percent of its population of 2.8 million people. The community largely came into existence starting in the early 1970s, around the same time as the establishment of the Indian community in New York City. Chicago holds a special significance for the Hindu community. It is here that the Hindu spiritual genius Swami Vivekananda delivered a historic speech on Hinduism at the World's Parliament of Religions in 1893. About a century later, in 1995, Chicago honored the Hindu leader by renaming a section of Michigan Avenue, a prominent street in the downtown area, as Swami Vivekananda Way.[292]

Chicago has its own Little India on a section of Devon Avenue in the northwestern suburbs. Devon Avenue is considered the most popular shopping district for the Indian immigrants of the greater Chicago area. It is filled with Indian restaurants, grocery stores, and video stores. The growing strength and political clout of the Indian community resulted in the designation of a stretch of Devon Avenue as Gandhi Way in 1991.

Chapter 9: Top Ten Challenges

India, despite its impressive economic gains in the past decade, faces a number of socioeconomic challenges that will likely prevent it from breaking out of third-world mode for the foreseeable future. About one-third of the population lives below the internationally accepted poverty line of $1 a day, and 80 percent of the population earns below $2 a day.[293] One out of three Indians cannot read or write. Some one hundred thousand villages in India do not have electricity. Nearly eighty million people light their houses using kerosene as the primary lighting source.[294] India sends its own satellites to space and has well-developed nuclear and missile programs. Yet an overwhelming number of its citizens has no access to proper healthcare, sanitation, or drinking water. Forty-seven percent of Indian children under the age of five are malnourished.[295] Less than a third of India's homes have a toilet.[296]

India ranks a dismal 128 out of the 177 countries in the Human Development Index[297] (HDI) computed by the U.N. Development Programme (UNDP). The HDI indicates a country's standard of living, taking into account parameters such as life expectancy, literacy, and income. In South Asia, only Sri Lanka has a ranking below one hundred.

India ranks 96 among 119 developing countries included in the Global Hunger Index (GHI).[298] That means India is among the top twenty-five malnourished countries in the world. China, which has a comparable population to India, ranks forty-seventh. The GHI, prepared by the International Food Policy Research Institute, takes into account three aspects of hunger: the availability of food, the nutritional status of children, and child mortality.

Table 37: India Versus China: Human Development Index

	IMR	MMR	Life	Poverty (%)	Literacy (%)	GDP	HDI	Rank
China	30	0.56	71.6	16.6	90.9	$5,003	0.755	85
India	63	5.40	63.3	34.7	61.0	$2,892	0.602	127

Source: UNDP; Infant Mortality Rate (IMR), Maternal Mortality Rate (MMR)

What does this all mean? Is India's recent economic boom real and sustainable? The simple answer is that many in India have missed out on the economic boom. For starters, India is growing at breakneck speed, second only to China, but the boom is very narrowly based and is concentrated mainly in urban areas in some key states. It is true that consumerism and capitalism are the new buzzwords in booming cities. However, three-quarters of India's population lives in rural areas. Although dynamic states like Karnataka and Maharashtra are forging ahead, northern states like Bihar, Madhya Pradesh, Rajasthan, and Uttar Pradesh, collectively referred to as the *Bimaru* states (*Bimar* means "sick" in Hindi), have been virtually untouched by the economic boom. The overwhelming majority of Indians, especially the rural and poor, have yet to see any improvement in their lives, and they continue to grapple with poverty, a lack of basic amenities like electricity and drinking water, rampant corruption, and a lack of educational and employment opportunities. Until the economic revolution trickles down to these people, India will continue to carry the label of a third-world country.

To be fair to the government, India has made giant strides since gaining its independence. All the social indicators have shown improvement. The percentage of people living under the poverty line has decreased considerably. India's per capita income stood at $460 in 2001. By 2025, the per capita income is expected to increase to $4,000 a year, pushing India from a low-income to a middle-income country.[299]The life expectancy at birth has increased from forty-four years in 1960 to sixty-four years in 2006. The infant mortality rate per thousand decreased from 236 in 1960 to 76.4 in 2006.[300]The adult literacy rate improved from 18 percent in 1951 to 65 percent today. India was able to eradicate or contain smallpox, malaria, polio, and leprosy. But India continues to trail its Asian neighbor and rival China on every key measure.

Poverty

India has fifty-three billionaires with a total wealth of $335 billion, according to the annual *Forbes* list of billionaires in 2008. India accounts for 5 percent of the world's billionaires.

Also, there are two million Indian households with an annual income of more than $100,000 a year. That number is growing at the rate of 14 percent a year. All this is good news for the country.

Table 38: The World's Billionaires (2008)

Rank	Name	Citizenship	Age	Net Worth ($ Billions)	Residence
1	Warren Buffet	U.S.A	77	62.0	U.S.A.
2	Carlos Slim Helu	Mexico	68	60.0	Mexico
3	William Gates III	U.S.A.	52	58.0	U.S.A.
4	Lakshmi Mittal	India	57	45.0	U.K.
5	Mukesh Ambani	India	50	43.0	India
6	Anil Ambani	India	48	42.0	India
7	Ingvar Kamprad	Sweden	81	31.0	Switzerland
8	K. P. Singh	India	76	30.0	India
9	Oleg Deripaska	Russia	40	28.0	Russia
10	Karl Albrecht	Germany	88	27.0	Germany

Source: Forbes.com

However, India also has the world's largest number of poor people in a single country. One-third of the Indian population, about 370 million people, lives below the internationally accepted poverty line, compared to only 85 million[301] in China, which has a bigger population. Nearly 80 percent of the population earns less than $2 a day.[302] To put this number in perspective, the federal minimum wage in the United States is currently $5.85 an hour and will reach $7.25 an hour by 2009. The Indian Planning Commission estimates that it will take a growth rate of 8–9 percent over a decade to reduce the poverty rate in India down to 11 percent.

Since independence, successive Indian governments have launched several schemes to alleviate poverty but have met with only partial success. After the Indian economy opened up in 1991, the level of poverty declined. The percentage of people living below the poverty line fell to 21.8 percent (2004–05) from 26.1 percent (1999–2000), according to the NSS estimates based on the Mixed Recall Period (MRP) consumption distribution data.[303]

In August 2005, the Indian parliament enacted a National Rural Employment Guarantee Act (NREGA) to tackle poverty in rural areas.[304] This ambitious multibillion-dollar program guarantees one hundred days of work per year for every rural household and pays a minimum daily wage of 60 rupees ($1.50) for mostly unskilled manual labor. Through this scheme, the government aims to reduce the poverty rate from the current 22 percent to 10 percent in the next seven years, stem the movement of people from rural areas to cities in search of work, and build rural infrastructure. In the 2007 budget, the federal government substantially increased government expenditure on agriculture, rural development, healthcare, and infrastructure development.

In addition to the rural jobs scheme, the government has also announced an ambitious social security program, which is aimed at benefiting about 390 million poor, nonunionized workers.[305] More than 90 percent of India's workers are not represented by organized trade unions. Under this plan, a nonunionized, casual worker will be entitled to life insurance and health and disability benefits. It is unlikely that the new plan can match the U.S. Social Security system in cost and scope.

The U.S. Social Security program, which is funded through payroll taxes, paid out $500 billion in benefits to around fifty million Americans in 2004. Workers contribute to the system during their careers and are entitled to benefits upon retirement, disability, or death. The U.S. Medicare program, which was created in 1965 as an amendment to the Social Security program, provides health insurance to Americans age sixty-five and older and currently covers thirty-nine million people. Another program, Medicaid, is a state-administered program that assists people with little or no income. These social programs have dramatically reduced poverty for the aged in America. It remains to be seen what impact the new Indian social security scheme is going to have on poverty in India.

Population Explosion

India is the second most populated country in the world after China. However, in terms of population density, India exceeds China, as India's land area is almost half of China's total land. Although India ranks fourth in the world in aggregate GDP in Purchasing Power Party (PPP) terms, its large population base results in very low rankings in per capita GDP. In 1950, the population of India stood at approximately 371 million. Since then, the population has more than tripled.[306]

Table 39: World Population (1950–2050) (Thousands)

	China	India	U.S.A.	World
1950	554,760	371,857	157,813	2,535,093
2000	1,269,962	1,046,235	278,357	6,124,123
2050	1,408,846	1,658,270	349,318	9,191,287

Source: United Nations Population Division

In 1999, India reached the alarming one billion population mark, or 17 percent of the global population. It should be noted that China reached the one billion mark in 1980. By 2016, the population of India is expected to be larger than the population of all the developed countries combined—that is, all the countries of Europe (including Russia), Australia, New Zealand, Japan, Canada, and the United States.

By 2050 or even sooner, India is expected to surpass China as the most populous country in the world and will remain that way thereafter.[307] China and India will most likely remain the only members of the one billion population club. According to U.N. projections, no other country will reach a population size of one billion. The world population is likely to increase by 2.5 billion by 2050, growing from the current 6.7 billion to 9.5 billion.[308] India entered the twenty-first century with close to one billion people, the majority of them lacking basic amenities like clean drinking water and basic healthcare.[309] India has a population growth rate of 1.6 percent, compared to China's growth rate of 0.6 percent.[310] India adds nearly nineteen million people (the combined population of Norway, Sweden, and Finland) to its population every year.[311]

Table 40: Number of Years for Population to Increase from Five Hundred Million to One Billion

Country	Years Taken	Time Period
China	33	1947 to 1980
India	34	1965 to 1999
World	304	1500 to 1804

Source: United Nations Population Division

Overpopulation is putting enormous pressure on India's already scarce natural resources, infrastructure, and public services like healthcare and education. Although India's food production has tripled since 1947, its population also tripled, thus neutralizing the benefits. The United Nations has warned that if the population growth doesn't slow down, India will likely face food and water shortages in the near future.

Also, the country is witnessing explosive growth in urban slum dwellers who are migrating from rural areas to big cities in search of better job opportunities. The problem is more acute in Mumbai, where half of its fifteen million people live in slums or makeshift townships. Mumbai is home to Asia's largest slum, Dharavi, which covers about 1.75 square kilometers of swampy, muddy land. It is home to more than one million people.[312] The Indian capital Delhi is home to close to two million slum dwellers.

To stem population growth, successive governments have implemented voluntary, state-funded family-planning programs, with a primary emphasis on contraception and female sterilization. So far, the results have been encouraging. The fertility rate (the average number of children a woman expects to have in her lifetime) has come down from 5.3 to 3.1 births per woman over the past three decades.[313] India's National Population Policy of 2000 set a goal of achieving a national average total fertility rate (TFR) of 2.1 by the year 2010.[314] But India has a long way to go when compared to China, where the implementation of the one-child policy was very effective in curbing its population. The policy limits urban couples to one child and rural families to two to control the population and conserve natural resources. This policy resulted in four hundred million fewer people in the past three decades.[315]

Pollution and Global Warming

Pollution is a fact of life in Indian cities. By some estimates, pollution threatens the health and livelihood of half of the population. India is one of the few major developing countries where one can see, smell, and taste pollution. A recent study[316] conducted by a prominent cancer institute concluded that 70 percent of the eighteen million inhabitants of Kolkota (formerly Calcutta) suffer from respiratory disorders caused by air pollution. The city also leads all Indian cities when it comes to lung cancer, at 18.4 cases per one hundred thousand people. Kolkota's pollution comes from high levels of auto emissions from vehicles older than fifteen years. The city's traffic policemen arguably brave some of the worst pollution in the world.

The Indian capital, Delhi, with a population of fourteen million people, presents one of the rare success stories in India's fight against pollution. Not long ago, Delhi was ranked fourth[317] among the forty-one most polluted cities in the world.

Acting on a public-interest litigation measure against the health risks posed by air, India's Supreme Court ordered the conversion of Delhi's entire public transport feet (consisting of buses, three-wheelers, and taxis) from diesel fuel to nonpolluting compressed natural gas (CNG). The order also banned vehicles older than fifteen years from operating within the city. The Supreme Court order was a blessing for Delhi, which has experienced a dramatic reduction in air pollution. It won the U.S. Department of Energy's first Clean Cities International

Partner of the Year award in 2003 for its bold efforts to curb air pollution and support alternative fuel initiatives. Despite pockets of success, however, India faces an uphill battle in its fight against pollution. India's economy is booming at 8 percent annually, driving the growth of private vehicles. For instance, Delhi adds one thousand new cars each day to its roads.[318]

To make problems worse, diesel-run vehicles are gaining popularity in India due to their lower operating costs as compared to gasoline-powered vehicles. Why is diesel fuel cheaper than gasoline in India? The Indian government artificially keeps diesel fuel prices lower than gasoline prices to help farmers and the transportation industry. India's Center for Science and Environment (CSE) has recently urged the government to take the tough measures needed to clean up the air.

India, along with China, is also drawing attention from world media on the matters of global warming and greenhouse gas emissions. According to a recent study by PricewaterhouseCoopers (PwC), India is likely to overtake the United States as the second-largest emitter of carbon by 2050, after China. Together, India and China are projected to account for around 45 percent of global carbon emissions by 2050.[319]

India ratified the Kyoto Protocol in 2002, the goal of which is to reduce worldwide greenhouse gas emission to 5.2 percent below 1990 levels between 2008 and 2012.[320] Most of the world's industrialized nations, with the exception of the United States and Australia, supported the Kyoto Protocol. However, as a developing nation, India is not required to reduce its emissions of greenhouse gases. India opposes any move to seek its commitment to reduce greenhouse gas emissions on the grounds that its per capita emission of carbon dioxide is just 1.2 metric tons.[321] That may be so. But in absolute terms, India figures among the top four emitters of carbon dioxide after the United States, China, and Russia. Since 1990, worldwide carbon dioxide emissions increased by 28 percent. About 21 percent of the world's emissions originate in the United States, followed by China, with 17 percent.

India accounts for 4.6 percent of the world's carbon dioxide emissions. Since 1990, India's emissions have nearly doubled.

A recent report by the U.N. Intergovernmental Panel on Climate Change (IPCC) states that India is likely to be among the first major nations to be affected by climate change. As per IPCC, one of the major world rivers on the endangered list is India's Ganges, which is the source of life for millions of people in the Indian subcontinent. The River Ganges gets its water from glaciers high in the Himalayas. Due to global warming, many of the glaciers are melting fast and could vanish in this century.

The panel warned that India would face a severe water crisis even if every available river and stream were harnessed to its full potential because of the expected increase in population. The gross per capita water availability will decline from 1,820 cubic meters per year in 2001 to 1,140 in 2050, a 38 percent drop.[322]Less rainfall, the melting of glaciers, and reduced groundwater are the likely reasons for the deteriorating situation.

India is increasingly turning to nuclear power technology to drive and fuel its economic development. Former French president Jacques Chirac, on a visit to India in 2006, enthusiastically supported India's efforts to gain access to nuclear fuel and civilian technology to fuel its growing energy needs.[323]

HIV/AIDS

An estimated 2.5 million Indians are infected with HIV/AIDS as per a survey backed by a U.N. organization.[324] That puts India in the third spot, behind South Africa (5.5 million) and Nigeria (2.9 million), in the list of nations affected the most by HIV/AIDS.[325] A total of 33.2 million people worldwide are living with HIV and 2.2 million people died of AIDS in 2007.[326] Former U.S. president Bill Clinton called India the epicenter of the global HIV/AIDS epidemic.[327] Until about a decade ago, India was in denial and downplayed the incidences of HIV.

In 1992, the government set up the National AIDS Control Organization (NACO) to oversee the formulation of policies relating to the prevention and control of AIDS. In 2001, then prime minister Vajpayee referred to AIDS as one of the most serious challenges facing the country.

Although antiretroviral drugs (ARVs) have proven to be effective in delaying the progression of HIV to AIDS, access to such drugs is very limited in India. The Clinton Foundation is providing financial and technical assistance to countries like India in their efforts to stop the spread of HIV/AIDS. The foundation struck a deal with two leading Indian drug companies under which the companies will make cheap ARVs available to sixty-two developing countries around the world.[328]

The southern Indian state of Andhra Pradesh is one of the worst-hit states. An estimated half a million to one million people of the state are infected with HIV, out of the population of seventy-eight million. To prevent the spread of the virus, the state government is seriously considering new a law making it mandatory for couples to take an HIV test before marriage.[329]

India's anti-AIDS drive faces several problems. Two of the biggest problems are a lack of awareness and the stigma associated with the disease. India's recent efforts to introduce sex education in schools to increase awareness about HIV received a setback when three major states, including Maharashtra, Gujarat, and Madhya Pradesh, opposed the move on the grounds that it would corrupt young minds.

Lack of Infrastructure

With the opening up of its economy to foreign trade and investment, India's infrastructure (or lack of it) has become a focus of attention. Much of the country's infrastructure is dilapidated and remains underdeveloped. The reasons are not difficult to comprehend. Until recently, the development of infrastructure was completely in the public-sector domain and was plagued by corruption, inefficiency, and lack of focus. Also, India spends only 5 percent of its GDP on infrastructure projects, compared to China, which spends 12 percent.[330]

India doesn't have enough electricity to meet its demand; its airports and ports are overflowing; roads are crumbling; and water shortages are common. Former U.S. ambassador to India David Mulford listed energy, infrastructure, and agriculture as India's three main challenges. As per some estimates, the investment required for infrastructure improvements in India would be $380 billion over the next five years.[331] Only recently has the Indian government woken up to the reality that its stellar economic performance can't be sustained unless its infrastructure development keeps pace with growth rates. Montek Singh Ahluwalia, the planning commission deputy chairman, is considered one of the architects of India's economic reforms, and he has called for greater public-private cooperation in infrastructure development.

India recently launched a massive $13.2 billion National Highways Development Project[332] (NHDP) to improve its road infrastructure. The project consists of two major components: the 5,486-kilometer Golden Quadrilateral, and the 7,300-kilometer North-South, East-West corridors. The ambitious Golden Quadrilateral project provides for four-lane national highways linking India's four major cities: Delhi, Mumbai, Chennai, and Kolkota.

Corruption

India ranks among the most corrupt nations in the world. A study by Transparency International found that as high as 62 percent of citizens had firsthand experience in paying bribes or "using a contact" to get a job done in a public office.[333] The Indian government loses billions of dollars to tax evasions each year. It is hard to a name a task involving the government that can be done without paying bribes. Whether it is getting a driver's license, getting a water connection, registering a plot, getting any kind of certificate (marriage, birth, or even death), lodging a report with the police, or any other task, greasing of the palms of the government officials involved is a prerequisite for getting the job done. India is perhaps one of the few major countries where one can get out of a traffic ticket by bribing the traffic police. Sadly, the people of India accept this as a fact of life. Former prime minister Rajiv Gandhi once remarked that for every rupee spent by the government for development, less than a tenth of that amount actually reaches the beneficiary.

India continues to fare badly in Transparency International's annual Corruption Perception Index (CPI). The CPI ranks 180 countries by their perceived levels of corruption, as determined by expert assessments and opinion surveys. The index focuses on corruption in the public sector and defines corruption as the abuse of public office for private gain. In the latest report, India's corruption ranking improved from eighty-eight in 2005 to seventy-two in 2007.[334] The improvement in ranking is partly attributed to the introduction of the new Right to Information (RTI) Act, which was enacted in 2005.[335] The goal of the RTI Act is to curb corruption by giving ordinary citizens the legal right to seek information from the government.

India also made some good progress in cutting down bureaucratic red tape. In 2003, it took eighty-nine days to start a new business. Now it takes only thirty-three days, in line with China.[336] India has yet to enact any laws to protect the identity of "whistleblowers." In 2003, Satyendra Dubey, a thirty-one-year-old engineer who was working on a high-profile national highway development project, was killed when he tried to expose rampant corruption.[337]Apparently his name was leaked from the complaint he had sent to the prime minister's office and the road network authority. In the letter to the prime minister's office he had requested that his name be kept secret. But the officials circulated his letter, along with details of his identity, among the bureaucracy.

Low Literacy Rates

Sixty years after gaining independence, about a third of India's population is still illiterate.[338] Also, there is a huge disparity between male and female literacy rates. Literacy rates are 73 percent for men and 48 percent for women.[339] The literacy rate is defined as the percentage of people in a country aged fifteen and over who can read and write. Compare this situation to the United States, where both male and female literacy rates stand at 97 percent. Even in China, the gap is not significant: 91 percent male literacy rate versus 87 percent female literacy rate. India did make some progress on the literacy front. In 1951, only 18 percent of the adult population was literate. Now the number stands at 65 percent.[340]

Low Life Expectancy/Infant Mortality/Maternal Mortality

India has a life expectancy of sixty-four, which is fourteen years lower than that of the United States. Life expectancy has increased from fifty-five in 1981 to sixty-four in 2006.[341] India's infant mortality rate of fifty-seven deaths per thousand live births[342] is very high compared to the United States (6.1) or China (21.1).

According to the latest data of the White Ribbon Alliance, about six hundred thousand women die every year due to complications from pregnancy and childbirth. India accounts for 130,000 of those deaths. Consider this. Every five minutes, a woman in India dies[343] from complications related to pregnancy and childbirth. The maternal mortality ratio in India is 450 per 100,000 live births, versus 45 per 100,000 live births in China.[344]

Child Labor/Human Trafficking

India is home to the largest number of child workers in the world. Children are employed in a variety of sectors, including agriculture, carpet weaving, match manufacturing, and food and hospitality. It is estimated that about thirteen million children work in the food and hospitality sector alone. Child labor is illegal in India, but these laws are very rarely enforced. A recent U.S. State Department Trafficking in Persons (TIP) report[345] estimates that tens of millions of Indians were subjected to forced labor and sex trafficking. The report placed India, China, and thirty-eight other countries on its "Tier 2" watch list, warning them that without improvements, they could be demoted to a "Tier 3" list, which would trigger sanctions.

Unemployment

India is facing a severe unemployment problem despite its fast economic growth in the past decade. The current unemployment rate stands at 7.2 percent, which translates to thirty-seven million[346] unemployed men and women. It is true that the country's burgeoning IT/BPO sector employs nearly two million people, but that number is a drop in the ocean when compared to India's huge labor force, which stands at 516 million.[347]

Normally, the labor force of a country consists of everyone of working age (fifteen to sixty-four). Agriculture continues to account for 50–60 percent of the labor force, whereas industry accounts for merely 12 percent.[348]

By contrast, China's manufacturing boom has provided employment for tens of millions of people. A study by TeamLease Staffing Solutions warned that if the current trends of employment generation continue, India would have 211 million unemployed in 2020, an unemployment rate of 30 percent. The bottom line is that India needs to look beyond the IT sector for creating jobs for its growing labor force. Until people in rural areas find alternatives to farm-based employment, the unemployment rate will continue to be high. In order to capitalize on "demographic dividend"[349](62 percent of India's population is in the working age group), India needs to emphasize skills development and encourage the creation of labor-intensive industries.

Epilogue

India has witnessed profound changes in the past decade and a half. It celebrated its sixtieth year of independence in 2007. The India of 2007 is vastly different from the India of 1947 or 1987. Now, urban India is looking more and more like mainstream America. There are more cars on the roads, more two-income households, more air travelers, more American-style malls and multiplexes, more usage of household appliances, more mobile phones, and more affluence. The youth are getting aggressive, the citizens are getting assertive, and—for better or worse—the old order is giving way to the new. Thanks to the proliferation of cable television and the Internet, dating, which was taboo until recently, is increasingly going mainstream in cities; French kissing in Bollywood movies is becoming more common.

India has recently witnessed the birth of a city-based cricket franchise sporting culture along the lines of the NBA and NFL. India was even introduced to the cheerleading culture when Washington Redskins cheerleaders performed at an inaugural cricket tournament held in Bangalore. For every popular American television show, there is a corresponding Indian show, whether it is *American Idol* or *Who Wants to Be a Millionaire.* While America is fascinated with Branjelina (the Hollywood couple Brad Pitt and Angelina Jolie), India is fascinated with Abhi-Aish (the Bollywood couple Abhishek Bachchan and Aishwarya Rai). The cultural integration of urban India and the United States is complete.

India is trying hard to break out of the third-world mold. The nation cheered when the U.S. government recently announced its intention to cut aid by 35 percent. The cut in aid followed the categorization of India as a *transforming* country instead of a *developing* one. That may be good news, but India faces a long, messy road ahead. Until the benefits of economic reforms trickle down to the poorest of the poor, India will continue to carry the label of third-world country. As the reform process enters the next phase, the government is coming under intense pressure to loosen remaining controls that are hampering growth. Retail, banking, and defense remain holdouts, whereas privatization and labor reforms are proceeding at a slower pace amid intense political debate. The good news? The gains India has made over the last decade and a half appear to be permanent. All political parties agree on the reforms; their differences are only in semantics.

India's finance minister, P. Chidambaram, has recently assured foreign investors of hassle-free clearances for their projects. "The red-tape is out and red carpet is in," he remarked.[350] Despite these assurances, India remains a tough place to do business. David Mulford, former U.S. ambassador to India, cautioned American investors not to expect instant results. "India is not a journey for the faint hearted, or for those who expect overnight success," he remarked. "You will need a strategy—a long term view—patience, and persistence. But one of the world's great markets is here."[351]

Despite the challenges it faces, India is forging ahead. These are arguably the best years for India and Indians around the world. There is optimism everywhere in the country, and even the poorest of the poor are exuding confidence. The world has finally woken up to India's potential. Every problem that India faces is viewed as an investment or growth opportunity by businesses around the globe. Ardent critics of India are becoming ardent admirers. Even Henry Kissinger, who orchestrated anti-India policies as secretary of state in the Nixon administration, is showering praise on India. India is just starting, and the best is yet to come. It is telling the world, "You ain't seen nothing yet." The world is bracing for the next economic superpower from Asia.

Appendix 1: Chronology of India

2500–1500 BC
Civilization flourishes in the Indus Valley. Two great cities, Mohenjo-daro and Harappa, are established.

1500 BC
Aryans invade India from the north and begin spreading around the Indus Valley and Ganges Valley. They bring with them the Vedic religion, which later evolves into Hinduism.

563–483 BC
Siddhartha Gautama founds and preaches Buddhism.

327 BC
Alexander the Great attacks India and defeats the local ruler, Darius III.

272–232 BC
Ashoka of the Mauryan dynasty rules India. Under Ashoka, Buddhism becomes the state religion.

AD 320–550

The Gupta dynasty reigns during this period. The period is referred to as the Golden Age of India in science, mathematics, astronomy, and religion. Kalidasa, India's celebrated Sanskrit poet and dramatist, lived during this time.

997–1027

Mahmud of Ghazni attacks India from Afghanistan and sacks several important Indian cities.

1191

Muhammad Ghori's army defeats a confederacy of northern Hindu kings in the second battle of Tarain. Prithviraj Chauhan, the last Rajput king of Delhi, is captured and killed.

1206

The Delhi Sultanate, the first Islamic state to be established in India, is founded by Qutbuddin Aibak.

1498

Portuguese explorer Vasco da Gama reaches Calicut.

1509–29

Krishna Deva Raya, the most powerful king of the Vijayanagara empire, reigns during this period.

1526

Babur defeats Ibrahim Lodhi in the first battle of Panipat and founds the Mughal empire.

1556–1605

Akbar reigns as emperor. He expands the Mughal empire by conquering Punjab, Rajasthan, Gujarat, Bengal, Kashmir, and Sind.

1565

An alliance of Deccan Muslim Sultans defeats and destroys the Vijayanagara empire in the decisive Battle of Talikota.

1600

Queen Elizabeth of England grants a charter to the East India Company, providing exclusive trading rights with India.

1628–58

Moghul emperor Shah Jahan rules India. He is most remembered for the construction of many magnificent buildings, including the Taj Mahal.

1658–1707

Aurangzeb, the last great Mughal ruler, reigns; he aspires to make India an Islamic state.

1737

Nadir Shah of Afghanistan captures Delhi; he leaves with the Kohinoor diamond and the Peacock Throne.

1757

British troops defeat the ruler of Bengal in the Battle of Plassey.

1760

British troops defeat the French in the Battle of Wandiwash.

1799

The British defeat Tipu Sultan in the Fourth Mysore War.

1802

Maharaja Ranjit Singh captures Amritsar and establishes a Sikh kingdom with Lahore as his capital.

1818

The British establish control over most of the Indian subcontinent.

1835

English education is introduced in India based on the recommendations of Thomas Macaulay.

1845–49

British forces annex the Sikh kingdom. They gain control of the Kohinoor diamond, which was later presented to Queen Victoria of England in 1950.

1853

The first railway on the Indian subcontinent runs over a stretch of twenty-one miles from Bombay to Thane.

1857

British Indian troops rebel against British rulers in the First War of Independence. Mutiny spreads throughout northern India.

1858

British troops quell the rebellion and recapture most areas seized by the rebels. The East India Company is dissolved, and India comes under the direct rule of the British Crown.

1869

Mohandas Karamchand Gandhi is born in Porbandar in western India.

1885

The Indian National Congress is formed at the initiative of Allan Octavian Home, a retired British official.

1914

Gandhi, now forty-five, returns to India after spending twenty years in South Africa. He sets up an ashram (retreat) along the Sabarmati River near Ahmadabad, Gujarat.

1919–20

Gandhi becomes the leader of the Congress Party; he initiates a program of nonviolent disobedience against the British government.

In Amritsar, British Indian troops under the command of Brigadier General Reginald Dyer fire on unarmed protesters, killing 379 and injuring 1,200.

1929
The Congress Party demands complete independence from British rule at the Lahore session. Jawaharlal Nehru becomes the president of the party.

1930
Gandhi leads a 165-mile protest march against the salt tax in a symbolic gesture of defiance against repressive British laws.

1931
Gandhi attends the second roundtable conference in London as the sole representative of the Congress Party.

1935
The British parliament passes the Government of India Act, providing more autonomy to Indians at the provincial level.

1940
The Muslim League, led by Mohammad Ali Jinnah, demands that a separate Muslim country be carved out of India.

1942
The Congress Party launches the "Quit India" movement, demanding an immediate end to British rule.

1945
World War II ends. In Britain, Clement Atlee of the Labor Party wins the parliamentary election and becomes the new prime minister. Atlee promises to end British rule of India.

1947

India and Pakistan become independent nations in August after two hundred years of British rule. Nehru becomes India's first prime minister. Freedom comes at an enormous cost, with over half a million people losing their lives in the communal bloodshed.

1948

Mahatma Gandhi is assassinated by a Hindu activist who believed that he was too sympathetic toward the Muslims.

1948–49

India and Pakistan fight over the disputed region of Kashmir.

1950

India adopts a new constitution and becomes a republic in the British Commonwealth.

1959

The Dalai Lama flees from Tibet to India after a Tibetan uprising against China fails.

1962

India loses a brief border war with China, marking the beginning of a chill in relations.

1964

Lal Bahadur Shastri becomes prime minister after Nehru's death.

1965

India and Pakistan fight a second war over the disputed region of Kashmir.

1966

Indira Gandhi, daughter of Jawaharlal Nehru, becomes prime minister.

1971

India supports the separatist guerillas of East Pakistan against the military rulers of West Pakistan. After a two-week war, Pakistani forces surrender to the Indian military. East Pakistan becomes the independent nation of Bangladesh.

1975

Indira Gandhi declares a state of emergency and arrests many political opponents.

1977

Indira Gandhi is defeated in the parliamentary elections. Morarji Desai forms India's first non-Congress government.

1978

India and China resume diplomatic relations.

1980

Indira Gandhi returns to power after winning the general election.

1984

Indian troops storm the Golden Temple, Sikhs' most holy shrine, to flush out militants campaigning for self-rule. In retaliation, Indira Gandhi is assassinated in Delhi by two of her Sikh bodyguards. Indira's son, Rajiv Gandhi, succeeds her as prime minister of India.

1989

Rajiv Gandhi is defeated in the ninth general elections. V. P. Singh, leader of the National Front coalition, becomes prime minister. The separatist movement in Indian-controlled Kashmir gains traction with support from the Pakistani military establishment.

1991

Rajiv Gandhi is assassinated at an election rally by a suicide bomber sympathetic to Sri Lanka's separatist LTTE group. Prime Minister Narasimha Rao and Finance Minister Manmohan Singh launch the first generation of economic reforms.

1992

Hindu activists demolish a sixteenth-century Muslim mosque in Ayodhya, claiming the site to be birthplace of their deity Lord Ram. Hundreds die in widespread communal violence following the destruction.

1996

The Congress Party is defeated in the general election and is replaced by a United Front government.

1997

Sonia Gandhi, the Italian-born widow of Rajiv Gandhi, steps into active politics. India celebrates fifty years of independence from British rule.

1998

The BJP coalition is elected to power. India conducts underground nuclear tests, and Pakistan responds with tests of its own within two weeks

1999

Pakistani troops and irregulars cross the Line of Control (LOC) in Kashmir and capture territory near Kargil. After three months of intense fighting, the Indian army evicts the intruders from its territories. The

BJP-led coalition scores a solid victory over the Congress Party in the general elections.

2000
President Bill Clinton makes a historic visit to India, marking the first trip by a sitting U.S. president in twenty-two years. India's population reaches one billion.

2001
India snaps diplomatic and transport links with Pakistan in the aftermath of a deadly attack on the Indian parliament, allegedly perpetrated by Pakistani-based militant groups. Both India and Pakistan amass hundreds of thousands of troops along the border amid mounting fears of all-out war between the nuclear neighbors.

2002
Communal violence erupts in Gujarat when fifty-nine Hindu activists die in a train fire. Over a thousand people, mainly Muslims, die in the ensuing communal riots.

2003
Prime Minister Vajpayee offers a "hand of friendship" to Pakistan. Both sides agree to resume air links after a two-year ban.

2004
Italian-born Sonia Gandhi leads the United Progressive Alliance to victory in the general election. Former finance minister Dr. Manmohan Singh, a Sikh, becomes India's prime minister.

2005
Indo-Pakistan relations get a further boost with the opening of a new bus service between

Srinagar in Indian-controlled Kashmir and Muzaffarabad in Pakistani-controlled Kashmir. China makes territorial concessions to India by giving up its claim on the Indian state of Sikkim.

2006

India and the United States sign a landmark nuclear agreement during President George W. Bush's visit to India. The nuclear deal allows India greater access to U.S. nuclear energy technology in return for agreeing to greater scrutiny of its civil nuclear program.

2007

Pratibha Patil becomes India's first woman president, a largely ceremonial post.

Appendix 2: Fifteen Events that Rocked India

1919: Jallianwala Bagh Massacre

On April 13, British Indian troops under the command of General Dyer open-fired on unarmed Indians protesting against the antisedition Rowlatt Act, leaving 379 dead and 1,200 injured. This gruesome incident represents a major turning point in India's struggle for independence from British rule.

1947: Partition of India

The partition of British India into the independent states of India and Pakistan is followed by one of the bloodiest migrations in history. Over ten million people cross the boundaries between India and Pakistan, and nearly five hundred thousand perish in the communal violence that followed the partition.

January 30, 1948: Gandhi's Assassination

Mahatma Gandhi, the hero of India's freedom struggle, is assassinated by a Hindu activist who disagreed with his ideology.

1962: Chinese Attack

India suffers a humiliating defeat at China's hands in a brief but bloody border conflict. India loses thirty-eight thousand square kilometers of its territory (the size of New Jersey and Connecticut combined) in the war.

January 11, 1966: Death of Prime Minister Lal Bahadur Shastri

Lal Bahadur Shastri, India's second prime minister, dies of a heart attack on foreign soil hours after signing a cease-fire agreement with Pakistani leader Ayub Khan in Tashkent.

June 25, 1975: Emergency Declaration

Prime Minister Indira Gandhi declares a state of emergency and suspends civil liberties. The twenty-one-month emergency period is considered one of the most controversial periods in the history of independent India.

October 31, 1984: Indira Gandhi's Assassination

Prime Minister Indira Gandhi is assassinated by two of her Sikh security guards in the garden of her home in Delhi in an apparent retaliation for ordering the storming of the Golden Temple (a Sikh holy shrine) in Amritsar in June. Her killing prompts communal riots in Delhi, leaving four thousand people dead.

December 3, 1984: Bhopal Gas Tragedy

In one of the worst industrial accidents in history, poisonous gas leakage from a chemical plant owned by Union Carbide (now a subsidiary of Dow Chemical) in Bhopal kills fifteen thousand and injures thousands more.

June 23, 1985: Air-India Midair Explosion

In what is considered one of the worst airborne terrorist attacks, Air India Flight 182 (named after the second-century Indian ruler Emperor Kanishka), en route from Montreal to New Delhi, explodes at an altitude of thirty-one thousand feet over the Atlantic Ocean near the Irish coast, killing all 329 people, mostly of Indian origin.

May 21, 1991: Rajiv Gandhi's Assassination
Rajiv Gandhi, the forty-six-year-old former Indian prime minister, is assassinated at an election rally in the town of Sriperumbudur, near Chennai, by a female Tamil Tiger suicide bomber.

December 16, 1992: Mosque Destruction
Hindu activists demolish a sixteenth-century Muslim mosque in Ayodhya, claiming the site to be the birthplace of Lord Ram. Hundreds die in widespread communal violence following the destruction.

December 24, 1999: Hijacking of Indian Airlines flight
A week before the arrival of the new millennium, an Indian Airlines Airbus plane on a routine flight from Kathmandu, Nepal, to New Delhi is hijacked in midair by a group of Kashmiri militants. The hijacking drama ends on New Year's Eve, after India agrees to release three hardcore militants from Indian prisons.

January 26, 2001: Gujarat Earthquake
A massive earthquake measuring 7.9 on the Richter scale devastates the Kutch district in the western Indian state of Gujarat, claiming twenty-five thousand lives. It is the most intense and devastating earthquake in India in almost half a century.

February 27, 2002: Gujarat Violence
The western Indian state of Gujarat witnesses communal riots after an express train carrying 1,500 Hindu activists was set on fire in Godhra, resulting in 59 deaths. In the ensuing communal violence, over 1,000 people, mostly Muslims, lose their lives.

December 26, 2004: Indian Ocean Tsunami

A massive 9.0 magnitude undersea earthquake with its epicenter off the west coast of Sumatra, Indonesia, triggers a series of deadly tsunamis (high tidal waves) that cause great destruction and death along the coastal areas bordering the Indian Ocean, within hours of the initial event. Over 225,000 people from eleven countries, including India, lose their lives, making the 2004 Boxing Day tsunamis one of the deadliest natural disasters in the history of mankind.

Appendix 3: India's Twelve Proudest Moments

1913: Nobel Prize
Rabindranath Tagore, India's most famous writer and poet, wins the Nobel Prize in Literature, becoming the first non-Westerner to win the coveted prize.

1928: Olympic Hockey Gold Medal
India wins the first of six consecutive Olympic gold medals in hockey in the 1928 Olympics held in Amsterdam.

1971: Military Victory in the Pakistan War
India scores a comprehensive military victory over Pakistan, resulting in the creation of the new nation of Bangladesh in the erstwhile region of East Pakistan.

1974: Nuclear Tests
India conducts its first nuclear test (nicknamed "The Smiling Buddha") at Pokhran in Rajasthan state, becoming the sixth nation in the world to test a nuclear device.

1975: India's Space Foray

India's first satellite is launched on a Russian rocket. It was named after fifth-century Indian astronomer Aryabhata.

1982: *Gandhi* Sweeps Oscars

Richard Attenborough's movie *Gandhi* wins eight Oscars, including Best Picture, Best Actor and Best Director.

1983: World Cup Cricket Victory

India wins the Cricket World Cup, defeating the mighty West Indies at Lord's Cricket Ground in London.

1984: First Indian in Space

Rakesh Sharma becomes the first Indian in space by spending eight days aboard the Soviet space station Salyut 7.

1994: Indian Wins Miss Universe Title

Sushmita Sen becomes the first Indian woman to win the coveted Miss Universe title at the 1994 pageant held in Manila, Philippines.

2006: Indian Women in Space

Sunita Williams becomes the second woman of Indian origin to venture into space, after Kalpana Chawla.

2007: Anand Becomes World Chess Champion

Vishwanathan Anand becomes the undisputed world chess champion after winning the unified World Chess Championship tournament in Mexico City.

2008: India Launches First Moon Mission

India successfully launches its first unmanned Chandrayaan 1 spacecraft to orbit the moon, joining a select group of nations (the United States, Russia, European Space Agency, Japan, and China) that have sent lunar missions.

Appendix 4: Bollywood (Movie Industry) Milestones

1913

India's first silent movie, *Raja Harishchandra*, is released by Dhundiraj Govind Phalke.

1931

India's first talkie (sound movie), *Alam Ara*, is released.

1944

Legendary actor Dilip Kumar makes his debut in Bombay Talkies production *Jwar Bhata*.

1951

Raj Kapoor's movie *Awaara* becomes a huge hit in India and a cult favorite in China and Russia.

1956

Bengali director Satyajit Ray's *Pather Panchali* wins the Best Human Document Award at the Cannes festival.

1957

Mehboob Khan's *Mother India* starring Nargis becomes the fist Indian movie to be nominated for an Oscar in the Best Foreign Language Film category.

1957

Guru Dutt's masterpiece *Pyaasa* is released. *Time Magazine* rates it one of the best one hundred films of all time.

1969

Actor Rajesh Khanna achieves overnight stardom with Shakti Samanta's *Aradhana*.

1973

Prakash Mehra's *Zanjeer* brings fame and success to actor Amitabh Bachchan.

1975

Ramesh Sippy's *Sholay* starring Amitabh Bachchan is released. The movie becomes the biggest blockbuster in the history of Bollywood.

1988

Mira Nair's *Salaam Bombay* is nominated for a Best Foreign Language Film Oscar.

1992

Satyajit Ray wins an Academy Award for Lifetime Achievement, weeks before his death.

1995

Aditya Chopra's *Dilwale Dulhania Le Jayenge* becomes one of the biggest box office hits of all times and propels actor Shah Rukh Khan into superstardom.

1996

Ramoji Film City opens in Hyderabad; it enters the *Guinness Book of World Records* as the largest film studio in the world.

1997
The first multiplex theater in India is opened in Delhi by PVR Cinemas.

1998
Shekhar Kapur's *Elizabeth* is released. The movie wins seven Oscar nominations, including Best Picture and Best Actress.

1999
Amitabh Bachchan is named the Greatest Star of the Millennium by a BBC online poll, ahead of Hollywood legends Alec Guinness and Marlon Brando.

2002
Gurinder Chadha's *Bend It Like Beckham* reaches the number-one spot at the British box office. Indian blockbuster movie *Lagaan* wins an Academy Award nomination in the Best Foreign Language Film category.

2002
Andrew Lloyd Webber's musical *Bombay Dreams* makes its debut in London. The musical features music by A. R. Rahman. In 2004, it makes New York Broadway debut.

2004
Aishwarya Rai makes her Hollywood debut in Gurinder Chadha's *Bride & Prejudice*

2007
Hollywood's first Bollywood movie, *Saawariya*, produced by Sony Pictures Entertainment, is released in November. The movie outperforms Tom Cruise's *Lions for Lambs* in the first week of its release.

Appendix 5: Fifty Prominent Indians of Present Times

Ambani, Anil (Born: 1959)

Anil Ambani is the chairman of Anil Dhirubhai Ambani Group, which includes Reliance Communications, Reliance Capital, Reliance Energy, and others. He was ranked sixth on the 2008 *Forbes* list of the world's billionaires, with a net worth of $42 billion.

Ambani, Mukesh (Born: 1957)

Mukesh Ambani is the chairman of Reliance Industries Limited, one of India's largest private-sector companies. He was ranked fifth on the 2008 *Forbes* list of the world's billionaires, with a net worth of $43 billion.

Anand, Vishwanathan (Born: 1969)

Vishwanathan Anand is an Indian chess grand master and one of the best-known non-Russian chess champions in the world. In 2000, he won the FIDE World Chess Championship, ending many years of

Russian domination of the game. In 2007, Anand won the World Chess Championship in Mexico City.

Bachchan, Amitabh (Born: 1942)

Amitabh Bachchan, considered the biggest Bollywood actor of the twentieth century, ruled the Hindi film industry for two decades starting the early 1970s. His first blockbuster movie, *Zanjeer*, released in 1973, propelled him to superstardom. In 2000, he became the first Bollywood star to be immortalized at Madame Tussauds wax museum in London.

Bhatia, Sabeer (Born: 1969)

Sabeer Bhatia cofounded Hotmail, a pioneering free web-based e-mail service, which was launched as an alternative to ISP-based e-mail in 1996. He sold the company to Microsoft, creating one of the greatest success stories of Indian entrepreneurship in the Silicon Valley.

Bhupathi, Mahesh (Born: 1974)

Mahesh Bhupathi is a professional tennis player who, like compatriot Leander Paes, is a dominant player in the ATP doubles circuit. In 1997, Bhupathi became the first Indian to win a Grand Slam title by winning the mixed-doubles tournament with Rita Hikari at the French Open.

Bose, Amar (Born: 1929)

Philadelphia-born Amar Bose is the founder of the Bose Corporation, known for its world-famous Bose speakers and other audio equipment. Born to Indian emigrants from Calcutta, Bose is a retired professor of electrical engineering at the Massachusetts Institute of Technology.

Chadha, Gurinder (Born: 1959)

Gurinder Chadha is a Kenya-born British film director of Indian descent known for her hit comedy movie *Bend It Like Beckham* (2002). The movie went on to become the first film by a nonwhite Briton to reach the number-one spot at the British box office. It also won a Golden Globe nomination for Best Film (Comedy/Musical) in 2002.

Chawla, Kalpana (Born: 1962; Died: 2003)

Kalpana Chawla was an Indian American astronaut who was one of the seven crew members killed in the space shuttle Columbia disaster. Chawla was posthumously awarded the Congressional Space Medal of Honor.

Chopra, Deepak (Born: 1946)

Deepak Chopra is one of the world's best-selling spiritual authors and the founder of the Chopra Center. Chopra, a trained physician from India, came to the United States in 1970 to practice medicine and later got involved in the field of mind-body medicine. His breakthrough book, *Quantum Healing*, brought him international recognition in 1989.

Dalai Lama (Born: 1935)

The Dalai Lama, the spiritual leader of the Tibetan people, won the Nobel Peace Prize in 1989 for his nonviolent struggle to gain autonomy for his homeland. Born and raised in Tibet, the Dalai Lama escaped with his followers to India in 1959 after China crushed the Tibetan national uprising. He currently runs the Tibetan government-in-exile from Dharamasala, which is home to more than 120,000 Tibetan refugees.

Desai, Kiran (Born: 1971)

Kiran Desai is an Indian novelist who, in 2006, became the youngest woman to win the prestigious Man Booker Prize for fiction for her novel *The Inheritance of Loss*. She is the daughter of famous writer and three-time Booker Prize nominee Anita Desai.

Dosanjh, Ujjal (Born: 1947)

India-born Ujjal Singh Dosanjh is a Canadian lawyer and politician, currently serving as a member of the Canadian parliament for Vancouver South. In 2000, Dosanjh became the premier of the province of British

Columbia, becoming the first Indo-Canadian to hold the post of provincial premier.

Gandhi, Sonia (Born: 1946)

Italian-born Sonia Gandhi is the leader of India's most powerful political party, the Indian National Congress (the Congress Party). She is the widow of former Indian leader Rajiv Gandhi and daughter-in-law of Indira Gandhi. In 2004, she led the party to a surprise victory in the general election.

Gupta, Dr. Sanjay (Born: 1969)

Dr. Sanjay Gupta is the chief medical correspondent for CNN. He is also a practicing neurosurgeon and faculty member of the department of neurosurgery at the Emory University School of Medicine.

Haque, Pramod

Delhi-raised Pramod Haque is the managing partner of Northwest Venture Partners, a venture capital firm based in Palo Alto, California. In 2004, he eclipsed Vinod Khosla to attain the top spot in the *Forbes* annual Midas List of the world's top venture capitalists.

Jindal, Bobby (Born: 1971)

Piyush "Bobby" Jindal is an Indian American Republican Party politician who, in 2007, made history by winning the Louisiana gubernatorial race. He became the first nonwhite governor of the state since 1870 and the first Indian American to head a state. The son of Indian immigrants from Punjab, Jindal was born and raised in Baton Rouge, Louisiana.

Kapoor, Anish (Born: 1954)

Anish Kapoor is an Indian-born, London-based sculptor who is famous for *Cloud Gate*, an enormous, shiny, stainless-steel sculpture, unveiled at the Millennium Park in Chicago in 2004.

Kapur, Shekhar (Born: 1945)

Shekhar Kapur is a Bollywood producer and director who directed Academy Award-winning movies *Elizabeth* (1998) and *Elizabeth: The Golden Age* (2007), which are based on the life of Queen Elizabeth I of England.

Khan, Amir (Born: 1965)

Amir Khan is a popular Bollywood actor who is widely acknowledged for his versatile acting prowess. Khan produced and acted in the movie *Lagaan*, which received the Best Foreign Language Film Oscar nomination. His recent movie *Rang De Basanti* (2006) was India's official entry for the 70th Academy Awards.

Khan, Shah Rukh (Born: 1965)

Shah Rukh Khan is today's most popular Bollywood actor, with a popularity and fan base akin to that of legendary actor Amitabh Bachchan. Khan, who shot to fame with a lead role in a 1988 television serial *Fauji*, made his debut in the 1992 hit film *Deewana*. His subsequent movies, *Baazigar*, *Darr*, and *Dilwale Dulhania Le Jayenge*, were all huge box-office successes and helped him reach stardom.

Lahiri, Jhumpa (Born: 1967)

Jhumpa Lahiri is a Pulitzer Prize-winning author of Indian descent. Her debut book, *Interpreter of Maladies*, a collection of short stories, won the 2000 Pulitzer Prize for fiction, making her one of the youngest recipients of the coveted prize. Lahiri's recent novel, *The Namesake*, was made into a feature film by Mira Nair.

Mallya, Vijay (Born: 1955)

Vijay Mallya is the chairman of United Breweries Group, the third-largest spirits company in the world. In 2005, he launched Kingfisher Airline, which gets its name from United Breweries' flagship beer brand, Kingfisher. Known for his flamboyant and flashy lifestyle,

Mallya is arguably the most charismatic Indian billionaire, invoking comparisons with Richard Branson.

Mehta, Deepa (Born: 1950)

Deepa Mehta is a Canada-based filmmaker known for her trilogy of controversial movies: *Fire* (1996), *Earth* (1998), and *Water* (2005). *Water*, Canada's entry for the Academy Awards, earned the Best Foreign Language Film nomination in 2007.

Mehta, Zubin (Born: 1937)

Zubin Mehta is one of the world's foremost conductors of Western classical music. Born in Mumbai, Mehta left India to attend the Academy of Music in Vienna. From 1978 to 1991 he was the music director of New York Philharmonic, conducting over a thousand concerts. In 2006, Mehta was among the five eminent artists to receive Kennedy Center Honors.

Mirza, Sania (Born: 1986)

Sania Mirza is a professional tennis player and the highest-ranked female tennis player from India. Mirza made a mark on the international tennis scene in 2005 by reaching the fourth round at the U.S. Open and the third round at the Australian Open. Mirza is now one of the most famous sports icons of southern Asia, with a large fan following.

Mittal, Lakshmi (Born: 1950)

Lakshmi Niwas Mittal is a London-based Indian billionaire industrialist whose company ArcelorMittal is the largest steel company in the world, controlling 10 percent of global steel production. He was ranked fourth (behind Warren Buffet, Carlos Slim Helu, and Bill Gates) on the 2008 *Forbes* list of the world's billionaires, with a net worth of $45 billion.

Mittal, Sunil (Born: 1957)

Sunil Mittal is the founder, chairman, and managing director of the Bharti Group, India's largest GSM-based mobile phone service provider with thirty million subscribers. He is arguably one of the most successful entrepreneurs in India's post-economic liberalization era.

Murthy, Narayana (Born: 1944)

Narayana Murthy is the cofounder and currently chief mentor of Infosys Technologies, India's premier software company. *The Economist* ranked him eighth on its list of the fifteen most admired global leaders in 2005.

Nair, Mira (Born: 1957)

Mira Nair is an Indian-born, New York-based film director known for producing several award-winning movies. Nair won international recognition for her debut movie, *Salaam Bombay*, which was nominated for an Academy Award in the Best Foreign Language Film category in 1988. Her other movies include *Monsoon Wedding* (2001) and *The Namesake* (2007).

Nooyi, Indra (Born: 1955)

Chennai-born Indra Krishnamurthy Nooyi is the chairwoman and chief executive officer of $32 billion PepsiCo, a global food and beverage company. She was ranked fifth on the *Forbes* list of the world's one hundred most powerful women in 2007.

Pachauri, Rajendra (Born: 1940)

Rajendra Pachauri is an Indian environmentalist and the chairman of the Intergovernmental Panel on Climate Change (IPCC). The IPCC, a U.N. body, is the world's top scientific authority on global warming and its impact. In 2007 the IPCC was jointly awarded the Nobel Peace Prize with former U.S. vice president Al Gore.

Paes, Leander (Born: 1973)

Leander Paes is an Indian tennis professional who mainly plays in ATP tour doubles events. Paes shot into prominence when he won the Wimbledon Junior title in 1990. In 1999, Paes paired up with compatriot Mahesh Bhupathi to reach the finals of four Grand Slam events, winning Wimbledon and the French Open.

Pandit, Vikram (Born: 1957)

Vikram Pandit is the current chief executive officer of Citigroup. Pandit worked for Morgan Stanley for two decades before leaving the company to start a hedge fund, Old Lane Partners, in April 2006. In July 2007, he sold the Old Lane hedge fund to Citigroup. In December 2007, he was named Citigroup's chief executive officer.

Prahalad, C. K. (Born: 1941)

Coimbatore Krishnarao Prahalad, an internationally known corporate strategist, is currently a distinguished professor of corporate strategy at the Ross School of Business, University of Michigan. He earned a top spot (ahead of Bill Gates, Alan Greenspan, and Michael Porter) on Suntop Media's Thinkers 50 list, a biennial ranking of the top fifty management thought leaders worldwide.

Premji, Aziz (Born: 1945)

Azim Hasham Premji is the chairman of Wipro technologies, one of India's largest software companies. Premji has been the richest Indian for the past several years and was rated among the hundred most influential people in the world by the *Time Magazine* in 2004.

Rai, Aishwarya (Born: 1973)

Aishwarya Rai is an Indian model, beauty pageant queen, and movie star, widely regarded as one of the most beautiful women and best-known Indian actress in the world. After being crowned Miss World in 1994, Aishwarya went on to pursue a highly successful career in Bollywood.

Ravi Shankar, Pandit (Born: 1920)

Pandit Ravi Shankar is a legendary sitar player and a composer who is arguably the most popular Indian musician in the world, with a music career spanning eight decades. Shankar's association with The Beatles, especially George Harrison, earned him international recognition and helped popularize Indian classical music in the West.

Roy, Arundhati (Born: 1961)

Arundhati Roy is an Indian novelist, writer, and activist. She won the Booker Prize in 1997 for her first novel, *The God of Small Things*. Since winning the Booker Prize, she has concentrated on social and political issues and emerged as a focal point in the antiglobalization and antinuclear movements.

Rushdie, Salman (Born: 1947)

Salman Rushdie is a controversial Mumbai-born British novelist known for great novels such as *Midnight's Children* (1981), which won the Booker Prize and brought him international fame. However, his fourth novel, *The Satanic Verses* (1988), earned him the ire of Muslims around the world.

Sarin, Arun (Born: 1954)

India-born Arun Sarin was the chief executive of Vodafone, Europe's largest mobile phone company. He is an alumnus of the Indian Institute of Technology, Kharagpur, and the University of California, Berkeley.

Sen, Amartya (Born: 1933)

Amartya Sen, a renowned Indian economist, was the winner of the Nobel Prize in Economics in 1998 for his work on poverty and famine. He is the sixth person of Indian origin to receive the coveted Nobel Prize.

Singh, Manmohan (Born: 1932)

Dr. Manmohan Singh is an economist turned politician who in 2004 became the first person from the minority Sikh community to become the prime minister of India. As finance minister under Prime Minister Narasimha Rao from 1991 to 1996, Singh was mainly responsible for launching groundbreaking economic reforms.

Shyamalan, M. Night (Born: 1970)

India-born, Philadelphia-raised M. Night Shyamalan is a Hollywood director and screenwriter who has often been referred to as a "modern-day Hitchcock" for his penchant to make low-budget horror movies and thrillers. His blockbuster movie *The Sixth Sense*, starring Bruce Willis, grossed $670 million at the worldwide box office, making it the second-biggest moneymaker of 1999.

Tata, Ratan (Born: 1937)

Ratan Tata is the chairman of the $22 billion Tata Group, one of India's largest private-sector conglomerates. The Tata Group includes Tata Steel, Tata Motors, Tata Consultancy Services, and numerous other companies.

Tendulkar, Sachin (Born: 1973)

Sachin Ramesh Tendulkar, nicknamed "The Master Blaster," is a current Indian cricket player rated as one of the greatest batsmen of all time. Tendulkar, who is often compared to cricketing legend Don Bradman, holds numerous world records in both Test and One Day International (ODI) cricket.

Tharoor, Shashi (Born: 1956)

Shashi Tharoor is an author, journalist, and former U.N. diplomat. Tharoor was India's official candidate for the post of U.N. secretary general in 2006, but he narrowly lost to South Korea's Ban Ki-moon.

Vajpayee, Atal Bihari (Born: 1924)

Atal Bihari Vajpayee, considered one of India's most charismatic political leaders of the post-independence era, was India's prime minister from 1998 to 2004. A moderate leader, Vajpayee often found his views at odds with the pro-Hindu political orientation of the party he founded. He left office after an electoral reverse in 2004.

Williams, Sunita (Born: 1965)

Sunita Williams is an Indian American astronaut who went into space onboard the space shuttle Discovery in 2006 and spent about seven months on the International Space Station, setting a record for the most time spent in space by a woman. She is the second woman of Indian origin to venture into space, after Kalpana Chawla.

Zakaria, Fareed (Born: 1965)

Mumbai-born Fareed Zakaria is the editor of *Newsweek International* and a political analyst for ABC News. He is the son of Rafiq Zakaria, an Indian politician and deputy leader of the Congress Party. Since 2002, he has been a regular member of ABC's *This Week with George Stephanopoulos* TV program.

Appendix 6: Twelve Indian Spiritual Leaders of All Times

Amritanandamayi, Mata (Born: 1953)

Mata Amritanandamayi, also known as the "hugging saint," is a spiritual leader and humanitarian who has gained international prominence for her practice of embracing people as a way to heal mind, body, and spirit.

Mahesh Yogi (Born: 1917; Died: 2008)

Maharishi Mahesh Yogi (the title *Maharishi* translates to "great seer"), India's best-known Hindu spiritual leader, introduced the transcendental meditation technique to the West. His transcendental meditation (TM) movement took off in the West in the 1970s after it was embraced by The Beatles and some Hollywood celebrities.

Prabhupada, Swami (Born: 1886; Died: 1977)

A. C. Bhaktivedanta Swami Prabhupada was the founder of the International Society for Krishna Consciousness (ISKCON), popularly known as the "Hare Krishna" movement, a twentieth-century Hindu religious movement. The movement became very popular among young people in the United States and Europe in the 1960s and 1970s.

Rajneesh, Osho (Born: 1931; Died: 1990)

Osho Rajneesh was a charismatic Indian spiritual leader who started a controversial new spiritual movement that still has many followers around the world. In 1981, he moved to the United States, where his followers built a massive ashram (retreat) in Oregon State. In 1986 he was deported from the United States for immigration violations and returned to Pune, where he died in 1990.

Ramanujacharya (Born: AD 1017; Died: AD 1137)

Ramanujacharya was a great Hindu philosopher and proponent of the philosophical doctrine of Vishishtadvaita, which differed from the philosophy of Shankaracharya. Whereas Shankaracharya's Advaita philosophy states that only god is real, the universe is not real, and god and individual are the same, Vishishtadvaita teaches that the god, the soul, and the universe are all real and that the universe comes out of god and returns to him in cycles. Ramanujacharya was instrumental in developing the Vaishnavism, a Hindu sect devoted to the worship of Lord Vishnu.

Ramdev, Guru (Born: 1965)

Guru Ramdev is India's leading yoga guru and practitioner of the ancient Indian medical science Ayurveda. He is widely credited with bringing yoga to the Indian masses through his unique *pranayama* (breathing) exercises.

Ravi Shankar, Sri Sri (Born: 1956)

Sri Sri Ravi Shankar is a spiritual leader, humanitarian, and founder of the Art of Living Foundation, an international nonprofit spiritual organization active in more than 160 countries around the world. Sri Sri Ravi Shankar, who was trained under renowned spiritual leader

Mahesh Yogi, popularized a powerful breathing-based technique called *Sudarshan Kriya* (healing breath).

Sai Baba, Sathya (Born: 1926)

Sathya Sai Baba, known as Swami, Bhagawan, or Baba, is India's most popular and enigmatic spiritual leader, with an estimated follower base of tens of millions of people spread across more than a hundred countries. His followers believe he is the reincarnation of fakir Shirdi Sai Baba, from whom he derives his name.

Saraswati, Dayananda (Born: 1824; Died: 1883)

Swami Dayananda Saraswati was a social reformer, religious leader, and founder of the Hindu reform movement the Arya Samaj (Society of Nobles). Throughout his life, Dayananda exhorted Hindus to go back to the Vedas (ancient Hindu religious scriptures) as the basis for Hinduism and to stop practices such as caste-based discrimination, idol worship, and child marriages.

Shankaracharya, Adi (Born: AD 788; Died: AD 820)

Adi Shankaracharya, also referred to as Jagadguru (universal teacher), was a famous Hindu philosopher and reformer who lived more than a thousand years ago. He had a profound influence on the growth of Hinduism at a time when the religion was losing appeal due to the influence of new religions. Shankaracharya is known for his Advaita (nondualistic Hindu philosophy). In his short life, spanning only thirty-two years, Shankaracharya is believed to have established four monasteries in the four corners of India—Kashmir, Dwaraka, Puri, and Sringeri—which are operational even today.

Teresa, Mother (Born: 1910; Died: 1997)

Mother Teresa was an Albanian Roman Catholic nun whose work on behalf of the poor in India and around the world made her an iconic figure in the latter part of the twentieth century. Mother Teresa was born Agnes Gonxha Bojaxhiu in Skopje, Macedonia, to parents of

Albanian descent. Moved by the plight of the poor and sick in the slums of Calcutta, she left her teaching position at a convent school in 1950 and founded The Missionaries of Charity, whose primary mission was to take care of the poorest of the poor. Mother Theresa's humanitarian work brought her international acclaim, including the Nobel Peace Prize in 1979.

Vivekananda, Swami (Born: 1863; Died: 1902)

Swami Vivekananda is one of the most influential and well-known Hindu spiritual leaders of nineteenth-century India. He played a major role in the Hindu reform movement. His famous speech on Hinduism at the World's Parliament of Religions held in Chicago in 1893 brought him instant celebrity in the West.

Appendix 7: Eighteen World Heritage Sites of India

Agra Fort

Agra Fort is a red sandstone monument located two kilometers from the famed Taj Mahal, beside the Yamuna River. Mughal emperor Akbar laid the foundation for this royal citadel, and construction took place between 1565 and 1571. It was in this fort that Shah Jahan, the deposed Mughal emperor, was imprisoned by his son, Aurangzeb.

Ajanta Caves

The Ajanta Caves are Buddhist caves located sixty-five miles from Aurangabad in the western state of Maharashtra. Once forgotten, they were accidentally discovered in 1819 by a British hunting expedition. These caves contain magnificent murals and carvings dating back from 200 BC to AD 250, depicting the life stories of Buddha.

Buddhist Monuments at Sanchi

The Buddhist monuments at Sanchi, forty kilometers from the central Indian city of Bhopal, are considered the most significant structures of ancient India. The site contains a number of Buddhist *stupas* (monasteries) and pillars built between the third century BC and twelfth century AD.

Chhatrapati Shivaji Terminus (Formerly Victoria Terminus)

The Chhatrapati Shivaji Terminus (CST), with its cathedral-like façade, is a historic landmark of Mumbai, India's financial capital. Built in 1878 in honor of Queen Victoria of England, the CST serves as a major railway station in Mumbai's busy suburban rail network. The CST is considered an outstanding example of Victorian Gothic Revival architecture in India. Initially known as Victoria Terminus (VT), the monument was renamed in 1996 in honor of the seventeenth-century Maratha ruler.

Elephanta Caves

The Elephanta Caves house rock-cut temples dating back to AD 600, in honor of the Hindu god Lord Shiva. Located on Elephanta Island, near Mumbai, the Elephanta Caves are a major tourist attraction for visitors to Mumbai.

Ellora Caves

The Ellora Caves, located twenty-nine kilometers from Aurangabad, house rock-cut temples representing the Buddhist, Jain, and Hindu religions; they showcase the spirit of religious tolerance that was the hallmark of ancient India. These rock-cut caves, believed to have come into existence between AD 350 and 900, house the magnificent Kailashnath Temple, honoring Lord Shiva.

Fatehpur Sikri

Fatehpur Sikri (City of Victory) is a historic city that served as the capital of Mughal ruler Emperor Akbar for a short period. Built in the second half of the sixteenth century and located thirty-seven kilometers from the historic city of Agra, Sikri had to be abandoned due to an insurmountable water shortage at the location. This deserted city contains many old structures and monuments and is among the major attractions of Agra.

Great Living Chola Temples
The Cholas ruled southern India between AD 900 and 1250, with Thanjavur as their capital. Cholas were great patrons of arts and culture. Thanjavur is home to the famed Brihadeeswara temple built by King Rajaraja Chola in honor of Lord Shiva. This tenth-century structure is a great example of the Chola dynasty's contribution to the Dravidian style of temple architecture.

Group of Monuments at Hampi
Hampi, once known as Vijayanagara (City of Victory), was the capital of the famed Vijayanagara empire that ruled southern India between AD 1343 and 1565. The empire reached its zenith during the reign of Krishna Deva Raya (AD 1509–30). Conquered in AD 1565 by a Deccan confederacy of Muslim rulers in the decisive Battle of Talikota, the city was thoroughly pillaged and then abandoned. Today, remains of the palaces, temples, and royal buildings lie scattered across an area of about twenty-six square kilometers. The once-thriving city, located 350 kilometers from Bangalore on the southern bank of the Tungabhadra River, attracts thousands of tourists every year.

Group of Monuments at Mahabalipuram
Mahabalipuram, located sixty kilometers from Chennai on the Bay of Bengal coast, was the main seaport of Pallava rulers from AD 600 to 900. It is home to some of the finest rock-cut temples, caves, massive chariots, sculptures, and a number of other monuments in the Dravidian style of architecture. The Shore Temple of Mahabalipuram is best known for its skilled craftsmanship and intricate carvings.

Group of Monuments at Pattadakal
Pattadakal was the capital of the Chalukya dynasty, which ruled from Badami from AD 543 to 763. Located twenty kilometers from

Badami, in the Bijapur district of present-day Karnataka state, this World Heritage Site contains a group of temples that display unique architectural features.

Humayun's Tomb, Delhi

The Humayun tomb was built in honor of Humayun, the second emperor of the Mughal empire, by his Persian-born wife in AD 1570. This monument is considered to be the first garden-mausoleum of India and inspired many architectural innovations, culminating in the construction of the Taj Mahal in AD 1653.

Khajuraho Group of Monuments

The Khajuraho temples, located in the central Indian state of Madhya Pradesh, were built during the rule of the Chandella dynasty between AD 950 and 1050. The name *Khajuraho* is derived from the Hindi word *khajur*, meaning "date palm." These medieval temples, famous for their erotic sculptures, are often described as shrines of love.

Mahabodhi Temple Complex at Bodh Gaya

The Mahabodhi Temple Complex is considered one of the holiest sites for followers of Buddhism. Initially built in the third century BC during the reign of Emperor Ashoka, this temple was rebuilt between the fifth and sixth century AD. Near the temple is the site of the famous Bodhi Tree, under which Prince Siddhartha Gautama meditated and attained enlightenment to become Buddha (awakened). The present Bodhi Tree is about 120 years old and grew from a sapling brought from Sri Lanka. Bodh Gaya attracts pilgrims from all over the world.

Qutb Minar and Its Monuments, Delhi

Qutb Minar, the most prominent landmark of Delhi, is India's highest stone tower. It is named after Qutubuddin Aibak, the trusted Turkish slave general of Muhammad Ghori, who ascended the Delhi throne in AD 1206, marking the beginning of Islamic rule in India. The tower was built in the early thirteenth century to celebrate the AD 1192 victory of Muhammad Ghori over the Hindu ruler of Delhi, Prithviraj Chauhan. The red sandstone tower is 72.5 meters (239 feet) high and tapers from 14.3 meters in diameter at the base to 2.75 meters in diameter at its peak.

Red Fort, Delhi

The Red Fort (*Lal Qila* in Hindi), the largest of Delhi's many famous monuments, was once the seat of power for the Mughal empire. It was built to serve as the royal fort palace for the fifth Mughal emperor Shah Jahan (also the builder of the Taj Mahal) when he moved his capital from Agra to the newly formed city of Shahjahanabad near Delhi in 1639. The area is now known as Old Delhi, as opposed to New Delhi, which was built by the British and now serves as the capital of independent India. The Red Fort gets its name from the thick walls of sandstone that surround it. Today, the Red Fort serves as a venue for the Indian prime minister's annual Independence Day speech to the nation. Opposite to the Red Fort is Jama Masjid, India's largest mosque, which was also built by Shah Jahan in 1656.

Sun Temple, Konark

The Sun Temple at Konark (*Kona* means "corner" and *Arka* means "sun") is a well-known attraction of the eastern Indian state of Orissa. Built in AD 1278 by Ganga King Narasimha Deva, the entire temple was designed as a chariot of the Sun God drawn by seven horses. The chariot has twelve pairs of gigantic ten-foot-diameter ornamented wheels. The temple is located along the shoreline of the Bay of Bengal and is close to both Puri (thirty-five kilometers) and state capital Bhubaneshwar (sixty-five kilometers). India's celebrated poet Rabindranath Tagore paid rich tributes to the Konark temple. He wrote of Konark: "Here the language of stone surpasses the language of man."[352]

Taj Mahal, Agra

The Taj Mahal (Crown Palace), considered "the embodiment of love," is indisputably the most celebrated monument of southern Asia. Located in Agra, this stunning mausoleum of white marble was constructed between 1631 and 1653 by Mughal emperor Shah Jahan is memory of his favorite wife, Mumtaz Mahal, a Persian princess who died during childbirth in AD 1631 at the age of thirty-nine.

Appendix 8: Other Tourist Attractions

Amarnath Cave Temple

The Amarnath Cave Temple, located at an altitude of four thousand meters in the Himalayan Mountains, is a popular pilgrimage site for Hindus. As per Hindu legend, the cave temple is the site where Lord Shiva recounted the secret of creation to his wife Parvati. The annual pilgrimage to this cave temple attracts tens of thousands of people. The trek from the city of Pahalgam to Amarnath Cave, a distance of forty-five kilometers, typically takes four to five days.

Badrinath Temple

The Badrinath temple, situated in the foothills of the Garhwal Himalayas, is home to a famous temple dedicated to Lord Vishnu. According to Hindu legend, Lord Vishnu came to this area called Badri Van (Berry Garden) to meditate. The temple is open only from April to October due to severe winter conditions.

Charminar, Hyderabad

The Charminar (Four Towers) is a prominent landmark of the southern city of Hyderabad. Built by Qutub Shahi in 1591, this fifty-four-meter-high monument is considered the masterpiece of Qutub Shahi architecture.

Golconda Fort, Hyderabad

Golconda Fort, ten kilometers west of Hyderabad, is among the most prominent fortress complexes in India. This medieval fort was built by three successive dynasties that ruled the region: the Kakatiyas, the Bahmanis, and the Qutub Shahis. The fortress sits on a granite hill 120 meters high. Golconda's glory ended when Mughal emperor Aurangzeb conquered and destroyed the fort in 1687, thus ending the illustrious rule of the Qutub Shahis. Today, much of the fort is in ruins, yet it remains a major tourist attraction.

Golden Temple, Amritsar

Amritsar is home to the Golden Temple, the holiest shrine of the Sikh religion. The temple was founded during the term of the fourth Sikh guru, Guru Ram Das (1574–81) and completed during the term of Guru Arjan Dev (1581–1606). The temple was rebuilt in its present form in 1776. Maharaja Ranjit Singh (1780–1839) gilded the roof of the temple with gold in 1802, and since then the temple has been known as the Golden Temple.

Haridwar and Rishikesh

Haridwar (Gateway to God), located in the foothills of the Himalayas in the northern Indian state of Uttarakhand, represents the point where the River Ganges reaches the plains. Haridwar is the site of many religious festivals, including Kumbh Mela, which happens once in twelve years. Rishikesh (Place of the Sages), located twenty-five kilometers from Haridwar, is another popular Hindu pilgrimage center that is dotted with several temples.

Kedarnath Temple

Kedarnath temple, located 3,500 meters above sea level in the northern Indian state of Uttaranchal, is dedicated to Lord Shiva. Due to extreme winter conditions, the temple only opens between April and November. It is widely believed that the temple was built five thousand years ago by the Pandavas, the heroes of the Hindu epic *Mahabharata*. It is here that the Pandavas did penance for killing their cousins and close relatives in the Battle of Kurukshetra and sought to meet Lord Shiva. Religious reformer Adi Shankaracharya renovated the temple in the eighth century. In close proximity to the temple is the Samadhi (final resting place) of Adi Shankaracharya.

Mathura and Vrindavan

Mathura, located 150 kilometers from Delhi, is widely known as the birthplace of Hindu god Lord Krishna, reincarnation of Lord Vishnu. Vrindavan (fifteen kilometers from Mathura) is where Krishna spent his childhood. Both Mathura and Vrindavan are major pilgrimage sites for devotees of Krishna.

Mount Kailas, Tibetan Plateau

Mount Kailas, considered the abode of Lord Shiva, is the holiest mountain in the world. According to Hindu mythology, Hindu god Lord Shiva sits in perpetual meditation at the top of the mountain with his wife Parvati. The famed peak, which stands at 22,000 feet, is located in Tibet.

Mysore Palace, Mysore

Mysore, located 159 kilometers southwest of Bangalore, is the erstwhile capital of Wodeyar, which ruled Mysore until 1950 when the kingdom became a state within the Indian Union. The spectacular Mysore Palace, designed by an English architect and constructed between 1897 and 1912, dominates Mysore's skyline. The palace is the venue for the famous Mysore Dasara festival, during which the entire palace is illuminated with thousands of bulbs.

Tirupati: Temple of Lord Venkateswara

Tirupati, located 130 kilometers from Chennai, is home to the famous Hindu temple of Lord Venkateswara. Considered the richest temple in India and the most popular pilgrimage site in the world after the Vatican, the sacred temple is located on the seventh peak of Tirumala Hill, which is 3,200 feet above sea level. Both the Pallavas of Kancheepuram (ninth century AD) and the Vijayanagara dynasty (fifteenth century AD) were active patrons of this ancient temple. The temple attracts tens of thousands of devotees each day.

Varanasi

The ancient city of Varanasi (also known as Banaras or Kashi), located on the west bank of the River Ganges, is considered India's holiest Hindu city and the oldest continuously inhabited city in the world. American author Mark Twain once wrote: "Banaras is older than history, older than tradition, older even than legend and looks twice as old as all of them put together."[353] The city is home to many temples dating back to the medieval period. The Kashi Vishwanath temple is the most famous temple of Varanasi.

Vivekananda Rock Memorial, Kanyakumari

The Vivekananda Rock Memorial is located in Kanyakumari, the southernmost tip of the Indian peninsula, where three oceans (Indian Ocean, Bay of Bengal, and Arabian Sea) meet. The Rock Memorial was built in 1970 to commemorate the visit of charismatic Hindu religious leader Swami Vivekananda, who had meditated here prior to his journey to the West to spread the Hindu philosophy in 1892. The memorial stands on Vivekananda's rock, about five hundred meters offshore.

Appendix 9: India's Top Twenty Metropolitan Cities

City	Population	Average Household Income ($)
Mumbai (Bombay)	16,368,000	6,326
Kolkata (Calcutta)	13,217,000	3,744
Delhi	12,791,000	9,982
Chennai (Madras)	6,425,000	4,797
Bengaluru (Bangalore)	5,687,000	4,102
Hyderabad	5,534,000	5,534
Ahmedabad	4,519,000	4,192
Pune	3,755,000	6,277
Surat	2,811,000	3,737
Kanpur	2,690,000	3,092
Jaipur	2,324,000	3,278
Lucknow	2,267,000	3,158
Nagpur	2,123,000	5,142
Patna	1,707,000	2,540
Indore	1,639,000	2,891
Vadodara	1,492,000	3,665
Bhopal	1,455,000	2,782
Coimbatore	1,446,000	4,844
Ludhiana	1,395,000	7,785
Kochi	1,355,000	3,965

Source: Investment Commission of India Web Site

Appendix 10: India's States and Union Territories (UT)

States/UT	Area (sq. km)	Population	Capital City	Language
Andhra Pradesh	275,069	76,210,007	Hyderabad	Telugu, Urdu
Arunachal Pradesh	83,743	1,097,968	Itanagar	Monpa
Assam	78,438	26,638,407	Dispur	Assamese
Bihar	94,163	82,878,796	Patna	Hindi
Chhattisgarh	136,034	20,975,956	Raipur	Hindi
Goa	3,702	1,343,998	Panaji	Konkani, Marathi
Gujarat	196,024	50,671,017	Gandhinagar	Gujarati
Haryana	44,212	21,144,564	Chandigarh	Hindi
Himachal Pradesh	55,673	6,077,900	Shimla	Hindi
Jammu & Kashmir	222,236	10,069,987	Srinagar, Jammu	Urdu
Jharkhand	79,714	26,909,428	Ranchi	Hindi
Karnataka	191,791	52,850,562	Bangalore	Kannada
Kerala	38,863	31,841,374	Thiruvananthapuram	Malayalam

Madhya Pradesh	308,600	60,385,118	Bhopal	Hindi
Maharashtra	307,713	96,752,247	Mumbai	Marathi
Manipur	22,327	2,293,896	Imphal	Manipuri
Meghalaya	22,429	2,318,822	Shillong	Khasi, Garo
Mizoram	21,081	891,058	Aizawl	Mizo
Nagaland	16,579	1,988,636	Kohima	Angami, Ao
Orissa	155,707	36,804,660	Bhubaneswar	Oriya
Punjab	50,362	24,358,999	Chandigarh	Punjabi
Rajasthan	342,239	56,473,122	Jaipur	Hindi Rajasthani
Sikkim	7,096	540,493	Gangtok	Lepcha, Bhutia
Tamil Nadu	130,058	62,405,679	Chennai	Tamil
Tripura	10,492	3,199,203	Agartala	Bengali
Uttarakhand	53,484	8,489,349	Dehra Dun	Hindi
Uttar Pradesh	240,928	166,052,859	Lucknow	Hindi
West Bengal	88,752	80,176,197	Kolkota	Bengali
Union Territories				
Andaman & Nicobar	8,249	356,152	Port Blair	Hindi
Chandigarh	114	900,635	Chandigarh	Hindi, Punjabi
Delhi	1,483	13,800,000	Delhi	Hindi
Dadra & Nagar Haveli	491	220,490	Silvassa	Gujarati
Daman and Diu	112	158,204	Daman	Gujarati
Lakshadweep	32	60,650	Kavaratti	Jeseri
Puducherry	480	974,345	Puducherry	Tamil, Telugu

Source: National Portal of India

Appendix 11: India at a Glance

GEOGRAPHY	
Location:	Bounded by the Himalayas (north), Bay of Bengal (east), Arabian Sea (west), and Indian Ocean (south)
Indian Standard Time:	GMT + 05:30; Telephone Code: +91
Area:	3.29 million sq. km (seventh-largest country in the world)
Neighboring Countries:	Pakistan (northwest); China, Bhutan, and Nepal (north); Myanmar, Bangladesh (east); Sri Lanka (south)
Coastline:	7,516.6 km (mainland, Lakshadweep, Andaman & Nicobar)
Climate:	Tropical climate (marked by high temperatures and dry winters)
Terrain:	The mainland comprises four regions: the Himalayas, plains of Ganga and Indus, desert region, and southern peninsula
PEOPLE	
Population:	1,147 million (15 percent of world population)
Population Growth Rate:	1.57 percent

Life Expectancy at Birth:	69.25 years
Median Age:	25.1 years
Religions	Hindus (80.5 percent), Muslims (13.4 percent), Christians (2.3 percent), Sikhs (1.9 percent)
Languages:	22 languages; Hindi (41 percent), Bengali (8.1 percent), Telugu (7.2 percent)
Literacy:	65 percent (2001 census)
GOVERNMENT	
Government Type:	Federal republic with a parliamentary system of government
Capital City:	New Delhi
Administrative Divisions:	28 states and 7 union territories
Independence:	August 15, 1947 (from British colonial rule)
Executive Branch:	President (head of state), prime minister (head of the government)
Legislative Branch:	Lok Sabha (House of People), Rajya Sabha (Council of States)
Political Parties	Indian National Congress, Bharatiya Janata Party, Communist Party of India-Marxist, and dozens of regional and small national parties
ECONOMY	
GDP (PPP):	$2.989 trillion (2007 est.); China: $6.991 trillion (2007 est.)
GDP Per Capita (PPP):	$2,700 (2007 est.); China: $5,300 (2007 est.)
GDP Real Growth Rate:	9.2 percent (2007 est.); China: 11.4 percent (2007 est.)
GDP Composition:	Agriculture: 17.6 percent, Industry: 29.4 percent, Services: 52.9 percent (2007 est.)

NATIONAL SYMBOLS	
National Flag Description:	Horizontal tricolor with deep saffron at the top, white in the middle, and dark green at the bottom. At the center is a navy blue wheel.
National Holidays:	January 26 (Republic Day), August 15 (Independence Day), October 2 (Mahatma Gandhi's Birthday)
National Symbols:	National bird: Indian peacock; national flower: lotus; national tree: Indian fig tree; national animal: magnificent tiger; national fruit: mango

Sources: CIA— *The World Factbook, U.S. Department of State, National Portal of India*

Bibliography

Aalgaard, Wendy. *East Indians In America*. Lerner Publications, 2005.

Ansari, Mark, and Liz Lark. *Yoga for Beginners*. Collins Living, 1999.

Einfield, Jann, ed. *History of Nations-India*. Greenhaven Press, 2003.

Friedman, Thomas. *The World Is Flat*. Farrar, Straus and Giroux, 2006.

Furbee, Mary. *The Importance Of Series-Mohandas Gandhi (The Importance Of Series)*. Lucent
Books, 2000.

Gandhi, Mohandas K. *The Story of My Experiments with Truth*. Navajivan, 1927.

Hiro, Dilip. *The Timeline History of India*. Barnes & Noble, 2002.

Ingram, Scott. *South Asian Americans (World Almanac Library of American Immigration)*. World Almanac Library, 2006.

Johnsen, Linda. *The Complete Idiot's Guide to Hinduism*. Alpha, 2001.

Kamdar, Mira. *Planet India: The Turbulent Rise of the Largest Democracy and the Future of Our World*. Scribner, 2008.

Lapierre, Dominique and Larry Collins. *Freedom at Midnight*. Vikas, 2001.

Meredith, Robyn. *The Elephant and the Dragon: The Rise of India and China and What It Means for All of Us*. W. W. Norton, 2008.

Ramesh, Jairam. *Making Sense of Chindia: Reflections of China and India*. India Research Press, 2005.

Sharma, Y. D. *Delhi and Its Neighborhood*. Archaeological Survey of India, 2001.

Spear, Percival. *The History of India, Vol. 2*. Penguin, 1990.

Radhakrishnan, Sarvepalli. *Indian Philosophy, Vol.1*. Oxford University Press, 1997.

Talbott, Strobe. *Engaging India: Diplomacy, Democracy, And the Bomb*, revised ed. Brookings Institution Press, 2006.

Tammita-Delgoda, Sinharaja. *A Traveller's History of India*, 3rd ed. Interlink Books, 2002.

Thapar, Romila. *The Penguin History of Early India*. Penguin, 2002.

Tharoor, Shashi. *Elephant, the Tiger, and the Cell Phone: The Emerging 21st-Century Power*. Arcade, 2007.

Tully, Mark and Zareer Masani. *India: Forty Years of Independence*. George Braziller, 1988.

Endnotes

[1] Quotes on India, National Portal of India. http://india.gov.in/myindia/quotes.php.

[2] Ibid.

[3] DominicWilson, Roopa Purushothaman, "DreamingWith BRICs: The Path to 2050," Goldman Sachs Global Economics Paper No: 99, October 2003.

[4] Das, Gurcharan, "The India Model," *Foreign Affairs*, July/August 2006, Council on Foreign Relations, Washington, D.C.

[5] Xinhua News Agency, "China Revises Its GDP Growth Rate in 1979–2004." January 10, 2006.

[6] Kux, Dennis. *India and the United States: Estranged Democracies 1941–1991*. University Press of the Pacific, 2002: 364.

[7] Panagariya, Arvind. "The Triumph of India's Market Reforms: The Record of the 1980s and 1990s." Cato Institute Policy Analysis No.554, November 2005.

[8] "Congress Party's Calculating Loyalist: Pamulaparti Venkata Narasimha Rao," *New York Times*, June 22, 1991.

[9] Ghosh, Arunabha, "India's Pathway through Financial Crisis," UNDP Human Development Report Office, GEG Working Paper, June 2004: 8.

[10] "India's debt rating raised to investment grade by S&P," *International Herald Tribune*, January 21, 2007.

[11] "Forex Reserves to touch $300 bn by March 2008: IEG," *The Economic Times*, December 30, 2007.

[12] Bulletin of the Atomic Scientists, Doomsday Clock Timeline. http://www.thebulletin.org.

[13] Polmar, Norman, "The Biggest Indian Naval Exercise," Military.com, July 2007.

[14] "Japan population starts to shrink," BBC News, December 25, 2005.

[15] "Clinton Warns India over HIV/AIDS," BBC News, December 1, 2006.

[16] Confederation of Indian Industry, Press Release, December 7, 2007.

[17] Mumbai will soon be global financial hub, *ExpressIndia.com*, 27 October 2006.

[18] "India needs help with civilian nuclear power, says Chirac," The Hindu, February 20, 2006.

[19] "New climate report warns time is running out," Greenpeace International, April 6, 2007, http://www.greenpeace.org/international/news/new-climate-impacts-report-fro.

[20] U.S. Department of State, Bureau of South and Central Asian Affairs, Background Note: India. http://www.state.gov/r/pa/ei/bgn/3454.htm; The CIA World Factbook.

[21] "Top 10 Tallest Mountains," Worldatlas.com. http://www.worldatlas.com/geoquiz/thelist.htm.

[22] The CIA World Factbook, 2008 population growth estimates.

[23] U.N. Population Division

[24] India at a Glance, National Portal of India. http://india.gov.in.

[25] Census of India, Office of the Registrar General & Census Commissioner, India, Census Data 2001. http://www.censusindia.gov.in.

[26] Katz, Morris. *The Journey*. Trafford Publishing, 2006:24.

[27] "Pope defends conversions in India," BBC News, November 7, 1999. http://news.bbc.co.uk.

[28] Sikhism Resource Site, "All About Sikhs: The Five K's." http://www.allaboutsikhs.com.

[29] The date for the Buddha's birth is contested. However, the majority of historians consider the year 563 BC to be the birth year of the Buddha.

[30] Buddha Dharma Education Association. http://www.buddhanet.net.

[31] Encyclopedia of World Biography on Vardhamana Mahavira. http://www.bookrags.com/biography/vardhamana-mahavira. BBC Religion & Ethics: Jainism

[32] "Gold loses its shine as high price hits Indian demand," *Times Online Business*, January 28, 2008. http://business.timesonline.co.uk/tol/business.

[33] Dash, Kishore. *McDonald's in India*. Thunderbird, The Garvin School of International Management, 2005: 18.

[34] Indian traditions: http://www.iloveindia.com. India culture: http://www.mapsofindia.com. Manas: Culture of India: http://www.sscnet.ucla.edu.

[35] "A Good Age for Yoga," *Washington Post*, September, 27 2005.

[36] "Evaluating Benefits of Yoga—American Council on Exercise (ACE) First," *Medical News Today*, October 2, 2005. http://www.medicalnewstoday.com/articles/31446.php.

[37] Statewide number of registered Ayurveda practitioners, http://www.ayurveda-herbal-remedy.com/ayurveda-infrastructure/hospital-dispensary.html.

[38] "Indian Matchmaking Portals Go Brick and Mortar," *Spiegel Online International*, April 6, 2007. http://www.spiegel.de/international.

[39] U.N. Educational, Scientific, and Cultural Organization (UNESCO), World Heritage, India, Properties Inscribed on the World Heritage List. http://whc.unesco.org/en/statesparties/in.

[40] "Reporters see wrecked Buddhas," BBC News, March 26, 2001.

[41] http://www.maduraimeenakshi.org.

[42] The New 7 Wonders of the World. http://www.new7wonders.com.

[43] "Pollution turns Taj Mahal yellow," ABC News Online, May 15, 2007. http://www.abc.net.au.

[44] Kamat's Potpourri, Important Proponents of the Bhakti Movement. http://www.kamat.com/indica/faiths/bhakti/bhakti.htm.

[45] MTV, Lata Mangeshkar: Full Biography, http://www.mtv.com/music/artist/mangeshkar_lata/artist.jhtml#bio.

[46] "'Bollywood' enters another dictionary," *The Hindu*, July 31, 2007.

[47] Central Board of Film Certification (CBFC), India, http://www.cbfcindia.tn.nic.in.

As per media reports, India made 1,091 movies in 2006, an all-time record, including Telugu (245), Hindi (223), and Tamil (163) movies; claim not yet verified by CBFC Web site.

[48] "Boom time for India's film industry; Country spends $2 billion on movies each year," *Variety*, November 27, 2007.

[49] Helmick, Alex, "Switzerland eyes Bollywood with incentives," World Radio Switzerland, February 29, 2008. http://www.worldradio.ch.

[50] Tourism Ireland, "Tourism Ireland Joins Trade Mission to India," January 16, 2006. Press Release, http://www.tourismireland.com.

[51] "IPL draws huge bids to own teams," *Newstrack India*, January 25, 2008. http://www.newstrackindia.com/newsdetails/2192.

[52] World Chess Federation (FIDE), FIDE Top Players List, July 2008, http://ratings.fide.com/toplist.phtml.

[53] "Stone-age tools dug out of 'tiger hole,'" *The Telegraph*, June 13, 2006.

[54] India at a Glance, National Portal of India, http://india.gov.in.

[55] UNESCO, World Heritage, Ajanta Caves, http://whc.unesco.org/en/list/242.

[56] Sharma, Y. D. *Delhi and its Neighborhoods*. Published by the Director General, Archaeological Survey of India, 2001: 17.

[57] About.com, Time's Man of the Year Winners, http://history1900s.about.com/library/weekly/aa050400a.htm.

[58] Nehru, Jawaharlal, Speech On the Granting of Indian Independence, August 14, 1947. Internet History Sourcebooks Project, History Department of Fordham University, New York. http://www.fordham.edu/halsall/mod/1947nehru1.html.

[59] Oracle Education Foundation, Prominent Figures of the 20th Century; Nehru announcing Gandhi's death (audio): http://library.thinkquest.org/C005803F/nehru.wav.

[60] Furbee, Mary. *The Importance Of Series—Mohandas Gandhi*. Lucent Books, 2000: 93.

[61] Ibid, p. 95.

[62] Election commission of India, Election Results—Full Statistical Reports. http://www.eci.gov.in.

[63] Bainham, Andrew, The International Survey of Family Law: 1995, Springer, 1997.

[64] "The Nehru/Gandhi dynasty," CBC News Online, May 13, 2004.

[65] Johri, Devika and Mark Miller, "Devaluation of the Rupee: Tale of Two Years, 1966 and 1991," Centre for Civil Society. http://www.ccsindia.org.

[66] War Chat, Indo-Pakistani War of 1971. http://www.warchat.org.

[67] Dolley, Steven, "Indian & Pakistani Nuclear Tests: Frequently Asked Questions," Nuclear Control Institute, June 9, 1998. http://www.nci.org/ip-faq.htm.

[68] "1984: Indian prime minister shot dead," BBC News.

[69] "Bhopal gas tragedy lives on, 20 years later," *The Christian Science Monitor*, May 4, 2004.

[70] "The Bombing of Air India Flight 182," CBC News Online, September 25, 2006. http://www.cbc.ca/news/background/airindia/bombing.html.

[71] Global Integrity Report, India: Corruption Timeline. http://report.globalintegrity.org/India/2007/timeline.

[72] Akbar, M. J., "The Kidnapping and after," *Dawn* Internet Edition, January 19, 2003.

http://www.dawn.com/weekly/books/archive/030119/books1.htm.

[73] "Economic Austerity Vowed for India," *New York Times*, June 23, 1991.

[74] "India Is Now in a New Ball Game," *New York Times*, July 8, 1991.

[75] "Major trading scandals in history," *Financial Post*, January 24, 2008.

[76] "Q&A: The Ayodhya dispute," BBC News, November 15, 2004.

[77] "Financier in India Accuses Premier," *New York Times*, June 17, 1993.

[78] "U.S. imposes sanctions on India," CNN World, May 13, 1998.

[79] "In Depth: South Asia: Gujarat Quake," BBC News, March 10, 2003.

[80] "Agra summit at a glance," BBC News, July 17, 2001.

[81] "PM extends 'hand of friendship' to Pakistan," *The Hindu*, April 19, 2003.

[82] "Gujarat hits at India's secular heart," *Asia Times Online*, April 6, 2002.

[83] National Human Rights Commission (NHRC), New Delhi, India. http://nhrc.nic.in/disparchive.asp?fno=150.

[84] "Mile by Mile, India Paves a Smoother Road to Its Future," *New York Times*, December 4, 2005.

[85] "BJP admits 'India Shining' error," BBC News, May 28, 2004.

[86] National Common Minimum Program of the Government of India, May 2004, http://pmindia.nic.in/cmp.pdf.

[87] "Senate Backs White House Plan for India Nuclear Deal," *Washington Post*, November 17, 2006.; "US House backs India nuclear deal," BBC News, July 27, 2006.

[88] Know India, States and Union Territories, National Portal of India, http://india.gov.in.

[89] Kronstadt, K. Alan, "India's 2004 National Elections," CRS Report RL32465.

[90] Election Commission of India, Election Results—Full Statistical Reports, http://www.eci.gov.in.

[91] GDP, GNI data: World Bank, Data & Statistics (GDP, GNI Data); GDP (2005, 2006): World Bank, Indian at a Glance; GDP growth rate of 9.2 percent (2007 est.): The CIA World Factbook.

[92] The CIA World Factbook; 2007 estimates.

[93] U.N. Development Programme (UNDP), Human Development Report 2007/2008, India Data Sheet. http://hdrstats.undp.org/countries.

[94] "India's GDP Growth May Slow for First Time in 3 Years (Update 3)," Bloomberg, February 7, 2008.

[95] World Bank: India at a glance, updated 9/28/07. http://devdata.worldbank.org/AAG/ind_aag.pdf

[96] Ibid.

[97] Investment commission of India.

[98] "Govt notifies guidelines for FDI in single brand retailing," *Hindu Business Line*, February 14, 2006.

[99] Goldman Sachs, "Dreaming with BRICs: The Path to 2050," Global Economics Paper No. 99. http://www2.goldmansachs.com/ideas/brics/book/99-dreaming.pdf.

[100] Singhal, Anupriya and Aoneha Tagore, "Big Industry Before Independence: 1860–1950," Centre for Civil Society. http://www.ccsindia.org.

[101] Johri, Devika and Mark Miller, "Devaluation of the Rupee: Tale of Two Years, 1966 and 1991," Centre for Civil Society. http://www.ccsindia.org.

[102] International Food Policy Research Institute (IFPRI), Green Revolution: Curse or Blessing? http://www.ifpri.org/pubs/ib/ib11.pdf.

[103] Dataquest, Sam Pitroda: Lifetime Achievement Award 2002, December 27, 2002

[104] "Economic Austerity Vowed for India," *New York Times*, June 23, 1991.; "India's Chief Urges U.S. Investment," *New York Times*, July 11, 1991.

[105] "India Is Now in a New Ball Game," *New York Times*, July 8, 1991.

[106] Panagariya, Arvind, "The Triumph of India's Market Reforms: The Record of the 1980s and 1990s," Cato Institute Policy Analysis No. 554, November 2005. http://www.cato.org/pubs/pas/pa554.pdf.

[107] Office of Development Commissioner (MSME), Government of India, List of Items Reserved for Exclusive Manufacture in Micro and Small Enterprises. http://www.smallindustryindia.com.

[108] India-U.S. Economic and Trade Relations; August 31, 2007; Congressional Research Service; CRS report to Congress; Michael F. Martin; K. Alan Kronstadt; pp 33–34.

[109] Investment Commission of India, Policies and Laws, Sector Caps and Entry Route.

[110] "India Drops a Ban on Foreign Trademarks," *New York Times*, January 31, 1992.

[111] Viswanath, P., "Implications of VAT for India: First the pains, then the gains," Avalon Consulting; VAT in India, http://finance.indiamart.com/taxation/vat_in_india.html.

[112] Bajpai, Nirupam, "Economic Crisis, Structural Reforms, and the Prospects of Growth in India," The Harvard Institute for International Development, Development Discussion Paper # 530, May 1996. http://hwww.cid.harvard.edu/hiid/530.pdf.

[113] Bajpai, Nirupam and Tianlun Jian, "Reform Strategies of China and India: Suggestions for Future Actions," The Harvard Institute for International Development, Development Discussion Paper # 564. http://www.cid.harvard.edu/hiid/564.pdf.

[114] Ahluwalia, Montek S., "Economic Reforms in India since 1991: Has Gradualism Worked?" *The Journal of Economic Perspectives*, 16.3 (Summer 2002).

[115] World Bank, Key Development Data & Statistics; GDP rates 8.4 percent (2003), 8.3 percent (2004), 9.2 percent (2005), 9.2 percent (2006).

[116] World Bank Key Development Data & Statistics, GNI per capita, Atlas method (current US$).

[117] Economic Survey 2007–08, Foreign Exchange Reserves, http://indiabudget.nic.in/es2007-08/chapt2008/tab61b.pdf; Ranade, Ajit, "A Decade of India's Economic Reforms," ABN AMRO, June 2001.

[118] India Ministry of Commerce & Industry, Fact Sheet on Foreign Direct Investment (FDI) from August 1991 to February 2008. http://dipp.nic.in/fdi_statistics/india_fdi_index.htm.

[119] The Fiscal Responsibility and Budget Management Bill, 2003, Bill No. 220-C, as passed by Lok Sabha. http://www1.worldbank.org/publicsector/pe/BudgetLaws/IndiaFiscalResponsibilityBill.pdf.

[120] Investment Commission of India, Infrastructure: Power Overview.

[121] Shaughnessy, Daniel E., "Fifty Years of International Food Aid—Time To Change?"

The Resource & Policy Exchange, RPX Publications & Speeches. http://www.rpex.org.

[122] Economic Research Service/USDA, "India Relaxes Restraints on Agricultural Imports," Agricultural Outlook, November 2000. http://www.ers.usda.gov; Landes, Maurice R., "The Elephant Is Jogging: New Pressures for Agricultural Reform in India," Amber Waves. http://www.ers.usda.gov/AmberWaves/February04.

[123] The CIA World Factbook; Economic Survey 2007–08, Employment in Organized Sectors.

[124] Manufacturing Sector, India Trade Center, Romania Portal. http://www.indiatradecenter.in/itc.

[125] Indian Demographic Scenario, 2025. http://www.iegindia.org/dispap/dis27.pdf.

[126] The CIA World Factbook (2007 est.)

[127] World Trade Organization, Country Profile: India, April 2008. http://stat.wto.org.

[128] India's Tata wins race for Corus, BBC News Business, January 31, 2007.

[129] "India to be world's 3rd largest car market by 2030: Study," *Financial Express*, December 1, 2005.

[130] U.S. Department of Transportation, Bureau of Transportation Statistics, World Motor Vehicle Production, Selected Countries. http://www.bts.gov.

[131] "India eyes 25 million automotive jobs," BBC News, April 30, 2007; Government of India Automotive Mission Plan, September 2006. http://www.dhi.nic.in/draft_automotive_mission_plan.pdf.

[132] Society of Indian Automobile Manufacturers (SIAM), http://www.siamindia.com.

[133] CII-McKinsey Report, "Made in India: The next big manufacturing exports opportunity." http://www.mckinsey.com/locations/india/mckinseyonindia/pdf/Made_in_India.pdf.

[134] "GM steering business to India," *International Herald Tribune*, April 17, 2007.

[135] "Chinese car market is world No 2," *BBC News*, January 11, 2007.

[136] "In India, the world's cheapest car debuts to fanfare, criticism," *Christian Science Monitor*, January 10, 2008.

[137] "Air India, Indian Airlines may merge," *USA Today*, February 21, 2006.

[138] "Airbus sees Indian passenger fleet rising 5-fold in 20 years," *The Hindu Business Line*, February 8, 2007.

[139] Economic Survey 2007–08, Growth of Civil Aviation. http://indiabudget.nic.in/es2007-08/chapt2008/tab129.pdf

[140] Investment Commission of India

[141] "India's national carriers fly under heavy burden," *International Herald Tribune*, June 28, 2005.

[142] Indian Railways, http://www.indianrailways.gov.in.

[143] "India may need 1,100 new aircraft in 20 years: Airbus," *Hindu Business Line*, February 6, 2007.

[144] Boeing News Release, Boeing, "Air India Celebrate Milestone with 737-800 Delivery," Seattle, November 30, 2006.

[145] Hyderabad Airport Web site.

[146] Economic Survey 2007–08, Number of Telephones. http://indiabudget.nic.in/es2007-08/chapt2008/chap97.pdf

[147] "Bharti Airtel Wafts Upward On Strong Profit Results," *Forbes*, January 30, 2008. http://www.forbes.com.

[148] "Vodafone Gets Final OK On Hutch Essar Deal," *Forbes*, May 7, 2007. http://www.forbes.com.

[149] Indian Pharmaceutical Industry Overview, http://www.pharmaceutical-drug-manufacturers.com/pharmaceutical-industry; "Growing at 9%p.a., Pharmaceutical Industry in India is Well Set for Rapid Expansion," *Medical News Today*, May 30, 2005. http://www.medicalnewstoday.com/articles/25348.php.

[150] Ram, Prabhu, "India's New 'Trips-Compliant' Patent Regime," *Chicago-Kent Journal of Intellectual Property*, 5.2 (Spring 2006).

[151] "TCS wins $35 mn Eli Lilly contract," *Economic Times*, November 13, 2006.

[152] U.S. Food and Drug Administration, "Pfizer Stops All Torcetrapib Clinical Trials in Interest of Patient Safety," FDA Statement, December 3, 2006; "End of Drug Trial Is a Big Loss for Pfizer," *New York Times*, December 4, 2006.

[153] "Frost & Sullivan Study Reveals the CRAMS Market in India to be Valued at US $895 Million in 2006 and Expected to Reach to Close to US $6.6 Billion by 2013," *Business Wire India Press Release*, April 23, 2007.

[154] "Pfizer, Ranbaxy settle Lipitor patent dispute," MSN Money Central, June 18, 2008.

[155] U.S. FDA, President's Emergency Plan for AIDS Relief. http://www.fda.gov/oia/pepfar.Htm.

[156] Confederation of Indian Industry, Press Release, December 7, 2007.

157 World Bank Key Development Data & Statistics 2005.

158 Investment Commission of India, Infrastructure: Power Overview.

159 Investment Commission of India, Natural Resources, Coal Overview.

160 "India's crude import bill surges 40%," *Rediff News*, May 27, 2008. http://www.rediff.com/money/2008/may/27oil2.htm.

161 Investment Commission of India.

162 BP Statistical Review of World Energy 2006.

163 Ibid.

164 Investment Commission of India

165 Ibid.

166 Reuters, "India's Mahindra Group to enter retail sector," October 10, 2007.

167 Growth Opportunities for Global Retailers, The A.T. Kearney 2007 Global Retail Development Index, http://www.atkearney.com/shared_res/pdf/GRDI_2007.pdf.

168 "Article at a glance: Tracking the growth of India's middle class," *McKinsey Quarterly*.

http://www.mckinseyquarterly.com/Tracking_the_growth_of_Indias_middle_class_2032_abstract.

169 "Indian State Orders Closure Of Reliance Retail Stores," *Forbes*, August 24, 2007. http://www.forbes.com.

170 "Wal-Mart and Bharti set joint venture," *Financial Times*, November 27, 2006. http://us.ft.com.

171 IBM, "IBM Chairman and CEO Announces Plans to Triple Investment in India over Next Three Years," Press Release, June 6, 2006.

172 "India's Edge Goes Beyond Outsourcing," *New York Times*, April 4, 2007.

[173] "IT exports to touch $80 b in three years," *Hindu Business Line*, May 13, 2008.

[174] "Steady Increase Seen in Tech Services Spending," *PC World*, May 18, 2008.

[175] National Association of Software and Service Companies (NASSCOM), Online Resource Center, Indian IT Industry–Fact Sheet. www.nasscom.org.

[176] The CIA World Factbook.

[177] Based on IIM Bangalore annual fee of 300,000 rupees for Indian nationals; conversion of 40:1 (rupees: dollar) used; U.S. tuition based on Harvard Business School annual tuition of $43,800.

[178] Software Engineering Institute, Carnegie Mellon, http://www.sei.cmu.edu/cmmi.

[179] "A New World Economy: The balance of power will shift to the East as China and India evolve," Business Week, August 22, 2005.

[180] "India cyber law comes into force," *BBC News*, October 18, 2000.

[181] "No use opposing offshoring—Study of Bay Area economy recommends finding ways to promote region's strengths," *San Francisco Chronicle*, July 16, 2004.

[182] "Outsourcing is good for US economy: Microsoft CEO," *Rediff Business*, November 9, 2006,

[183] In the book, The World Is Flat: A Brief History of the Twenty-First Century, Thomas L. Friedman explains what globalization means to American students by recounting a warning he offered to his teenage daughters: "Girls, when I was growing up, my parents used to say to me, 'Tom, finish your dinner. People in China and India are starving.' My advice to you is: Girls, finish your homework. People in China and India are starving for your jobs."

[184] "Number of U.S. tech jobs rises despite fears of outsourcing," *USA Today*, April 24, 2007.

[185] "Bush Urges Americans to Welcome India as Competitor," *New York Times*, March 3, 2006.

[186] Binder, Alan S., "Offshoring: The Next Industrial Revolution?" *Foreign Affairs*, March/April 2006, Council on Foreign Relations, Washington, D.C.

[187] Office of the Governor, State of Georgia Release, "Wipro Technologies to Open New Software Development Center in Atlanta—Plans to Hire from Local Universities," August 27, 2007.

[188] "Hyderabad IT giants on hiring spree," *IBN Live*, April 19, 2006.

[189] Cyber Media Dice Press Release, April 5, 2007, http://www.cybermedia.co.in/press/pressrelease35.html.

[190] "Insecurities over Indian outsourcing," CNET News, April 26, 2005,

http://news.cnet.com.

[191] "India's Edge Goes Beyond Outsourcing," *New York Times*, April 4, 2007.

[192] "Drug Company Eli Lilly Outsources Clinical Data To India," *Information Week*, November 20, 2006.

[193] Nicholas Piramal Press Release, Mumbai, India, January 12, 2007.

[194] "Some U.S. hospitals outsourcing work," MSNBC, December 6, 2004.

[195] Teleradiology Solutions, http://www.telradsol.com.

[196] Government of India, Ministry of Commerce & Industry, Press Release, June 1, 2007. http://commerce.nic.in/pressrelease/pressrelease_detail.asp?id=2064.

[197] "This UK patient avoided the NHS list and flew to India for a heart bypass. Is health tourism the future?" *Guardian*, February 1, 2005.; "India Fosters Growing 'Medical Tourism' Sector," *Financial Times*, July 2, 2003. http://yaleglobal.yale.edu/display.article?id=2016.

[198] "Here is the US news from Bangalore," BBC News, February 2 2007.

[199] "E-tutoring takes rapid strides," *Mumbai Mirror*, December 27, 2007.

[200] Tutor Vista Web site, http://www.tutorvista.com; "Multinationals lead India's IT revolution," BBC News, January 24, 2007.

[201] "Contract with India: Legal outsourcing," *Financial Post*, April 25, 2008.

[202] "Canadians to outsource legal services to India," *Legalwise*, March 4-10, 2008; issue 958,

[203] 2008 Global Outsourcing 100, The International Association of Outsourcing Professionals™

[204] Tata Consulting Services Annual Reports and Company Web site.

[205] Wipro Annual Reports, SEC Filings, http://www.wipro.com; Forbes, The World's Billionaires 2008, http://www.forbes.com.

[206] Wipro Annual Reports, SEC Filings, http://www.wipro.com.

[207] World Semiconductor Trade Statistics, News Release, May 31, 2005. http://www.wsts.org/plain/content/view/full/2076.

[208] "Companies Losing Interest in Offshore Captive Centers," *IT Business Edge*, May 9, 2007. http://www.itbusinessedge.com.

[209] "GE sets tongues wagging in India," *Asia Times Online*, November 12, 2004.

[210] Accenture, "Accenture's Growing Presence in India," Message from Chairman & CEO, February 2007. http://http://www.accenture.com.

[211] Microsoft India Development Center Web site.

[212] "IBM may rival India's top offshore IT firms in head count," *Computer World*, April 4, 2007. http://www.computerworld.com.

[213] GE Global Research Web site, http://www.ge.com/research/grc_3.html.

[214] "Oracle to add 1,400 jobs in India," *International Herald Tribune*, January 11, 2006; Oracle Corporation, The Oracle In India Story, http://www.oracle.com.

[215] All India Council for Technical Education (AICTE), http://www.aicte.ernet.in/ApprovedInstitute.htm

[216] Hogg Robinson Group 2006 Hotel Survey, http://www.hrgworldwide.com/Portals/0/Documents/HRG_UK_hotel_survey_2006.pdf.

[217] "Bangalore selected most favourite offshore destination in Asia-Pacific," *Deccan Herald*, July 5, 2007, http://www.deccanherald.com/Content/Jul52007/state2007070511107.asp?section=updatenews.

[218] Partha Iyengar, "IT Outsourcing to India - Analysis of Cities," Gartner Report, http://www.gartner.com/teleconferences/attributes/attr_106290_115.pdf.

[219] The Non-Aligned Movement: Description and History, http://www.nam.gov.za.

[220] Montgomery, Michael, "Atoms for Peace," Center for Investigative Reporting, April 10, 2008. http://centerforinvestigativereporting.org/articles/atomsforpeace.

[221] Davis Cup Official Web site.

[222] "China commemorates 40th anniversary of first test of hydrogen bomb," *People's Daily Online*, June 18, 2007. http://english.people.com.cn/200706/17/eng20070617_385146.html.

[223] Canadian Coalition for Nuclear Responsibility, Canadian Nuclear Cooperation with India & Pakistan, David Martin Nuclear Awareness Project, http://www.ccnr.org.

[224] India and Pakistan: New Missiles Increase the Risk of Nuclear War, Wisconsin Project on Nuclear Arms Control, The Risk Report, Volume

1 Number 6 (July-August 1995), http://www.wisconsinproject.org/countries/india/india-pak-missile-war.html.

[225] U.S. Department of State, Visit to the U.S. by Foreign Heads of State and Government, http://www.state.gov/r/pa/ho/c1792.htm; Rajiv Gandhi visited the United States in 1985 and 1987 and visited the Soviet Union in 1985, 1986, 1987, and 1989.

[226] Federation of Indian Chambers of Commerce and Industry, India-Israel Economic and Commercial Relations; Embassy of India Tel Aviv, Country Brief on Israel; Khan, M. Shamsur Rabb, "Indo-Israel Defense Cooperation: A Step in the Right Direction," Institute of Peace & Conflict Studies (IPCS). http://www.ipcs.org.

[227] "India's 'Look East' policy pays off," *Asia Times Online*, October 11 2003.

[228] Federation of Indian Chambers of Commerce and Industry, Thailand, "India Close to Concluding FTA for Trade in Goods," Press Releases, June 26, 2007. http://www.ficci.com/press/306/THAILAND.pdf.

[229] U.S. Census Bureau, Foreign Trade Statistics, http://www.census.gov/foreign-trade/balance.

[230] "S. Korean Strongly Backed to Lead U.N.," *Washington Post*, October 3, 2006.

[231] War Chat, Indo-Pakistan War of 1971, http://www.warchat.org.

[232] Earlier visits were by presidents Dwight Eisenhower (1959) and Richard Nixon (1969). http://www.indianembassy.org/indusrel/clinton_india/home.html.

[233] Nuclear Control Institute, "Reagan Administration to Approve Nuclear Exports to India Despite Ban in Nuclear Non-Proliferation Act," July 21, 1983. http://www.nci.org.

[234] Slough, Neil, Paul Miesing, and Rodger Brain, "The Ten Big Emerging Market Initiative a Decade Later: Measurements and Commentary." http://www.albany.edu/~pm157/research.

235 Rao, P. V. Narasimha, Address to joint meeting of U.S. Congress, Embassy of India, May 18, 1994, Washington, D.C.

236 Talbott, Strobe, "Engaging India: Diplomacy, Democracy, and the Bomb," Brookings Institution Press.

237 Reidel, Bruce, "American Diplomacy and the 1999 Kargil Summit at Blair House," Center for the Advanced Study of India, University of Pennsylvania, 2002: 11. www.ccc.nps.navy.mil/research/kargil/reidel.pdf.

238 "Narayanan's tough speech upsets government," *Rediff News*, March 23, 2000.

239 "Clinton hails India ties," BBC News, September 18, 2000.

240 "India's PM Calls to be Ready to Fight Terrorism," *Voice of America News*, May 22, 2002.

241 "India offers half-hearted criticism of US war on Iraq," *World Socialist Web Site*, March 25, 2003, http://www.wsws.org/articles/2003/mar2003/indi-m25.shtml.

242 World Socialist Web site, "Washington presses India to send troops to Iraq," June 30, 2003. http://www.wsws.org/articles/2003/jun2003/indi-j30.shtml.

243 Vaypayee, Atal Bihari, "Next Steps in Strategic Partnership with USA." http://www.indianembassy.org/pic/pm/vajpayee/2004/pm_jan_13_2003.htm.

244 "U.S. Will Celebrate Pakistan As a Major Non-NATO Ally," *New York Times*, March 19, 2004.

245 "India riled by US-Pakistan ties," *BBC News,* March 20, 2004.

246 Bush, George W., "President, Indian Prime Minister Singh Exchange Toasts," White House Press Release, July 18, 2005.

247 "Bush visit to India centers on nuclear pact," *CNN.com*, March 1, 2006.

[248] Bush, George W., "President Discusses Strong U.S.-India Partnership in New Delhi, India," White House Press Release, March 3, 2006.

[249] Ibid.

[250] "US firms seek opportunities in India," *BBC News*, November 29, 2006.

[251] Blank, Stephen, "Primakov's Russian/India/China Triangle Nears Realization," *Eurasia Daily Monitor*, 2.79, April 25, 2005; published by The Jamestown Foundation

[252] "Russia and India's complex friendship," *BBC News*, January 26, 2007.

[253] "Gandhi Lands in China to Renew Old Friendship," *New York Times*, December 20, 1988.

[254] Kampani, Gaurav, "From Existential to Minimum Deterrence: Explaining India's Decision to Test," *The Nonproliferation Review*, Fall 1998. http://cns.miis.edu/pubs/npr/vol06/61/kampan61.pdf.

[255] Embassy of People's Republic of China in India, "China, India renew aviation agreement," April 15, 2005.

[256] "Sikkim is part of India, concedes Chinese envoy," *Times of India*, June 22, 2008.

[257] Voice of America, "China Hosts More Than 40 African Leaders in Bid to Seal Deals," November 2, 2006.

[258] "China, Pakistan, and the Bomb: The Declassified File on U.S. Policy, 1977–1997," National Security Archive Electronic Briefing Book No. 114, March 5, 2004. http://www.gwu.edu/~nsarchiv.

[259] "India begin historic cricket tour," *BBC News*, March 10, 2004.

[260] U.N. Resolution, August 13, 1948. http://www.jammu-kashmir.com/documents/jkunresolution.html.

[261] U.S. Department of State, "Country Reports on Human Rights Practices," Released by Bureau of Democracy, Human Rights, and Labor. http://www.state.gov/g/drl/rls/hrrpt.

262 "Indian PM's bid for Peace Mountain," CNN International, June 13, 2005.

263 The CIA World Factbook.

264 "India Presses Oil-Rich Gulf Nations to Offer Imported Workers Minimum Wage," Fox News, March 26, 2008.

265 India-Brazil-South Africa (IBSA) Trilateral Web site, http://www. ibsa-trilateral.org.

266 2006 American Community Survey.

267 Ibid.

268 Homeland Security Office of Immigration Statistics, Persons Naturalized by Region and Country of Birth. http://www.dhs.gov/ xlibrary/assets/statistics/publications/natz_fr_07.pdf.

269 2006 American Community Survey; Mean earnings: $101,108 for Asian Indians.

270 Institute of International Education, Opendoor 2007 Fast Facts. http://www.opendoors.iienetwork.org.

271 Matthews, Christine M., "Foreign Science and Engineering Presence in U.S. Institutions and the Labor Force," CRS Order Code 97-746, Updated July 23, 2008.

272 Panagariya, Arvind, "The Indian Diaspora in the United States," Economic Times, May 23, 2001. http://www.columbia.edu/~ap2231/ ET/et26-may01.htm.

273 American Association of Physicians of Indian Origin (AAPI).

274 "Immigrants Behind 25 Percent of Startups," Washington Post, January 3, 2007.

275 "Indian-Americans book years of success," USA Today, April 19, 2007.

276 Scripps Howard National Spelling Bee, Champions and Their Winning Words, 1925 through 2005. http://www.spellingbee.com/ bwg/statschamp.shtml; Indian American Champions: Nupur Lala

(1999), George Abraham Thampy (2000), Pratyush Buddiga (2002), Sai R. Gunturi (2003), Anurag Kashyap (2005), Sameer Mishra (2008).

[277] U.S.-India Friendship.net, Members of Congressional Caucus, list updated as of March 2007. http://www.usindiafriendship.net.

[278] U.S. Census Bureau, State Population Estimates by Selected Race Categories, July 1, 2007. http://www.census.gov/popest/states; Louisiana's state population: 4,293,204, Asian population: 61,801.

[279] Lal, Vinay, "Establishing Roots, Engendering Awareness: A Political History of Asian Indians in the United States." http://www.sscnet.ucla.edu/southasia/Diaspora/roots.html.

[280] "Indian American population may reach 4.5 mn in 2010," *Rediff News*, August 22, 2006.

[281] American Association of Physicians of Indian Origin (AAPI).

[282] "U.S. Plan to Lure Nurses May Hurt Poor Nations," *New York Times*, May 24, 2006.

[283] Source: Open Doors 2006: International Students in the United States.

[284] Institute of International Education, Opendoor 2007 Fast Facts. http://www.opendoors.iienetwork.org.

[285] U.S. Department of Homeland Security, Office of Immigration Statistics, Characteristics of Specialty Occupation Workers (H-1B): fiscal year 2003, Issued November 2004. http://www.uscis.gov/files/article/FY03H1BFnlCharRprt.pdf.

[286] "Bill Gates to Congress: Let us hire more foreigners," CNET News, March 12, 2008.

[287] Matloff, Norman, "On the Need for Reform of the H-1B Non-Immigrant Work Visa in Computer-Related Occupations," *University of Michigan Journal of Law Reform*, December 12, 2003. http://www.cs.ucdavis.edu/~matloff/Mich.pdf.

[288] "Indian-Americans book years of success," *USA Today*, April 19, 2007.

[289] "600,000 more Indians in US," *Rediff News*, November 28, 2006.

[290] NYC Taxicab Handbook, Schaller Consulting.

[291] Asian American Federation of New York Census Information Center, Census Profile: New York City's Indian American Population. http://www.aafny.org/cic/briefs/indianamer.pdf.

[292] Vivekananda Vedanta Society, Swami Vivekananda Statue, July 13, 1998; Press Release From the Consulate General of India, Chicago, IL, USA.

[293] UNDP, Human Development Report 2007/2008. http://hdrstats.undp.org/countries.

[294] "Low-cost lamps brighten the future of rural India," *Christian Science Monitor*, January 3, 2006.

[295] UNDP, Human Development Report 2007/2008, http://hdrstats.undp.org/countries; Children underweight for age (percent under age 5): 47 percent.

[296] "India Rising," BBC World Service.

[297] UNDP, 2007/2008 Human Development Index rankings. http://hdr.undp.org/en/statistics.

[298] International Food Policy Research Institute (IFPRI), 2006 Global Hunger Index (GHI)—ranking of countries, 2006. http://www.ifpri.org.

[299] 2000, 2005 and 2006 data from World Bank Key Development Data & Statistics; 2025 projection based on comments of India's finance minister, P. Chidambaram. http://www.business-standard.com/india/storypage.php?tp=on&autono=29803; GNI per capita using Atlas method (current US$).

[300] World Bank Key Development Data & Statistics.

[301] "India Rising," BBC World Service.

[302] UNDP, Human Development Report 2007/2008. http://hdrstats. undp.org/countries/data_sheets/cty_ds_IND.html.

[303] Economic Survey 2007–2008, Poverty Ratios by URP and MRP. http://indiabudget.nic.in/es2007-08/chapt2008/chap103.pdf; Based on the Uniform Recall Period (URP)—consumption distribution data, poverty declined from 36 percent in 1993–94 to 27.5 percent in 2004–05.

[304] "Landmark Indian jobs bill passed," BBC News, August 23, 2005.

[305] "Social security for Indian poor," BBC News, May 24, 2007.

[306] U.N. Population Division, Population Growth in India Since Its Independence. http://www.un.org/esa/population/pubsarchive/india/indgrow.htm.

[307] U.S. Census Bureau, Population Division, International Database, Country Rankings.

http://www.census.gov/ipc/www/idb/ranks.html.

[308] U.S. Census Bureau, International Database, World Population Information. http://www.census.gov/ipc/www/idb/worldpopinfo. html.

[309] Economic Survey 2007–2008, Access to Safe Drinking Water in Households in India (1981: 38.2 percent, 1991: 62.3 percent, 2001: 77.9 percent). http://indiabudget.nic.in/es2007-08/chapt2008/tab96. pdf.

[310] The CIA World Factbook; 2008 estimates.

[311] U.S. Census Bureau, International Database. http://www.census. gov/ipc/www/idb/country/inportal.html;

In the calendar year 2005, India had twenty-six million births and eight million deaths; net increase in population is eighteen million.

[312] "Growth gives hope to India's poor," BBC News, April 18, 2006.

[313] UNDP, Human Development Report 2007/2008, http://hdrstats. undp.org/countries/data_sheets/cty_ds_IND.html; Fertility rate: 5.3 (1970–75), 3.1 (2000–05)

[314] World Health Organization, Regional Office for Southeast Asia, "India and Family Planning: An Overview." http://www.searo.who. int/linkfiles/family_planning_fact_sheets_india.pdf.

[315] "Has China's one-child policy worked?" BBC News, September 20, 2007. http://news.bbc.co.uk/2/hi/asia-pacific/7000931.stm.

[316] "Air pollution suffocates Calcutta," BBC News, May 3, 2007.

[317] United Nations Environment Programme (UNEP), CNG conversion: Learning from New Delhi. http://ekh.unep.org/?q=node/1737.

[318] Center for Science and Environment, Press Release, November 6, 2007. http://www.cseindia.org/AboutUs/press_releases/press_20071106.htm

[319] PricewaterhouseCoopers (PwC), "The World in 2050: Can rapid global growth be reconciled with moving to a low carbon economy?"

[320] "Climate change: The big emitters," BBC News, July 4, 2005. http://news.bbc.co.uk/2/hi/science/nature/3143798.stm.

[321] UNDP, The Human Development Index—going beyond income, Table 4: Carbon dioxide emissions. http://hdrstats.undp.org/countries/data_sheets/cty_ds_IND.html.

[322] "India on brink of water crisis, says climate panel," *Times of India*, April 27, 2008.

[323] "France and India in Nuclear Deal," *BBC News South Asia*, February 20, 2006.

[324] World Health Organization, AIDS Epidemic Update. http://data.unaids.org/pub/EPISlides/2007/2007_epiupdate_en.pdf.

[325] "India now third on world's AIDS list," *Times of India*, July 7, 2007.

326 World Health Organization, AIDS Epidemic Update. http://data. unaids.org/pub/EPISlides/2007/2007_epiupdate_en.pdf.

327 "Clinton Warns India over HIV/AIDS," BBC News, December 1, 2006.

328 "Clinton's Foundation Brokers AIDS Deal," *New York Times*, November 30, 2006.

329 "Compulsory HIV tests for couples," BBC News, December 19, 2006.

330 China numbers from "Building BRICs of growth," *Economist*, June 5, 2008, http://www.economist.com; India numbers from "India Needs More Infrastructure Spending: Official," *Forbes.com*, April 12, 2008.

331 Investment Commission of India.

332 National Highway Authority of India, Financing of NHDP. http://www.nhai.org/nhdpfinance.htm.

333 Transparency International India, India Corruption Study 2005. http://www.cmsindia.org/cms/events/corruption.pdf.

334 Transparency International 2005, Corruption Perceptions Index. www.transparency.org.

335 Ministry of Personnel, Public Grievances and Pensions, Government of India, Right to Information Act. http://www.persmin.nic.in/RTI/welcomeRTI.htm.

336 World Bank Key Development Data & Statistics.

337 "Why was Satyendra Dubey betrayed?" *Rediff News*, December 10, 2003.

338 Economic Survey 2007–2008, State-Wise Literacy Rates, Ministry of Finance. http://indiabudget.nic.in/es2007-08/chapt2008/tab94.pdf.

339 The CIA World Factbook.

340 Economic Survey 2007–2008, State-Wise Literacy Rates, Ministry of Finance. http://indiabudget.nic.in/es2007-08/chapt2008/tab94.pdf

341 India numbers from Economic Survey 2007–2008; China and U.S. numbers are 2008 estimates from The CIA World Factbook.

342 India numbers from Economic Survey 2007–2008, UNICEF India Statistics; China and U.S. numbers are 2008 estimates from The CIA World Factbook.

343 White Ribbon Alliance for Safe Motherhood—India.

344 UNDP, Human Development Report 2007/2008, Country Factsheets. http://hdrstats.undp.org/countries; MMR rates of 450 (India) and 45 (China).

345 U.S. Department of State, Trafficking in Persons Report 2008. http://www.state.gov/g/tip/rls/tiprpt/2008.

346 The CIA World Factbook.

347 Ibid.

348 The CIA World Factbook (2007 est.); Based on Economic Survey 2007–2008, the labor force stood at 419 million in 2004–05.

349 Economic Survey 2007–2008, Section 10.24. http://indiabudget. nic.in.

350 "India proposes free trade agreement with Gulf countriesnews," domain-b.com, November 14, 2006. http://www.domain-b.com/ economy/trade/20061114_agreement.html

351 "US firms seek opportunities in India," *BBC News*, November 29, 2006.

352 Orissa Tourism. http://www.indiatourism.com/orissa-tourism/ konark-temple.html

353 History of Varanasi. http://www.varanasicity.com/history-of-varanasi.html

Index